DE QUINCEY'S COLLECTED WRITINGS

NEW AND ENLARGED EDITION

IN FOURTEEN VOLUMES

PORTRAIT OF THOMAS DE QUINCEY.

From a painting by Sir J. Watson Gordon. P.R.S.A.

In National Portrait Gallery. London.

THE COLLECTED WRITINGS

OF

THOMAS DE QUINCEY

NEW AND ENLARGED EDITION

BY

DAVID MASSON,

PROFESSOR OF ENGLISH LITERATURE IN THE
UNIVERSITY OF EDINBURGH

VOL. V

BIOGRAPHIES AND BIOGRAPHIC SKETCHES

CHARLES LAMB

EDINBURGH

ADAM AND CHARLES BLACK

1890

AMS PRESS
NEW YORK

Reprinted from the edition of 1889-90, Edinburgh
First AMS EDITION published 1968
Manufactured in the United States of America

Reprinted from a copy in the collections of the Harvard
College Library.

Library of Congress Catalogue Card Number: 68-58566

AMS PRESS, INC.
New York, N. Y. 10003

CONTENTS OF VOL. V

EDITOR'S PREFACE

THE papers included in this volume, like those in the last, were written at different points of De Quincey's life, and are culled from different periodicals. The long opening paper, entitled "Dr. Parr, or Whiggism in its Relations to Literature," but containing a great deal more than could be guessed from that title, and altogether one of the most fascinating specimens of De Quincey in what may be called his mischievous biographico-satirical vein, was a contribution to *Blackwood* in 1831. The amusing little paper called "Anecdotage" was one of his contributions to the *London Magazine* in 1823; the pleasant little biographic sketch of the Marquess Wellesley appeared in *Tait's Magazine* in 1846; "Coleridge and Opium-Eating" is a very interesting *Blackwood* paper of 1845; and the fine paper on Charles Lamb was written in 1848 for the *North British Review*. Of the two sketches of Professor Wilson, the first and more careful is of date 1829, and has been resuscitated from the columns of a long-defunct weekly once known as the *Edinburgh Literary Gazette*, while the other and slighter is of date 1850, and from the later and less-forgotten Edinburgh weekly called *Hogg's Instructor*. The valuable but strangely whimsical sketch entitled "Sir William Hamilton" was a contribution in 1852 to the same *Hogg's Instructor;* and the two closing papers of more distant historical range, entitled "Charlemagne" and "Joan of Arc," take us back respectively to *Blackwood* of 1832 and *Tait* of 1847. While further particulars in this chronology may be reserved for notes at the beginnings of the papers severally, it is well that the reader should be aware beforehand that in this volume, as in the last, there are brought together products of De Quincey's pen on different occasions, and in different sets of circumstances, through many years of his busy literary life.

The first seven of the biographic sketches, it will be observed, relate to persons and subjects contemporary with De Quincey himself, so that in treating them he could draw from his own observations and recollections, and not merely, as in most of the biographies in last volume, from books and tradition. These seven papers, accordingly, have been arranged pretty much in the order of their subjects. Dr. Parr comes first, as, though quite within De Quincey's memory and known to De Quincey by actual contact, yet on the whole more an eighteenth-century object than a figure of the nineteenth ; Miss Hawkins's Anecdotes, though some of them are scraps from the Johnsonian world of the eighteenth century prior to Parr's connexion with it, may follow Parr, as coming from the memory of a lady who was Parr's junior ; after which, in the Marquess Wellesley, Coleridge, Lamb, Professor Wilson, and Sir William Hamilton, we are distinctly among De Quincey's coevals. The last four, indeed, were personal friends of his, of whom he had again and again made mention in his writings, and of three of whom,—Coleridge, Lamb, and Wilson,—we have already had sketches from him in his Autobiographic Reminiscences. This reappearance of Coleridge, Lamb, and Wilson in the present volume, to be sketched again, with Sir William Hamilton now in their company, is, indeed, a feature of the volume that cannot escape remark. It is worth some attention on De Quincey's own account.

In few lives, of notable intellectual distinction otherwise, is there such evidence as in De Quincey's of the possession, in almost inordinate degree from the first, of the beautiful quality of affection for individual living contemporaries, rising into sustained veneration for the two or three of these who could be regarded as topmost and supreme. The first living contemporary to whom De Quincey bowed in adoring allegiance was Wordsworth. O ! how, in his boyhood, he had yearned towards that man in the Lakes, whom he had not yet seen ; and how, in later years, becoming a denizen of the Lakes himself, he tried to wind his own life, ivy-like, round that stationary oak ! Hardly less, and indeed larger on that side of his nature which inclined him to speculative philosophy and scholarly erudition, was his allegiance to Coleridge, his acquaintanceship with whom had preceded that with Wordsworth, though it was less continuous in the sequel. Those two, Wordsworth and Coleridge, were De Quincey's chiefs in the England of his own prime ; but there were other and minor, or at all events later and different, attachments. The gentle Charles Lamb, who won all hearts, had won De Quincey's by special kindness to De Quincey himself in London, no less than by the charms of his peculiar literary genius. Then, how De Quincey,—from the moment that he and his magnificent physical contrast, the athletic Wilson, had been brought into companionship in the Lake district, trudging together for days, the strangest of possible couples, over its roads and mountains,—how the little De Quincey took to this Hercules-Apollo as somehow his pre-destined brother, and admired him and loved him ! The friendship with Wilson led to De Quincey's first visit to Edinburgh in 1814, under Wilson's convoy, and so, by ramification, to acquaintanceship with some of Wilson's Edinburgh friends, Sir William Hamilton in the number. These are by no means all ; there were others to whom, in various places and on various grounds, De Quincey had related himself by more or less of enthusiastic liking. Not, of course, but that these personal likings and admirations of De Quincey were counterbalanced by equally strong, and perhaps equally numerous, personal antipathies. There were contemporaries of De Quincey, eminent in their day, to whom his antipathy was open and constant, to the pitch in some cases of the violently unreasonable, or even the rancorous and malicious,—partly perhaps from the same constitutional necessity that determined his sympathies and reverences, but sometimes too visibly from reckless political partisanship. Now, when De Quincey, after his thirty-six years of silent student-life, broke forth as a man of letters, seeking a liveli-hood by contributions to magazines and other miscellanies, and when, as it happened, his most available matter, and the most acceptable for popular effect, in this new industry, con-

sisted to a large extent of such reminiscences as he could
draw from his own life,—accounts of celebrities he had seen
and known, and of the impressions they had made on himself,—was it so wonderful that Wordsworth, Coleridge,
Charles Lamb, Wilson, and others of his highest favourites,
on the one hand, with now and then a black sheep, or a
blackish sheep, from the other list, should form the subjects
of his articles? It is to his credit that, though he did now
and then bring in a victim from the list of those he disliked,
or liked but slenderly and thought over-rated,—*e.g.* Dr. Parr,
—the larger proportion of his published recollections concerned those whom he could speak of affectionately and
admiringly, and were testimonies intended for their honour.
Here, however, is a peculiarity distinguishing De Quincey
from the herd of common eulogists. Not only does he never
make a swan out of a demonstrably inferior bird, but he is
critically frank, humorously shrewd and clear-sighted, in his
exhibitions of the swans themselves. From the first moment
of his introduction to Wordsworth, intense to idolatry as had
been his youthful worship of the very name of Wordsworth,
one can see that his attachment even to this most stately and
exacting of his seniors was not that of a slavish adherent,
conscious of being himself a nobody, but that of an independent younger intellect, becomingly deferential in the
presence of greatness, but that could observe sharply, reason
coolly, detect foibles, and be amused by them, even
while it yielded homage. So through De Quincey's intercourse with Coleridge. The demigod remained a demigod, but a demigod clouded and obscured. So, too, in the
other cases. When De Quincey sat and conversed with
Lamb, it was with De Quincey's eyes that he was looking all
the while at the delightful humourist and essayist, finding
that he was really as delightful and as good as all people
said he was, but nevertheless taking his measure. Then, to
come from the seniors to De Quincey's friends of his own
age, does any one think that, while he and Wilson were
walking together amid the scenery of the Lakes, and the
physically smaller of the two men had to look up a foot or
two every time he wanted to share the laugh on the jovial
face of the larger, there were not moments when the smaller

man had to resort mentally to his private intellectual gauge
for testing the worth of his radiant comrade's ideas on all
deeper matters in comparison with what he himself carried
in stock? Hence, accordingly, in all those celebrated
sketches by De Quincey of the contemporaries he admired
and honoured most, the presence always of a critical element,
—the interfusion of qualifying comment or actual banter
with the eulogy, the hinting or specifying of defects, the
relapse from the subject of the eulogy as he might deservedly
appear to the public through his public performances to the
man himself on that closer inspection against which not even
Adam, as the angel told him, could be quite safe,—

"Thy mate, who sees when thou art seen least wise."

Not the less, however, although De Quincey's admirations of
those who in his reckoning were the best of his contemporaries were thus all avowedly reasoned admirations, admirations of limited liability, have we to note his loyalty to
them.   Of this the re-expression of so many of them in the
present volume is a strong proof.   In the various sketches
of Wordsworth which may be read in previous volumes
there has been no deficiency of criticism of Wordsworth
personally ; and in one of them there is a special account of
those harshnesses of Wordsworth's character and demeanour
which had caused De Quincey's estrangement from him at
last.   In like manner we have heard of De Quincey's quarrel
with Coleridge on the precious question of their relative
degrees of guilt in the matter of opium-eating, and have seen
the worst that De Quincey had to say of his old friend in
that connexion.   Nor in the previous sketches of Charles
Lamb and Wilson was the *amari aliquid* totally wanting.   In
the return to these four in the present volume, however,
there is no increase of the critical mood, but rather a proclamation of unabated fidelity to the old allegiances.   There
is, indeed, no express new paper on Wordsworth (a paper of
1845 on Wordsworth's poetry having to be reserved for a
future volume because of its non-biographical character) ;
but every mention of Wordsworth's name, or quotation from
him, attests continued loyalty to that surviving patriarch of
English poetry.   Coleridge had been dead eleven years when

De Quincey penned the article entitled "Coleridge and
Opium-Eating"; but that article, despite its title, is in the
main a parting tribute to the memory of the man whom De
Quincey still believed to have been, in some intellectual
respects, the most extraordinary Englishman of his generation.
The paper on Charles Lamb surpasses what De Quincey had
previously written about Lamb for beauty and completeness
of appreciation. To learn what De Quincey really thought
of his magnificent friend Wilson, the Christopher North of
Blackwood, one must go rather to the two sketches of Wilson
in the present volume, and especially to the first of them
than to the brief sketch included in the series of the Autobiographic Reminiscences. Finally, it is in the present
volume, for the first time, that we see De Quincey in actual
contact with Sir William Hamilton, and learn, though in the
oddest fashion in which such an abstruse subject was ever
handled for the entertainment of readers of popular periodicals, what De Quincey thought of that since famous Scottish
philosopher, his enormous and miscellaneous scholarship, and
the worth of his slashing innovations upon the Scholastic
Logic.

From Christopher North and Sir William Hamilton to
pass to Charlemagne and Joan of Arc is certainly a long leap
backwards. The closing papers on these subjects, however,
have really their proper place among De Quincey's biographical sketches; and one reason for placing them last in
the volumes containing the Biographic Sketches is that they
seem to form a fit transition to the "Historical Essays and
Researches" which are to come in the next two volumes.
Both papers are worth reading. In the "Charlemagne," after
some excellent introductory observations on History in general,
De Quincey fastens on the great Frankish conqueror and
emperor of the eighth and ninth centuries, chiefly with the
view of contrasting him with Napoleon Bonaparte, the French
conqueror and emperor of the eighteenth and nineteenth.
De Quincey's prejudice against the modern French generally
having been notoriously one of his most extravagant characteristics, and Napoleon Bonaparte in particular having
been notoriously one of his life-long abominations, the contrast is so furiously to the disadvantage of the modern French

as compared with the Franks, and of Napoleon as compared with Charlemagne, that a careful reader may do well to adjourn the question for further investigation, only thanking this advocate for his eloquent pleading on one of the sides. The reception of the "Joan of Arc" may be different. Here, as if to vindicate himself from the imputation of being incapable of doing justice to the French or to anything in French History, De Quincey calls upon all Frenchmen to listen to what he, an Englishman, after Voltaire's old French ribaldries and the hesitancies of M. Michelet and other later Frenchmen, will say in honour of the heroic maid. It is the passages of fine lyrical prose at the opening and the close of the paper that chiefly recommend it now, and cause it to be remembered as De Quincey's. A good deal of the intermediate matter (of facetious disputation with M. Michelet, and what not) may seem unpleasantly out of key.

D. M.

DR. SAMUEL PARR;

OR,

WHIGGISM IN ITS RELATIONS TO LITERATURE.[1]

SECTION I

THE time is come when, without offence, the truth may be
spoken of Dr. Parr.[2] Standing too near to a man's grave,

[1] Originally published in *Blackwood's Magazine* for January, February, May, and June 1831, under the title, "Dr. Parr and His Contemporaries," and in the guise of a review of these three books :—(1) *The Works of Samuel Parr, D.D.*, with Memoirs, &c., by John Johnstone, M.D., in 8 vols., London 1828 ; (2) *Memoirs of Dr. Parr*, &c., by the Rev. William Field, in 2 vols., London 1828 ; (3) *Parriana ; or Notices of the Rev. Samuel Parr, LL.D.*, by E. H. Barker, Esq., London 1828. De Quincey, besides changing the title of the papers in his reprint of them in 1857 for the sixth volume of his Collective Writings, revised them carefully, making alterations, omissions, and additions. He also threw the original footnotes to the papers, or most of them, into an Appendix, as they appear in this volume.—M.

[2] Twenty-five years ago, I felt strong scruples in approaching the
subject of Dr. Parr, so much had a *partisan* interest invested the
Doctor : he was known, in fact, too well, and too polemically. But
mark how things change : at this moment it may be questioned
whether one reader in three thousand of readers belonging to this
present generation is likely to be aware who the Doctor was, or upon
what pretensions rest his claims to commemoration. Most people will
suppose him to be that Parr whose glorification arises from having
started in the trade of living during the reign of Henry VII and
wound up the concern during that of Charles II. But they will find
themselves mistaken. The Doctor belonged entirely to the Georgian
era : and his reputation is built upon that variety of scholarship

all writers who have trained themselves to habits of liberal
sympathy and of generous forbearance—all, in short, but the
very juvenile and thoughtless, or the very malignant—put a
seal upon their lips. Grief, and the passionate exaggerations
of grief, have then a title cheerfully recognised to indulgent
consideration. On this principle, I prescribed to myself
most willingly a duty of absolute silence at the time of Dr.
Parr's death,[1] and through the years immediately succeeding.
The sorrow of his numerous friends was at that time keen
and raw. For a warm-hearted man—and Dr. Parr was such
—there is an answerable warmth of regret. Errors and
indiscretions that made themselves painfully felt amongst his
living associates are then no longer remembered ; virtues
are brought forward into high relief ; talents and accomplishments are excusably magnified beyond all proportions of truth ; and even frailties that operated most
injuriously upon the comfort of his friends are now
regarded as mere natural expressions of a flesh-and-blood

which connects itself with full-blown pedantry. He was a pedagogue ;
and among the last of that generation that sternly contended for the
necessity of unlimited flagellation. He flagellated many distinguished
scions of aristocratic families, both Whigs and Tories, many of whom
thought vindictively on the subject of the Doctor, and were of
opinion that the reverend gentleman would have benefited much by
receiving tithes, which so sternly he exacted upon all other subjects of
culture, from the inhuman amount of scourgings annually reported as
"reaped" in his own private practice. A pedant, it may be thought,
can have no historic value. But even amongst pedants there are
better and worse ; more and less meritorious. Extraordinary erudition, even though travelling into obscure and sterile fields, has its own
peculiar interest. And about Dr. Parr, moreover, there circled
another and far different interest. His profession as a schoolmaster,
his reputed learning, and his political creed as a Whig, brought him
into direct personal intercourse with the great Whig leaders in Parliament. By looking forward to Section the Second of this paper on Parr,
my reader will find that (however scandalous such a fact may seem)
Dr. Parr corresponded with one-half of our British Peerage, with
select members of the royal family, and with the Episcopal Bench of
that Church which daily he insulted. But a deeper interest will
arise by anticipation when I promise him an access through this
same pedant to the letters of Fox in relation to the principles of
Burke. Such letters, on such a theme, will hang with gold bullion
even the records of a pedant.

[1] He was born in 1747, and died in 1825.—M.

humanity, that uttered itself in a language of fiery strength. These extravagances are even graceful under the immediate impulses which prompt them ; and for a season they are, and ought to be, indulged. But this season has its limits. Within those limits the rule is—*De mortuis nil nisi bonum.*[1] Beyond them, and when the privilege of recent death can no longer be sustained, this rule gives way to another—*De mortuis nil nisi demonstrabile.* This canon has now taken effect with regard to Dr. Parr. The sanctities of private grief must surely have received a sufficient homage, now that the grief itself has submitted to the mitigations of time. Enough has been conceded to the intemperance of sorrowing friend-

---

[1] "*De mortuis nil nisi bonum*" :—This famous canon of charity ("*Concerning the dead let us have nothing but what is kind and favourable*") has furnished an inevitable occasion for much doubtful casuistry. The dead, as those pre-eminently unable to defend themselves, enjoy a natural privilege of indulgence amongst the generous and considerate ; but not to the extent which this sweeping maxim would proclaim ; since, on this principle, in cases innumerable tenderness to the dead would become the ground of cruel injustice to the living : nay, the maxim would continually counterwork itself ; for too inexorable a forbearance with regard to one dead person would oftentimes effectually close the door to the vindication of another. In fact, neither history nor biography is able to move a step without infractions of this rule ; a rule emanating from the blind kindliness of grandmothers, who, whilst groping in the dark after one individual darling, forget the collateral or oblique results to others without end. These evils being perceived, equitable casuists began to revise the maxim, and in its new form it stood thus—"*De mortuis nil nisi verum*" ("*Concerning the dead let us have nothing but what is true*"). Why, certainly that is an undeniable right of the dead ; and nobody in his senses would plead for a small *percentage* of falsehood. Yet, again, in that shape, the maxim carries with it a disagreeable air of limiting the right to truth. Unless it is meant to reserve a small allowance of fiction for the separate use of the living, why insist upon truth as peculiarly consecrated to the dead ? If all people, living and dead alike, have a right to the benefits of truth, why specify one class, as if in silent contradistinction to some other class, less eminently privileged in that respect ? To me it seems evident that the human mind has been long groping darkly after some separate right of the dead in this respect, but which hitherto it has not been able to bring into reconciliation with the known rights of the living. Some distinct privilege there should be, if only it could be sharply defined and limited, through which a special prerogative might be recognised as amongst the sanctities of the grave.

ship: the time has at last arrived for the dispassionate appreciation of unbiassed equity.

Many are the years which have passed away since I first set eyes upon Dr. Samuel Parr. Off and on through the nine or ten years preceding, I had heard him casually mentioned in Oxford, but not for any good. In most cases, the occasion which suggested the mention of his unamiable name was some pointless parody of a Sam-Johnsonian increpation, some Drury-Lane counterfeit of the true Jovian thunderbolts. In no instance that I recollect had there appeared any felicity in these fulminations of Dr. Parr. With an unlimited licence of personal invective, and with an extravagance of brutality not credible, except in the case of one who happened to be protected by age and by his petticoats, — consequently with one power more than other people enjoy, who submit themselves to the restraints and decencies of social intercourse,—the Doctor had yet made nothing of his extra privilege : not so much as once had he attained a distinguished success. There was labour, indeed, and effort enough, preparation without end, and most tortuous circumgyration of periods ; but from all this sonorous smithery of harsh words, dark and pompous, nothing adequate emerged, — nothing commensurate, — but simply a voluminous smoke : for the Doctor was a patron of tobacco in a degree which made him the horror of ladies, and which in all respects reached a point of excess not often heard of except on the right bank of the Rhine and the left bank of the Danube. In smoke the Doctor's day commenced ; in smoke it closed ; smoke literal and abominable to his ox and his ass, to his man-servant and his maidservant, and to the stranger that was within his gates. But to me there seemed always to settle a smoke symbolical upon the whole sum of the Doctor's life—all that he did, and all that he tried to do. At length a day arrived on which the Fates had resolved that I should see Dr. Parr in the flesh.

The scene of this little affair was a front drawing-room in the London mansion of a Chancery barrister, Mr. Basil Montagu, eminent in himself, and foremost amongst Dr. Parr's friends. Here was collected a crowd of morning visitors to Mrs. Montagu : time—say 3 P.M. on a summer day in the year 1812 : and in a back drawing-room was heard, at intervals, the clamorous laugh of Dr. Samuel Parr, then recently arrived from the country upon a visit to his London friend. The miscellaneous company assembled were speedily apprised *who* was the owner of that obstreperous laugh—so monstrously beyond the key of good society ; it transpired, also, *who* it was that provoked the laugh, and in a subdued key sometimes accompanied that laugh ; it was the very celebrated *Bobus* Smith. And, as a hope was expressed that one or both of these gentlemen might soon appear amongst us, most of the company lingered, in the very reasonable expectation of seeing Dr. Sam,—but I myself on the very doubtful chance of seeing Mr. Bobus. Many of my junior readers, who cannot count back so far as to the year in question (1812), are likely to be much at a loss for the particular kind of celebrity which could possibly illustrate a name so little known to these present days as this of Bobus Smith. I interrupt, therefore, my little account of Dr. Parr, with the slightest outline of Mr. Smith's story and his pretensions. Bobus, then, was a brother of the Rev. Sydney Smith, already at that time well known as a wit and humorist, but through the next thirty and forty years even more so. Mr. Robert Smith, however, even then held the higher place in the esteem of his own domestic circle, for originality and power. How he came to be known as *Bobus* arose naturally thus : Robert being Latinised by adding the ordinary termination *us*, it was a playful expression of analogy to Latinise the familiar abbreviation *Bob* by the same process, as *Bob^{us}*. At Cambridge, where he had drawn public attention upon himself by Latin philosophic verses, framed on the model externally of Lucretius (*i.e.* as regards archaic forms of language), and otherwise much in the spirit of the Lucretian grandeur as to Orphic enthusiasm and fiery movement,—all these metrical essays, having been signed *Bob^{us} Smith*, had naturally made him known to the public under that signature.[1] But these were the playful ἀγωνίσ-

---

[1] "*That signature*" :—the first syllable not being pronounced short, as in the English name *Bob*, but long, as in *Bobus*, the dative plural of the word *bos* by contraction for *bovibus*.

μᾰτα, the rope-dancing trials of skill, that belonged to the earlier stages of his manhood. His maturer years exposed a loftier scale of ambition. Already, in the year 1808 or 1809, I had been told (whether truly or not) that Mr. Bobus had some years before announced his determination to do two little things, neither of which is easy, but one of which may be viewed as a sort of stepping-stone to the other ; so that the two jointly may be easier to do than the last singly. The first was—to create a fortune of sufficient magnitude in Bengal. Secondly, by and through the leverage of that Indian fortune, to vault by a hop-step-and-jump into the post of prime minister. A man armed with such a spirit of learned judgment upon life as Mr. Bobus could not be ignorant that to such a grand result there must co-operate not merely many a splendid intellectual gift, but also many a splendid gift of fortune—many a splendid connexion— many a splendid opportunity—many a splendid combination of chance and skill : and yet, with all this knowledge, Mr. Bobus was willing to stand the risk of the dice ; or else, in open defiance of the dice, was willing to throw himself, in faith upon his own intellectual supremacy, such as he conceived it to be. At last the fortune was made ; secondly, it was remitted ; and then, thirdly, Mr. Bobus thought of remitting himself. " *He's coming !* " said a whisper from somebody, that might upon consideration be Mr. Bobus himself. " *He's coming !* " echoed many whispers. " *He's come !* " was at last announced. And all the world of those in the secret stood on tiptoe, waiting for the result. He took the necessary steps for prosecuting his self-created mission : he caused himself to be returned to Parliament for some close borough ; he took his seat ; on a fitting occasion he prepared to utter his maiden oration ; for that purpose he raised himself bolt upright upon his pins ; all the world was hushed : you might have heard not merely a pin, but even a needle, drop. At this critical moment of his life, upon which all his vast cloud-built fabrics of ambition were suspended, when, if ever, he was called upon to converge all his energies, suddenly his presence of mind forsook him ; he faltered ; rudder and compass slipped away from him ; and —oh ! Castor and Pollux !—Bobus floundered ! nor, from that day to this, has he been heard of in the courts of ambition. This catastrophe had occurred some time before the present occasion ; and an event which entirely extinguished the world's interest in Mr. Bobus Smith had more than doubled my own. Consequently I waited with much solicitude. At length the door opened ; which recalls me from my digression into the high-road of my theme : for not Mr. Bobus Smith entered, who would have compelled me to continue the digression, but simply Dr. Parr, who in one moment compelled me to close it.

Nobody announced him ; and we were left to collect his name from his dress and his conversation. Hence it happened that for some time I was disposed to question myself whether this might not be Mr. Bobus even (little as it could be supposed to resemble him) rather than Dr. Parr, so much did he contradict all my rational preconceptions. "A man," said I, "who has insulted people so outrageously, ought not to have done this in single reliance upon his professional protections ; a brave man, and a man of honour, would here have carried about with him, in his manner and deportment, some such language as this :—' Do not think that I shelter myself under my gown from the natural consequences of the affronts I offer ; mortal combats I am forbidden, sir, as a Christian minister, to engage in ; but, as I find it impossible to refrain from occasional licence of tongue, I am very willing to fight a few rounds in a ring, with any gentleman who fancies himself ill used.' " Let me not be misunderstood ; I do not contend that Dr. Parr should often, or regularly, have offered this species of satisfaction. But I *do* insist upon it that no man should have given the very highest sort of provocation so wantonly as Dr. Parr is recorded to have done, unless conscious that, in a last extremity, he was ready, like a brave man, to undertake a short turn-up, in a private room, with any person whatsoever whom he had insulted past endurance. A doctor who had so often tempted (which is a kind way of saying—had merited) a cudgelling ought himself to have had some ability to cudgel. Dr. Johnson assuredly would have acted on that principle. Had volume the second of that same folio with which he floored Osborne happened to lie ready to the prostrate man's grasp, nobody can suppose that Johnson would have disputed Osborne's right to retaliate ; in which case a regular succession of rounds would have been established. Considerations such as these, and Dr. Parr's undeniable reputation (granted even by his most admiring biographers) as a sanguinary flagellator throughout his long career of pedagogue, had prepared me— nay, entitled me—to expect in Dr. Parr a huge carcase of man, fourteen stone at the least. Even his style, pursy and bloated, and his sesquipedalian words, all warranted the same expectation. Hence, then, my surprise, and the perplexity I have recorded, when the door opened, and a little man, in a most plebeian wig (far, indeed, from that wig of his which the " Edinburgh Review" of eight or nine years earlier had described as the mighty astonishment, or, in Greek, the μέγα θαῦμα of barbers), cut his way through the company, and made for a *fauteuil* standing opposite to the fire. Into this he *lunged ;* and then forthwith, without preface or apology, began to open his talk upon the room. Here arose a new marvel, and a greater. If I had been scandalised at Dr. Parr's want of thews and bulk, conditions so indispensable for enacting the part of Sam Johnson, much more, and with better reason, was I now petrified with his voice, utterance, gestures, and demeanour. Conceive, reader, by way of counterpoise to the fine classical pronunciation [1] of Dr. Johnson, an infantine lisp—the worst I ever heard—from the lips of a man above sixty, and accompanied with all sorts of ridiculous grimaces and little stage gesticulations. As he sat in his chair, turning alternately to the right and to the left, that he might distribute his edification in equal proportions amongst us, he seemed the very image of a little French gossiping abbé.

Yet all that I have mentioned was, and seemed to be, a trifle by comparison with the infinite pettiness of his matter. Nothing did he utter but little shreds of calumnious tattle— the most ineffably silly and frivolous of all that was then

[1] Boswell, whose ear was peculiarly quick, and whose sensibilities, to the better and the worse, in this accomplishment were fastidiously cultivated—for, in his English residences, he made a diligent use of his numerous introductions to the *élite* of English society—has somewhere noticed expressly the singular beauty which distinguished Dr. Johnson's accentuation and intonation of English.

circulating in the Whig *salons* of London against the Regent.
I ought, by the way, to have prefaced my little narrative by
mentioning that about this summer of 1812 the Whig party
had perfected their sense of a perfidy to themselves on the
part of the Regent. In 1810 it happened that George III
accomplished as a king what is called the *golden* jubilee. The
twenty-fifth year of any connexion—as, for instance, of a
marriage—is called the *silver* jubilee ; but the fiftieth year
the *golden*. This had been celebrated with peculiar enthusiasm
by the nation ; and it was supposed that the nervous
sympathies of the king had been too powerfully called into
activity by such parts of the festivities as could not, with
every care, be wholly withdrawn from his participation. Out
of this excitement arose a second insanity. On the first,
when the Prince of Wales was a very young and indiscreet
man, Mr. Pitt's party was not disposed to have lodged much
power in his Royal Highness's hands, and none at all as due
by any constitutional right. But things were altered now :
the Florizel [1] that had been sowing his wild oats in the
former lunacy was now an elderly man ; his *Perditas*, one
and all, were dead and buried ; and, what was of even more
importance, it seemed too probable (as in fact happened) that
this second lunacy would not depart unless in company with
life. The new Regent might now, therefore, be regarded as
virtually king. This trebled his value to that party which
should now succeed in winning his confidence. But on such
a question what room for a doubt ? Surely that party
which had stood by him through life possessed a paramount
claim on his gratitude. True ; but paramount to all private
claims was that of Britain and of Europe. Was the war in
Spain to be maintained or not ? The Whigs had so used
this great question as an engine of partisan attack upon their
opponents that it had become impossible for *them*, with any
colour of consistency, to do otherwise than withdraw the
British armies from the Peninsula. That one point settled

---

[1] " *The Florizel* " :—See Shakspere's "Winter's Tale." At this great
distance of time, when seventy years or so have intervened, it becomes
necessary to mention that the beautiful Mrs. Robinson, who was the
first love of the Prince of Wales, originally caught his eye in performing the part of *Perdita* in this exquisite drama.

the case ; and upon that argument, just at this time in 1812, the wrath of the Whig party was culminating.

He began precisely in these words : " Oh! I shall tell you " (laying a stress upon the word *shall*, which still further aided the resemblance to a Frenchman) " a sto-hee " (lispingly for story) _" about the Pince Thegent " (such was his nearest approximation to *Prince Regent*). " Oh, the Pince Thegent! —the Pince Thegent!—what a sad, sad man he has turned out! But you *shall* hear. Oh, what a Pince!—what a Thegent!—what a sad Pince Thegent!" And so the old babbler went on, sometimes wringing his hands in lamentation, sometimes flourishing them with French grimaces and shrugs of shoulders, sometimes expanding and contracting his fingers like a fan. After an hour's twaddle of this scandalous description, suddenly he rose, and hopped out of the room, exclaiming all the way, " *Oh, what a Pince !—Oh, what a Thegent! Is it a Thegent, is it a Pince, that you call this man ? Oh, what a sad Pince ! Did anybody ever hear of such a sad Pince !—such a sad Thegent !—such a sad, sad Pince Thegent ? Oh, what a Pince !* " &c., da capo.

Not without indignation did I exclaim to myself, on this winding-up of the scene, " And so this, then, this lithping slander-monger, and retailer of gossip fit rather for washer-women over their tea than for scholars and statesmen, is the champion whom his party would propound as the adequate antagonist of Samuel Johnson! Faugh!"——— I had occasion, in this instance, as in so many others which I have witnessed, to remark the conflict between the natural and the artificial (or adopted) opinions of the world, and the practical triumph of the first. A crowd of ladies were present ; most of them had been taught to believe that Dr. Parr was a prodigious scholar, and in some mysterious way, and upon something not exactly known or understood, except by learned men, a great authority. Accordingly, upon his first entrance, all of them were awed—deep silence prevailed—and the hush of indefinite expectation. Two minutes dispersed that feeling ; the Doctor spoke, and the spell was broken. No sooner was the style and tendency of Dr. Parr's gossip apparent than a large majority of those present broke up into little parties, entered upon their own affairs, and, by a tacit

convention, agreed to consider the Doctor as addressing himself exclusively to the lady of the house and her immediate
circle. Had Sam Johnson been the talker nobody would
have presumed to do this; secondly, nobody would have
been so indiscreet as to do this—he would not have acknowledged weariness had he felt it; but, lastly, nobody would
have wished to do this—weariness was impossible in the
presence of Sam Johnson. Neither let it be said that perhaps
the ladies present were unintellectual, and careless of a
scholar's conversation. They were not so ; all were tinctured
with literature, and one or two of distinguished talents. And
I can undertake to say that any man of tolerable colloquial
powers, speaking upon a proper topic, would have commanded
the readiest attention. As it was, every one felt (if she did
not even whisper to her neighbour), " Here, at least, is nothing
to be learned."

Such was my own first interview with Dr. Parr ; such its
issue. And now let me explain my drift in thus detailing
its circumstances. Some people will say, the drift was doubtless to exhibit Dr. Parr in a disadvantageous light—as a petty
gossiper, and a man of mean personal appearance. No, by
no means. Far from it. I, that write this paper, have myself a mean personal appearance ; and I love men of mean
appearance.[1] Having one spur more than other men to seek
distinction in those paths where nature has not obstructed
them, they have one additional chance (and a great one) for
giving an extended development to their intellectual powers.
Many a man has risen to eminence under the powerful reaction
of his mind in fierce counter-agency (sometimes even, more
nobly, in grand benignant indifference) to the scorn of the
unworthy daily evoked by his personal defects, who with a

[1] In a letter of Southey's to his brother, Lieutenant Southey, of
date Keswick, Nov. 12, 1808, he wrote—"Little Mr. De Quincey is
at Grasmere. He was here last week, and is coming again. I wish
he was not so little, and I wish he would not leave his greatcoat always
behind him upon the road. But he is a very able man, with a head
brimful of information." At the date of that letter De Quincey was
but twenty-three years of age. But the same impression of his extremely diminutive appearance accompanied him through life, until,
the compensating boyish bloom of his face in his earlier years having
given way to seams and wrinkles under the wear and tear of his later,
he struck every one as " a little druid wight of withered aspect."—M.

handsome person would have sunk into the luxury of a careless life under the tranquillising smiles of continual admiration. Dr. Parr, therefore, lost nothing in *my* esteem by showing a meanish exterior. Yet even this was worth mentioning, and had a value in reference to my present purpose. I like Dr. Parr : I may say, even, that I love him, for some noble qualities of heart that really *did* belong to him, and were continually breaking out in the midst of his singular infirmities. But this, or a far nobler moral character than Dr. Parr's, can offer no excuse for giving a false elevation to his intellectual pretensions, and raising him to a level which he will be found incapable of keeping when the props of partial friendship are withdrawn. My object is to value Dr. Parr's claims, and to assign his true station both in literature and in those other walks of life upon which he has come forward as a public man. With such a purpose before me, it cannot be wholly irrelevant to notice even Dr. Parr's person, and to say that it was at once coarse and in some degree mean ; for his too friendly biographers have repeatedly made his personal appearance the subject of flattery, and more than once have expressly characterised it as " dignified,"—which it was *not*, according to any possible standard of dignity, but far otherwise ; and it is a good inference (is it not ?) from such a mis-statement to other mis-statements grosser and more injuriously misleading. His person was poor, and his features were coarse and ignoble, with an air, at the same time, of drollery, that did not sit well upon age or the gravity of his profession. Upon one feature, indeed, Dr. Parr valued himself exceedingly ; this was his eye. He fancied that it was peculiarly searching and significant : he conceited, even, that it frightened people, and had a particular form of words for expressing the severe use of this basilisk function: " I *inflicted* my eye upon him," was his phrase in such cases.[1] But the thing was all a mistake ; his eye could be borne very well ; there was no mischief in it. Doubtless, when a nervous gentleman in a pulpit, who was generally the subject of these inflictions, saw a comical-looking old man from below levelling one eye at him, with as knowing an expression as he could throw into it, mere per-

[1] See De Quincey's Appended Note to this page.—M.

plexity as to the motive and proper construction of so unseasonable a personality might flutter his spirits, and, to
the vain, misjudging operator below, might distort this
equivocal confusion, arising out of blank ignorance of his
meaning, into the language of a conscious and confessing
culprit. Explanations would be of rare occurrence ; for
some would not condescend to complain ; and others would
feel that the insult, unless it was for the intention, had
scarcely body enough and tangible shape to challenge inquiry.
To remonstrate would only be to let Dr. Parr know that he
had succeeded in lodging an affront, and also to give him an
opportunity for redoubling it. They would anticipate that
the same man who, in so solemn a situation as that between
a congregation and their pastor, could offer such an affront,
would be apt to throw a fresh ridicule upon the complaint
itself, by saying—"Fix my eye upon you, did I ? Why,
that's all my eye with a vengeance.   Look at you, did I ?
Well, sir, a cat may look at a king."   This said in a tone of
sneer ; and then, with sneer and strut at once, "I trust, sir
—humbly, I take leave to suppose, sir—that Dr. Parr is not
so obscure a person, not so wholly unknown in this sublunary
world, but he may have licence to look even at as great a
man as the Reverend Mr. So-and-so."   And thus the worthy
Doctor would be confirmed in his mistake that he carried
about with him, in his very homely collection of features, an
organ of singular power and effect for detecting hidden guilt.

A mistake, at all events, it was ; and his biographers have
gone into it as largely under the delusions of friendship as
he under the delusions of vanity.   On this, therefore, I
ground what seems a fair inference—that, if in matters so
plain and palpable as the character of a man's person and
the cast of his features it has been possible for his friends to
fall into gross errors and exaggerations, much more may we
count upon such fallacies of appreciation in dealing with the
subtler qualities of his intellect, and his less determinable
pretensions as a scholar.   Hence I have noticed these lower
and trivial misrepresentations as presumptions for suspecting
more weighty instances of the same exaggerating spirit.   The
animus which prompted so unserviceable a falsification of the
real case is not likely to have hesitated when coming upon

ground more important to Dr. Parr's reputation, and, at the same time, much more susceptible of a sincere latitude of appraisement, even amongst the neutral. I call the whole estimates to a new audit, and submit the claims of Dr. Parr to a more equitable tribunal. I would anticipate the award of posterity ; and it is no fault of mine that, in doing so, it will be necessary to hand the Doctor down from that throne in the cathedral of English clerical merit, on which the intemperate zeal of his friends has seated him for the moment, into some humble prebendal stall. Far more agreeable it would naturally have been to assist in raising a man unjustly depreciated than to undertake an office generally so ungracious as that of repressing the presumptuous enthusiasm of partisans, where it may *seem* to have come forward, with whatever exaggerations, yet still in a service of disinterested friendship, and on behalf of a man who, after all, was undeniably learned. The disinterestedness, however, of that admiration which has gathered about Dr. Parr is not so genuine as it may appear. His biographers (be it recollected) are bigots, who serve their superstition in varnishing their idol ; they are Whigs, who lose no opportunity of undervaluing Tories ; they are religious Dissenters, who value their theme quite as much for the collateral purpose which it favours of attacking the Church of England as for its direct and avowed one of lauding Dr. Parr. Moreover, in the letters (which, in the undigested chaos of Dr. Johnstone's collection, form three volumes out of eight [1]), Dr. Parr himself obtains a mischievous power, which, in a more regular form of composition, he would not have possessed, and which, as an honest man, we must presume that he would not have desired. Letters addressed to private correspondents, and only by accident reaching the press, have all the licence of private conversation. Most of us, perhaps, send a little treason or so at odd times through the post-office. In all this there is no blame. *Hanc veniam petimusque damusque vicissim.* Such an indulgence we claim for ourselves, and allow to our antagonists · we give and we take interchangeably. But publication is

[1] *The Works of Samuel Parr, LL.D. : with Memoirs of his Life and Writings and a Selection from his Correspondence,* by John Johnstone, M.D., 8 vols., London, 1828.—M.

another thing. Rash insinuations, judgments of *ultra* violence, injurious anecdotes of loose or no authority, and paradoxes sportively maintained in the certainty of a benignant construction on the part of the individual correspondent—all these, when printed, become armed, according to circumstances of time and person, with the power of extensive mischief. It is undeniable that through Dr. Parr's published letters are scattered some scores of passages which, had he been alive, or had they been brought forward in a formal address to the public, would have called forth indignant replies of vehement expostulation or blank contemptuous contradiction. And many even of his more general comments on political affairs, or on the events and characters of his times, would have been overlooked only upon the consideration that the place which he occupied, in life or in literature, was not such as to aid him in giving effect to his opinions.

In many of these cases, as we have said already, the writer had a title to allowance which those who publish his letters have *not*. But there are other cases which call for as little indulgence to him as to them. In some of his political intemperances, he may be considered as under a twofold privilege : first, of place—since, as a *private* letter-writer, writing in his study things meant to be read in his correspondent's drawing-room, he must be held as within the protection and the licence of his own fireside ; secondly, of time—since, on a general rule of construction, it may be assumed that such communications are not deliberate, but thrown off on the spur of the occasion ; that they express, therefore, not a man's settled and abiding convictions, but the first momentary impulses of his passion or his humour. But in many of his malicious sarcasms and disparaging judgments upon contemporaries who might be regarded as competitors with himself, either for the prizes of clerical life or for public estimation, Dr. Parr could take no benefit by this liberal construction. The sentiments he avowed in many cases of this description were not in any respect hasty or unpremeditated ebullitions of a momentary impulse. This is evident ; because uniformly, and as often almost as he either spoke or wrote upon the persons in question, he gave vent to the same bilious jealousy in sneers or libels of one uniform character ; and, if he forbore to do this in his open and avowed publications, the fair inference is that his fears or his interest restrained him ; since it is notorious, from the general evidence of his letters and his conversation, that none of those whom he viewed with these jealous feelings could believe that they owed anything by possibility to his courtesy or his moderation.

For example, and just to illustrate my meaning, in what terms did he speak and write of the very eminent Dean of Carlisle, the late Dr. Isaac Milner ? How did he treat Bishop Herbert Marsh ? How, again, the illustrious Bishop Horsley ?[1] All of them, I answer, with unprovoked scurrility. Not one had offered him any slight or offence ; all were persons of gentlemanly bearing, though the last (it is true) had shown some rough play to one of Parr's pet heresiarchs ; all of them were entitled to his respect by attainments in various directions superior to his own ; and all of them were more favourably known to the world than himself, by useful contributions to science or theologic learning. Dean Milner had ruined his own activities by eating opium ; and he is known, I believe, by little more than his continuation down to the Lutheran period of that Ecclesiastical History which had been originally undertaken by his brother Joseph,[2] and by the papers which he contributed to the London Philosophical Transactions. But his researches and his accomplishments were of wonderful extent ; and his conversation is still remembered by multitudes for its remarkable compass, and its almost Burkian quality of elastic accommodation to the fluctuating accidents of the occasion,[3] so that his contributions were not drawn from recollections of past studies that fitted in by accident to an alien call, but were felt to be a natural and spontaneous *growth* under the inspirations of the moment. The dean was not much in the world's eye : at intervals, indeed, he was to be found at the

---

[1] Dr. Isaac Milner, 1751-1820 ; Bishop Herbert Marsh, 1758-1839; Bishop Samuel Horsley, 1733-1806.—M.

[2] *History of the Church of Christ*, by Joseph Milner, 5 vols., 1794. *Additions by Isaac Milner*, 1819.—M.

[3] See De Quincey's Appended Note to this page.—M.

tables of the great ; more often he sought his ease and consolations in his honourable academic retreat, as the head of
Queen's College, Cambridge. There he was the object of
dislike to a particular intriguing *clique* that had the ear of
Dr. Parr. He was also obnoxious to the great majority of
mere worldlings, as one of those zealous Christians who are
usually denominated *evangelical;* that is to say, in common
with the Wilberforces, Thorntons, Hoares, Babingtons, Gis-
bornes, &c., and many thousands of less distinguished persons
in and out of Parliament, Dean Milner assigned a peculiar
emphasis, and a more significant interpretation, to those
doctrines of original sin, the terms upon which redemption
is offered,—to regeneration, sanctification, &c.,—which have
the appearance of being the *characteristic* parts in the
Christian economy. Whether otherwise wrong or right in
these views, it strikes us poor lay critics (who pretend to no
authoritative knowledge on these great mysteries) that those
who adopt them have at all events a *primâ facie* title to be
considered less worldly, and more spiritual-minded, than the
mass of mankind ; and such a frame of mind is at least an
argument of fitness for religious contemplations, in so far as
temper is concerned, be the doctrinal (or merely intellectual)
errors what they may. Consequently, for our own parts,
humbly sensible as we are of our deficiencies in this great
science of Christian philosophy, we could never at any time
join in the unthinking ridicule which is scattered by the
brilliant and the dull upon these peculiarities. Wheresoever, and whensoever, we must freely avow that evidences of
real nonconformity to the spirit of this impure earth of ours
command our unfeigned respect. But *that* was a thing which
the worthy Dr. Parr could not abide. He loved no high or
aerial standards in morals or in religion. Visionaries, who
encouraged such notions, he viewed (to express it by a learned
word) as ἀεροβατοῦντας, and as fit subjects for the chastisement of the secular arm. In fact, he would have persecuted
a little upon *such* a provocation. On Mr. Pitt and the rest
who joined in suspending the *Habeas Corpus* Act Dr. Parr
was wont to ejaculate his pastoral benediction in the following after-dinner toast—" *Qui suspenderunt, suspendantur !* "
And afterwards, upon occasion of the six bills provoked by

the tumults at Manchester, Glasgow, &c., his fatherly blessing was daily uttered in this little caressing sentiment—" Bills for the throats of those who framed the bills!" On the same principle, he would have prayed fervently—had any Isaac Milner infested his parish—" Let those who would exalt our ideals of Christianity be speedily themselves exalted!" And, therefore, if any man inquires upon what grounds it was that Dr. Parr hated with an intolerant hatred —scorned, and sharpened his gift of sneer upon—the late Dean of Carlisle, I have here told him "the reason why"; and reason enough, I think, in all conscience. For be it known that, over and above other weighty and obvious arguments for such views, Dr. Parr had a standing personal irritation connected with this subject—a continual "thorn in the flesh"—in the relations subsisting between himself and his principal, the incumbent of his own favourite and adopted parish. As the position of the parties was amusing to those who were in possession of the key to the right understanding of it—viz. a knowledge of their several views and opinions —I will pause a moment to describe the circumstances of the case.

Dr. Parr, it is well known, spent a long period of his latter life at Hatton, a village in Warwickshire. The living of Hatton belonged to Dr. Bridges, who, many a long year ago, was well known in Oxford as one of the fellows in the magnificently-endowed College of Magdalen; that is to say, Dr. Bridges was the incumbent at the time when some accident of church preferment brought Dr. Parr into that neighbourhood. By an arrangement which I do not exactly understand, the two doctors, for their mutual convenience, exchanged parishes. I find it asserted by Dr. Johnstone that on Dr. Parr's side the exchange originated in a spirit of obliging accommodation. It may be so: although the word *accommodation*, which forced itself slowly upon the hazy intellect of Shakspere's Bardolph as "that by which a man is, or may be thought to be, accommodated," does not certainly appear to have ever found a place in the practical vocabulary of Dr. Parr. However, one pointed reservation was made by Dr. Bridges (whether in obedience to church discipline or to his private scruples of conscience, I cannot say): viz. that

once in every year (according to my remembrance, for a series
of six consecutive Sundays) he should undertake the pulpit
duties of the church.   On this scheme the two learned clerks
built their *alterni fœdera regni*[1] ; and, like two buckets, the
Drs. Bridges and Parr went up and down reciprocally for a
long succession of years.   The waters, however, which they
brought up to the lips of their parishioners were drawn from
two different wells ; for Dr. Bridges shared in the heresy of
the Dean of Carlisle.   Hence a system of energetic (on Dr.
Parr's side, we may say of fierce) mutual counteraction.
Each, during his own reign, laboured to efface all impressions
left by his rival.   On Dr. Bridges's part, this was probably,
in some measure, a necessity of conscience ; for he looked
upon his flock as ruined in spiritual health by the neglect
and ignorance of their pastor.   On Dr. Parr's, it was the
mere bigotry of hatred, such as all schemes of teaching are
fitted to provoke which appeal to a standard of ultra-perfec-
tion, or exact any peculiar sanctity of life.   Were Bridges
right, in that case, it was clear that Parr was wrong by vital
defect.   But, on the other hand, were Parr right, then
Bridges was wrong only by superfluity and pardonable re-
dundance.   Such was the position, such the mutual aspects,
of the two doctors.   Parr's wrath waxed hotter and hotter.
Had Dr. Bridges happened to be a vulgar sectarian, of narrow
education, of low breeding, and without distinguished connexions, — those *etesian* gales or annual monsoons which
brought in his periodical scourge would have been hailed by
Parr as the harbingers of a triumph in reversion.   Yielding
the pulpit to his rival for a few Sundays, he would have
relied upon the taste of his parishioners for making the
proper distinctions.   He would have said—"You have all
eyes and ears—you all know that fellow ; you all know me :
need I say more ?   Pray, don't kick him when he comes
again."   But in the present case this sort of contempt was
out of the question.   Dr. Bridges was a man of fortune ;
travelled and accomplished ; familiar with courts and the
manners of courts.   Even that intercourse with people of
rank and fashion which Parr so much cultivated in his latter
years, and which, to his own conceit, placed him so much in

[1] Their compact of alternate sovereignty.

advance of his own order, gave him no advantage over Dr. Bridges. True, the worthy fanatic (as some people called him) had planted himself in a house at Clifton near Bristol, and spent all his days in running up and down the lanes and alleys of that great city, carrying Christian instruction to the dens of squalid poverty, and raising the torch of spiritual light upon the lairs of dissolute wretchedness. But, in other respects, he was a man *comme il faut*. However his mornings might be spent, his *soirées* were elegant, and it was not an impossible event to meet a prince or an ambassador at his parties. Hence it became vexatiously difficult to treat him as a person of no social consideration. In that view he was the better man of the two. And Parr's revenge, year after year, was baulked of its food. In this dilemma of impotent rage, what he could he did! And the scene was truly whimsical. Regularly as Dr. Bridges approached, Dr. Parr fled the country. As the wheels of Dr. Bridges were heard muttering menacingly in advance, Dr. Parr's wheels were heard groaning sullenly in retreat. And, when the season of this annual affliction drew to a close, when the wrath of Providence was spent, and the church of Hatton passed from under the shadows of eclipse into renovated light, then did Dr. Parr—cautiously putting out his feelers to make sure of the enemy's retreat—resume the spiritual sceptre. He congratulated his parish of Hatton that their trials were over ; he performed classical *lustrations*, and Pagan rites of expiation ; he circled the churchyard nine times *withershins* (or inverting the course of the sun) ; he fumigated the whole precincts of Hatton Church with shag tobacco ; and left no stone unturned to cleanse his little Warwickshire fold from its piacular pollution.

This anecdote illustrates Dr. Parr's temper. Mark, reader, his self-contradiction. He hated what he often called "rampant orthodoxy," and was never weary of running down those churchmen who thought it their duty to strengthen the gates of the English Church against Popish superstitions (or what *they* viewed as such), on the one hand, or against Socinianism on the other. Yet, let anything start up in the shape of zealous and fervid devotion—right or wrong—and let it threaten to displace his own lifeless

scheme of ethics, or to give a shock of galvanism to his
weekly paralytic exhortations ; let but a scintillation appear
of opposition in that shape, and who so ready to persecute
as Dr. Parr ? Fanaticism, he would tell us, was what he
could not bear : the rights of the Church must be supported
with rigour ; if needful, even with severity.   He was also a
great patron of the Church as against laymen ; of the parson
as against the churchwarden ; of the rector's right to graze
his horse upon the graves ; of the awful obligation upon his
conscience to allow of no darned or ill-washed surplice ; of
the solemn responsibility which he had undertaken in the
face of his country to suffer no bell-ringing except in canonical
hours ; to enforce the decalogue, and also the rubric ; to obey
his ecclesiastical superiors within the hours of divine service ;
and, finally, to read all proclamations or other state documents sent to him by authority with the most dutiful submission, simply reserving to himself the right of making
them as ridiculous as possible by his emphasis and cadence.
In this fashion Dr. Parr manifested his reverence for the
Church Establishment ; and for these great objects it seemed
to him lawful to persecute.[1]   But, as to purity of doctrine,
zeal, primitive devotion, the ancient faith as we received it
from our fathers, or any service pretending to be more than
lip service—for all such questionable matters it was incumbent upon us to show the utmost liberality of indifference on
the most modern and showy pattern, and, except for Popery,
to rely upon Bishop Hoadly.   This explanation was necessary to make the anecdote of Dr. Bridges fully intelligible ;
and that anecdote was necessary to explain the many scornful
allusions to that reverend gentleman which the reader will
find in Dr. Johnstone's collection of letters ; but, above all, it
was necessary for the purpose of putting him in possession of
Dr. Parr's character and position as a member of the Church
of England.

To return from this digression into the track of our
speculations : Dean Milner and Dr. Bridges stood upon the
same ground in Dr. Parr's displeasure.   Their offence was
the same, their criminality perhaps equal ; and it was
obviously of a kind that, for example's sake, ought not to be

[1] See De Quincey's Appended Note to this page.—M.

overlooked.   But Herbert Marsh was not implicated in
their atrocities. No charge of that nature was ever preferred
against *him*.   His merits were of a different order, and,—
confining my remarks to his *original* merit, and that which
perhaps exclusively drew upon him the notice of Mr. Pitt's
government, — not so strictly clerical.   His earliest public
service was his elaborate account of the regal conferences at
Pilnitz, and his consequent justification of this country in
the eyes of Europe on the question, then pending between
her and the French Republic, with which party lay the *onus*
of first virtual aggression, and with which therefore, by implication, the responsibility for that deluge of blood and
carnage which followed.[1]   This service Herbert Marsh performed in a manner to efface the remembrance of all former
attempts.   His next service was more in the character of his
profession : he introduced his country to the very original
labours in theology of Michaelis, and he expanded the compass
and value of these labours by his own exertions.[2]   Patriots,
men even with the feeblest sense of patriotism, have felt grateful to Dr. Marsh for having exonerated England from the guilt
of creating a state of war lightly—upon a weak motive—upon
an unconsidered motive—or indeed upon any motive or reason
whatsoever ; for a reason supposes choice and election of the
judgment, and choice there can be none without an acknowledged alternative.   Now it was the triumphant result of
Dr. Marsh's labours that alternative there was practically
none, under the actual circumstances, for Great Britain ; and
that war was the mere injunction of a flagrant necessity,
coupling the insults and the menaces of France with what
are now known to have been the designs, and indeed the
momentary interests, of the predominant factions at that
epoch.   Herbert Marsh has satisfied everybody almost but
the bigots (if any now survive) of Jacobinism as it raged in
1792 and 1793, when it held its horrid Sabbaths over the
altar and the throne, and deluged the scaffolds with innocent

---

[1] *History of the Politics of Great Britain and France from the
time of the Conference at Pilnitz to the Declaration of War against
Great Britain.*   2 vols.   1800.—M.
[2] Michaelis's *Introduction to the New Testament*, translated from
the German, with notes, etc.   6 vols.   1793-1801.—M.

blood. All but those he has satisfied. Has he satisfied Dr.
Parr ? No. For those who governed his fluctuating conscience were the parliamentary leaders from whom he
expected a bishopric (and would very possibly have got it,
had some of them lived a little longer in the first decade of
this century, or he himself lived to the end of the third).[1]
Hence it does not much surprise me that, in spite of his
natural and creditable horror on the judicial murder of the
French king, he relapsed into Jacobinism so fierce that two
years after a friend, by way of agreeable flattery, compliments
him as being only "*half* a *sansculotte*"; a compliment, however, which he doubtless founded more upon his confidence
in Dr. Parr's original goodness of heart, and the almost
inevitable contagion of English society, than upon any
warrant which the Doctor had yet given him by words or
by acts for so advantageous an opinion. Well, therefore,
might Herbert Marsh displease Dr. Parr. He was the open
antagonist of those through whom only the fortunes of
sansculottes, thorough-bred or half-bred, had any chance of
thriving; and he had exposed the hollowness of that cause
to which the Doctor was in a measure sold.

As to Horsley, his whole life, as a man of letters and a
politician, must have won him the acceptable tribute of Dr.
Parr's fear and hatred; a tribute which Dr. Parr paid as
duly as his assessed taxes. Publicly, indeed, he durst not
touch him; for the horrid scourge which Horsley had
wielded at one time, in questions of scholarship and orthodoxy, still resounded in his ears. But in his letters and
conversation Dr. Parr fretted for ever at his eminence, and
eyed him grudgingly and malignly; and those among his
correspondents who were not too generous and noble-minded
to pay their court through his weaknesses evidently were
aware that a sneer at Bishop Horsley was as welcome as a
basket of game. Sneers, indeed, were not the worst: there
are to be found in Dr. Parr's correspondence some dark insinuations, apparently pointed at Horsley, which involve a
sort of charges that should never be thrown out against any
man without the accompaniment of positive attestations.
What may have been the tenor of that bishop's life and

[1] See De Quincey's Appended Note to this page.—M.

conversation I do not take upon myself to say. It is little probable, at this time of day, under the censorious vigilance of so many unfriendly eyes, and in a nation where even the persons upon the *judicial* bench exhibit in their private lives almost a sanctity of deportment, that a dignitary of the English Church will err by any scandalous immorality. Be that, however, as it may, and confining our view to Horsley in his literary character, I must say that he is far beyond the reach of Dr. Parr's hostility. As a polemic and a champion of his own Church, he was above the competition of any contemporary divine. As a theologian, he reconciles the nearly contradictory merits of novelty and originality with well-meditated orthodoxy ; and I may venture to assert that his *Sermons* produced a greater impression than any English book of pure divinity for the last century.[1] In saying this, I do not speak of the sale ; what that might be I know not ; I speak of the strength of the impression diffused through the upper circles, as apparent in the reverential terms which, after the appearance of that work, universally marked the sense of cultivated men in speaking of Bishop Horsley—even of those who had previously viewed him with some dislike in his character of controversialist. Let the two men be compared ; not the veriest bigot amongst the Dissenters, however much he would naturally prefer as a companion, or as a subject for eulogy, that man who betrayed the interests of his own Church to him who was its column of support and ornament, could have the hardihood to insinuate that Dr. Horsley was properly, or becomingly, a mark for the scurrilities of Dr. Parr. In what falls within the peculiar province of a schoolmaster, I think it probable (to make every allowance which candour demands) that Dr. Parr had that superior accuracy which is maintained by the practice of teaching. But in reach and compass of intellect in those mixed branches of speculative research which belong equally to divinity and to metaphysics (as in the Platonic philosophy), in philosophic scholarship, and generally in vigour of style and thought, I suppose Horsley to have had, in the eyes of the public no less than in the realities of the

---

[1] His *Sermons* were published in 1810-1822 in four volumes, and again in 1829 in two volumes.—M.

case, so prodigiously the advantage that none but a sycophant or a false friend would think of suggesting seriously a comparison so disadvantageous to Dr. Parr. But, at all events, let the *relations* of merit be what they may in Horsley, certainly his absolute merit is unquestionable ; and the continued insults of Dr. Parr are insufferable.

Upon these justifying grounds—viz. special attacks past counting, besides a general *system* of disparagement and contumely towards the most distinguished pretensions in Church and State, unless ranged on the side of the Whigs— I stand for a sufficient apology in pressing the matter strongly against Dr. Parr.[1] Not Tories only, but all who resist anarchists (for that Dr. Parr did not blazon himself in that character was due to the lucky accident which saved him from all opportunities of *acting* upon his crazy speculations), have an interest in depressing to their proper level those who make a handle of literature for insidious party purposes, polluting its amenities with the angry passions proper to our civil dissensions, and abusing the good-nature with which we Tories are always ready to welcome literary merit without consideration of politics. In order to appraise Dr. Parr satisfactorily, let us pursue him through his three characters, the triple *role* which he supported in life : first, of Whig politician ; secondly, of scholar (or, expressing our meaning in its widest extent, of literary man) ; and, finally, of theologian.

There are, in every populous community, many different strata of society, that lie in darkness, as it were, to each other, from mere defect of mutual intercourse ; and in the literary world there are many chambers that have absolutely no intercommunication. Afterwards, when thirty or sixty years have passed away—by means of posthumous memoirs, letters, anecdotes, and other literary monuments—they are all brought, in a manner, face to face ; and we, their posterity, first see them as making up a whole, of which they themselves were imperfectly conscious. Every year makes further disclosures ; and thus a paradox is realised, that the more we are removed from personal connexion with a past age of literature oftentimes the better we know it.

[1] See De Quincey's Appended Note to this page.—M.

Meantime, as an appropriate close to this preliminary section, I will put a question—and in a cursory way discuss the proper answer to it—upon Dr. Parr, as a man of the world, and ambitious candidate for worldly distinctions ; in short, as the architect of his fortunes. Was he, in *this* light, an able and successful man ? Or, separating the two parts of that question, which do not *always* proceed concurrently, if he were not successful in a degree corresponding to his own wishes and the expectations of his friends,—if it is notorious that he missed of attaining those prizes which he never hesitated to avow as the objects that stimulated his ambition,—in what degree are we to ascribe his failure to want of talent, to misdirection of his talent, to a scrupulous and fastidious integrity, to the injustice of his superiors, or, finally, to mere accidents of ill luck ? One man in each ten thousand comes into this world, according to the homely saying, " with a silver spoon in his mouth " ; but most men have a fortune to make, a station to create. Taking life as a whole, luck has but little sway in controlling its arrangements. Good sense and perseverance, prudence and energy, these are the fatal deities that domineer over the stars and their aspects. And, when an *ambitious* man's coffin knocks at the gates of the tomb, it is a question not unimportant, among other and greater questions, What was he on beginning life—what is he now ? What has been his success in playing for the great stakes of his profession or his trade? By his own confession, often and most frankly repeated, Dr. Parr was an ambitious man on the vulgarest scheme : what, then, in *his* case, will be the answer to these questions ?

The prizes which the Doctor set before his eyes from his earliest days were not very lofty, but they were laudable ; and he avowed them with a *naïveté* that was amusing. They were two—a mitre and a coach-and-four. " I am not accustomed," says he (writing to an Irish bishop), " to dissemble the wishes I once had " (this was said in 1807, when he had them more than ever) " of arriving at the profits and splendour of the prelacy, or the claims to them which I believe myself to possess." The bishopric he did not get ; there he failed. For the coach-and-four he was more fortunate. At the very latest period of his life, when the shades of death were fast gathering about him, he found himself able to indulge in this luxury ; and, as his time was obviously short, he wisely resolved to make the most of it ; and, upon any or no excuse, the Doctor was to be seen flying over the land at full gallop, and scouring town and country with four clerical-looking long-tailed horses. We believe he even meditated a medal, commemorating his first ovation by a faithful portrait of the coach and his own episcopal wig in their meridian pomp. He might have been represented in the act of looking out of the window, and "inflicting his eye" upon some hostile parson picking his way through the mud on foot. On the whole, I really rejoice that the Doctor got his coach and his four resounding coursers. The occasional crack of the whip must have sounded pleasantly in his ears at a period when he himself had ceased to operate with that weapon—when he was no more than an *emeritus* professor—and could be saluted no longer as Samuel μαστιγοφόρος.[1] So far was well ; but still, I ask, how came it that his coach panels wanted their appropriate heraldic decoration ? How was it that he missed the mitre ? Late in life, I find him characterising himself as an "unpreferred, calumniated, half-starving country parson" ; no part of which, indeed, was true : but yet I demand—how was it that any colourable plea existed, at that time of his career, to give one moment's plausibility to such an exaggeration ? Let us consider.

Dr. Parr was the son of a country practitioner in the humbler departments of medicine. Parr senior practised as a surgeon, apothecary, and accoucheur. From him, therefore, his son could expect little assistance in his views of personal aggrandisement. But *that* was not necessary. An excellent Latin scholar, and a man who brought the rare sanction (sanctification, I was going to say) of clerical countenance to so graceless a party as the Whigs, who in those days had scarcely a professional friend to say grace at their *symposia*, must, with any reasonable discretion in the conduct of his life, have been by much too valuable a resource on the Whig establishment to run any risk of neglect. The single clerk, the one sole *reverend* man of letters, who was borne

---

[1] The *scourge-bearer :* this is the epithet applied to the lunatic Telamonian Ajax by Sophocles.

upon their books, must have had a priceless value in the eyes
of that faction, when "taking stock," and estimating their
alliances.   To them he must have been what the *Emperor of
Morocco* is to the collector of butterflies.   To have lost this
value, to have forfeited his hold upon their gratitude, and
actually to have depreciated as he grew older and better
known to the world, implies too significantly some gross
misconduct, or some rueful indiscretions.   The truth is this—
and for Parr's own honour, lest worse things should be
thought of him than the case really warrants, his friends
ought to make it known—though a man of integrity, he could
not be relied upon ; in a muster of forces, he was one of the
few that never could be absolutely reckoned on and made
sure of.   Neither did his scruples obey any known law ; he
could swallow a camel, and strain at a gnat ; and his caprice
was of the most dangerous kind,—not a woman's caprice,
which is the mere mantling of levity, and readily enough
obeys any fresh impulse, which it is often easy to apply in an
opposite direction.   Dr. Parr's caprices grew upon another
stock ; they were the fitful outbreaks of steady, mulish
wrong-headedness ; products of a blind belief that, in order to
show his independence now and then, like a true mule, he
must lie down with his burden at some critical point of the
road, and refuse to budge an inch farther.   This was a constitutional taint, for which he was indebted to the accoucheur.
That original old mule overruled his son to the end of his
long life, and controlled his reiterated opportunities of a certain and brilliant success, by the hereditary taint in the blood
which he transmitted to him, in more perhaps than its original strength.   The true name for this infirmity is, in the
vulgar dialect, *pig-headedness.*   Stupid imperturbable ad-
herence, deaf and blind, to some perverse view that abruptly
thwarted and counteracted his party, making his friends
stare, and his opponents laugh—*that* was the key to Dr.
Parr's lingering preferment.   And I believe, upon a considerate view of his whole course, that he threw away ten
times the amount of fortune, rank, splendour, and influence
that he ever obtained, and with no countervailing indemnity
from any moral reputation, such as would have attended all
consistent sacrifices to high-minded principle,—on the con-

trary, with harsh opposition and expressions of powerful disgust from friends in every quarter, all conscious that, in such
instances of singularity, Dr. Parr was merely obeying a
demon, that now and then mastered him, of wayward, restive,
moody self-conceit, or else the blind spirit of contradiction.
Most of us know a little of such men, and occasionally suffer
by such men in the private affairs of life—men that are unusually jealous of slights, or insufficient acknowledgments of
their personal claims and consequence. They require to be
courted, petted, caressed ; they refuse to be compromised or
committed by the general acts of their party ; they must be
specially consulted, else they read a lesson to the whole party
on their error, by some shocking and revolting act of sudden
desertion, which, from a person of different character, would
have been received as perfidy. Dr. Johnstone himself admits
that Parr was "jealous of attention and indignant at neglect,"
and on one occasion endeavours to explain a transaction of
his life by supposing that he may have been "hurried away
by one of those torrents of passion of which there are too
many instances in *his* life." Of the father, Parr obstetrical,
the same indulgent biographer remarks that he was "distinguished by the rectitude of his principles" ; and in another
place he pronounces him, in summing up his character, to
have been "an honest, well-meaning Tory," but, at the same
time, confesses him to have been "the petty tyrant of his
fireside,"—an amiable little feature of character that would
go far to convince his own family that "rectitude of principles" was not altogether incompatible with the practice of a
ruffian.

Tory, however, Parr senior was *not :* he was a Jacobite,
probably for the gratification of his spleen, and upon a conceit that this arrayed him in a distinct personal contest with
the House of Hanover ; whereas, once confounded amongst
the prevailing party of friends to that interest, as a man-mid-
wife, he could hardly hope to win the notice of His Britannic
Majesty. His faction, however, being beaten to their heart's
content, and his own fortune all going overboard in the
storm, he suddenly made a bolt to the very opposite party—
he ratted to the red-hot Whigs ; and the circumstances of the
case, which are as we have here stated them, hardly warrant

us in putting a very favourable construction upon his motives. As was the father, such was the son : the same right of rebellion reserved to himself, whether otherwise professing himself Jacobite or Whig ; the same peremptory duty of passive obedience for those of his household ; the same hot intemperances in politics ; the same disdain of accountableness to his party leaders ; and, finally, the same " petty tyranny of the fireside." This last is a point on which all the biographers are agreed : they all record the uncontrollable ill temper and hasty violence of Dr. Parr within his domestic circle. And one anecdote, illustrating his intemperance, I can furnish myself. On one occasion, rising up from table, in the middle of a fierce discussion with Mrs. Parr, he took a carving-knife, and, applying it to a portrait of that lady, hanging upon the wall, he drew it sharply across the jugular, and cut the throat of the picture from ear to ear, thus murdering her in effigy.

This view of Parr's intractable temper is necessary to understand his life, and in some measure to justify his friends. Though not (as he chose himself to express it, under a momentary sense of his slow progress in life, and the reluctant blossoming of his preferment) " a half-starved parson," yet most unquestionably he reaped nothing at all from his long attachment to Whiggery, by comparison with what he would have reaped had that attachment been more cordial and unbroken. and had he, in other respects, borne himself with more discretion, and, above all, had he abstained from offensive personalities. This was a rock on which Parr often wrecked himself. Things, and principles, and existing establishments, might all have been attacked with even more virulence than he exhibited, had his furious passions allowed him to keep his hands off the persons of individuals. Here lay one class of the causes which retarded his promotion. Another was his unbecoming warfare upon his own Church. " I am sorry," said one of his earliest, latest, and wisest friends (Bishop Bennet)—" I am sorry you attack the Church, for fear of consequences to your own advancement." This was said in 1792. Six years later, Bennet, who had a confidential post in the Irish Government, and saw the dreadful crisis to which things were hurrying—viz. at a moment

when two formidable insurrections were impending—found
it necessary to break off all intercourse with Dr. Parr ; so
shocking to a man of principle was the careless levity with
which this minister of peace and his immediate associates,
themselves in the bosom of security amongst the woods of
Warwickshire, scattered their firebrands of inflammatory
language through the public at a period of so much awful
irritation. Afterwards, it is true, when the Irish crisis
had passed, and the rebellion was suppressed, Bennet's
respect for Parr as a scholar led him to resume his correspondence. But he never altered his opinion of Parr as a
politician : he viewed him as a man profoundly ignorant in
politics, a mere Parson Adams in the knowledge of affairs
and the real springs of political action or political influence ;
but unfortunately with all the bigotry and violent irritability
that belong to the most excited and interested partisan ;
having the headlong passions of a mob united with the ignorance of the desert ; coupling the timid simplicity of the dove
with the fierce instincts of the serpent.

The events of his life moved under this unhappy influence.
Leaving college prematurely upon the misfortune of his
father's death,[1] he became an assistant at Harrow under the
learned Dr. Sumner. About five years after, on Dr.
Sumner's death, though manifestly too young for the situation, he entered into a warm contest for the vacant place of
head-master. Notwithstanding the support of Lord Dartmouth
and others, he lost it ; and, unfortunately for his peace of
mind, though fancying, as usual, all sorts of intrigues
against himself, yet in the real circumstances of the election
he was not able to detect one argument of injustice. The
pretensions of Benjamin Heath, his successful competitor,
were such as to disabuse all the world of any delusive conceit
that justice had not been done. Parr, it must be remembered,
then only twenty-five years old, had in no single instance
distinguished himself ; nor had he even fifty years after—
no, nor at the day of his death—given any evidences to the
world that he was comparable to Heath as a Grecian. The
probable ground of Heath's success was a character better fitted
to preside over a great school (for even the too friendly

[1] See De Quincey's Appended Note to this page.—M.

biographers of Parr admit that he did not command the respect of the boys), and his better established learning.
Naturally enough, Parr was unwilling to admit these causes,
so advantageous to his rival, as the true ones. What, then,
is *his* account of the matter ? He says that he lost the election by a vote which he had given to John Wilkes in his
contest for Middlesex. To John Wilkes—mark *that*, reader !
Thus early had this "gowned student" engaged his passions
and his services in the interest of brawling, intriguing
faction.

This plan failing, he set up a rival establishment in the
neighbourhood of Harrow, at Stanmore ; and never, certainly, did so young a man, with so few of the ordinary
guarantees to offer—that is to say, either property, experience, or connexions—meet with such generous assistance.
One friend lent him £2000 at two per cent, though his
security must obviously have been merely personal. Another
lent him £200 without any interest at all. And many
persons of station and influence, amongst whom was Lord
Dartmouth, gave him a sort of countenance equally useful to
his interests by placing their sons under his care. All came
to nothing, however ; the establishment was knocked up,
and clearly from gross defects of management. And, had
his principal creditor pressed for repayment, or had he
shown less than the most generous forbearance, which he
continued through twenty-one years (in fact, until the repayment was accomplished without distress), Parr must have
been ruined ; for in those days there was no merciful indulgence of the laws to hopeless insolvents ; unless by the favour
of their creditors, they were doomed to rot in prison. Now,
in this one story we have two facts illustrated, bearing upon
our present inquiry : first, the extraordinary good luck of
Parr ; secondly, his extraordinary skill in neutralising or
abusing it.

What young man, that happens to be penniless at the
age of twenty-five, untried in the management of money,
untried even as the *presiding* master in a school, would be
likely to find a friend willing to intrust him, on his personal
responsibility (and with no prospect for the recovery of his
money, except through the tardy and uncertain accumula-

tion of profits upon an opposition school), with so large a sum as £2000 ? Who, in an ordinary way, could count upon the support of a nobleman enjoying the ear and confidence of royalty ? Lastly, who would so speedily defeat and baffle, by his own unassisted negligence and flagrant indiscretions, so much volunteer bounty ? At this time of his life, it strikes me, in fact, that Dr. Parr was mad. The students at Stanmore were indulged in all sorts of irregularities. *That*, perhaps, might arise from the unfortunate situation of the new establishment—too near to its rival ; and in part, also, from the delicate position of Parr, who, in most instances, had come under an unfortunate personal obligation to the young gentlemen who followed him from Harrow. But in his habits of dress and deportment, which drew scandal upon himself, and jealousy upon his establishment, Parr owed his ill success to nobody but himself. Mr. Roderick, his assistant, and a most friendly reporter, says that at this time he "brought upon himself the ridicule of the neighbourhood and passengers by many foolish acts ; such as riding in high prelatical pomp through the streets on a black saddle, bearing in his hand a long cane or wand, such as women used to have, with an ivory head *like a crosier*, which was probably the reason why he liked it." We see by this he was already thinking of the bishopric. "At other times he was seen stalking through the town in a dirty striped morning-gown : *Nil fuit unquam sic impar sibi.*" When we add that Dr. Parr soon disgusted and alienated his weightiest friend amongst the residents at Stanmore—viz. Mr. Smith, the accomplished rector of the place—we cannot wonder that little more than five years saw that scheme at an end.[1]

The school at Stanmore he could not be said to leave ; it left *him :* such was his management that no fresh pupils succeeded to those whom the progress of years carried off to the universities. When this wavering rushlight had at length finally expired, it became necessary to think of other plans, and in the spring of 1777 he accepted the mastership of Colchester School. Even there, brief as his connexion was with that establishment, he found time to fasten a

[1] See De Quincey's Appended Note to this page.—M.

quarrel upon the trustees of the school in reference to a lease ; and upon this quarrel he printed (though he did not publish) a pamphlet. Sir William Jones, his old school-fellow, to whom, as a lawyer, this pamphlet was submitted, found continual occasion to mark upon the margin such criticisms as these, "*too violent—too strong.*" This was probably the mildest mode of telling Dr. Sam that he was growing libellous.[1]

But, luckily, he was soon called away from these miserable feuds to a more creditable sort of activity. In the summer of 1778 the mastership of the public Grammar School at Norwich became vacant : in the autumn Parr was elected ; and in the beginning of 1779 he commenced his residence in that city. Thus we see that he was unusually befriended in all his undertakings. As a private speculator at Stanmore, as a candidate for Colchester, as a candidate for Norwich, he was uniformly successful, as far as it is possible that encouragement the most liberal, on the part of others, can overrule a man's own imprudence. The mastership of Norwich has certainly been considered a valuable prize by others. How it happened that Parr found it otherwise, or whether mere restlessness and love of change were his governing impulses, does not appear ; but it is certain that in August 1785 he sent in his resignation ; and at Easter 1786 he went to reside at the parsonage house of Hatton, in the County of Warwick, where he opened a private academy. And, though, as old age advanced, he resigned his pupils, Hatton continued to be his place of residence.

This, then, was the haven, the perpetual curacy of Hatton, into which Dr. Parr steered his little boat, when he had already passed the meridian of his life.[2] And (except upon a visit) he never again left it for any more elevated abode. For a philosopher, we grant that a much happier situation cannot be imagined than that of an English

---

[1] See Appended Note last cited.—M.

[2] By *meridian* I here mean the month which exactly bisected his life. Dr. Parr lived about eleven months less than eighty years ; and he was about two months more than forty when he came to live at Hatton.

rural parson, rich enough to maintain a good library. Dr.
Parr was exactly in those circumstances : but Dr. Parr was
no philosopher.   And assuredly this was not the vision
which floated before his eyes at Stanmore when he was
riding on his "black saddle," in prelatical pomp, with his
ivory crosier in his fist.   The coach-and-four and mitred
panels must then have flourished in the foreground of the
picture.   But at that time he was between twenty-five and
thirty ; now he was turned forty—an age when, if a man
should not have made his fortune, at least he ought to see
clearly before him the road by which it *is to be* made.   Now,
what was Parr's condition at this time, in respect to that
supreme object of his exertions ?   We have no letter on
that point in this year, 1786 ; but we have one in 1782,
when it does not appear possible that his situation was
materially different.   Writing to a man whom he valued,
but then under a cloud of distress, and perhaps wishing to
excuse himself for not sending him money, he thus states
the result of his labours up to that date :—"You desire my
confidence ; and I therefore add that the little progress I
have made in worldly matters, the heavy loss I have sustained by the war, the inconsiderable advantages I have
gained by a laborious and irksome employment, and the
mortifying discouragements I have met with in my clerical
profession, have all conspired to depress my spirits and
undermine my constitution.   I was content to give up
ecclesiastical preferment while I had a prospect of making
some comfortable provision for my old age in my business
as a teacher ; but the best of my years have now elapsed,
and I am, through a most vexatious and trying series of
events, not a shilling richer than when I went to Stanmore.
I have this very week closed an account on which I stood
indebted near £2000, which I was obliged to borrow when
I launched into active life.   My house at Stanmore I sold
literally for less money than I expended on the repairs only.
To this loss of more than £1000 I am to add near £700,
which I *may* lose entirely, and *must* lose in a great measure,
by the reduction of St. Vincent and St. Kitt's.   My patience,
so far as religion prescribes it, is sufficient to support me
under this severity of moral trial.   But the hour is past in

which I might hope to secure a comfortable independency ; and I am now labouring under the gloomy prospect of toiling, with exhausted strength, for a scanty subsistence to myself and my family. It is but eighteen months that I could pronounce a shilling my own. Now, indeed, *meo sum pauper in œre* [though poor, I am without debt]—but my integrity I have ever held fast."

Possibly ; but integrity might also have been held fast in a deanery ; and certainly Dr. Parr will not pretend to hoax us with such a story as that "integrity" was all that he contemplated from his black saddle in Stanmore. Undoubtedly, he framed to himself some other good things, so fortunately arranged that they could be held *in commendam* with integrity. Such, however, was the naked fact, and I am sorry for it, at the time when Dr. Parr drew near to his fortieth year—at which age, as all the world knows, a man must be a fool if he is not a physician, and a physician for mind, body, and estate. Pass on, reader, for the term of almost another generation : suppose Dr. Parr to be turned of sixty, and the first light snows of early old age to be just beginning to descend upon him, and his best wig to be turning grey ;—were matters, we ask, improved at that time ? Not much. Twenty years from that Easter on which he had entered the gates of Hatton—viz. in 1806-7—had brought him within hail of a bishopric ; for his party were just then in power. Already he could descry his sleeves and his rochet ; already he could count the pinnacles of his cathedral ;—when suddenly Mr. Fox died, and his hopes evanesced in spiral wreaths of fuming Orinoco. Unfortunate Dr. Parr ! Once before he had conceived himself within an inch of the mitre ; *that* was in the king's first illness, when the regency intrigue gave hopes, at one time, that Mr. Pitt would be displaced. Dr. Parr had then been summoned up to London ; and he had gone so far as to lay down rules for his episcopal behaviour. But the king suddenly recovered ; many a grasping palm was then relaxed abruptly ; and, alas for Dr. Parr ! whether people died or recovered, the event was equally unfortunate. Writing, on August 25, 1807, to the Bishop of Down, he says, "If Mr. Fox had lived and continued in power, he certainly would have made me a bishop."

Now, if Dr. Parr meant to say that he had a distinct promise to that effect, that certainly is above guessing ; else I should almost presume to guess that Mr. Fox neither would, nor possibly could, have made Dr. Parr a bishop. It is true that Mr. Fox meant to have promoted the Bishop of Llandaff of that day, who might seem to stand in the same circumstances as a literary supporter ; at least Lord Holland said to a friend of mine, " Had our party remained in office, we should have raised the Bishop of Llandaff to the Archbishopric of York." But then why ? Lord Holland's reason was this—" For he " (meaning Dr. Watson) " behaved very well, I can assure you, to us " (meaning by *us* the whole Fox and Grenville coalition). Now, this reason (I fear) did not apply, in Mr. Fox's mind, to Dr. Parr ; he had behaved violently, indiscreetly, foolishly, on several occasions ; he had thoroughly disgusted all other parties ; he had not satisfied his own. And once, when, upon a very frivolous reason, he gave a vote for Mr. Pitt at the Cambridge election, I am satisfied myself that he meditated the notable policy of ratting,—conceiving, perhaps, that he would be cherishing a romantic punctilio of honour in adhering to a doomed party ; and the letter of Lord John Townshend on that occasion convinces me that the Whigs viewed this very suspicious act in that light. Even Dr. Johnstone, I observe, doubts whether Mr. Fox would have raised Dr. Parr to the mitre ; and, as to everybody else, they shuddered at his very name. The Chancellor, Lord Thurlow, gave him a hearty curse, *more suo*, instead of a prebend ; and Lord Grenville assigned, as a reason against making him a bishop, his extreme unpopularity with his own order.[1] As one proof of that, even the slight distinction of preaching a visitation sermon had never once been offered to Dr. Parr,—so he himself tells us in 1816, when he had completed his seventieth year,—notwithstanding he had held preferment in five different counties. Nor was it, in fact, offered for six years more ; and then, being a hopeful young gentleman of seventy-six, he thought proper to decline the invitation.

Next for the emoluments of his profession.— Was he better off as regards *them ?* Else, whence came the coach-

---

[1] See De Quincey's Appended Note to this page.—M.

and-four ?   I answer that, by mere accidents of good luck, and the falling-in of some extraordinary canal profits, Dr. Parr's prebend in the cathedral of St. Paul's, given to him by Bishop Lowth upon the interest of Lord Dartmouth, produced him in his last year or two an unusually large sum ; so that he had about £3000 a-year ; and I am glad of it. He had also an annuity of £300 a-year, granted by the Dukes of Norfolk and Bedford, in consideration of a subscription made for Dr. Parr by his political friends.   But this was a kind of charity which would hardly have been offered had it not been felt that in the regular path of his profession he had not drawn, nor was likely to draw, any conspicuous prizes.   In fact, but for the two accidents I have mentioned, his whole regular income from the Church, up to a period of advanced age, when Sir Francis Burdett presented him to a living of about £200 per annum, was £93 on account of his living, and £17 on account of his prebend.

Such were the ecclesiastical honours, and such the regular ecclesiastical emoluments, of Samuel Parr.   I do not grudge him the addition, as regards the latter, which, in his closing years, he drew from the liberality of his friends and the accidents of luck.   On the contrary, I rejoice that his last days passed in luxury and pomp ; that he sent up daily clouds of undulating incense to the skies ; and that he celebrated his birth-day regularly with ducal game and venison from the parks of princes : finally, I rejoice that he galloped about in his coach-and-four, and am not angry that, on one occasion, he nearly galloped over myself.

Still, I rejoice that all these luxuries came to him irregularly, and not at all, or (if at all) indirectly and by accident, through the Church.   As regards *that*, and looking not to the individual, but entirely to the example, I rejoice that, both for her honours and emoluments, Dr. Parr missed them altogether.   Such be the fate of all unfaithful servants, in whatsoever profession or office of trust !   So may *those* be still baffled and confounded who pass their lives in disparaging and traducing their own honourable brethren, and who labour (whether consciously and from treachery, or half-consciously and from malice and vanity) for the subversion of institutions which they are sworn, pledged, and paid to defend !

My conclusion, therefore, the *epimuthion* of my review, is this : that, considered as a man of the world, keenly engaged in the chase after rank and riches, Dr. Parr must be pronounced to have failed,—that his rare and late successes were casual and indirect, whilst his capital failures were due exclusively to himself. His two early bosom friends and schoolfellows, Dr. Bennet and Sir W. Jones, he saw raised to the rank of a bishop and a judge, whilst he was himself still plodding as a schoolmaster. And this mortifying distinction in their lots was too obviously imputable, not to any more scrupulous integrity in *him*, soothing as that hypothesis was to his irritated vanity, but solely to his own hotheaded defect of self-control—baffling the efforts of his friends, and neutralising the finest opportunities. Both of those eminent persons, the bishop as well as the judge, deeply disapproved of his conduct ; though they agreed in candour, and in the most favourable construction of his meaning ; and though they allowed him the largest latitude for his politics—one of them being what is termed a liberal Tory, and the other an ardent Whig. And yet, with the full benefit of this most latitudinarian privilege, he could not win their toleration to his indiscretions. So that, purely by his own folly, and in headstrong opposition to the concurring tendencies of his opportunities and his extra advantages, Samuel Parr failed utterly as an ambitious man of the world. It remains to inquire how much better he succeeded as a politician, a scholar, and a divine.

SECTION II

READER ! perhaps you have heard of churls who, being embarked in some magnificent ship upon an East India voyage, have manifested no interest at all in the partners of their hopes and hazards. Far be such apathy from myself and my friends ! The merest *poco-curante* or misanthrope, whom long freezing experience of the world has brought to the temper of fixed and contemptuous disregard for man as a species, not seldom makes an exception in favour of the particular John, William, or James, whom accident has embarked in the same enterprise, or associated in the same perils, with himself. Dan Dancer, the miser, who would not have risked a half-crown upon a fire-escape or a life-boat for ten generations whom he had not personally known, nevertheless fought the battles of the paupers in his own neighbourhood, and headed them in their campaigns for rights of common and turbary with the most disinterested heroism. Elwes, the prince of misers, sometimes laid aside his narrow cares for the duties of a patriot. No man so memorably selfish who has not, on some occasion of his life, felt the social instinct which connects his else contemptible race, and acknowledged the duties which grow out of it. As to the good and generous, they cannot travel so much as a Jewish Sabbath-day's journey in company with another, participating in common purposes for the time, and liable to common inconveniences of weather or accident, and even to common possibilities of danger, without recognising something beyond a stranger's claim to offices of kindness or courtesy in the transient relations of a fellow-traveller.

Yet these are, in their nature, felt to be perishable con-nexions. Neighbourhood is a relation either purely of accident, or of choice not primarily determined by consideration of neighbours. And the brief associations of public carriages or inns are as evanescent as the sandy columns of the Great Desert, which the caprices of the wind build up and scatter, shape and unshape, within the brief revolution of a minute. Seldom, indeed, does a second sun shine upon fellow-travellers in modern England. And neighbourhood, if a more durable tie, is often one even less consciously made known to the parties concerned. If, then, connexions casual as these, where the *vinculum* of the relation is so finely spun as to furnish rather a verbal classification to the logician than a practical subject of duties to the moralist, are yet acknowledged by the benevolent as imposing some slight obligations of consideration and service, much more ought an AUTHOR to find, in the important circumstances which connect the ministers of the press, in their extensive fellowship of duties, rights, powers, interests, and necessities, a bond of fraternal alliance, and more than fraternal sympathy. Too true it is that authors are sometimes blockheads, and by the remotest of possibilities even knaves. Too commonly it happens that, in the occasions and the motives which originally drew them into authorship, there is little or nothing to command respect. *Venter largitor ingeni* : the stomach, that keen developer of talent, is the great feeder of the metropolitan press ; and, amongst the few who commence authors upon arguments less gross and instant, there are not many who do so from impulses that are exclusively noble.

Considerations such as these are at war with all sentiments of regard for the mere hacks of the press, who, having no *natural* summons to so fine a vocation, pervert literature —the noblest of professions—into the vilest of trades. But, wherever *that* is not *primâ facie* presumable, wherever circumstances allow us to suppose that a man has taken up the office of author with adequate pretensions, and a proper sense of his responsibilities, every other author of generous nature will allow him the benefit of that privilege which all over the world attaches to co-membership in any craft, calling, or guild whatsoever—even those which are illiberal or mechanical ; *a fortiori* in those which are intellectual. Surgeons bleed surgeons for love, physicians assassinate physicians gratis. Superannuated actors are everywhere free, I believe, of the theatre. And an author who has exercised his craft in a liberal, courteous, and honourable spirit, is entitled in that character to the indulgence of all professional authors, and above all he is entitled to entire amnesty as respects his politics. These are claims which I cheerfully allow to Trojan and Tyrian—to Whig and Tory alike ; and I come to the consideration of Dr. Parr as a scholar and as an author with perfect freedom from all prejudice, anxious to give him the fullest benefit of his real merits, and dismissing all unpleasant recollections of that factious and intemperate character which, most superfluously, he put forward in politics and divinity.

Dr. Parr as an author ! That very word in my ear sounds ridiculous, apart from every question upon the quality or value of what he wrote. As a literary man, as a scholar, prepared by reading and research for appreciating a considerable proportion of the past or the current literature, Dr. Parr, I willingly concede, stood upon somewhat higher ground than the great body of his clerical brethren. But even this I say with hesitation ; for it is scarcely to be believed, except by those who have gone with an observing eye into English society, how many rural clergymen go down to their graves unheard of by the world, and unacquainted with the press, unless perhaps by some anonymous communication to a magazine, or by an occasional sermon—who have beguiled the pains of life by researches unusually deep into some neglected or unpopular branches of professional learning. Such persons, it is true, are in general unequally learned ; so indeed are most men ; so, beyond all men, was Dr. Parr. I do not believe that he possessed any one part of knowledge accurately, unless it were that section of classical learning which fell within his province as a schoolmaster. The practice of a long life naturally made him perfect in that—perfect, at least, in relation to the standard of that profession. But how small a part of classical researches lie within the prescriptive range of a practising schoolmaster ! The duties of an academic professor may have a wider compass ; but it must be a pure labour of supererogation in a teacher of any school for boys if he should make his cycle of study very comprehensive. Even within that cycle, as at this time professed by some first-rate teachers, was Dr. Parr master of everything ? In some of its divisions was he even master of anything ? For example, how much did he know—has he left it upon record, in any one note, exegetical or illustrative, upon any one obscure or disputed passage of any one classic, that he knew anything at all in the vast and interminable field of classical antiquities ? The formulæ of the Roman calendar were, of course, known to him as a writer of Latin epitaphs ; for the chronology of the grave, as I shall have occasion to notice a little further ahead, has its own special varieties of delicate scientific caprice. But these niceties are soon learned from Morcellus.[1] And even on that subject—even on the practi-

[1] S. T. Morcelli, an Italian writer on "Inscriptions," 1737-1821. —M.

cal applications of chronology to the usages of daily life, or to
the severe requisitions of law—was Dr. Parr the learned man
that common fame reputed him to be ? To take one case
amongst a thousand, when the year 1800 brought up a question [1] in its train—Was it to be considered the last year of the
eighteenth century, or the first of the nineteenth ?—did Dr.
Parr come forward with an oracular determination of our
scruples, or did he silently resign that pleading to the
humble hands of the laureate—Pye ? Or again, shifting
from questions of time to those of space, has Dr. Parr contributed so much as his mite to the very interesting, important, and difficult subject of classical geography ? Yet these
were topics which lay within his beat as a schoolmaster. If
we should come upon the still higher ground of divinity and
Christian antiquities, perhaps upon those it might appear
that Dr. Parr had absolutely no pretensions at all. But, not
to press such questions too closely or invidiously, whatever
might be the amount of his attainments under these heads,
were it little or were it much, scanty as the measure of my
faith in them, or co-extensive with the vaunts of his friends
—still all this has reference only to his general capacity as a
man of letters ; whereas we are called upon to consider Dr.
Parr also as an author. Indeed we have now no other
means for estimating his *posse* as a scholar than through his
esse as a writer for the press.

This is my task ; and this it is which moves my mirth,
whilst it taxes the worthy Doctor and his friends with a
spirit of outrageous self-delusion. Dr. Parr as an author !
And what, now, might happen to be the Doctor's works ?
For I protest, upon my honour, that I never heard their
names. Was ever case like this ? Here is a learned doctor,
whose learned friend has brought him forward as a first-rate
author of his times, and yet nothing is extant of his writing,
beyond an occasional preface, or a pamphlet on private
squabbles. But are not his *Opera Omnia* collected and published by this friendly biographer, and expanded into eight

---

[1] " *Brought up a question* " :—Which question was virtually again
brought up by the year 1850 : are we to regard that year *last* of the
first bisection in the nineteenth century, or *first* of the *last* bisection ?
And every fifty years the same exact question will recur.

enormous tomes ?   True ; and the eight tomes contain,
severally, the following hyperbolical amount of pages :—

		PAGES.
Vol. I	. . . . .	850
II	. . . . .	701
III	. . . . .	715
IV	. . . . .	718
V	. . . . .	715
VI	. . . . .	699
VII	. . . . .	680
VIII	. . . . .	656
Total	. . .	5734

Yes ! five thousand seven hundred and thirty-four octavo
pages, many of them printed in a small type, are the apparent amount of Samuel Parr's works in the edition of Dr.
Johnstone ; and it is true, besides, that the very *élite* of his
papers is omitted—such as his critical notices of books in the
Monthly and Critical Reviews or the " British Critic," and
his essay on the word *Sublime*, addressed to Mr. Dugald
Stewart.   Add what is omitted, and the whole would be
little short of seven thousand pages.   And yet, spite of that,
not one " *work* " of Dr. Parr's is extant which can, without
laughter, assume that important name.   The preface to
Bellenden is, after all, by much the weightiest and most
regular composition, and the least of a fugitive tract.[1]   Yet
this is but a *jeu d'esprit*, or classical prolusion.   And I
believe the case to be unexampled, that, upon so slender a
basis, a man of the world, and reputed a man of sense,
should set up for an author.   Well might the author of the
" Pursuits of Literature " (1797) demand—" What has Dr.
Parr written ?   A sermon or two, rather long ; a Latin preface to Bellendenus (rather long too), consisting of a cento of
Latin and Greek expressions, applied to political subjects ;
another preface to some English Tracts ; and two or three
English pamphlets about his own private quarrels : and this
man is to be compared with Dr. Samuel Johnson ! ! "
    Certainly the world had never before seen so great a

---

[1] An edition of the *De Statu Prisci Orbis* of the Scottish scholar
William Bellenden was published in 1787, with a preface by Dr.
Parr.—M.

pomp of pretension rising from so slight a ground. The
delusion was absolutely unrivalled, and prevailed throughout
Dr. Parr's long life. He and his friends seemed constantly
to appeal to some acknowledged literary reputation, estab·
lished upon foundations that could not be shaken, and
notorious to all the world. Such a mistake, and in that
extent, was never heard of before. Dr. Parr talked, and his
friends listened, not only as giving and receiving oracles of
moral wisdom, but of wisdom owned to be such by all the
world ; whereas this *auctoritas* (to borrow a Roman word for
its Roman sense), whether secretly due to the Doctor or not,
evidently could not exist as a fact, unless according to the
weight and popularity of published works by which the
world had been taught to know him and to rank him.
Starting originally from the erroneous assumption, insinuated
by his preposterous self-conceit, that he was Johnson redi-
vivus, he adopted Johnson's colloquial pretensions—and that
was vainglorious folly ; but he also conceived that these
pretensions were familiarly recognised—and that was frenzy.
To Johnson, as a known master in a particular style of
conversation—not the very best within the whole classified
range of styles, not the most difficult, not the most instructive, but a finished specimen of its particular kind — everybody gave way ; and upon all questions with *moral* bearings
he was supposed to have the rights and precedency of a
judicial chair. But this prerogative he had held in right of
his works,—works, not which he merely *ought* to have written
(see Dr. Johnstone's "Memoirs of Parr," p. 464), but which
he *had* written, printed, and published. Strange that Dr.
Parr should overlook so obvious a distinction ! Yet he *did*
so for fifty years. Dining, for instance, at Norfolk House,
the duke having done him the honour to invite him to the
same table with the Prince of Wales, such was his presumption in the presence of the heir-apparent, of the premier peer
of England, and of all the illustrious leaders from the
Opposition side of the two Houses, that he fully believed it
to be his vocation to stand forward as the spokesman of the
company. It gave him no check, it suggested no faltering
scruple, that Mr. Fox was on one side the table, and Sheridan
on the other. His right he conceived it to be to play the

foremost part, and to support the burden of conversation between his royal highness and the splendid party assembled to meet him. Accordingly, on some casual question arising as to the comparative merits of Bishop Hurd and Archbishop Markham as Greek scholars, in which the prince delivered a plain and sensible evidence in favour of the latter from facts of his own youthful experience, Parr strutted forward, with the mingled licence of Jacobinism and paradox, to maintain a thesis against him. " I," said the Prince of Wales, "esteem Markham a much greater, wiser, and more learned man than Hurd, and a better teacher ; and you will allow me to be a judge, for they were both my preceptors." Here was a direct opinion ; and the prince afterwards gave reasons for it equally direct. A simple answer, as brief as the original position, was all that good breeding or etiquette allowed. But Dr. Parr found an occasion for a *concio*, and prepared to use it. " Sir," said he, " is it your royal highness's pleasure that I should enter upon the topic of their comparative merits as a subject of discussion ? "—" *Yes*," said the prince.—" Then, sir," said Dr. Parr, " I differ entirely from your royal highness in opinion." One would suppose, by his formal preparation, that Dr. Parr was some sergeant-at-law rising to argue a case before the judges at Westminster. The prince, however, had permitted him to proceed : under the special appeal made to him, what else could he do ? And, by way of acknowledging this courteous allowance, with the true soul of a low-bred democrat, Parr starts with a point-blank contradiction of his royal highness, put as broadly and coarsely as he knew how.[1]

Perhaps there are not ten men in Europe, occupying at the time no higher station than that of *country* schoolmaster, who would have had the front—in the presence of the Prince of Wales, or the Dauphin of France—to step before the assembled wits of Paris or London, and the great leaders of parties, as the rightful claimant of the royal ear, and natural representative of the illustrious party assembled at Norfolk House—all distinguished by high birth, talents, or station. Brass, triply bronzed, was requisite for this. " Thou art the great toe of this society ; because that thou, being

[1] See De Quincey's Appended Note to this page.—M.

lowest, basest, meanest, still goest foremost." Arrogance
towards his fellow-claimants was not enough for Dr. Parr,
unless he might also be arrogant towards the prince. In
high-bred society, all disputation whatsoever—nay, all continued discussion—is outrageously at war with the established
tone of conversation ; a dispute must be managed with much
more brilliancy, much more command of temper, a much
more determinate theme, and a much more obvious progress
towards a definite result in the question at issue, than are
commonly found—not to prove grievously annoying to all
persons present, except the two disputants. High-breeding
and low-breeding differ not more in the degrees of refinement
which characterise their usages than in the good sense upon
which these usages have arisen. Certainly, mere good sense
is sufficient, without any experience at all of high life, to
point out the intolerable absurdity of allowing two angry
champions to lock up and sequestrate, as it were, the whole
social enjoyment of a large party, and compel them to sit "in
sad civility" witnesses of a contest which can interest the
majority neither by its final object nor its management.
Social pleasure is the end and purpose of society ; and whatsoever interferes with that should be scourged out of all
companies. But, if disputing be intolerable, what shall we
say of blank contradiction offered to a Prince of Wales—not
in prosecution of some point of public service, but as an
elegant condiment to the luxuries of colloquial intercourse ?
To turn your back upon the king, to put a question to him,
to pull out your watch in his presence—all these are notorious trespasses against the etiquette of courts, and reasonably
so ; because they are all habits which presuppose a carelessness of demeanour incompatible with that reverence and
decorous homage which should never slumber in the presence
of a king, considered not as an individual, but as a state
creature, embodying the majesty of a great nation. A Prince
of Wales, or whosoever occupies that near relation to the
throne, has the same sanctity of public character ; and a man
of sense, though a red-hot republican from the banks of the
Potomac, would as little allow himself to forget *that* as to
insult a judge upon the bench. It is not the prince as an
individual that is considered, but the prince as representative

of a great nation; it is not the judge personally that is
regarded, but the sanctities of law and justice.

Had the matter in dispute been some great question of
constitutional policy, or in any way applicable to the prince's
future behaviour in life, or in many other circumstances that
might be imagined, we can suppose a sort of propriety in the
very breach of propriety. But the question was, in this
case, too trivial to justify the least eccentricity of manner.
He who courts the character of an *abnormis sapiens* (an
uncouth rustic philosopher) should be careful that his inde-
corums and singularity cover some singular strength of
character or some weight of fine sense. As it was, Dr. Parr
was paradoxical and apparently in the wrong; the prince
direct and rational. With what disadvantage to Dr. Parr,
on this occasion, and afterwards in his relation to Queen
Caroline, do we recall the simple dignity of Dr. Johnson,
when presented to George III ! Dr. Parr's introduction was
at a dinner-table, Dr. Johnson's in a library ; and in their
separate styles of behaviour one might fancy each to have
been governed by the presiding genius of the place. Johnson
behaved with the dignity of a scholar and a loyal son of the
Muses, under the inspiration of "strong book-mindedness" [1] ;
Parr with the violence of a pedagogue under the irritations
of wine and indigestion. In reality, Dr. Parr's effrontery
was chiefly to be traced to that one fact in his life—that for
forty years he swayed the sceptre of a pedagogue. Native
arrogance was the root ; but the "bright consummate
flower" was unfolded and matured by his long reign as a
tyrant over schoolboys. To borrow his own words, with
one slight omission, in speaking of a Cambridge head, his
"manners and temper were spoiled by the pedantries, and
pomposities, and fooleries which accompany the long exercise
of petty archididascalian authority."

"*Archididascalian authority*" ! Thanks to Dr. Parr for
one, at least, of his sesquipedalian words ; for *that* one contains the key to his whole life, and to the else mysterious
fact that a pamphleteer, a party pamphleteer, a pamphleteer
in the service of private brawls, trod the stage, on all occasions, with the air of some great patriarch of letters or polemic

[1] See De Quincey's Appended Note to this page.—M.

champion of the Church. Who could believe that Dr. Parr's friend and biographer, in the very act of publishing eight volumes entitled " *Works* of Dr. Parr," should yet have no better answer to the contemptuous demand from the "Pursuits of Literature"—"What has Dr. Parr written ?"—than simply an expression of regret (vol. i. p. 464) "that, with such powers, and such means of gathering information from every quarter, Dr. Parr did NOT produce some great work on some great subject." He goes on to lament that Parr did not, "like Clarendon, give the history of that awful period of which he saw the springtide, and in part the issue ; or, like Burnet, that he did not relate, in a familiar manner, the transactions of the period in which he lived ; or, like Tacitus, paint in caustic and living colours the atrocities of some of which he was a witness, and deliver, as an everlasting memorial to posterity, the characters of those who bore a part in them." But, with submission, Posterity are a sort of people whom it is very difficult to get at ; whatever other good qualities Posterity may have, accessibility is not one of them. A man may write eight octavos, specially addressed to Posterity, and get no more hearing from the wretches than had he been a stock and they been stones. As to those "everlasting memorials" which Dr. Johnstone and Thucydides talk of, it is certainly advisable to "deliver" them— but troublesome and injurious to the digestive organs.

Another biographer, who unites with Dr. Johnstone in lamenting "that he (viz. Parr) did not undertake some work of a superior kind calculated for permanent utility and more durable fame," goes on in the following terms :—" It is hinted, however, by a periodical writer, that he *could not* produce more creditable works ; and for this reason—that he was, as it were, overlaid with acquired knowledge ; the flood of his memory burst in on his own original powers and drowned them." But, in that case, I would venture to hope that some *Humane Society*, like that on the banks of the Serpentine, will arise to save hopeful young men from such sad catastrophes ; so that "acquired knowledge" may cease to prove so fatal a possession, and native ignorance be no longer a *conditio sine quâ non* for writing "creditable works." Meantime, whatever were the cause, the fact, we see, is

admitted by Dr. Parr's best friends—that he did not write
any great, durable, or creditable work ; and the best excuse
for him which Dr. Johnstone's ingenuity can devise is that
neither Archbishop Markham nor Dean Cyril Jackson wrote
anything better.   True : but the reason which makes such
an excuse not entirely available to the case is this, that
neither the archbishop nor the dean arrogated that place and
authority in letters which they had not won : they had both
been employed in the same sort of labour as Dr. Parr ; they
had severally assisted in the education of a great prince, and
they were content with the kind of honour which that procured them.   And, for Cyril Jackson in particular, he was
content with less : for he persisted to the last in declining
the mitre which he had earned.   No : the simple truth is, as
we have stated, that Dr. Parr assumed his tone of swagger
and self-sufficiency in part, perhaps, from original arrogance
of nature, and a confidence which he had in his own powers,
but chiefly from a long life of absolute monarchy within the
walls of a schoolroom.   The nature of his empire was absolute and unlimited despotism in the worst form, described by
Aristotle in his " Politics " as *Pambasileia.*   There is no
autocrat so complete, not the Czar of all the Russias, as one
or other of these two tyrants—first, the captain of a king's
ship, or, secondly, the head-master of a grammar school.
Both of them are irresponsible, ἀνυπεύθυνοι, in the utmost
degree.   And, for Parr in particular, not only was he an
autocrat, but, if he is not greatly belied, he was a capricious
and Algerine tyrant, who went the whole length of his
opportunities for showing partial favour, or inflicting vindictive punishment.   And he had this peculiarity, that, whilst
other tyrants find a present gratification in their severities,
but shrink from their contemplation, Parr treated *his* as
Plato's suppers—they were luxuries for the moment, and
subjects of sweet consolatory exultation in the retrospect.
Long after a man had entered the world as an active citizen,
Dr. Parr used to recall, as the most interesting tie which
could connect this man with himself, that at some distant
period he had flogged him ; and from one biographer it
appears that, in proportion to his approbation of a boy, and
the hopes with which he regarded him, were the frequency

and the severity of his flagellations.   To a man who reigned
in blood, and banqueted (like Moloch) upon children's cries,
we may suppose that resistance was unheard of : and hence,
I repeat, the despotic arrogance with which he came abroad
before the world.   But what, it will be asked, on the side
of the public, gave success to this arrogance ?   How was it
that in his lifetime this insolence of assumption prospered ?
Partly, I answer, through the insolence itself : in all cases
that does wonders.   The great majority of men are ready
to swear by any man's words, if he does but speak with
audacity.

In process of time, however, this resource will fail a man,
unless reinforced by auxiliary means ; and these I conceive
to have lain in two circumstances, without which Parr never
would have gained a height so disproportioned to his performances.   In the *first* place, Parr was a Whig ; and the
Whigs, as then the party militant, made much of all who
stuck by *them*.   Hence the excessive compliments which
flowed in upon Dr. Parr from Edinburgh, and from persons,
such as Dugald Stewart, who had otherwise no particular
value for the whole class of Dr. Parr's pretensions.   The
Whigs are wise in their generation ; and, like the Dissenters
from the Church of England, they make men sensible that it
is good to be of their faction ; for they never forsake those
who adhere faithfully to *them*.   Dr. Parr, indeed, was rather
a slippery partisan ; but this was not generally known.   His
passions carried him always back to Whiggism ; and his
general attachment was notorious, whilst his little special
perfidies or acts of trimming were secrets to all but a very
few.   A *second* circumstance in the Doctor's favour was this
—that, as a schoolmaster, he was throwing into public life a
continual stream of pupils, who naturally became partisans
and obstinate *proneurs*.   In some instances, he educated both
father and son ; and, though it is true that here and there
an eccentric person retains too lively a remembrance of past
flagellations, and is with some difficulty restrained from
cudgelling or kicking the flagellator, still, as a general case,
it may be held that such recollections of the boy do not
weigh much in the practice of the man.   Most certain it is
that, had Dr. Parr been other than an active Whig in

politics—or had he not been a schoolmaster of ancient and extensive practice—he never could as a literary man have risen so abruptly above the natural level of his performances as in fact he did. And, now that he is dead, and the activity of such adventitious aids is rapidly beginning to fail him, he will sink doubtless even more abruptly to his just standard than ever he rose above it; or, perhaps by the violence of such a natural reaction, will be carried very much below it : *which fate is now* (1857) *realised.*

There is another scale, from which it is probable that some persons may have taken their literary estimate of the Doctor—viz. the scale avoirdupois. For it is very possible that, upon putting the eight volumes of *works* (as edited by Dr. Johnstone) on a butcher's steelyard, it may have been ascertained that they draw against a weight of three stone six pounds. Infinite levity in particular cases amounts practically to ruinous gravity; a vast host of fluttering pamphlets, letters, and stray leaves, make up one huge geological boulder. It becomes necessary, therefore, to state the substance of the whole eight volumes. Briefly, then, the account stands thus :—Volume I. contains Memoirs (with some Extracts from Letters). The two last contain Correspondence. Three other volumes contain Sermons : of which two volumes are mere parish discourses, having no more right to a place in a body of literary works than the weekly addresses to his congregation of any other rural clergyman. Thus, out of six volumes, one only is really privileged to take its rank under the general title of the collection. The two remaining volumes (the third and fourth) contain Dr. Parr's miscellaneous pamphlets, with some considerable omissions not accounted for by the editor. These two volumes are, in fact, all that can properly be described as of a literary nature : and to these I shall resort for matter in the close of my review.

Meantime, I am satisfied that the correspondence of Dr. Parr and his friends, for the very reason that it was written with no view (or no uniform view) to the press, is that part of the whole collection which will be read by the greatest number of readers, and with most interest by all readers. I shall throw a glance on such parts of this correspondence as have a value in reference to the development of Dr. Parr's character, or have any separate interest on their own account.

Among the earliest of the literary acquaintances which Dr. Parr had the opportunity of forming was that of Dr. Johnson. Writing in 1821 (January 6) to Mr. Joseph Cradock, who had said a few days before that perhaps, upon the death of Dr. Strahan, he himself "must be the oldest of Dr. Johnson's friends who knew him intimately during the last five or six years of his life," Dr. Parr takes occasion to retrace the nature of his own connexion with that eminent person :—" Well, dear sir, I sympathise with you in your " pleasure and in your pride, when you represent yourself as " the oldest remaining scholar who lived upon terms of in- " timacy with Samuel Johnson. You saw him often, and " you met him often, in the presence of Goldsmith, Garrick, " Sir Joshua Reynolds, and other literary heroes. I acknow- " ledge the great superiority of your claims. Lord Stowell,[1] " I should suppose, will stand in the next place ; and I " challenge for myself the third. For many years I spent a " month's holidays in London, and never failed to call upon " Johnson. I was not only admitted, but welcomed. I " conversed with him upon numberless subjects of learning, " politics, and common life. *I traversed the whole compass of* " *his understanding ;* and, by the acknowledgment of Burke " and Reynolds, I distinctly understood the peculiar and

---

[1] "*Lord Stowell*" :—On revising these pages for a generation in advance by more than thirty years of many who are chiefly concerned in their notices, it has become necessary to explain that Lord Stowell, originally Sir William Scott, was the brother of the great Chancellor, Lord Eldon, and equally distinguished as a lawyer, though in a very different field. He was the oracle of the Admiralty Courts ; and, the business of those courts being prodigiously enlarged by the war, and by the furious struggle between our British orders in council and the Napoleon decrees issued at Berlin and Milan, naturally it happened that Lord Stowell fell under the widest circle of cognisance, and con- sequently of hostile (sometimes of malignant) interpretation from the continental publicists and jurists—all to a man bought and paid for by Napoleon. His reputation, at one time most splendid, rests generally upon the expansion which he gave to the principles of international law, and, amongst his countrymen, upon the scholar-like elegance and sustained dignity of his judicial style.

" transcendental properties of his mighty and virtuous mind.
" I intended to write his life.   I laid by sixty or seventy
" books for the purpose of writing in such a manner as
" would do no discredit to myself.   I intended to spread my
" thoughts over two volumes quarto ; and, if I had filled
" three pages, the rest would have followed.   Often have I
" lamented my *ill fortune* in not building this monument to
" the fame of Johnson, and (let me not be accused of arro-
" gance when I add) my own."

William Wordsworth, when he dedicated, in a few lines
at once modest and dignified, his "Excursion" to the present (now, 1857, the *late*) Lord Lonsdale, with that accurate
valuation of words which is one of his greatest poetical
accomplishments, offers it as

> "A token (*may it prove* a monument !)
> Of high respect," etc.

A token, or pledge of his attachment, the poem was, at any
rate, by the mere act of dedication ; whether it should also
be a monument, a monumental token, that was for posterity
to determine ; and, if others were at liberty to anticipate
such a result, the author, at least, was not.   And, at all
events, the mere logic of the case made it inevitable that
whatever proved a monument to the fame of Dr. Johnson
should be such also to the fame of him who raised it ; for, of
a structure which should happen to be durable as a record of
Dr. Johnson, it is mere tautology to say that it must also be
durable as the workmanship of Dr. Parr.   One and the same
work could not have a divided character, or a separate
destiny, in its different relations ; could not be immortal as
a record, and at the same time perishable as a memorial of
the recorder.

But can it be imagined that Dr. Parr's clumsy masonry
could raise a monument to anybody ?   For Dr. Johnson, in
particular, all that he could have done with effect would
have been a short *excursus* or appendix to Boswell, on the
pretensions of Johnson as a classical scholar.   These were
greater than it is the custom to suppose.   Dr. John Johnstone, indeed, somewhere has thought fit to speak of him in
that character as immeasurably inferior to Parr.   This is

not true. Certainly, I am satisfied that Dr. Johnson was no very brilliant Grecian; the haste and trepidation which he showed in declining Dr. Burney's application for assistance on the Greek tragedians sufficiently establish *that*. But there is no reason to suppose that, in this part of scholarship, Dr. Parr had the least advantage of him: if he had, why are the evidences of his superiority so singularly wanting? or in what corner of forgotten literature are we to seek them? As Latin scholars, both were excellent: Parr, from practice, had the greater command over the delicacies and varieties of prose diction; Johnson, from natural talent, had by much the greater facility in verse. Elaborate ingenuity is far more in request for metrical purposes in Latin—knowledge of the idiom for prose. It might be shown, indeed, that exquisite facility in the management of thoughts, artifices of condensation or of substitution, of variation or inversion, are for the writer of Latin verse transcendent to any acquaintance with the Latin idiom: the peculiar treatment of an idea, which metre justifies and vindicates from what would else seem affectation, creates its own style. Johnson, in those relics of his Latin verses which have been preserved. benefited by that advantage; Parr, writing in Latin prose, and writing purely as a rhetorician, was taxed in the severest degree for a command over the idiomatic wealth of the language, and, for what is still less to be obtained from dictionaries, for a command over a Latin structure of sentence, and over the subsidiary forms of connexion and transition. In the preface to Bellenden, he answered the demand upon him, and displayed very unusual skill in the accomplishments of a Latin scholar. Latin composition, in fact, if we except bell-ringing, was the one sole thing, in the nature of accomplishments, which Dr. Parr seems to have possessed. Among the fine arts, certainly, I admit, that he understood bell-ringing thoroughly,[1] and I was on the point of forgetting to add that in the art of slaughtering oxen,[2] which he cultivated early as an amateur, his merit was conspicuous. Envy itself was driven to confess it; and none but the

[1] See De Quincey's Appended Note to this page.—M.
[2] Ταυροκτονεῖν is the word of Sir W. Jones; but bulls, unless for Pagan sacrificial purposes, were nowhere, and at no time, slaughtered.

blackest-hearted Tory would go about at this time of day to deny it. Still, of these three accomplishments, one only seems available to a biography of Dr. Johnson; and that would barely have sufficed for the least important chapter of the work.

After all, was Parr really intimate with Johnson? I doubt it: for he must in that case have submitted to a kind of dissimulation bitter to a proud spirit. He was a Jacobite by inheritance: that would have pleased Dr. Johnson well; but then by profession he was a Whig—a sort of monster which the Doctor could not abide, and which he deduced genealogically from Satan; and (worse than that!) he was a Whig renegado—such a combination of monstrous elements in a man's character as none of us can abide. To be a Whig is bad—to be a traitor is bad—but to be a Whig *and* a traitor is too much for humanity. Such features of his character Parr must have dissembled; and this would at once pique his self-love, and limit his power. One anecdote, rich in folly and absurdity, is current about an interview between Johnson and Parr, in which the latter should have stamped whenever the other stamped, and, being called upon to explain this sonorous antiphony, replied, that he could not think of allowing his antagonist to be so much as a stamp ahead of him. Miss Seward, I think, was in the habit of telling this story, though Sir Walter Scott has not recorded it in his edition of that lady's works. But she was one of the dealers in marvels, for ever telling of "gigantic powers" and "magnificent displays" in conversation, beyond anything that her heroes were seen to have effected in their writings. I remember well that she used to talk of a particular dispute between Johnson and Parr, which in her childish conceit (for she had not herself been present) was equal to some conflict between Jupiter and one of the Titans. Possibly it was the stamping dispute, which we may be assured was a fiction. No man—least of all Sam Johnson— falling into any gesticulation or expression of fervour from a natural and uncontrollable impulse, would bear to see his own involuntary acts parodied and reverberated as it were in a cool spirit of mimicry; that would be an insult; and Johnson would have resented it by flooring his man *instanter*,

—a matter very easy indeed to him ; for in every sense he was qualified to "take the conceit" out of Dr. Parr. Or, perhaps, though I rather incline to think that Miss Seward's dispute turned upon some political question, the following, as recorded by Parr himself ("*Parriana*," p. 321), might be the particular case alluded to :—" Once, sir, Sam and I " (*i.e.* Sam Johnson) " had a vehement dispute upon that most " difficult of all subjects—the origin of evil. It called forth " all the powers of *our* minds. No two tigers ever grappled " with more fury ; but we never lost sight of good manners. " There was no Boswell present to detail our conversation. " Sir, he would not have understood it. And then, sir, " who do you think was the umpire between us ? That " fiend Horsley."

Miserable fudge ! " Grappling like tigers " upon the origin of evil ! How, but by total confusion of mind, was that possible upon such a question ? One octavo page would state the outline of all that has ever been accomplished on this subject ; and the German philosopher Kant, whom Dr. Parr professed to have studied, and from whom he borrowed one polysyllable, and apparently one solitary idea, has in a short memoir sketched the outline of all past attempts (especially that of Liebnitz), and the causes of failure. Libraries may be written upon any question ; but the whole *nodus* of this particular question lies in a brief series of six sentences ; and as yet no real advance has been made in solving it. As to Dr. Johnson, it happens that we all know what *he* could do in this matter, for he has given us the cream of his meditations in a review of Soame Jenyns.[1] Trifling more absolute, on a philosophic subject, does not exist. Could Dr. Parr do better ? Had he one new idea on the question ? If so, where is it ? I remember obscurely some sentence or other of purest commonplace on this point in one of his sermons. Further on I may have an occasion for producing it. At present it is sufficient to say that as philosophers only could Parr and Johnson ever converse upon equal terms. Both being equally blind by natural constitution of mind, and equally unprepared by study or reading in that department, there was no room for differ-

[1] See *ante*, vol. iii, p. 20.—M.

ences between them, except such as were extra-essential or alien to the subject. On every other topic that could have arisen to divide them, Johnson, with one grasp of his muscular hand, would have throttled the whole family of Parrs. Had Parr presumed to talk that sort of incendiary politics in which he delighted, and which the French Revolution ripened into Jacobinism, Johnson would have committed an assault upon him. As that does not appear to have happened, I venture to suppose that their intercourse was but trifling ; still, for one who had any at all with Johnson, many of his other acquaintance seem a most incongruous selection. The whole orchestra of rebels, incendiaries, state criminals, all who hated the Church and State, all who secretly plotted against them, or openly maligned them, the faction of Jacobinism through its entire gamut—ascending from the first steps of disaffection or anti-national feeling to the full-blown activity of the traitor and conspirator—enjoyed a plenary indulgence from the curate of Hatton, and were inscribed upon the roll of his correspondents. I pause with a sense of shame in making this bold transition from the upright Sam Johnson, full of prejudice, but the eternal champion of social order and religion, to the fierce Septembrisers who come at intervals before us as the friends, companions, or correspondents (in some instances as the favourites) of Dr. Parr. Learning and good morals are aghast at the association !

It is singular, or at first sight it seems so, that brigaded with so many scowling republicans are to be found, as occasional correspondents of Dr. Parr, nearly one-half of our aristocracy—two or three personages of royal blood, eight dukes, five marquises, six-and-twenty earls, thirteen viscounts, one-and-thirty barons or courtesy lords ; to say nothing of distinguished women—a queen, several duchesses, countesses, and daughters of earls, besides baronesses and honourables in ample proportion. Many of these, however, may be set down as persons systematically (oftentimes insolently) negligent of political principles in correspondents of no political power. The covert meaning in such cases is this : Oh, as to political principles, my friend, yours, it is true, are rotten and detestable ; so that, if you occupied any

considerable station that gave weight to your opinions, I
should be obliged to *cut* you : but confessedly you are
nobody ; so that I can conscientiously retain your acquaintance, whilst disregarding your little impotent treasons, as so
much babble uttered by a child of three years old. But
what are we to think of ten judges (besides Lord Stowell)
addressing, with the most friendly warmth, one who looked
upon all their tribe as the natural tools of oppression ; and
no fewer than forty bishops, and four archbishops, courting
the notice of a proud priest who professed it as an axiom
that three out of every five on the Episcopal Bench were
perfect knaves. Oh for a little homely consistency !
and, in a world where pride so largely tyrannises, oh
for a little in the right place ! Dr. Parr did not in
so many words proclaim destruction to their order as a
favourite and governing principle ; but he gave his
countenance to principles that would, in practice, have
effected that object, and his friendship to men that pursued no other.

His Royal Highness the Duke of Sussex opens the correspondence, according to the present arrangement of the
letters—if that may be called arrangement where all is
anarchy. At first I anticipated, from this precedency
granted to a prince, that the Peerage and the Red Book
would dictate the principle of classification ; this failing,
I looked to the subject, and next to the chronology. But
at length I found that pretty much the same confusion
obtains as in a pack of cards that has first of all been
accurately arranged in suits and then very slightly shuffled.
In such a case, strong symptoms occur of the sorting, continually disturbed by weak symptoms of the shuffling : two
or three hearts, crossed by two or three spades ; and a
specious promise of diamonds, suddenly thrown into the
shade by a course of clubs. Letters from the same person
are usually thrown together, and sometimes a vein of the
same subject prevails through a considerable tract of pages.
Then suddenly all changes ; a new *stratum* crops out ; and
a printer's devil seems to have determined the order of
succession.

The Duke of Sussex, who has actually placed the bust of

a hack dissenting book-maker,[1] rather than that of Aristotle
or Lord Bacon, as the presiding genius of his fine library in
Kensington Palace, could not, of course, find any objections
to Dr. Parr in his hostility to the Church of England.   His
royal highness is probably indifferent on this point ; whilst
others, as Mr. Jeremy Bentham, could hardly fail to honour
this defect in " *Church-of-Englandism.*"   The duke's letters
are amiable and pleasing in their temper, but otherwise (for
want of specific subject) not very interesting.   Mr. Bentham,
in more senses than one the Lucifer of the radical politicians,
is still less so ; and simply because he affects the humorous,
in a strain of very elaborate and very infelicitous trifling,
upon the names of Parr and Fox (which he supposes to have
been anticipated by Homer, in the address to Paris, Δύσπαρι,
&c., and in the description of Thersites, Φοξὸς ἐὴν κεφαλήν,
&c.)   In a second letter (February 17, 1823), which abun-
dantly displays the old gentleman's infirmity,—who (like
Lord Byron) cannot bear a rival in the public interest, no
matter whether otherwise for good or for bad,—there is one
passage which, amusing on its own account, furnishes also an
occasion for bringing forward one of Parr's most extravagant
follies in literature.   It is this :—" The 1st of March," says
Mr. Bentham, " or the 1st of April, comes out a number of the
" European Magazine, with another portrait of ME by another
" hand ; *considerable expectations are entertained of this likewise.*
" When you see a copy of a print of the House of Lords at
" the time of the Queen's trial in the hand of Bowyer, and
" expected to come out in a month or two, you will (if
" Bowyer does not deceive me) see the phiz of your old
" friend " [Jeremy, to wit] " among the spectators ; and
" these, how small soever elsewhere, will, in this print,

---

[1] " *Book-maker* " :—I trust that in so describing Dr. Rees I do him no
wrong.   The doctor was understood to be the editor of an immense
encyclopædia, originally charged to the public at £80,—latterly, I believe, at about 80 shillings.   Southey, who was an admirable judge of
such compilations, had received a copy as a present from the very
liberal proprietors in its early or 80-*pound* stage ; and he privately
showed me such transformations and specious creations worked by
paste and scissors as are elsewhere unexampled.   [Abraham Rees,
D.D., 1743-1825, was editor of *Rees's Cyclopædia*, completed in 45
volumes quarto in 1819.—M.]

" forasmuch as their station is in the foreground, be greater
" than lords. Oddly enough made up the group will be.
" Before me he had got an old acquaintance of mine of
" former days—Sir Humphry Davy : he and I might have
" stood arm-in-arm. *But then came the servile poet and*
" *novelist; and then the ultra-servile sack-guzzler.*[1] Next to
" him, the old radical. What an assortment !" Certainly
a strange lot of clean and unclean beasts were in that ark at
that time, what with Mr. Bentham's " assortment "—what
with the *non mi recordo* Italians—the lawyers, *pro* and *con*—
and some others that I could name. But, with regard to
Mr. Jeremy's companions in Bowyer's print, does the reader
take his meaning ? I will be " as good as a chorus " to him,
and interpret. The " servile poet and novelist," then, is Sir
Walter Scott ; the " ultra-servile sack-guzzler," Mr. Southey,
a pure and high-minded man ; the " old radical," Mr. Corporal Cobbett. Now, with regard to the last of these, Dr.
Parr considered him a very creditable acquaintance. He
visited the corporal at Botley ; and the corporal wrote him a
letter, in which he talked of visiting Hatton. (What a
glorious blunder, by the way, if the old ruffian had chanced
to come whilst Dr. Bridges was on duty !) Cobbett would
do : but, for Sir Walter, in Dr. Parr's estimation he was
stark naught. One reason may be guessed at—the Queen ;
there may have been others, but this was the main reason,
and the reason of that particular year. Well, so far we
can allow for the Doctor's spite. Queen Caroline was
gracious and confiding towards the Doctor, until, by some
mysterious offence, he had incurred her heavy displeasure.[2]
It was natural that a person in Parr's rank should be grateful
for her notice, and that a person of Parr's politics should
befriend her cause. In that same degree, it was natural,
perhaps, that he should dislike Sir Walter Scott, and look
with jealousy upon his public influence as pledged to the
service of her enemies. Both were in this case party men,

---

[1] " *Sack-guzzler* " :—The reason for this particular reproach must
be sought in the antique mode of payment to the laureate (not yet, I
believe, obsolete)—viz. so much money and so much wine ; the wine
being *sherry*, the main element in *sack*.

[2] See De Quincey's Appended Note to this page.—M.

with the single difference in Sir Walter's favour that he was
of the right party ; a fact that Dr. Parr could not be expected to appreciate.   But was any extremity of party
violence to be received as an apology for the Doctor's meanness and extravagant folly in treating so great a man (which
uniformly he did) as a miserable pretender in literature ?
Not satisfied with simply lowering or depreciating his merits,
Dr. Parr spoke of him as an errant *charlatan* and impostor.
Discussing Sir Walter's merits as a poet, there is room undeniably for wide difference of estimates.   But he that can
affect blindness to the brilliancy of his claims as a novelist,
and generally to the extraordinary grace of his prose, must
be incapacitated for the meanest functions of a critic by
original dulness of sensibility.   Hear the monstrous verdict
delivered by this ponderous mechanist of style, when adjudi-
cating the *quantum meruit* of a writer who certainly has few
rivals among ancient or modern classics in the rare art of
narrating with brilliancy and effect :—" Dr. Parr's taste,"
says a certain Irish poet, a Rev. Mr. Stewart, of whom or his
works the reader probably now hears for the first time—
" Dr. Parr's taste was exquisite, his judgment infallible.   One
" morning he sent for me to attend him in his library.   I
" found him seated at one side of the fire, Mrs. Parr leaning
" against the mantel on the opposite side, and a chair placed
" for me between them.   ' Mrs. Parr,' he began, ' you have
" seen Moore in this spot some time ago ; *you now see Mr.*
" *Stewart !*—The race of true poets is now nearly extinct.
" There is you ' (turning to me), ' and Moore, and Byron,
" and Crabbe, and Campbell—I hardly know of another.' "
[All these, observe, were Whigs !]   " ' You, Stewart, are a
" man of genius, of real genius, and of science, too, as well as
" genius.   I tell you so.   It is here, it is here,' shaking his
" head, and sagaciously touching his forehead with his
" finger.   ' I tell you again, it is here.   As to Walter Scott,
" his jingle will not outlive the next century.   It is namby-
" pamby.' "   Dr. Parr is here made to speak of Sir Walter
merely as a poet ; but for the same person, in any other
character, he had no higher praise in reserve.   In the poetry
of Sir Walter I pardon the Doctor for taking little interest.
But what must be the condition of feeling in that writer who,

without participating probably in the Doctor's delusions, could yet so complacently report to the world a body of extravagances which terminated in placing himself, an author unknown to the public, conspicuously above one amongst the most illustrious writers of his age ! Dr. Parr might perhaps plead, as the apology for *his* share in such absurdities, the privilege of his fireside, kindness for a young friend, and a sudden call upon him for some audacity to give effect and powerful expression to his praise ; but Mr. Stewart, by recording them in print, makes himself a deliberate party, under no apology or temptation whatsoever, to the whole injustice and puerility of the scene.

Mr. Bentham, Dr. Parr, and Mr. Douglas of Glasgow, are probably the three men in Europe who have found Sir Walter Scott a trifler. Literature, in fact, and the fine arts, hold but a low rank in the estimate of the modern utilitarian republicans. All that is not tangible, measurable, ponderable, falls with them into the account of mere levities, and is classed with the most frivolous decorations of life : to be an exquisite narrator is tantamount to dressing well ; and a finished work of art is a showy piece of upholstery. In this vulgarity of sentiment Dr. Parr could not entirely accompany his coarsest friends ; for he drew largely on their indulgence himself as a trespasser in the very worst form—he was guilty of writing superfluous Latin with fluency and striking effect. It is certain, however, that the modern school of reformers had an injurious effect upon Dr. Parr's literary character, by drawing out and strengthening its harshest features. His politics became more truculent, and his intellectual sensibilities coarser, as he advanced in years. How closely he connected himself with these people I shall show in the sketch of his political history. For the present I turn with pleasure to his more elegant, though sometimes not less violent, friends amongst the old established Whig leaders. These, in their very intemperances, maintained the tone, breeding, and cultivation of gentlemen. They cherished and esteemed all parts of elegant letters, and, however much they have been in the habit of shocking our patriotism or constitutional principles, seldom offered annoyance to our tastes as scholars and men of letters.

Foremost amongst these, as foremost in politics, stood
Charles Fox. His letters in this collection are uniformly in
the unpretending manner which he courted : what we have
too generally to regret is the absence of Dr. Parr's answers,
especially to those letters of Mr. Fox or his friends which
communicated his *jeux d'esprit* in Greek verse. Meantime, as
perhaps the most interesting passage in the whole collection
of Dr. Parr's correspondence, I will make the following
extract from a letter in which Mr. Fox states the final
state of his feelings with regard to Edmund Burke : the
immediate occasion being a plan, at that moment agitated,
for raising a monument to Burke's memory. The date of
this memorable letter is February 24, 1802 :—

" Mackintosh wrote to me upon the subject you mention ;
" and I think he took my answer rather more favourably
" than he was strictly warranted to do. When he said I
" would second the proposition, I told him *support* was my
" word.—The truth is, though I do not feel any malice
" against Burke, nor would I have in any degree thwarted
" any plan for his advantage or honour : though I feel the
" greatest gratitude for his continued kindness to me during
" so great a part of our lives, and a strong conviction that I
" owe to his friendship and conversation a very great portion
" of whatever either of political or oratorical merit my friends
" suppose me to have displayed : notwithstanding all this, I
" must own that there are some parts of his conduct that I
" cannot forgive so entirely as perhaps I ought, and as I wish
" to do.—His public conduct may have arisen from mistaken
" motives of right, carried to a length to which none but
" persons of his ardent imagination would have pursued
" them. But the letter to the Duke of Portland and Lord
" Fitzwilliam, with the worst possible opinion of me, is what
" I never can think of without sensations which are as little
" habitual to me as to most men. To attempt to destroy me
" in the opinion of those whom I so much value, and in
" particular that of Fitzwilliam, with whom I had lived in
" the strictest friendship from our infancy,—to attempt it,
" too, at a time and in a way which made it almost certain
" that they would not state the accusation to me, and con-
" sequently that I should have no opportunity to defend

" myself,—this was surely not only malice, but baseness in
" the extreme ; and, if I were to say that I have quite for-
" given it, it would be boasting a magnanimity which I can-
" not feel.—In these circumstances, therefore, I think that
" even not opposing, much more supporting, any motion
" made in honour of his memory as an individual amongst
" the rest, without putting myself forward as a mover or
" seconder, is all that can be expected or desired of me by
" those who are not admirers of hypocrisy. I shall have
" great pleasure, however, in seeing your plan for an epitaph
" for him, and will tell you freely my opinion of it, both in
" general and in the detail. He was certainly a great man,
" and had very many good as well as great qualities ; but
" his motto seems the very reverse of μηδὲν ἄγαν (nothing in
" excess) ; and, when his mind had got hold of an object, his
" whole judgment, as to prudent or imprudent, unbecoming
" or indecent, nay, right or wrong, was perverted when that
" object was in question. What Quintilian says of Ovid,
" ' Si ingenio temperare quam indulgere maluisset,' was emi-
" nently applicable to him, even with respect to his passions.
" ' Si animi sui affectibus temperare quam indulgere
" maluisset, quid vir iste præstare non potuerit ?' [1] would be
" my short character of him. By the way, I do not know
" that affectibus is the right word ; but I know no other."

Monstrous as we must consider this view of Burke's conduct, which, under every provocation from the underlings of
Mr. Fox's party, continued irreproachably honourable towards those whom he had been compelled (and whom others [2]
had been compelled) to abandon,—still, under the perverse prejudices which had possession of Mr. Fox, we must allow his
temper and his conduct, as here stated by himself, to have
been sincere, manly, and liberal. That he did not speak
with more fervour of admiration, in summing up the claims
of a man so immeasurably beyond his contemporaries in the

[1] This man, had he chosen to control rather than to humour the
impulses of his native mind, what was there beyond his power of
attainment ?

[2] Let that be deeply remembered : let it not for a moment be overlooked—which gives so violent a wrench to the whole pleading of
Charles Fox—that Burke was not the only member of the Whig Club
who had left it under a conscientious compulsion.

fineness and compass of his understanding, is not to be imputed to jealousy of his powers, or to the smothered resentments which Mr. Fox acknowledges—but entirely to the extreme plainness, simplicity, and almost homely character of his own mind, which laboured under a specific natural inaptitude for appreciating an intellect so complex, subtle, and elaborate, as that of Burke.

We see how readily he clings to the slang notion of Burke's "*imagination*" as the key to all differences between them ; and how resolutely he mistakes, for an original tendency to the violence of extremes, what in fact was the mere breadth and determinateness of principle which the extremity of that crisis exacted from a mind of unusual compass. Charles Fox had one grandeur, one originality, in his whole composition, and that was the fervour, the intensity, the contagious vehemence of his manner ; which alone, in the absence of all other merit, might avail to plant a man on the supreme eminence as an orator.   Let me draw attention to a most remarkable and significant feature in Charles Fox's idiosyncrasy.   He could not endure his own speeches when stripped of the advantage they had in a tumultuous and self-kindling delivery.   "I have always hated the thought," says he to Dr. Parr, "of any of my speeches being published." Why was *that*?   Simply because, in the mere *matter*, he could not but feel himself that there was nothing to insure attention, nothing that could give a characteristic or rememberable expression to the whole.   The thoughts were everybody's thoughts.   Burke's, on the other hand, were so peculiarly his own that they might have been sworn to as private property in any court of law.

How was Dr. Parr affected by this great schism in politics, the greatest which ever hinged upon pure difference of abstract principle ?   A schism which was fatal to the unity of the Whig Club could not but impress new determinations on the political bias, conduct, and language of every Whig partisan.   At the time of the Bellenden Preface, it was a matter of course that Parr should praise Burke ; he was then the ally of Fox, and the glory of the Whigs.   But what tone of sentiment did Dr. Parr maintain towards this great man after he had become alienated from the revolutionary cause

which he himself continued to patronise, alienated from the
party which he continued to serve? For previous to that
change his homage was equivocal. It might be to the man,
or it might be to his partisan position.

There are many ways of arriving at a decision. In
letters, in tracts (Letters on Fox's *James II*), and in recorded
conversations, Dr. Parr's sincere opinions on this question (a
question as comprehensive as any personal question ever can
have been) were repeatedly obtained. He wrote, besides, an
inscription for Burke's public monument ; and this, which
(in common with all his epitaphs) was anxiously weighed and
meditated in every syllable, happens to have been the most
felicitous in the opinion of himself and his friends amongst
all which he executed. What was its prevailing tone? " I
remember," says Parr himself, when writing to Lord Holland,
" one or two of Mr. Burke's admirers said to me that it was
cold ; and I answered that I had indeed been successful ; for,
as I really did not feel warmth, I had not attempted to
express it." Perhaps in these words Dr. Parr, with a cour-
tier's consideration of the person whom he was addressing,
has done some injustice to himself. Enough remains on
record, both in the epitaph and elsewhere, to show that he
had not indeed attained to a steady consciousness of Burke's
characteristic merits ; cold or warm, he was incapable of
rising to that high level ; but it is manifest that he struggled
with a reluctant instinct of submission to the boldest of
Burke's views, and fought up against a blind sense of
Burke's authority as greater than on many accounts suited
him to admit.

Even in this personal accident, as it may seem, taken in
connexion with the fetters of party, lay a snare to the
sobriety of Parr's understanding. The French Revolution,
with him as with multitudes beside, unhinged the sanity of
his moral judgments. Left to the natural influences of
things, he, like many of his political friends, might have
recovered a steady equilibrium of mind upon this great
event, and " all which it inherited." He might have
written to others, as Lady Oxford (once the most violent of
democrats, but sickened by sad experience of continental
frenzies) had occasion to write to *him*—" Of Burke's writ-

ings and principles I am now a very great admirer ; he was a great lover of practical liberty.   In my days of darkness, prejudice, and folly, I never read a line of Burke ; but I am now, thank heaven, in a state of regeneration."   Obstinacy, and (except by occasional starts) allegiance to his party, made this noble confession of error impossible to Dr. Parr.   And the intellectual results to one who lived chiefly in the atmosphere of politics, and drew his whole animation from the fluctuations of public questions, were entirely mischievous.   To those who abided by the necessities of error which grew upon any systematic opposition to Burke, the French Revolution had destroyed all the landmarks of constitutional distinctions, and impressed a character of indeterminate meaning upon ancient political principles.   From that time forward, it will be seen, by those who will take the trouble to examine, that Dr. Parr, struggling (as many others did) between the obscure convictions of his conscience and the demands of his party or of his personal situation, maintained no uniform opinions at all ; gave his faith and his hopes by turns to every vagrant adventurer, foreign or domestic, military scourge or political reformer, whom the disjointed times raised into a casual notoriety ; and was consistent in nothing but in those petty speculations of philology which, growing out of his professional pursuits, served at last no end so useful as that of relieving the unamiable asperities of his fierce political partisanship.

SECTION III

How painful it is to all parties—judges or juries, government or the public in general, the culprit or his friends— when a literary man falls under the lash of the law !   How irritating to himself and others that he should be transported —how distressing that he should be hanged !   Such fates, however, befell some of Dr. Parr's dearest connexions : he lived to see his most valued pupil expatriated, in company with felons, to the land of the kangaroo and the ornithorhynchus ; and he lived to accompany another friend (who also by one biographer is described as a pupil) to the foot of the gallows.[1]

I mention not these things by way of reproach to Dr. Parr's memory. The sufferings of his unhappy friends, *after* they came into trouble, called out none but the good qualities of his nature. Never, indeed, was Samuel Parr seen to greater advantage than when animating the hopes, supporting the fortitude, or ministering to the comforts, of the poor dejected prisoner in his gloomy cell, at a time when self-reproaches had united with the frowns of the world to make the consolations of friendship somewhat more than usually trying to the giver, and a thousand times more precious to the receiver. If all others forsook the wretched, and fled, Dr. Parr did not; his ear was open to the supplications of those who sat in darkness and sorrow; and, wherever the distress was real, remembering that he himself also was a poor frailty-laden human creature, he did not think it became him too severely to examine in what degrees guilt or indiscretion had concurred to that effect. Sam Parr! these things will make the earth lie light upon your last abode; flowers will flourish on its verdant roof; and gleams of such remembrances extort an occasional twinge of compunction even from me—at the very moment when I am endeavouring with the gentlest of knoutings quietly to *perstringe* your errors.

Sam Parr! I love you. I said so once before. But *perstringing*, which was a favoured word of your own, was a no less favoured act. You also in your lifetime perstringed many people, some of whom perstringed you, Sam, smartly in return; some kissed the rod, and some disdained it in silence. Complaint, therefore, on your behalf would be unreasonable; that same *parresia*,[2] which in your lifetime furnished a ground for so many thousand discharges of the same Grecian pun on your own name (each duly delivered by its elated author as the original explosion) obliges me to deal frankly with your too-frequent errors, even when I am

---

[1] The references here are to (1) Joseph Gerrald, tried at Edinburgh in March 1794 for sedition, and sentenced to transportation, (2) the case of a young Mr. Oliver, hanged at Stafford in 1797 for murder committed in a love-frenzy.—M.

[2] "*Parresia*" (Παῤῥησία):—The Greek word for *freedom of speech*.

most impressed by the spectacle of your Christian benignity.
Indeed, the greater your benignity, the better is my title to
tax those errors which so often defeated it.   For why, let
me ask of Dr. Parr's friends, should he choose to testify his
friendship to men in standing by them and giving his countenance to their affliction rather than in the wiser course—
so suitable to his sacred calling—of interposing his gentler
counsels between their frantic designs and the dire extremities which naturally conducted to that affliction?   In
Gerald's case, he certainly *had* counselled and warned him of
the precipice on which he stood, in due season.   But to
Gerald, as to the chamois-hunter of the Alps, danger was a
temptation even for its own sake : he hungered and thirsted
after political martyrdom.   And it is possible that in that
case Dr. Parr found no grounds of self-reproach.   *Possible*, I
say.   Even here I speak doubtingly : because, if Dr. Parr
applied sedatives to Gerald's fiery nature in 1794, he had
certainly in 1790-92 applied stimulants ; if, finally, when
Mr. Pitt and the French Reign of Terror showed that no
trifling could be allowed, he pulled vainly at the curb-rein
(as his letters remain to show), originally it is beyond all
doubt that he used the spur.   Violence and intemperance, it
is true, in Mr. Gerald were constitutional ; yet there can be
little doubt that, for the republican direction which they
took, his indiscreet tutor was nearly altogether answerable.

Joseph Gerald was a man of great talents : his defence in
the Edinburgh court shows it ; and I have the assurance of
an able critic, who was himself present at its delivery in
March 1794, that no piece of forensic eloquence on record
better deserved the profound attention with which it was
received.   Under happier auspices than Dr. Parr's, how distinguished a citizen might this man have become ! [1]   As to
Mr. Oliver, it is Dr. Parr's own statement of the case (a
statement which, at this day, I presume, few persons will be
found to believe) that he was condemned and executed for
drinking Mr. Fox's health and reading Tom Paine's writings ;
in short, for being a Jacobin.   The little trifling circumstance that he was also a murderer with Dr. Parr weighs
nothing at all.   Take, then, his own representation.   Who was

---

[1] See De Quincey's Appended Note to this page.—M.

it that countenanced the reading of Tom Paine, criticising his infamous books *as counterpoises to those of Burke,* and as useful in bringing out a neutral product ? Who was it that gave to Warwickshire (Mr. Oliver's part of the country), nay, to all England, the one sole example of a "budge doctor," [1] arrayed in the scarlet robes of the English universities, and a public instructor of the young English aristocracy, speaking cautiously and respectfully of this shallow dogmatist, who, according to his power, laid the axe to all civil government throughout the world. Who, but one man, clothed in the character of a Christian minister, could have been blinded by party violence to the extent of praising in a qualified manner, and naming amongst creditable writers, the most insolent theomachist and ruffian infidel of ancient or modern times ? If Dr. Parr's friends acted upon Mr. Paine's principles, propagated Mr. Paine's principles, and suffered in public estimation, even to the extent of martyrdom, as champions of those principles, nobody can suppose that, in selecting and professing a faith so full of peril, they could be other than greatly influenced by the knowledge that a learned doctor in the Church of England, guide and tutor to themselves, had publicly spoken of that Mr. Paine as an authority not altogether without high claims to consideration.

But I have insensibly wandered into political considerations at a point of my review where the proper object before me was—Dr. Parr as a man of letters. For this I have some excuse, considering that politics and literature so naturally blended in Dr. Parr's practice of authorship that perhaps not one of his most scholarlike performances but is richly interveined with political allusions and sarcasms, nor again one of those most professedly political which did not often turn aside to gather flowers from the fields of the Muses, or

---

[1] "*Budge doctor*":—Milton's "Comus." *Budge* is a species of fur ; furriers can best describe it. But generally the expression has the same value as when we say *the ermined judge ;* the use of which phrase is expressly to remind the professional dignitary that we are not speaking of him in his private and extra-official capacity, when he might be entitled to play the fool according to his pleasure, but as one clothed with solemn national responsibilities, whose very costume should at every moment have recalled those responsibilities to his remembrance.

herbs of " medicinable power " from the gardens of philosophy.   The truth is, the Doctor wrote as he lived ; now
bending to momentary gusts of passion ; then recovering
himself through cloudy glimpses to a higher standard of
professional duty ; remembering by fits that he was officially
a teacher, spiritual and intellectual ; by fits forgetting himself into a fiery partisan.

However, as I shall consider Dr. Parr's politics under a
separate and peculiar head, I will, for the present, confine
myself more rigorously to his literary character, difficult as it
really is to observe a line of strict separation which the good
Doctor himself is for ever tempting or provoking us to forget.

As a man of letters, then, what was it—what power,
what accomplishment, what art—that Dr. Parr could emblazon
upon his shield of pretence, as characteristically his own ?
Latin : Latin *quoad* knowledge ; Latin *quoad* practical skill.
" Reading," said he, " reflection, the office of a teacher, and
much practice in composition, have given me a command
over the Latin sufficient for the ordinary purposes of a
scholar."   This was his own estimate of himself : it was
modest—ostentatiously modest ; and possibly he would not
have made it, had he been addressing anybody but a Whig
lord, taught from his earliest youth to take his valuation of
Dr. Parr from a party who regarded him as their champion
and martyr.   Yet, again, it is not impossible that he was
sincere ; for the insincere will make a general profession of
humility in the abstract, and yet revolt from the test of
individual comparisons : they confess how much they fall
short of their own ideal ; but, as to John, Thomas, or William,
they would spurn a claim of superiority offered for *them.*
Now, Dr. Parr sometimes goes so far in his humility as to
" name names ": Sir William Jones, Sir George Baker,—*these*
I am sure of,—and I think Bishop Lowth, were amongst the
masters of Latinity to whom he somewhere concedes the palm
for this accomplishment, on a question of comparison with
himself.   I must profess my own hearty dissent from such a
graduation of the honours.   Sir George Baker, from his
subjects, is less generally known.[1]   He was an Etonian, and
wrote at least with facility ; but medicine has a Latin of her

---

[1] Sir George Baker, M.D., 1722-1809.—M.

own. As to the other two, who are within everybody's reach, I contend that, maugre their reputation, they do not write good Latin. The kind of Latin they affect is in bad taste : too florid, too *rotund*, too little idiomatic ; its structure is vicious, and evidences an English origin. Of Lowth[1] I say this even more determinately than of Sir W. Jones.[2] Some day or other I shall make a great article on this subject, and I shall then illustrate largely ; for, without illustration, such a discussion is as empty and aerial as a feast of the Barmecide.

Meantime, whatsoever the mechanic hounds may say who now give the tone to education, the art of writing Latin finely is a noble accomplishment, and one, I will take upon me to say, which none but a man of distinguished talent will succeed in. All the scholarship in the world will not avail to fight up against the tyranny of modern idioms and modern fashions of thought : the whole composition will continue to be redolent of lamps not fed with Roman oil, but with gas— base gas—unless in the hands of a man vigorous and agile enough to throw off the yoke of vernacular custom—

" Heavy as frost, and deep almost as life."

No custom cramps and masters a man's freedom so effectually as the household diction which he hears from all around him. And that man who succeeds (like Dr. Parr) in throwing his thoughts into ancient moulds does a greater feat than he that turned the Euphrates into a new channel for the service of his army.

This difficulty is in itself a sufficient justification of modern Latin, coupled, as it is, with so useful an activity of thought. But, apart from that, will any man contend that the establishment of a great commonwealth can be complete without artists in Latinity ? Even rogues, swindlers, hangmen, are essential to the proper *mounting* of a great metropolis : a murderer or two, perhaps, in the complete subdivision of employments, would not be amiss in casting the parts for a full performance of social life. Assuredly, it cannot be

[1] Bishop Robert Lowth, 1710-1787.—M.
[2] Sir William Jones, 1746-1794. See De Quincey's Appended Note to this page.—M.

denied that all sorts of villains, knaves, prigs, and so forth, are essential parts in the equipage of civil life. Else why do we regard police as so indispensable a function of organised society ? for without corresponding objects in the way of scoundrels, sharks, crimps, pimps, ringdroppers, &c., police-officers would be idle superfluities, and liable to general disgust.

But, waiving the question as stretched to this extent, for artists who work in Latin I may plead one more reason than is likely to occur in general—viz. an argument applied to our just national pride. Is it not truly shameful that a great nation should have occasion to go abroad for any odd bit of Latin that it may chance to want in the way of inscription for a triumphal monument, for a tomb, for a memorial pillar, for a public or official gift ? Conceding for the moment, but only for the moment, that Latin is of little other application, is it to be endured that we should be reduced to the necessity of importing our Latin secretary ? [1] For instance, I will mention one memorable case. The Czar Alexander, as all the world knows, one fine day in the summer of that immortal year 1814, went down to Oxford, in company with our own Regent, the King of Prussia, the Hetman of the Cossacks, and a long roll of other princely personages, with titles fatiguing to the memory, and names appalling to orthography. Some were entertained at one college, some at another. The emperor's billet fell upon Merton College ; and, in acknowledgment of the hospitality there shown, some time afterwards he sent to the warden and fellows, through Count Lieven, his ambassador to the Court of London, a magnificent vase of Siberian jasper. This vase wanted an inscription—a Latin inscription, of course. This inscription was to be worked in Russia, and the workmen stood resting upon their tools until this should come out from England. Now, under these circumstances, John Bull ! conceive the shame and the scandal if Oxford, the golden seat of classical erudition, under the very eyes of the Czar and his ambassador, had been obliged to resort to some coxcomb on the Continent for the small quantity of Latin required ! What would Mrs. Grundy have said ? What would the Hetman have said ? And Woronzoff, and Kutusoff, and

[1] See De Quincey's Appended Note to this page.—M.

Doctoroff, and Tchitchzakoff? Indeed, I cannot think it altogether becoming to Oxford that Cambridge should have furnished the artist; for Dr. Parr it was who undertook and executed the inscription, which, after all, exhibited too Spartan a nakedness to have taxed any man very severely, except for the negative quality of forbearance; and the scandal, as between the two universities, is actually on record and in print, of a chancellor of the one (Lord Grenville) corresponding with a doctor of the other, for a purpose which exclusively concerned Oxford. Perhaps the excuse may be that Oxford was not interested as a body in an affair which belonged strictly to the warden and fellows of an individual college.[1] And, at all events, the *national* part of the scandal was averted.

On this subject, which furnishes so many a heartache to a patriotic Englishman, I would beg to throw a hasty glance. John Bull, who piques himself so much and so justly on the useful and the respectable, on British industry, British faith, British hardware, British morals, British muskets (which are by no means the best specimens of our morals, judging by the proportion that annually bursts in the hands of poor savages), and, generally speaking, upon British arts, *provided only they are the useful and the mechanical arts*—this same John Bull has the most sheepish distrust of himself in every accomplishment that professes a purpose of ornament and mere beauty. Here he has a strong superstition in favour of names ending in *ano* and *ini*. Every foreigner, indeed, but more especially every Italian—it is John's private faith —is by privilege of nature a man of taste, and, by necessity, a knave. Were it only of music that he thought this, and only of Italian foreigners, perhaps he might not be so far amiss. Oh the barbarous leaning of British taste as regards music! Oh the trashy songs which pollute our theatres, and are allowed to steal into the very operas of Mozart! Not merely, however, in arts, technically so called, but in every branch of ornamental knowledge, everything that cannot be worked in a loom, weighed on a steelyard, measured by an ell-wand, valued by an auctioneer, John Bull secretly distrusts himself and his own powers. He may talk big

[1] See De Quincey's Appended Note to this page.—M.

when his patriotism is irritated ; but his secret and sincere opinion is that nature has made him a barbarian as regards the beautiful—if not for sensibility, at any rate for executive skill—and that, in compensation of this novercal usage, fortune has given him a long purse, to buy his beauty ready-made.   Hence it is, that, whilst openly disavowing it, John is for ever sneaking privately to foreigners, and tempting them with sumptuous bribes to undertake a kind of works which many scores of times would be better done by domestic talents.   Latin, we may be sure, and Greek, fall too much within the description of the ornamental to be relished by John of home manufacture.   Whenever, therefore, a great scholar was heard of on the Continent, him John Bull proceeded to buy or to bargain for.   Many were imported at the Reformation.   Joseph Scaliger was courted in the succeeding age.   A younger friend of his, Isaac Casaubon, a capital scholar, but a dull man, and rather knavish, was caught. Exultingly did John hook him, play with him, and land him.   James I. determined that he would have his life written by him ; and, in fact, all sorts of uses were meditated and laid out for their costly importation.   But he died without doing anything that he would not have done equally well upon the Continent.   The whole profit of the transaction rested with the Protestant cause ; which, but for English gold, Casaubon might ultimately have abandoned for the honours and emoluments of Rome.   Cromwell himself, perfect John Bull as he was in many a nobler feature, here also preserved the national faith.   He would have his martial glories recorded.   Well : why not ?—especially being one who had Milton at his right hand.   But no ; he thought little of *him*—he would buy a foreigner.   In fact, he was in treaty for several ; and I will venture to say that Salmasius himself was not more confounded upon finding himself suddenly seized, bound, and whirled at Milton's chariot-wheels, in a field where he was wont to career up and down as supreme and unquestioned *arbiter*, than Cromwell was on hearing that his own secretary, a Londoner born, and manufactured at Cambridge, had verily taken the conceit out of the vainglorious but all-learned Frenchman.   It was just such another conflict as we see in " As You Like It " between

Orlando and the Duke's wrestler, as well for the merits of the parties as for the pleasant disappointment to the lookers-on. For even on the Continent all men rejoiced at the humiliation of Salmasius. Charles II, again, and his favourite ministers, had heard of Des Cartes as a philosopher and Latinist, but apparently not of Lord Bacon, except as a lawyer. King William, though in the age of Pearson, and Stillingfleet, and Bentley, in the very rare glances which he condescended to bestow on literature, squinted only at Grævius, Gronovius, and other Dutch professors of humanity on a ponderous scale. And, omitting scores of other cases which might be brought in illustration, even in our own day, the worthy George III, thinking it would be well to gain the *imprimatur* of his own pocket university of Göttingen before he made up his mind on the value of the books used in the great schools of England, despatched a huge bale of grammars, lexicons, vocabularies, elementary selections, to that most concinnous and rotund of professors, Mr. Heyne. At Cæsar's command, the professor slightly inspected them ; and, having done so, in revenge of private feuds with English critics, he drew up an angry verdict on their collective merits. And thus it happened that his Majesty came to have but an indifferent opinion of English school literature. Now, in this instance we see the John Bull mania pushed to extremity. For surely Dr. Parr, on any subject whatever, barring Greek, was as competent a scholar as Master Heyne. And, on this particular subject, the jest is apparent,—that Parr was, and Heyne was not, a schoolmaster.[1] Parr had cultivated the art of teaching all his life ; and it were hard indeed if labours so tedious and heavy might not avail a man to the extent of accrediting his opinion on a capital question of his own profession. Speaking seriously, since the days of Busby, that great man who flogged so many of our avi, abavi, atavi, and tritavi,[2] none among the schoolmasters of Europe could, in those days, stand forward as competitors in point of scholarship with Parr. Scholars more eminent, doubtless, there had been, but not among those who wielded the ferule ; for

---

[1] See De Quincey's Appended Note to this page.—M.

[2] " Dr. Busby ! a great man, sir,—a very great man ! He flogged my grandfather."—*Sir Roger de Coverley.*

Dr. Burney of Greenwich, and Dr. Butler of Shrewsbury, had not then commenced their reigns. How pointed, then, was the insult, in thus transferring the appeal from a golden critic at home to a silver one abroad ; or rather, how strong the prejudice which could prompt such an appeal to one who probably meditated no insult at all. And let no man say, on *this* occasion, that Parr, being a Jacobin, could not be decently consulted on the scruples of a king ; for Heyne was a Jacobin also, until Jacobinism brought danger to his windows. If the oracle at Hatton *philippised,* the oracle of Göttingen philippised no less, and perhaps with much less temptation, and certainly with less conspicuous neglect of his own interest. Well for him that his Jacobinism lurks in ponderous Latin notes, whilst Dr. Parr's was proclaimed to the world in English !

It is fitting, then, that we people of England should always keep a man or two capable of speaking with our enemies in the gate when they speak Latin ; more especially when our national honour in this particular is to be supported against a prejudice so deep, and of standing so ancient. These, however, are local arguments for cultivating Latin, and kept alive by the sense of wounded honour. But there are other considerations, more permanent and intrinsic to the question, which press equally upon all cultivated nations. The language of ancient Rome has certain indestructible claims upon our regard : it has a peculiar merit *sui generis,* in the first place ; and, secondly, circumstances have brought it into a singular and unexampled relation to the affairs and interests of the human race.

Speaking carelessly of Latin, as one of two ancient languages, both included in the cycle of a perfect education, and which jointly compose the entire conservatory of all ancient literature that now survives, we are apt to forget that either of these languages differs from the other by any peculiar or incommunicable privilege : and, for all the general advantages which can characterise a language, we rightly ascribe the preference in degree to the Greek. But there are two circumstances, one in the historical position of the Latin language, and one in its own internal character, which unite to give it an advantage in our esteem, such as

no language besides (not even the Grecian) ever did, or, in
the nature of things, ever *can* possess. They are these :—
The Latin language has a *planetary* importance ; it belongs
not to this land or that land, but to all lands where the
human intellect has obtained its rights and its development.
It is the one sole *Lingua Franca :* that is, in a catholic
sense, it is such for the whole humanised earth, and the
total family of man. We call it a dead language. But
how ? It is not dead as Greek is dead, as Hebrew is dead,
as Sanscrit is dead—which no man uses in its ancient form
in his intercourse with other men. It is still the common
dialect which binds together that great *imperium in imperio*
—the republic of letters. And, to express in a comprehensive way the relation which this superb language bears to
man and his interests, I would say that it has the same
extensive and indifferent relation to our planet which the
moon has amongst the heavenly bodies. Her light, and the
means of intercourse which she propagates by her influence
upon the tides, belong to all nations alike. How impressive
a fact would it appear to us, if the great Asiatic family of
nations, from Teheran, or suppose from Constantinople and
Cairo (which are virtually Asiatic), to Pekin and the remotest
islands on that quarter of Asia, had some one common language through which their philosophers and statesmen could
communicate with each other over the whole vast floor of
Asia ! Yet this sublime masonic tie of brotherhood we ourselves possess, we members of Christendom, in the most
absolute sense. Gradually, moreover, it is evident that we
shall absorb the whole world into the progress of civilisation.
Thus the Latin language is, and will be still more perfectly,
a bond between the remotest places. Time also is connected
by this memorable language as much as space ; and periods
in the history of man, too widely separated from each other
(as might else have been imagined) to admit of any common
tie, are, and will continue to be, brought into connexion by
a vinculum so artificial (and, generally speaking, so fluctuating) as a language. This position of the Latin language,
with regard to the history of man, would alone suffice to
give it an overpowering interest in our regard. But,
secondly, as to its intrinsic merits,—the peculiarity of its

structure, and the singular powers which arise out of that structure,—I must leave that topic undiscussed. This only let me say,—that, for purposes of elaborate rhetoric, it is altogether unrivalled; the exquisitely artificial mould of its structure giving it that advantage. And, with respect to its supposed penury of words, I beg to mention the opinion of Cicero, who, in three separate passages of his works, maintains that in copiousness it has the advantage of the Greek.

Many questions arise upon the qualities of Parr's Latin in particular, and upon the general rules of style which he prescribed to himself. The far-famed author of the "Pursuits of Literature"[1] has stigmatised the preface to Bellendenus (we beseech you, courteous reader, to pronounce the penultimate short[2]—that is, lay the accent on the syllable *lend*) as "*a cento of Latin quotations*"; in which judgment there is a double iniquity; for, beyond all other human performances, the "Pursuits of Literature" *is* a cento, and, in any fair sense, Parr's preface is *not*. In fact, with all its undeniable ability, all its cloudy amplifications, tortuous energy of language, and organ notes of profounder eloquence leaping at intervals through the "sound and fury" of his political vaticinations—merits which sufficed to propel that bulky satire through nearly a score of editions—yet, at this day, it cannot be denied that the "Pursuits of Literature" was disfigured by much extravagance of invective, much licence of tongue, much mean and impotent spite (see his lying attempt to retort the jest of Colman by raising a Greek dust[3]), but, above all (and in a degree which took all colour of decency from his sneers at Parr), by a systematic pedantry without parallel in literature. To Parr it was open, at least, to have retorted that in no instance had *he* left it a matter of doubt what language it was that he professed to be writing, whether it were Greek enamelled upon an English ground, or a substratum of Greek tesselated by English. That boast was something: more by a good deal than the learned satirist

---

[1] Thomas James Mathias, 1757-1835. The *Pursuits of Literature* appeared in 1794.—M.

[2] For an account of this Bellendenus see De Quincey's Appended Note to this page.—M.

[3] See De Quincey's Appended Note to this page.—M.

could pretend to. Such a *mosaic* as his hyper-Manippean satire was never seen by man ; unless, indeed, it were in one imitation (the " Millennium "), where the author, apparently determined to work in more colours than his master, had strewed his pages with Arabic and Persic, and actually pressed upon the particular and indulgent notice of the Lord Mayor and Aldermen in common council assembled various interesting considerations in Coptic.

By such an accuser, then, Parr could not justly be thrown upon his defence. But really, at any bar, he did not need a defence. Writing professedly as a rhetorician, he caught at the familiar commonplaces of Roman rhetoric, and golden ornaments of Ciceronian mintage, just as in English we point our perorations with the gorgeous tropes of Jeremy Taylor, relieve the austerity of our didactic speculations with the great harmonies of Milton, or lock up our sentences with massy keystones of Shaksperian sentiment. Thus far the famous Preface was no further arrayed in borrowed plumage than really became it as an avowed *bravura* of rhetorical art, deliberately unfolding its " dazzling fence " in passages of effect, and openly challenging admiration as a solemn agonistic effort of display and execution. What probably misled the unfriendly critic were the continued references in the margin to Cicero, or other masters of Latinity. But these were often no acknowledgments for obligations, but simply sanctions for particular uses of words, or for questionable forms of phraseology. In this Dr. Parr was even generous ; for, though he *did* sometimes leave traps for the unwary— and this he acknowledged with a chuckling laugh—still, in many more instances, he saved them from the snares which were offered by these suspicious cases in Latinity.

Dismissing, however, in his own contemptuous words this false and malicious exception to Dr. Parr's preface,— " Quare suo, per me licet, sale nigro ii delectentur, suæque superbiæ morem gerant, qui me dictitant, veluti quendam ludimagistrum, ex alienis orationibus librum meum composuisse "—it is very possible that there may be others with better foundation. Amongst these there is one which I have heard most frequently pressed in conversation, and it is connected with a *quæstio vexatissima* on the general principles of modern Latin diction : was not the style hybrid—that is, a composite style, owned by no one age in particular, but made up by inharmonious contributions from many ? I answer firmly—No. Words there are, undoubtedly—single words, and solitary phrases, and still oftener senses and acceptations of words — which can plead no Ciceronian authority.[1] But the mould—the structure—the τύπος of the sentence, *that* is always Roman, always such as Cicero would have understood and countenanced. Nay, many passages there are which Cicero could not have beat for his ears. Every sentence or period moves upon two principal determinations : its external connexion in the first place—how does it arise, upon what movement of the logic or the feeling from the preceding period ? and, secondly, its own internal evolution. These *moments* (to speak dynamically) in the construction of sentences according to their treatment (but, above all, in a language the most exquisitely artificial that human necessities have created) become the very finest tests of their idiomatic propriety. In the management of these primary elements in the art of composition, Parr is a master. As to words, or separable parts, which a stroke of the pen can remove and supply, the effect, upon the whole, is little, and to modern ears, untrained by colloquial use to apprehend spontaneously the discordant association of archaisms and neologisms, scarcely any at all. Yet, it is observable that to words only, and single phrases, the purists in Latin composition have most unwisely directed their attention.

Above all, the Ciceronian purists were famous in their day : a volume might be written on their history. Fierce sectarianism bred fierce latitudinarianism. Was a writer Ciceronian in his words and phrases ? *That*, for some critics, was the one demand. On the other hand, many piqued themselves on throwing off a restriction so severe, and for certain subjects so disadvantageous. Some valued themselves on writing like Tacitus ; some, with larger and more natural taste, like Livy. Some even were content with a model as modern as Lipsius or Strada.[2]

In such disputes all turns upon the particular purpose

[1] See De Quincey's Appended Note to this page.—M.
[2] Justus Lipsius, 1547-1606 ; Famianus Strada, 1572-1649.—M.

which a writer has in using the Latin idiom. Why, on what considerations, honouring what old prescriptive usage, or looking to what benefit, has an author used Latin at all? For, evidently, in forgoing his own mother tongue, he has wilfully forfeited much ease and some power. His motives, therefore, must be very determinate in a choice so little for his own immediate interest. If,—which is the commonest case,—he writes Latin merely as a *Lingua Franca*, as the general language of the literary commonwealth of Christendom, and, therefore, purely to create an extended circulation for his thoughts, it is probable that his subject in these days will be derived from some branch of science, or, at all events, some theme treated didactically; for, as an orator, an essayist, or, generally, as a *bellettrist*, he can find no particular temptations in a language which, whilst it multiplies his difficulties, must naturally limit his audience. On a mere calculation of good sense, we may predict that his subject will, in nine cases out of ten, be one which is paramount, by its matter, to all considerations of style and manner. Physics, for example, in some one of its numerous branches; mathematics; or some great standing problem of metaphysics. Now, in such a case, if there be one rule of good taste more pressing than another, it is this: to reject all ornaments of style whatever—in fact all style; for, unless on a question which admits some action of the feelings, in a business of the pure understanding, style, properly defined, is impossible. Consequently, classical Latin, whether of the golden, silver, or brazen age, is, in such a case, equally to be rejected.

Why is it that in law Latin we say *murdravit*, for he murdered— *warrantizo*, *homagium*, and so forth? Simply because the transcendent *matter* in all legal discussions, the great interests of life and property which law concerns, the overruling importance of the necessities to which law ministers, making intelligibility and distinction of cases to be the absorbing consideration, cannot but throw into the shade every quality of writing which does not co-operate to that end; and, for those qualities which have a tendency even to clash with it, cannot but reduce them to the rank of puerile levities. The idea of *felony*, under its severe and exclusive limitation, according to our jurisprudence, could not be adequately reached by any Ciceronian term whatsoever ; and, this once admitted, it is evident that the filigree frost-work of classical fastidiousness must be allowed to melt at once before the great domineering influences of life in its elementary interests. Religion again, how much has *that* been found to suffer in the hands of classical precisians, to whom the whole vocabulary of Christianity—all the technical terms of its divine economy, all its idioms, such as *grace, sanctification, sacrament, regeneration,* &c. — were so many stones of offence and scandal as regarded the terms, even where they did not reject the conceptions. Now, one law of good sense is paramount for all composition whatsoever— viz. that the subject, the very ideas, for the development of which only any composition at all became necessary, must not suffer prejudice, or diminution, from any scruples affecting the mere accessories of style or manner. Where both cannot co-exist, perish the style—let the subject-matter (to use a scholastic term) prosper ! [1]

This law governs every theme of pure science, or which is capable of a didactic treatment. For instance, in natural philosophy, where the mere ideas under discussion, the bodies, the processes, the experiments, the instruments, are all alike almost in a region unknown and unsubjected to any jurisdiction of the classical languages, how vain, how puerile the attempt to fight up against these natural, and for us insurmountable, difficulties, by any system of clever equivocations, or ingenious compromises between the absolute barbarisms of the thing and their nearest classical analogies. By such misdirected sleight-of-hand what is effected ? We sacrifice one principle, without propitiating the other. Science, defrauded of her exactness, frowns ; and the genius of classical elegance does not smile. Precision is wilfully forfeited ; and no real ornament is gained. Wheresoever a man writes not for a didactic purpose, but for effect, —wheresoever the composition is not a mere means for conveying truths, but its own end and final object as a *power,*— there only it may be allowable to attempt a happy evasion of some modern barbarism by means of its nearest Roman

[1] See De Quincey's Appended Note to this page.—M.

equivalent. For example, in a sepulchral inscription, one of the finest modes of the serious epigram, where distinction for the understanding is nothing, and effect for the natural sensibilities is all in all, Dr. Parr might be justified in saying that a man died by a *ballista*, as the nearest classical weapon of offence to that which was really concerned in the fatal accident. But the same writer, treating any question of natural philosophy, could never have allowed himself in so vague a term. To know that a man perished under a blow from some engine of war acted on by a mechanical force, without distinguishing whether gun or pistol, bomb, mortar, howitzer, or hand-grenade, might be all that was required to engage the reader's sympathy. Some little circumstantiality, some slight specification of details, is useful in giving direction and liveliness to a general tone of commiseration; whilst too minute an individualisation of objects, not elevated enough to sustain any weight of attention, would both degrade the subject and disturb the natural current of the feelings, by the disproportionate notice it would arrogate under the unwieldy periphrasis that might be necessary to express it. But, on the other hand, in pure physics, the primary necessity of rigorous distinction would demand an exact designation of the particular implement; size, weight, bore, mode of action, and quantity of resistance, might here all happen to be of foremost importance. Something, in fact, analogous to all this, for the case itself, and for the law which it suggests, may be found in the art of gardening, under its two great divisions of the useful and the ornamental. Taste was first applied to the latter. From the art of gardening, as cultivated for picturesque effects, laws and principles of harmonious grouping, of happy contrast, and of hidden co-operation in parts remote from each other, were soon derived. It was natural that some transfer should be attempted of these rules to the humbler province of kitchen-gardens. Something was tried here, also, of the former devices for producing the picturesque; and the effects were uniformly bad. Upon which two classes of critics arose: one who supposed kitchen-gardens to be placed altogether out of the jurisdiction of taste; and another, who persisted in bringing them within it, but unfortunately by

means of the very same rules as those which governed the
larger and more irregular province of pleasure-gardens. The
truth lay between the two parties. The last were right in
supposing that every mode of exhibiting objects to the eye
had its own susceptibilities (however limited) of beauty, and
its own rules of good taste. The first, on the other hand,
were equally right in rejecting the rules of the picturesque
as applicable to arrangements in which utility and convenience presided. Beauty, "wild without rule or art, *enormous*
bliss" (that is, bliss which transcends all *norma*, or artificial
regulation), which is Milton's emphatic summing up of the
luxuries of Eden, obeys a much wider law, and in that proportion more difficult to be abstracted than the elegance of
trim arrangement. But even this has its own appropriate
law of ornament ; and the mistake is to seek it by translation from some province differing essentially, and by its
central principle, from itself. Where it is possible (as in
ornamental gardening on the English plan it is) to appear as
an assistant, and in subordination to nature, making her the
principal artist, and rather directing her efforts than positively interfering with them, there it is certain that the wild,
the irregular, the illimitable, and the luxuriant, have their
appropriate force of beauty ; and the tendency of art is no
more than simply to assist their development, and to sustain
their effect, by removing whatever is inharmonious. But,
in a system of which utility is the object, utility must also
be the law and source of the beauty. That same convenience
which dictates arrangement and limitation as its own subsidiary instruments ought to dictate these same principles as
the presiding agents for the creation of appropriate ornaments. Instead of seeking a wild picturesque, which delights
in concealing, or in revealing only by fits, the subtle and
half-evanescent laws under which it grows, good taste suggests imperatively, as the object we should court, a beauty of
the architectural kind, courting order and symmetry, avowing, not hiding, its own artifices, and absolutely existing by
correspondence of parts.

Latin composition falls into the same or analogous divisions, and these divisions obey the same or corresponding
rules. The highest form of Latin composition,—ornamented

Latin, which belongs to a difficult department of the higher *belles lettres*,—clothes itself, by natural right, in the whole pomp and luxury of the native Roman idiom. Didactic Latin of any class, in which the subject makes it impossible to sustain that idiom for two consecutive sentences, abandons it professedly, and creates a new law for itself. Even the art of annotation, a very extensive branch of purely didactic Latin, and cultivated by immense numbers of very able men, has its own peculiar laws and proprieties, which must be sought in the works of those who have practised it with success.[1]

For an example in support of what I have been saying, and illustrating the ludicrous effect which arises from a fastidiously classical phraseology employed upon a subject of science, I might refer my readers to the collection of letters between Leibnitz and various correspondents in different parts of Europe, published at Hanover by Feder, among which are some extra superfine letters by a certain Italian abbé.

It is really as good as a comedy to see the rope-dancing tricks of agility by which this finical Italian *petit-maitre* contrives to talk of electricity, retorts, crucibles, and gas, in terms that might have delighted the most delicate ears of Augustan Rome. Leibnitz pays him some compliments, as he could do no less, upon his superfine apparel; but evidently he is laughing in his sleeve at the hyperbolical pains and perspiration that each paragraph of his letters must have cost him. This Italian simply carried a pretty common mistake to a ridiculous excess. The notion is universal that, even in writing upon scientific subjects, it is right to strive after classical grace in that extent to which it shall be found attainable. But this is false taste. Far juster, better, and more self-consistent, is the plain, unpretending Latin of the great heroes of philosophy—Lord Bacon, Des Cartes, and Leibnitz.[2] They court no classical ornaments, no rhetorical phrases; yet the Latin idiom, though not studiously courted, is never harshly violated. Philosophic ideas, philosophic

[1] Amongst whom, by the way, Bentley stands foremost, whilst Porson is the least felicitous in giving a scholar-like expression to his notes.

[3] See De Quincey's two Appended Notes to this page.—M.

dogmas, of modern birth, are not antedated by giving them Pagan names. Terms of modern science, objects of modern discovery, are not disguised in a ridiculous masquerade of classical approximations, presenting a conjectural travesty, rather than a just and responsible translation by fair equivalents. The interests of the sense, and the demands of the primary purpose, are everywhere made the governing considerations ; and, whilst the barbarisms of some amongst the schoolmen are never imitated, and no idioms positively modern are adopted, the pure Roman idiom is only so far courted as it favours the ends of expedition and precision. In short, I shall not much err in making this general assertion,—that a philosophic Latin style, suited to the wants of modern speculation and modern research, has gradually matured itself in the hands of the great philosophic reformers : an ancient language has bent to the pressure of new circumstances, and of modern revolutions in thinking ; and it might be shown that it has, in fact, thrown off a new and secondary idiom, neither modern nor antique, and better fitted for despatch, though less showy, than that of ancient Rome ; and this secondary idiom has been created in the same way, and by the same legitimate agency, as any language whatsoever—viz. by the instincts of feeling, and the necessities of the human mind. Voluntarily and consciously, man never did, nor could, create a language.

The great men I speak of, as all men engaged in that function, were controlled by circumstances existing out of themselves—viz. the demands of human thinking, as they have gradually been unfolded, and the needs of experimental philosophy. In maturing their product, that neutral diction of philosophy which is neither modern nor ancient, they were themselves controlled by the circumstances I state ; yet, again, as they started with a scholar-like knowledge of the ancient Roman idiom, they have reciprocally so far reacted upon these circumstances, and controlled their natural tendency, as not to suffer their own vernacular idioms to impress themselves upon their new diction, or at all to mould its shape and character.

Into these discursive notices I have allowed myself to wander, from the interest which attaches to every phasis of so imperishable a monument of Roman power as survives for all cultivated nations in the Roman language, and also from its near connexion with my immediate subject. Recalling myself, however, into that branch of my theme which more particularly concerns Dr. Parr, who wrote little (if anything) in the neutral or didactic form of the Latin idiom, but came forward boldly as a performer on the great classical organ of that majestic language—I have said that, in my judgment, he was a skilful performer ; I will add that, notwithstanding his self-depreciation, possibly not sincere, he was much more skilful than those who have been most accredited for this accomplishment in modern England; particularly he was superior, as a master of Latinity, to Sir William Jones and Bishop Lowth, the two most celebrated English composers in Latin through the latter half of the eighteenth century.

Whilst thus limiting my comparison of Parr to English competitors for the same sort of fame, I am reminded that Reiske, the well-known editor of the Greek Orators,[1] a hasty and careless but a copious scholar, and himself possessing a fluent command over the Latin language, has pronounced a general censure (preface to Demosthenes) of English Latinity. In this censure, after making the requisite limitations, I confess that reluctantly I concur. Not that the Continent does not keep us in countenance by its own breed of bald composers ; but our English deficiencies are the more remarkable when placed in collision with the unquestionable fact that in no country upon earth have the gentry, both professional and non-professional, and the majority even of the higher aristocracy, so large a tincture of classical knowledge. What is still more remarkable, some of our first-rate scholars have been our poorest masters of Latinity. In particular, Taylor, the civilian,[2] and, forensically speaking, the able editor of Demosthenes,[3] whose style it was, to the best of my remembrance, in connexion with some ill-natured sneer at Wolff, that

[1] J. J. Reiske, 1716-1774.—M.

[2] *" Civilian "* :—The ridiculous abuse of this word *civilian* in our days obliges me to explain that I mean by *civilian* one of three separate characters :—1. the student, 2. the teacher or professor, 3. the forensic practiser, of the civil (or Roman) law.

[3] John Taylor, LL.D., 1704-1766.—M.

furnished the immediate provocation to Reiske's remark, wrote meanly in Latin ; and Porson, a much greater scholar than any of these men,[1] was, as a Latinist, below the meanest of them. In fact, he wrote Latin of any kind—such Latin even as was framed on his own poor ideal—with singular want of freedom and facility : so much may be read in the very movement of his disjointed style.   But (more than all *that*) his standard and conception of Latin style were originally bad, and misdirected. A compass so wide as that of Parr was far beyond Porson's strength of pinion.   He has not ventured, in any instance that I am aware of, to trust himself through the length of three sentences to his own impulses, but, in his uniform character of annotator, timidly creeps along shore, attached to the tow-line of his text, and ready to drop his anchor on the least summons to stretch out to sea.   In this, however, there is something equivocal : timidity of thinking may per-haps be as much concerned in his extreme reserve as penury of diction.   In reality, the one mortal taint of English Latinity is, that it is a translation, a rendering back, from an English archetype.   In that way, and upon any such a prin-ciple, good Latin never can arise.   It grows up by another process.   To write like an ancient Roman, a man must *think* in Latin.   From its English shape, the thoughts, the con-nexions, the transitions, have *already received a determination* this way or that, unfitting them for the yoke of a Latin con-struction.   Even the most absolute fixtures (to use that term) in an English structure must often be unsettled, and the whole framework of the period be taken to pieces and recast in a thoroughly Latin composition.   The interrogative form must often be changed to the absolute affirmative, and *versâ vice ;* parenthetical intercalations must often be melted down into the body of the sentence ; qualifications and restraints added or omitted ; and the whole thought, its succession and connexion, altered, before it will be fitted to receive a direct Latin character.

This part of my subject, and, in connexion with it, Dr. Parr's singular command of the Latin idiom, I might easily illustrate by a few references to the Bellenden Preface ; and there is the more propriety in a studious use of this preface

---

[1] Richard Porson, 1759-1808.—M.

because Parr himself declared to one of his friends (Dr. Johnstone's Memoirs, p. 263), "There are in the preface almost all the phraseological beauties I know of in Latin."

But this task belongs to a separate paper on modern Latinity. At present I hasten to a class of the Doctor's Latin compositions in which his merits are more conspicuous —because more characteristically his own.

In the EPITAPHS of Dr. Parr, as amongst the epitaphs of this country, where a false model has prevailed—the lapidary style and arrangement, and an unseasonable glitter of rhetoric—there is, in one direction, almost a unique body of excellence. Indeed, from these inscriptions I believe it possible to abstract all the *negative* laws which should preside in this species of composition. The defect—a heavy defect—is in the *positive* qualities. Whatsoever an epitaph ought *not* to be, that too frequently it is; and, by examining Dr. Parr's in detail, we shall find, from the uniformity of his abstinence in those circumstances which most usually offer the matter of offence, that his abstinence was not accidental, and that *implicitly*—that is, by involution and silent implication—all the canons of a just theory on this branch of art are there brought together and accumulated. This is no light merit; indeed, when one reflects upon it, and considers how many and how able men have failed, I begin to think that Sam was perhaps a greater man by the intention of nature than my villainous prejudices have allowed me to suppose. But, with this concession to the *negative* merits of the Doctor, let it not be thought illiberal in me to connect a repetition of my complaint as to the defects of the τὸ *affirmative* in this collection. Every art is there illustrated which can minister to the gratification of the judgment: the grand defect is in all that should affect the sensibility. It is not enough in an epitaph that it does not shock or revolt my taste or sense of propriety—of decorum—and the *convenances* arising out of place, purpose, occasion, or personal circumstances. The absence of all this leaves me in the condition for being suitably affected: I am ready to be affected; and I now look for the τὸ *positive* which is to affect me. Everything has been removed by the skilful hand of the composer which could interfere with, or disturb, the sanctity or tenderness of my emotions : " And now then," the ground being cleared, "why don't you proceed to use your powers of pathos ? " The Grecian *epigrammata* — that matchless bead-roll of tender expressions for all household feelings that could blossom amongst those for whom no steady dawn of celestial hopes had risen—that treasury of fine sentiment, where the natural pieties of the human heart have ascended as high as a religion so meagre could avail to carry them—do not rely for their effect merely upon the chastities of their composition. Those graces act simply in the way of resistance to all adverse forces; but their *absolute* powers lie in the frank language of natural grief, trusting to its own least elaborate expression, or in the delicacies of covert and circumstantial allusion.   Of this latter kind we have occasionally an example in Dr. Parr himself.   When he numbers, not the years only, and months, but the *hours*, even, of a young man's life, he throws the attention indirectly on the affecting brevity of his career, and on the avaricious love in the survivors clinging tenaciously to the record of his too fugitive hours, even in their minutest fractions.   Applied to elder persons, this becomes too much of a mechanical artifice. But the pointed expression, by any means or artifice whatever, of the passions suited to the occasion, is far too rare in the Parrian inscriptions.   One might suppose even that pious grief and tender *desiderium*, the final cause and the efficient cause at once of epitaphs, were, in Dr. Parr's estimate, no more than a *lucro ponamus*, something indifferent to their essence, and thrown in casually as a *bonus* beyond what we are entitled to expect.

Meantime, allowing for this one capital defect, all the laws of good composition, and of Latin composition in particular, are generally observed by Dr. Parr.   In particular, he objected, and I think judiciously, to the employment of direct *quotations* in an epitaph.   He did not give his reasons ; perhaps he only felt them.   On a proper occasion, I fancy that I could develop these reasons.   At present it is sufficient to say that quotations always express a mind not fully possessed by its subject, and abate the tone of earnestness which ought to preside either in very passionate or in very severe composition.   A great poet of our own days,

in writing an ode, felt that a phrase which he had borrowed
ought not to be marked as a quotation ; for that this reference to a book had the effect of breaking the current of the
passion.[1] In the choice of his Latinity, also, Dr. Parr prescribed to himself, for this department of composition, very
peculiar and very refined maxims. The guide whom he chiefly
followed was one not easily obtained for love or money,—
Morcellus de Stylo Inscriptionum. Yet sometimes he seems to
have forgotten his own principles. An epitaph was sent for
his approbation, written by no less a person than Louis
XVIII. All the world is aware that this prince was a man
of cultivated taste, and a good classical scholar, and, in
particular, minutely acquainted with Horace. The prince
was, however, for such a task, something too much of a
Catholic bigot ; and he disfigured his epitaph by introducing
the most unclassical Latinity of the Vulgate. Nevertheless,
Dr. Parr thought proper to approve of this. Now I admit,
and the spirit of my remarks already made on the Latinity
for scientific subjects will have shown that I admit, cases in
which classical Latin must systematically bend to modern
modifications. I admit, also, that the Vulgate translation,
from the sanctity of its authority in the Romish Church,
comes within the privileged class of cases which have created
a secondary order of Latinity, deserving to be held classical
in its own proper jurisdiction. Sepulchral inscriptions for
Christian countries being usually in churches, or their consecrated purlieus, may be thought by some to fall peculiarly
within that line. But I say—No. It would be so, were the
custom of monumental inscription wholly, or in its first
origin, a religious one ; whereas epitaphs are primarily a
matter of usage and sentiment, not at all prescribed by religion, but simply checked and modified by the consecrated
place in which they are usually sculptured, and by the religious considerations associated with the contemplation of
death. This is my opinion, and ought to be Dr. Parr's ; for,
in writing to Sir Joshua Reynolds on the subject of an

1 This poet was Wordsworth ; the particular case arose in the
" Ode on the Intimations of Immortality " ; and I will mention frankly
that it was upon my own suggestion that this secondary and revised
view was adopted by the poet.

epitaph for Dr. Johnson, amongst other judicious reflections upon the general subject of Latin inscriptions, he says, "If Latin is to be the language, the whole spirit and the whole phraseology ought to be *such as a Latin writer would use.*" Now, the Vulgate translation of the Scriptures would have been nearly unintelligible in the ages of classic Rome, and nowhere more so than in that particular passage which fell under Dr. Parr's examination.

The laws of the Epitaph, a peculiar and most interesting branch of monumental inscription, and the modification of these laws as applied to *Christian* cemeteries, present a most attractive subject to the philosopher and the man of taste in conjunction. I shall relegate the inquirer to an essay on this subject by Wordsworth, the sole even tentative approximation which I know towards a philosophic valuation of epitaphs upon fixed principles. His essay is beautifully written, and finely conceived.[1] The central principle of an epitaph he states thus (I do not pretend to quote, speaking from a recollection of many years back) :—It expresses, or ought to express, the most absolute synthesis of the generic with the individual : that is to say, starting from what a man has *in common* with all his species, the most general affections of frail humanity—its sufferings and its pleasures, its trials and triumphs, its fears and awful hopes—starting from this as the indispensable ground of all *general* sympathy, it goes forward to what a man has most peculiar and exclusive to himself—his talents and their special application, his fortunes, and all the other incommunicable circumstances of his life, as the ground for challenging a separate and peculiar attention. The first element of an epitaph claims the benefit of participation in a catholic interest ; the second claims it in that peculiar degree which justifies a separate and peculiar record. This most general idea of an epitaph, or sepulchral inscription, which is valid for all religions, falls in especially with the characteristic humility of the Christian. However distinguished amongst his earthly peers, yet, in the presence

---

[1] Wordsworth's *Essay upon Epitaphs :* originally furnished to Coleridge in 1810 for his Lake periodical called *The Friend,* and afterwards printed by Wordsworth among his Notes to his Poems. —M.

of that Being whose infinity confounds all earthly distinctions, every man is bound to remember, in the first place,
those great bonds of a common mortality—a common frailty
—and a common hope, which connect him with the populous
"nations of the grave." His greatest humiliation, but also
his most absolute glory, lies in that mysterious incarnation
of an infinite spirit in a fleshly robe which makes him heir
to the calamities of the one, but also co-heir to the imperishable dowry of the other. As the basis, therefore, of any
interest which can connect him with the passing reader, and
as an introductory propitiation also to the Christian *genius
loci*, he begins by avowing his humanity — his absolute
identity with what is highest and lowest, wisest and simplest,
proudest and meanest, in all around him.

This principle must preside in every epitaph alike.
There is another equally important which should govern the
conclusion ; and, like that which I have just been urging, as,
on the one hand, it is prompted by universal good taste, and
therefore claimed its rights even under a Pagan mythology,
so, on the other, it lends itself, with a peculiar emphasis,
to the characteristic tone of a Christian epitaph. It is
this :—We may observe that poets of the highest class,
whether otherwise delighting or not in the storm and
tumultuous agitation of passion, whether otherwise tragic or
epic in the constitution of their minds, yet, by a natural
instinct, have all agreed in tending to peace and absolute
repose, as the state in which only a sane constitution of feelings can finally acquiesce. And hence, even in those cases
where the very circumstances forbade the absolute tranquillity of happiness and triumphant enjoyment, they have
combined to substitute a secondary one of resignation. This
may be one reason why Homer has closed his chief poem
with the funeral rites of Hector : a section of the " Iliad "
which otherwise has appeared to many an excrescence. Perhaps he was unwilling to leave us with the painful spectacle
of the noble and patriotic martyr dragged with ruffian
violence round the funeral pyre of Patroclus, the coming
desolation of Troy in prospect, the frenzy of grief in its
first tempestuous career amongst the Trojan women and
children, and the agitations of sympathy in the reader as yet

untranquillised. A final book, therefore, removes all these stormy objects, leaving the stage in possession of calmer objects, and of emotions more elevating, tranquillising, and soothing :—

" Ὣς οἵγ᾽ ἀμφίεπον τάφον Ἕκτορος ἱπποδάμοιο."

"So tended they the grave [ministered to the obsequies] of Hector, the tamer of horses."

Or, to give it with the effect of Pope's rhythmus—

> "Such honours Ilion to her hero paid ;
> And peaceful slept the mighty Hector's shade."

In one sense, indeed, and for that peculiar auditory whom Homer might contemplate—an auditory sure to merge the universal sense of humanity in the local sense of Grecian nationality—the very calamities of Troy and her great champion were so many triumphs for Greece ; and, in that view, it might be contended that the true point of repose is the final and absolute victory of Achilles ; upon which supposition the last book really is an excrescence, or at least a sweeping ceremonial train to the voluminous draperies of the " Iliad," in compliance with the religious usages of ancient Greece.   But it is probable that my own view of the case is more correct ; for there is other and independent evidence that Homer himself was catholic enough in his sensibilities to sympathise powerfully with Hector and Priam, and means his hearers to do so.   Placing himself, therefore, at least for the occasion, in the neutral position of a modern reader whose sympathies are equally engaged for Greece and for Troy, he felt the death of Hector as an afflicting event, and the attending circumstances more as agitating than as triumphant, and added the last book as necessary to regain the key of a disturbed equanimity.   In " Paradise Lost," again, this principle is still more distinctly recognised, and is practically applied to the case by an artifice even more elaborate.   There the misery, the anguish, at one point of the action—the despair—are absolute ; nor does it appear at first sight how, or by what possibility, the reader can repossess himself of the peace and fortitude which even the sullen midnight of Tragedy requires, much more the large sunlight of the Epopee.   Paradise was lost ; that

idea ruled and domineered in the very title ; how was it to
be withdrawn, or even palliated, in the conclusion ?   Simply
thus :—If Paradise were lost, Paradise was also regained ;
and though that reconquest could not, as an event, enter into
the poem without breaking its unity in a flagrant manner,
yet, proleptically, and in the way of vision, it might.   Such
a vision is placed by the archangelic comforter before
Adam ; purged with euphrasy and rue, his eye beholds it ;
and, for that part which cannot artistically be given as a
visionary spectacle, the angel interposes as a solemn narrator
and interpreter.   The consolations which in this way reach
Adam reach the reader no less ; and the reader is able to
unite with our general father in his thankful acknowledgment :—

> " Greatly instructed shall I hence depart ;
>   Greatly *in peace of mind.*"

Accordingly, spite of the triumphs of Satan — spite of Sin
and all-conquering Death, who had left the gates of Hell for
their long abode on Earth — spite of the pollution, wretchedness, and remorse, that had now gained possession of man —
spite of the far-stretching taint of that contagion which (in
the impressive instances of the eagle and the lion) too evidently showed itself by " mute signs " as having already
seasoned for corruption earth and its inheritance [1]—yet, by
means of this one sublime artifice, which brings together the
Alpha and Omega, the beginning and end of time, the last
day of man's innocence and the first of his restoration, it is
contrived that a twofold peace—the peace of resignation and
the peace of hope—should harmonise the key in which the
departing strains of this celestial poem roll off ; and its last
cadences leave behind an echo, which, with the solemnity of
the grave, has also the halcyon peace of the grave, and its
austere repose.   A third instance we have—even more direct
and unequivocal, of the same principle, from this same poet,
not only involved silently in his practice, but also consciously contemplated.   In the " Samson Agonistes," though

----

[1] See the fine incidents (*Paradise Lost*, Book XI) of the earliest
hostility among animals, which first announce to Adam the immeasur-
able extent of *his own* ruin.

a tragedy of most tumultuous catastrophe, it is so contrived, by the interposition of the chorus, who, fixing their hopes in the heavens, are unshaken by sublunary griefs, not only that all should terminate

"In peace of spirit and sublime repose,"

but also that this conclusion should be expressly drawn out in words as the great moral of the drama ; by which, as by other features, it recalls, in its most exquisite form, the Grecian model which it follows, together with that fine trans- figuration of moral purpose that belongs to a higher, purer, and far holier religion.

Peace, then, severe tranquillity, the brooding calm, or γαλήνη of the Greeks, is the final key into which all the storms of passion modulate themselves in the hands of great poets.

"In war itself—war is no ultimate end." [1]

All tumult is for the sake of rest—tempest, but the harbinger of calm—and suffering, good only as the condition of perma- nent repose.   Peace, in a double sense, may be supposed inscribed on the portals of all cemeteries : that peace, in the first place, which belongs to the grave as the final haven after the storms of life—and in this sense the sentiment belongs equally to the Pagan, the Mahometan, and the Chris- tian ; secondly, the peace of resignation to the will of God, in the meek surrender at his call of those on whom our pro- foundest affections had settled.   This sentiment belongs pre- eminently, if not exclusively, to Christianity ; is known, I presume, in some sense, to the Mahometan ; but not at all to the Pagan.   And this it is in which Christian epitaphs should terminate.   Hence it is peculiarly offensive to a just taste, were no higher principle offended, that despair—or obstinate refusal of consolation—should colour the expression of an epitaph.   The example which (if I remember rightly) Wordsworth alleges of this capital fault, is from the famous monument erected by Sir Brooke Boothby, a Derbyshire baronet, to his only daughter, a very beautiful and intellectual child, about eight years old.   The closing words of the in-

---

[1] Coleridge's *Wallenstein.*

scription are to this effect :—"The wretched parents embarked their all upon this frail bark, *and the wreck was total.*" Here there are three gross faults : first, it is an expression of rebellious grief, courting despair, and within the very walls of a Christian church abjuring hope ; secondly, as a movement of *violent* passion, it is transient. Despair cannot long sustain itself ; hence it is pointedly out of harmony with the *durability* of a marble record. How puerile to sculpture laboriously with the chisel, and thus invest with a monumental eternity, any sentiment whatever which must already have begun to fade before the sculptor has finished his task ! Thirdly, this vicious sentiment is expressed figuratively—that is, fancifully. Now, all action of the fancy is out of place in a sepulchral record. No sentiment is *there* appropriate except the weightiest, sternest, and most elementary ; no expression of it except the simplest and severest.

"Calm passions *there* abide, majestic pains."

These great laws of feeling, in this difficult and delicate department of composition, though perhaps never contemplated distinctly *as* laws by Dr. Parr, yet seem to have been impulsively obeyed by many of his epitaphs. And, with regard to the *expressions* of his thoughts, except to the extent of a single word—as, for instance, *velificari,* in which the metaphorical application has almost obliterated the original meaning—I remember nothing figurative, nothing too gay, nothing luxuriant ;—all is chaste, grave—suited to the solemnity of the situation. Had Dr. Parr, therefore, written under the additional restraints *connected with the additional powers* of verse, and had he oftener achieved a distinguished success in the pathetic, he would, as an artist in monumental inscriptions, have held a place amongst the highest class.[1] Meantime, his merits are the less memorable, or likely to leave an impression on our literature, that they are almost invariably negative ; painfully evading faults which are not known or suspected *as* faults by most readers, and resisting temptations to rhetorical displays that, even if freely indulged, would for the multitude have had a peculiar fascination.

[1] See De Quincey's Appended Note to this page.—M.

Section IV

About the year 1789 Dr. Parr was involved in two literary broils : the one purely aggressive on *his* part, the other nearly so ; though, as usual, the Doctor coloured them to his own mind as measures of just retaliation.   The first arose in his wanton republication of a pamphlet, written by Bishop Warburton,[1] but afterwards suppressed by his orders ; and to this pamphlet he united another, " by a Warburtonian," meaning Bishop Hurd [2] ; prefixing to the whole a preface, and a most rhetorical dedication, from his own pen, in which he labours to characterise both the bishops, but especially the living one, in terms that, whilst wearing some show of justice, should also be as sarcastic and as injurious as possible.   The mere act of reviving what the authors themselves had been painfully anxious to suppress is already sufficiently offensive, and expressive of a spiteful mind, had the preface even been spared.   What was the provocation to a piece of mischief so puerile ?   Listen to the Doctor, and you will suppose that no motive but the purest and most philanthropic had governed him.   Leland and Jortin, two dissenting clergymen, respectably learned as regarded the amount of their learning, and usefully learned as regarded its application [3] ;—these men had, by the Bishop of Gloucester (Warburton), and by his sycophant, the Bishop of Worcester (Hurd), as Parr alleged, been cruelly undervalued · Leland had been " most petulantly insulted, and Jortin most inhumanly vilified."   Well—and what then ?   Better men than ever stood upon *their* pins have been insulted, hustled, floored, smashed, and robbed.   Besides, hard words break no bones.   And why could not the two dissenters have settled their own quarrels with the two bishops ?   In effect, they *had* done so.   Why must Dr. Parr intrude his person into the row, long after it was extinct, and when three out of four parties nominally interested were in their graves ?   Oh, but, says Dr. Parr, the example was the thing ; neither of

[1] Warburton, 1698-1779.—M.   [2] Hurd, 1720-1808.—M.
[3] John Leland, D.D., 1691-1766 ; John Jortin, D.D., 1698-1770. —M.

the offenders had been punished ; and their impunity, if tolerated, would encourage future bishops to future assaults upon future dissenters, when future Parrs for redressing the wrong might not be at hand.   He was resolved to deter others from supposing " that what has been repeatedly and deliberately done in secret will not, sooner or later, be punished openly."   Finally, coming nearer to the true purpose of the whole, he avows that " it was intended to *lessen the number of those who speak too well of Bishop Hurd.*"

Vain and tortuous disguises of malice self-betrayed ! Now, let us hear the true lurking motives to this almost unprincipled attack, which Dr. Parr so studiously masked under pretexts of public purposes.   One writer tells us that Parr, on a visit to Hartlebury (the Bishop of Worcester's villa), had been dismissed with little ceremony, and with hospitable attentions either none at all, or so chilling as to pique his pride.   This anecdote, however, I have reason to think, refers to a period subsequent to the original offence. Perhaps that offence might arise in a case where the bishop drew upon himself the ferocious resentment of Parr by hesitation in passing one of Parr's friends, then a candidate for holy orders.   Even this resentment, however, was possibly no more than the first expression of Parr's secret mortification at the bishop's private opinion of his sermon on education.   Nothing in this world travels faster than the ill-natured judgments of literary men upon each other ; and Parr probably heard from a thousand quarters that Hurd had expressed his dislike to the style, or the preposterous length of this " vernacular sermon."   That this anecdote is true nobody doubts who remembers the pointed manner in which Parr himself notices, in his dedication, Bishop Hurd's " rooted antipathy to *long vernacular sermons from Dr. Parr.*"

Of such quality are often the true motives even of good men, when their personal feelings are roused.   The whole pretence of Parr was a fiction.   Jortin and Leland were already avenged.   Both had retaliated upon Hurd, and, as Parr fancied, with success.   The one, he said, had " chastised " Hurd with " wit "—the other had " baffled " him with " argument."   So many cudgellings for one crime were out of all proportion.   " These two excellent men," says Parr, " were not to be annoyed again and again by the poisonous arrows of slander." Neither was this excellent bishop to be "again and again" pulled up to the public bar, and annoyed for having annoyed *them*. "Tit for tat" all the world over; and, if a man, "being fap," as Pistol observes, and also too lively with young blood, will "try conclusions," and perhaps "assault and batter" a leash of worthy men, he must pay. But, *having* paid (as, suppose, five pounds), then, at Bow Street or anywhere else, he is held entitled to his five pounds' worth of battery. He has bought it, settled the bill, and got a stamped receipt. For *them* to claim further payment entitles *him* to further battery.

But one argument shall put down Dr. Parr's pretences. Were Jortin and Leland the only parties to whom Hurd or Warburton had furnished actionable matter? Not by a hundred. They had run amuck at all the men who lay in their path. To go no further than one of Parr's friends: Bishop Lowth and Hume had been assaulted with more injustice than either of those for whom Parr stood forward. Hurd had called Hume "a puny dialectician." Now, this was insolence. Hume, even as a *litterator*, was every way superior to the bishop; but, as a dialectician, Hume to Hurd was a Titan to a pigmy. The "Essay on Necessary Connexion," which was the seed that has since germinated into the mighty forest of German philosophy, was hardly in one sentence within Hurd's comprehension. As to Lowth, we would not quarrel with those who should fasten a quarrel upon *him*.

But, if that is our way of thinking, it was not Parr's. He was incensed at Hurd for his depreciation of Lowth; he was incensed with him, and justly, for his affected contempt of Hume; he was incensed with another worthy bishop for insidiously calling Lardner[1] "industrious," as though, in raising such a pile as the "Credibility of Gospel History" (originally counting seventeen octavo volumes), he had no other merit than that of supporting his "wife and family." Why then, my Sam, did you not visit for these offences? This question, so far as it regards Hume, Sam answers himself. "Leland and Jortin," says he, "had a right to expect

[1] Nathaniel Lardner, D.D., 1684-1768.—M.

from their clerical opponent a milder and more respectful
treatment than that given to a sceptic who scoffed at all the
principles of religion." [1] By no means, doctor ; I beg your
pardon. Leland and Jortin had a right to fair play, and to
so much every man, *Tros Tyriusve*, has the same right. But,
once for all, let us hear an answer to this. If Leland and
Jortin had a privileged case by comparison with Hume, and
a claim upon Hurd's forbearance, much more had Lowth a
privileged case as regarded Parr, and a claim, if any man
could have, upon his vindictive friendship ; for Lowth had
been Parr's earliest patron. How comes it, then, that he
left Lowth to the protection of Providence ? Lowth, it will
be said, redressed his own wrongs. True, he did so ; but so
did all of them—Hume, Jortin, Leland, &c. Supposing,
therefore, Dr. Parr sought a case for his Quixotism in which
he might avenge a man that was past avenging himself, why
did he not "perstringe" his patron, Lowth, for taking
liberties with Richard Bentley ? This case was a very bad
one ; the "petulance" of Hurd could not be worse than the
petulance of Lowth ; and what a difference in the objects of
their attack ! Finally, let us remember this : Milner, the
papist of Winchester, had the audacity publicly to denounce
Porteous, Bishop of London, as a bigot and falsifier of facts ;
Bishop Hoadly and Bishop Shipley, as Socinians ; Halifax,
Bishop of Durham, as a papist (thus literally applying to Dr.
Halifax the very identical aspersion which he had himself
wiped off from Bishop Butler, in his edition of that prelate's
works) ; Dr. Rennell as a knave ; and the Bishops Barring-
ton, Watson, Benson, and Sparke, as insincere believers in
the Protestant faith. This ruffian, for such he really was,
Dr. Parr addressed in a long letter meant for the press.
But he never printed his letter ; and, now that it *is* printed,
what do we find ? An expostulation running over with
courtesy, forbearance, and unreasonable concessions ; no
sneering, no threats. So mild was Dr. Parr in defending
outraged truth—so furious in avenging his wounded self-
love ! [1]

Such was the famous attack on Hurd, in its moving

[1] See De Quincey's two Appended Notes to this page.—M.

impulse.   As to its literary merit, doubtless that is considerable.   Perhaps the author of the " Pursuits of Literature " went too far in styling it " astonishing and splendid." Assuredly it is in bad taste—not so much for its excess of antithesis, simply considered ; *that* is rightly defended by Mr. Field, as a legitimate engine of rhetorical effects ; but for the effort and visible straining which are often too palpably set forth in finding matter suitable for loading the opposite scales of the antithetic balance.   However, it is a *jeu d'esprit* of great ability, and may give to an English reader some notion of the Bellenden Preface.

The other feud of this period forms a singular chapter in the secret history of books.   Dr. White, the Oxford Professor of Arabic, had preached, for one year, the Bampton Lectures.[1] They were much admired.[2]   But all at once a discovery was made that a part of these lectures had been written by a Mr. Badcock, a dissenting clergyman, recently dead, who latterly had ceased to be a dissenter, having conformed to the Church of England.   This discovery, so painful and discreditable to the Arabic professor, was made through a bond for £500 given by Dr. White to Mr. Badcock, which B.'s sister endeavoured to recover, and which the professor was weak enough to resist.   The ground which he took was plausible—that the bond had been given, not for work done, but for work *to be* done.   At the very time when this affair broke out, Dr. Parr happened to arrive at Oxford.   White was his intimate friend.   But it is difficult to imagine a sort of conduct less reconcilable with the obligations of friendship than that which Parr adopted.   Without delay, without consulting Professor White, he avowed his peremptory disbelief in Badcock's claim ; but on what ground ?   On the ground that he was himself the contributor of a very considerable share of these lectures.   Never did man do a more critical injury to a friend ; and, were it not that the irritations of

---

[1] Joseph White, D.D., 1746-1814.   His Bampton Lectures were preached in 1784, and published that year.— M.

[2] Gibbon, in his fifty-second chapter, had spoken of White in high terms : " He sustains," says he, " the part of a lively and eloquent advocate, and sometimes rises to the merit of an historian and philosopher."

jealous vanity, with constitutional incontinency of secrets, seem to have overpowered and surprised his better resolutions, I should be compelled to pronounce it perfidy. Whatsoever help of this nature one literary man gives to another carries with it an implied obligation to secrecy ; otherwise, what else results than that, under the mask of giving a partial assistance to a friend's literary fame, the writer has, in fact, been furnishing himself with the means of crushing it entirely. He has given perhaps a trifle that he might take away the whole ; for, after such an exposure, the man has credit for nothing at all as *certainly* his own. And this injury was, as I have said, critically timed. Coming at the moment of Mr. Badcock's claim, about which much doubt prevailed, and was likely to prevail, from the death of the only person who could effectually meet the denial of White, Dr. Parr's claim at one and the same time authenticated itself and Badcock's ; that is, it doubly shattered White.

Meantime, Parr's claim was a true one. Mr. Kett (so well known in Oxford by the name of Horse Kett, from his *equine* physiognomy) thus states at once the extent of Parr's contributions and their value : " Whether I consider the " solidity of the argument, the comprehension of thought, or " the splendour of style, I think them, upon the whole, the " most able and elegant parts of the lectures. In point of " quantity they are considerable, as they are more than a " *fifth* of the whole, without reckoning the corrected passages. " But their intrinsic excellence is such that any person, " with such materials, might not only have obtained a great " deal of present applause, but lasting fame. They are in " the highest style of composition, as they are of a philo- " sophical and refined cast, and make many of the other " parts of the lecture with which they are connected appear " nothing more than loose and florid declamation."

Laborious investigations, conferences, and explanations followed ; in which, it appears to me, that Dr. Parr behaved with little generosity, and White with much duplicity.[1] One incident is remarkable : Dr. Parsons, of Baliol College, one of the arbiters or referees, at length withdrew himself from the service he had undertaken, but in so pointed and

[1] See De Quincey's Appended Note to this page.—M.

significant a manner as to satisfy myself that he also had very considerable right of property in these lectures, which his honour or his kindness had obliged. him to dissemble, and that, in some one of Parr's reclamations, in making which (though perfectly sincere) he relied confessedly on a very vague recollection, or a still vaguer discrimination of styles, Parr had unintentionally been trespassing on ground which Parsons secretly knew to be his own.   This is my own private opinion.   To the parties interested never was any literary broil so full of vexation.   Cabals were gathering at Oxford in the interest of White on the one hand, or of Dr. Gabriel of Bath on the other; the public journals took up the affair, with their usual imperfect information; private characters suffered; old friendships were dissolved for ever; and, finally, no party reaped either profit or honour from this contest for the proportions of property in a book which has long since been consigned to oblivion (however unjustly) by the whole world—whether hostile or friendly.

But, after all, the worst scandal of this transaction settled not upon any individual so much as upon the professional body of divines in general.   That part of the correspondence which got abroad admitted the public ruinously behind the curtain, and exhibited the writers concerting their parts, and arranging their passages of display, their clap-traps, and *coups-de-théâtre*, in a manner but little creditable to their singleness of heart, or simplicity of purpose.   They had the air at one time of attorneys, scheming to obtain a verdict for Christianity; at another, of martinets, arranging the draperies of their costume, or of *figurantes*, attitudinising for effect.   We must be particularly brilliant, says White, in that part where we attack Gibbon.   Alas! for the ancient faith—the primitive devotion—that burned in the evangelists and martyrs, in Hilarion or Paul, in Wycliffe or Luther!   How little room did *that* allow for any thoughts about self, or calculations of literary credit!   Dr. Parr, however, was no party to this huckstering traffic in devotional feeling, or this manufacture of spiritual thunder.   Hypocrisy was not *his* failing; whatever was the value of his religious opinions, his devotional feelings were thoroughly sincere.   But he suffered from the connexion in which his name appeared; and, as regarded the duties of a friend, his character has suffered in this transaction permanently, from his own indiscretions, and from the infirmity of his too ungenerous vanity.

To sum up Dr. Parr's pretensions as a man of letters :—I have already sufficiently acknowledged that his talents were splendid, and fitted, under suitable guidance, to have produced a more brilliant impression on his own age than they really did, and a more lasting one on the next age than they ever will. In his lifetime, it is true that the applauses of his many pupils, and his great political friends, to a certain extent, made up for all deficiencies on his own part ; but now, when these vicarious props are withdrawn, the dispro portion is enormous, and hereafter will appear to be more so, between the talents that he possessed and the effects that he accomplished. This result is imputable, in part, to his own want of exertion, and the indolence with which he shrank from undertaking any labour of great compass or research, the very best of his performances being mere *velitations*, skirmishes, or academic exercises ; and in part, also, it is imputable to a cause less open to moral reproach—namely, the comparative poverty of his philosophic understanding, between which and his talents there was no equilibrium. He gave a bright and gaudy colouring to truths which were too often trite, mean, or self-evident. And the impression was ineradicable, in a keen observer's mind, of a perpetual swell, glitter, and false inflation, beyond the occasion, and without a corresponding activity or power of thought. His architecture was barbaresque—rich in decoration at times, colossal in proportions, but unsymmetrical, and reposing on no corresponding foundations. It is very possible, and not uncommon, to have a poor understanding combined with fine talents. I do not say that Dr. Parr's understanding was a poor one ; but it was in no sense emphatically a fine one, not habitually profound, not philosophically subtle. Unquestionably it was mismatched, in point of natural vigour, with his talents—that is, with his powers of giving effect to his thoughts, and realising his conceptions. The splendours of Burke, yoked, as they were, with the very finest, subtlest, and most combining intellect that ever yet has been applied to political philosophy, awoke no sense of disparity or false

balance in his powers.   But, in the case of Parr, we feel
that, having once tasted the luxury of his periodic sentences,
with their ample volume of sound and self-revolving rhythmus
—having enjoyed his artful antithesis, and solemn antilibra-
tion of cadences—we have had the cream of his peculiar
excellences, and may exclaim, with Romeo, that it is time to
be gone, because "the sport is at the best."

As to that other cause which co-operated to the effect I
have been stating—viz. Parr's indolence, or unpersevering
industry—his excuse was the less that his stomach (where it
is that most men fail) was as strong as the shield of Telamonian Ajax, and his spirits, even under attacks of illness,
were indomitable ; he himself styles them "*lion* spirits."
Heavens ! what an advantage in that temperament above the
general condition of literary men !   Coleridge, for example,
struggling with the ravages of opium through forty years,
and with the *res angusta domi* in a degree never known to
Parr, has contrived to print a score of octavo volumes.   And,
were all his contributions to the "Morning Post" and
"Courier" collected, and his letters, many and long, together
with his innumerable notes on the fly-leaves and margins of
books, he would appear to have been a most voluminous
author, instead of meriting the reproach (which too often I
have been fated to hear) of shameful indolence and waste of
stupendous powers.   Of Dr. Parr's very criminal indolence
there was but one palliation : much of his life had passed in
the labours of the school-room ; and his leisure from those
was excusably turned to purposes of relaxation.   Still he had
latterly a long period of immunity from toils of every kind ;
he had a library of above ten thousand volumes ; he had
increasing wealth ; and, for years, he toiled not, neither did
he spin.   As to his execrable handwriting, that is rather an
explanation than a justification of his sterility.   Pretty often
he had the aid of volunteer amanuenses ; and was he at any
time too poor to have paid a secretary ?   Beginning with
some advantages for literary research so much beyond those
of Gibbon, in his far greater familiarity with the languages
of ancient books, why should Dr. Parr, the apologist of
universities against Gibbon, not have left behind him a
monument of learned industry as elaborate as that of his

opponent ? On the whole, I fear that Dr. Parr, as an author, must always be classed with those who have spent their vigour upon *certamina ludicra*, mock fights, mimic rehearsals, and shadowy combats ; that his knowledge and the sweat of his brow have been laid out upon palaces of ice, incapable of surviving the immediate atmosphere under which they arose, and dissolving with the first revolution of the seasons, rather than upon the massy Roman masonry that might have sustained his influence to a distant posterity. This may seem his misfortune, but then it was a misfortune to have been foreseen. And, for the more intrinsic qualities of his works, it will be recorded in their very fate that, if their execution was sometimes such as to challenge a permanent interest, their matter was unable to support so great a distinction ; and that, perhaps, of all known works, they are best fitted to illustrate the critical objection of *materiem superabat opus* (the workmanship transcended the material) ; and, finally, with regard to their author, that hardly any writer, of age so mature, of education so regular, and of pursuits so solemn and professional, had derived his subjects from occasions so ephemeral, or his excitement from motives so personal.

It remains that I should speak of Dr. Parr as a politician and as a divine : and fortunately the transcendent character of the facts will bring those inquests within the range of a short trial and a self-evident verdict.

First, as a politician. The French Revolution found Dr. Parr a Jacobin ; *found*, I say, not made. Of this there is abundant presumption. To give his vote for Wilkes, he faced a situation of considerable risk ; he was unwigged, and probably saved his life by escaping through a back window to his horse. Considering that he was then the *Reverend* Samuel Parr, this argued no trivial sympathy with the seditious agitator. It is true that a constitutional question was at issue in the case of Wilkes's expulsion ; but it does not appear that Parr gave his countenance to Wilkes the purist of the constitution so much as Wilkes the demagogue, and loved him upon the principle laid down by Junius— viz. ' so long as he was a thorn in the king's side." Besides, right or wrong in politics, ought an impure scoffer like

Wilkes, by common repute [1] the author of an obscene " Essay on Woman," to have commanded the volunteer and ardent support of a clergyman ? Was this decent ? Such, however, were Parr's earliest attachments, and such the leonine ardour with which he displayed them. In a better cause I should have admired his courage ; for he seems to have been resolved to go to Brentford,[2] in the spirit of Luther, though there had been " as many devils there as tiles upon the roofs of the houses."

Well, in the fulness of time came the French Revolution. The first persons to sing public pæans of congratulation in this country were the dissenters of Birmingham—moving under the domineering influence of Dr. Priestley. What followed is known to all whose recollections stretch back to those tumultuous days. Dr. Priestley's house was stormed and sacked by the Birmingham mob ; his philosophical apparatus (as a private one, matchless) destroyed ; his papers, letters, philosophical MSS., scattered to the four winds ; and the angry philosopher himself, by a fierce levanter of indignation, driven westwards to America. These scenes passed in too close neighbourhood to Dr. Parr for a temper so combustible as his to escape kindling at the flame of party fury. We may be sure also that he took the side of Priestley : to the extent of pity for his misfortunes, all good men did so ; but, as an approver of the conduct which provoked these misfortunes, I may almost venture to say that, amongst the fifteen thousand clergymen of the Church of England, Dr. Parr stood altogether alone. Every person of sober mind, whilst commiserating Dr. Priestley as an unfortunate man, and esteeming him as a very ingenious one, could view him in no other light than as the victim of his own folly and misguided passions. Political frenzy had prompted him to acts of defiance against a mob as fanatical in one direction as himself in another ; with this difference, however, that *their*

---

[1] At the time of writing this I had no reason (which now, on revision, I have) for doubting Wilkes's participation in the authorship.

[2] " *Brentford* " :—This gloomy place, on the left bank of the Thames, about seven miles to the west of Hyde Park Corner, is the county town of Middlesex ; consequently, *there* it was the voting for Wilkes went on.

fanaticism pointed to a very much more seasonable policy than the fanaticism of the celebrated experimentalist. The mob had retorted as an insulted and irritated mob may be expected to retort. They who play at bowls must look for rubbers. And Dr. Parr, by mixing in the game, wantonly drew upon himself a participation in the danger ; or at least a participation in the terror ; for, after all, he seems to have been more frightened than hurt. Great was his panic ; schooled by Dr. Priestley's losses, he sent off his books hastily to Oxford. They suffered from the hurried removal ; and at Oxford, where they were indifferently sheltered, they suffered still more. This lesson might have done him good service, had his temper allowed him to profit by it. But neither fear nor interest was ever able to check *his* fanaticism. With such a temper, we may suppose that he was blinded to all sense of his own errors by the dazzling light with which his anger invested the errors of the opposite party. At an after period the Doctor's cries ascended to heaven in print against the mob and their criminal politics. Yet such is the temper of this world that, if a grave philosopher, by shaking his fist, and other acts of bravado, should happen to provoke a company of mischievous boys to reply with a shower of stones, people in general suffer their resentment to settle upon the philosopher for his wanton provocation, rather than on the boys for that lapidary style of retort in which their wrath has been trained to express itself.

This affair, taken singly, being mixed up with considerations of persons and neighbourhood, might, after all, but indifferently represent the condition of Dr. Parr's politics. Other ebullitions of his feelings about the same period were less equivocal. On Mr. Burke, for the crime of writing his memorable book on the French Revolution, he inflicted the whimsical punishment of inverting his portrait — that is, suspending it with the head downwards. The insolent tyranny of this act is remarkable. Mr. Burke had held up his "protesting hand" against the Revolution ; and he, if ever any man upon any question, had explained the philosophic grounds of his protest. It seemed, therefore, that, with or without reasons, no dissent was tolerated from Dr. Parr's views. For, as to Mr. Burke's vehemence, it was no more than the natural warmth of sincerity. Precisely the same sentence of degradation, I believe, was executed upon Mr. Windham, and for the same offence. This was intelligible, and was equity, if not justice. Equal acts merited equal treatment. But in a third case the same degradation, by greatly extending the construction of guilt, warranted much larger inferences against Dr. Parr's motives. The third criminal was Paley ; on *his* portrait, also, sentence of inversion was passed and executed ; and for years it hung at Hatton in that position. What, then, had been Paley's crime ? *Audi facinus majoris abollæ;* he had literally been guilty of writing *" Reasons for Contentment."* The title explains its object. At a crisis of universal political irritation, when Paine's works and the French Revolution had combined to diffuse a spirit of change, and when the indefeasible evils of poverty were made handles of disaffection, being charged upon the institutions of the land, Dr. Paley had exerted himself to dissipate such delusions ; to rouse the ignorant to a sense of the real blessings which they enjoyed under equal laws administered by a popular government ; and thus to save them as well from secret discontents as from publicly lending themselves to the purposes of designing incendiaries. This was the service which he did, or attempted ; and for this only, neither more nor less, he incurred the wrath of Parr. I may add that he was never forgiven. The following record of his feelings in regard to Paley he left behind him for publication :—" I never thought Paley an honest man : he had great sagacity, wit, and science ; some good humour ; but he was *vain, inconsistent"* [odd objections to come from Samuel Parr] : " he was also, it appears, . . ." [*i.e.* something too bad for Parr's executors to print], "and selfish."

No one fact can better illustrate the furious disaffection of Dr. Parr. Simply because a man applied his great talents to a purpose of the highest charity, which could no otherwise serve the existing ministers, even remotely and mediately, than by first of all serving[1] many thousands of his humble

---

[1] *" Serving his countrymen"* :—I do not mean to assert that Paley *did* in any effectual sense accomplish this service ; neither is the spectacle a pleasant one, of rich people, such as Paley and

countrymen directly and essentially, he became with Dr. Parr a marked man. After this it will not be surprising that even the Whiggish correspondents of Parr found occasion to remind him that England was not the country in sober sadness which it suited their party tactics to represent; that he was interpreting too literally the violences of their public polemics; and that England did in fact continue to be,—what she had so long been esteemed by all the world, except her eternal enemies,—the ark to which were confided the dearest interests of man.

In 1794 war had begun to rage; the revolutionary frenzy had produced its bloodiest excesses; the gloom had terrifically deepened; and the French reign of terror, by a very natural reaction on all the rest of Europe, produced a corresponding system of vigilance and coercion in all regular governments, which must now be admitted to have been too harsh and despotic, if viewed apart from the extremities of the occasion. Questions which depend for their adjudication upon the particular estimate which is taken of the impending dangers allow room for great latitude of opinion amongst honest men. From mere differences of bodily temperament, men of the sanest judgments take radically different views of the very broadest cases that can arise; and, starting as he did from Whiggish principles, Dr. Parr is entitled to a large indulgence in his construction and valuation of Mr. Pitt's policy. We ought to allow, therefore, most readily for the fervour of interest which he took, not merely as a private friend to some of the parties concerned, but also as a constitutional politician, in the state trials which occurred at that period. For poor Gerald, as a splendid pupil of his own, as an unfortunate man betrayed into calamity by generous enthusiasm, and as a martyr to most disinterested indiscretions, Parr was entitled to feel the very warmest concern. I and others, of principles very adverse to Dr. Parr's, are of opinion that Gerald was most harshly, nay, unconstitutionally, treated. He was tried (through accidental connexion

Hannah More, sitting in luxurious saloons, and lecturing their poor, hard-working fellow-countrymen upon the enormity of the blessings which they enjoy. But Paley's *purpose* was to all appearance honest and patriotic.

with an Edinburgh club) in Scotland, and under a super-annuated law of Scotland, which had arisen out of another condition of things, and was never meant for our times ; it was a mere accident that such a law should be unrepealed ; and a verdict was obtained against him that the rest of the empire could not have countenanced. This was a case beyond any other to merit a pardon, even in the opinion of those who thought Mr. Gerald a turbulent democrat, since undoubtedly the verdict was in some measure obtained surreptitiously. Conduct that, on one side the Border, was then punish-able with transportation, on the other was confessedly, at the very utmost, a misdemeanour. Under these circumstances, to have enforced the sentence, and to have thrown a man of genius and a scholar into the society of ruffians, and the very refuse of jails, was doubtless an unjustifiable harshness. Warmth, therefore, and earnestness might be expected from Dr. Parr, in behalf of his unhappy friend. But nothing short of childish defect in self-government could have allowed Dr. Parr to insult the very person to whom he looked for a mitigation of the sentence. Yet this he did. Writing to Mr. Windham, as Home Secretary, for the exertion of his influence with Mr. Pitt, he told him with a bullying air that Mr. Gerald was as able a man as Mr. Pitt, and a great deal more learned. What followed ? Mr. Windham had been acquainted with the doctor, and was the very man to have felt for the peculiar hardship of Mr. Gerald's case. But of an application in this spirit he could not allow himself to take any official notice. A formal answer was returned ; and Mr. Gerald's sentence was permitted to take its course. Was Windham right ? I think *not*. The merits of Gerald's position should not have suffered from the intemperance of his advocate. Did Windham's error tend to neutralise that of Parr ? Not at all. Parr's political enthusiasm had then risen to the height of fanaticism, which set at nought all ordinary discretion.

However, the truth must be told : the first anti-Gallican war, though supported (as I shall always maintain) by the *élite* of British society, by the property and education of the land, did not unite all hearts in its cause. There was still room left for honest recusants ; though it is undoubtedly true that most of those who did actually stand forward conspicuously in that character were so upon any but laudable motives.   Unless where they happened to be betrayed by natural defects of discretion, and original incapacity for calculating consequences—a case which I believe to be that of Dr. Parr—nearly all the sturdy recusants to Mr. Pitt's policy moved upon the very worst impulses of anti-national feeling. Pitiably blind they were in some rare instances ; but in more desperately unpatriotic.   Still, I repeat that room was left for honest dissent up to a certain point ; and there are not a few, even now, amongst those whose patriotism was never tainted, and who gave to Mr. Pitt the fullest benefit of their accession as regarded principles, that yet question the policy of a military league against the infant republic of France—as being that which in effect, by furnishing to France the occasion for resistance, finally developed her yet unconscious strength.

But a few short years sufficed to place all this upon new foundations.   If ever, in this world, a nation had one heart and one soul, it was the British nation in the spring of 1803. A poet (William Wordsworth) who had deeply protested against the first French war at this crisis exclaimed, addressing the men of Kent, who had reason to look for the first attack—

" We *all* are with you now from shore to shore ! "

No need of sagacity at this time : blind instinct was sufficient to develop the views of the Consular government, and to appreciate the one sole policy which circumstances commanded.   And here it was the Whigs (I mean the Whigs in Parliament) lost themselves, and riveted that national distrust which had first commenced with the schism in the Whig Club.   They would not change their tone ; they would not open their eyes to the new state of things ; but continued to palliate the worst atrocities of the enemy, and to prophesy a long heritage of shame and defeat for ourselves.   At that period it was many times remarked that the long habit of expressing sympathy with the national foes insensibly moulded the feelings of the Opposition to a tone of bitterness against a nation that spurned their abject counsels, and of too evident mortification at the spectacle of our military triumphs. To prophesy evil for his own nation is an unwise course for any man; it gives his vanity, and perhaps his personal enmities, an interest in the national disasters, and at all events disturbs the currents of his patriotic sympathies. Strange as it may sound, there have been Englishmen to whom it was thought necessary by their families cautiously to break the shock of the great news of Waterloo, so violent was the grief anticipated at the final prostration of their idol. We could mention one man, well known in his day as a miscellaneous author, and not an unamiable man (though a coxcomb) in his character of literary patron, who, being accidentally at a dinner-party on the day when that mighty catastrophe reached Norfolk, was kept in ignorance of the news by an arrangement concerted separately with each of the guests (amongst whom was Wordsworth) as he happened to arrive: it was understood that this precaution was requisite to insure his attendance at dinner.

No such case ever has occurred in France. The martial successes of France in the days of Louis XIV, when the unhappy Palatinate was twice given up to desolation by French marshals, obtained the cordial sympathy of the whole people, no less than the still more atrocious acts of Napoleon. No excess of profligacy and injustice connected with martial trophies has ever damped the unity of patriotic joy amongst the French: no sanctity of defensive warfare has ever availed to insure it amongst the English. And, generally, this may express no more than that freedom of thought amongst ourselves which presents all public topics under every variety of phasis. But, as there are cases in morals upon which good feeling precludes all variety of judgment, so in politics there are rare crises upon which the good and evil of posterity so essentially depend that any diversity of feeling is irreconcilable with the very lowest stage of patriotism. Absolute conformity is required by simple honesty; and no toleration exists for dissenters of any class.

Such a case existed from 1803 to 1815, and more eminently than ever before in the history of mankind. What was Dr. Parr's behaviour? I shall not go into it at length: to see a good man wandering so grievously from the path of his

clear duty, is afflicting ; and a few instances will tell in what
channel his feelings ran. In the spring of 1814, when all
Christendom was exulting in the approaching destruction of
the destroyer, Dr. Parr writes thus to Mr. Coke :—" My
" indignation at the English Government, as the real and
" implacable disturbers of the peace of Europe, increases
" daily and hourly ; and from that malignant spirit which
" began to act in 1793, and is now reinforced by the accession
" of such an auxiliary as the Prince Regent [ah, that sad
" *Pince Thegent !*], I forebode the most disastrous consequences.
" My fear is that the allies will be overruled by the earnest-
" ness, or cajoled by the bribes, of the Prince Regent and his
" minions." So, then, upon this view of things, Jena, Aus-
terlitz, Borodino, the outrages upon Spain, Portugal, Germany,
Russia, were not French — they were British acts. But
patience !

In what way it was that Dr. Parr received the Waterloo
news we learn from no express record ; but, indirectly, we
can easily collect it. About two months before that battle,
he anticipated such an event as what was most to be abominated. The horizon already reddened with the dawn of
that coming retribution ; already it was believed that to
England, in reward of her matchless perseverance, would be
assigned the exterminating sword [1] ; and Dr. Parr—sharing
that belief, but abjuring the moral hopes of that belief—
sickens at the prospect. Worse than this we cannot say of any
man. I may add, however, that his condition of feeling on
these subjects continued pretty uniform. He wrote violently
against assassination, and the exception often urged in
favour of tyrannicide. But how exclusively the benefit of
even this doctrine was applied to our enemy may be judged
by this :—Mr. Percival was murdered in the summer of
1812 by a stranger (Bellingham), not known to him even by
sight ; Dr. Parr's attention is attracted by no one consideration but the excuses which might be offered for the assassin.
The Duc de Berri is murdered, without even the shadow of
a provocation, by one whom he also did not know ; Dr. Parr
assures his correspondent that he (not the murderer, as one

[1] " *The exterminating sword* " :—See Wordsworth's "Sonnet on
Waterloo."

would naturally wish to understand the passage, but the murdered prince) was a " vulgar ruffian." Again, as another illustration of his fanatic violence, Mr. Hone publishes parodies on the Scriptures [1] : as a politician after his own heart, though in a conscious opposition to the decorums of his sacred profession, and to his own sincere reverence for religion, Dr. Parr encourages and sanctions him by a money subscription. And we find the Duke of Bedford, who forfeited the distinction of representing his sovereign in his own county solely by a participation in the same expression of approbation, directly justifying his conduct (upon which, in some views, he felt a doubt) by Dr. Parr's example. Not, certainly, that the duke would have laid any stress upon Dr. Parr's authority in a question merely political; but, where the politics of the case had been complicated with a point of religious casuistry, — viz. how far it was right to take a *judicial* notice of scoffs pointed at the religious creed of the land,—his grace had naturally supposed that path to be safe which had been trodden by a professional divine. I might accumulate many more cases ; but enough is here cited to show that, as a politician, Dr. Parr stood aloof from his country in the hour of her most memorable trials, and dishonoured his grey hairs by absolute fanaticism that lost sight finally even of his religious principles.

This leads me to the view of Dr. Parr as a divine ; in which it had been my intention to show that in every part of his life he allowed the principles of his theology to be biassed by his political prejudices. Dissenters of all classes were welcome to him, whether their dissent began originally' upon religious or political views, because in any case it terminated in hostility to the state. Upon examining Dr. Parr's sermons, I find too little of a regular chain or system of religious principles to sustain the review which I meditated : and of the correspondence yet published too small a part turns upon theological questions to do much in supplying this defect. I shall content myself for the present, therefore, with observing that, whilst he dwelt with ludicrous self-congratulation upon the support he gave to orthodoxy in

---

[1] William Hone, 1779-1842. For the "Parodies" here mentioned he was tried in December 1817, but acquitted.—M.

the purest trifles, he really betrayed the interests of his
Church in its two capital interests,—as against the Roman
Catholics on the one hand, and the Socinians on the other.
Long and laboured were his pleadings for the Roman
Catholics, and for the relaxation of the penal laws against
them, in his notes upon Mr. Fox's "History"; and on the
other hand he attacked the Archbishop of Dublin, otherwise
a friend and admirer, in a rancorous tone, for denying the
title of Christianity (in which denial he is countenanced by
many a score of learned and pious men) to Socinianism.
Finally, he left for posthumous publication a printed record
of his dissatisfaction with Anti-Socinian and Anti-Arian
arguments; and he has left repeated evidence, apart from
his known leaning to Socinian views, that he had not in any
stage of his life adopted any system at all which could properly class him with the believers in the Trinity.

Dr. Parr in one point showed himself superior to a
popular error. Even Archbishop Laud, but more memorably
another Primate (Wake) of the following century, had fallen
into the weakness of supposing that the English Church and
the Gallican could terminate their differences as if by a
compact of mutual concession. But no treaty of compromise could restore the real "Catholic unity"; no remedy
could in that way be applied to the evils of schism in the
Christian Church. Towns and territory may be the subject
of cession, but not truth. And of this Dr. Parr was fully
sensible. Yet in other aspects of the same weak passion
for a hollow name of peace Dr. Parr was often as blind as
others. Pity that he had not more uniformly remembered
the spirit of a maxim which he sometimes quoted from
Grotius—that he so loved Peace as not to sacrifice Truth.
He persuaded himself often that the differences of men in
religious matters were in a large proportion verbal: a
common, a very common, but a very shallow maxim. On
the contrary, from my earliest days I have remarked that,
for one verbal dispute which passes for a real one, there are
ten disputes undoubtedly *real* which are popularly dismissed
as verbal. "*Tu fis,*" says Boileau,

"Tu fis dans une guerre si triste et si longue
Périr tant de Chrétiens—*martyrs d'une diphthongue.*"

Martyrs of a diphthong ?   Yes.   But Boileau, as much as anybody, maintained that this single diphthong was the occasion that the Church "sentit trembler *la verité Chrétienne*": the whole peculiar truth of Christianity reposed upon that one diphthong—for it made the whole difference between the Catholic ὁμοούσιος and the Arian ὁμοίουσιος: so mighty are the differences which may be involved, not in a word only, but even in a syllable ; and so truly did Boileau, therefore, but destructively to his own argument, characterise even *that* as "une sillabe *impie.*"   (Sat. xii.)

I have questioned the systematic perfection, the orbicularity (so to speak), of Dr. Parr's classical knowledge. Much more certainly might I question the coherency, as a whole, of his divinity.   What he adopted in this department was taken up casually and independently : his theology was not the fruit of laborious investigation at the fountainheads.   It was gleaned here and there, separately, by fragments, from chance authors, and not finally fused or harmonised.

Finally, and as the sum of my appreciation, I should say that, speaking of him as a moral being, Dr. Parr was naturally good and conscientious, but (in a degree which sometimes made him *not* conscientious) the mere football of passion.   As an amiable man, I must add that, by the testimony of his best friend, he was a domestic nuisance ; he also, as well as his father, says Dr. Johnstone, was "the tyrant of the fireside."   As a scholar, he was brilliant ; but he consumed his power in gladiatorial displays, and has left no adequate monument of his powers.   As a politician, he sank his patriotism in the spirit of a partisan, and forgot to be an Englishman in his fanaticism for the ultra Whigs.   And, last of all, as a divine, for the sake of those sectaries whom charity enjoined him to tolerate, he betrayed that Church which it was his holiest duty to defend.

POSTSCRIPT IN 1857 [1]

In the paper on Dr. Parr a careless reader may fancy that I, being a Tory, am illiberal enough to assume that Whiggism is in itself a matter of reproach. But in this he would be doing me great injustice ; for it happens that I have placed on record my own peculiar views of the relation subsisting between the doctrine of the Tories and that of the Whigs,[2]— which views represent them as separately forming the two hemispheres which jointly compose the total truth. In a paper on that subject I contend that, when Charles Fox undertook a History of our English Revolution with the purpose of glorifying the Whigs in contradistinction to the Tories as the heroes of that great event, he made shipwreck of all political philosophy. The misconception was total. A Trinitarian, I there said by way of illustration, and an anti-Trinitarian cannot both be right : in such a case the affirmation of either is the negation of the other. But in very many cases this is far otherwise. The Whig and the Tory, for instance, are both right, and both equally right. Not only so, but the one is right only because (and so long as) the other is right. Singly, the Tory would be wrong. Singly, the Whig would be wrong. But, taken jointly, they

[1] What is here necessarily given as a postscript to the paper on Dr. Parr formed a portion of the preface prefixed by De Quincey in 1857 to the volume of his collected writings containing that paper.—M.

[2] De Quincey here refers to a paper of his which appeared in *Tait's Edinburgh Magazine* for December 1835 and January 1836, under the title "A Tory's Account of Toryism, Whiggism, and Radicalism." He did not live to republish that paper, but it will be given in a future volume of this edition.—M.

compose that synthesis which realises and embodies the total constitutional truth. The Whig takes charge of the constitutional forces in one direction ; the Tory in another. And it would be as absurd to invest either party with a superior function as to imagine the centripetal force more important than the centrifugal in the planetary system of motions. Were the Whig withdrawn, instantly the Tory would become a redundant and destructive power ; and *vice versâ*. Both Whig and Tory shared *equally* in our Revolution. Meantime, not one act in a thousand done or proposed by the Whig or Tory party concerns them *as* Whigs or *as* Tories. For instance, to each of these parties at different periods foreign politics have presented a ruinous snare. During the four last years of Queen Anne the Tories played the most treasonable part. That was early in the eighteenth century. Almost in the corresponding years of the nineteenth century the very same false and treacherous part was played by the Whigs ; but in this respect more criminally by far, inasmuch as the danger was incomparably greater from 1803 to 1812 than from 1703 to 1712. The enemy at whose feet the Whigs would have laid us prostrate from 1807 to 1815 was Napoleon, with a servile Europe at his back : whereas, in the corresponding case of the preceding century, the enemy was Louis XIV, menaced by a growing confederacy of our allies.

The reader understands, therefore, that I do not (and could not consistently) disparage or anywhere condemn Dr. Parr *as* a Whig. Those acts which reflect shame and reproach upon his character and the claims of his clerical profession had no connexion with Whig principles : very often they were acts discountenanced, or at the least *not* countenanced, by his own political party. But, in those rarer cases where the acts really *had* such a partisan countenance, the party concerned in the first place was not the Whigs as opposed to the Tories, but the *Outs* as opposed to the *Ins*. It was with no reference to their party creed that Messrs. Fox, Grey, Tierney, Sheridan, &c., oftentimes lent their support to Dr. Parr : not at all ; it was simply as the party in *opposition* (whether Whigs or Tories), pulling an oar against the party in *office :* pledging, therefore, no principles whatever in Dr. Parr's behalf, but simply weight of influence. Finally, in those very rare cases where the Whig party *as* Whigs avowed their patronage to an act or to a book of Dr. Parr's, there was still room left for this objection : that it was the act of a schismatical Whig party,—of one section dividing against the other, and leaving it doubtful which was the true depositary of Whiggism, which the spurious.

APPENDED NOTES

GENERAL NOTE.

THE errors of the press, and the errors of the *redacteur* himself, are very serious in Dr. Johnstone's large and costly work. Let me take the liberty of counselling him, if from a Tory he will accept counsel, to change the whole form of his labours—in German phrase to reproduce them in an *umbearbeitung*, or thorough recast on the following plan, as soon as ever the sale of the present arrangement shall have been sufficient to warrant him in doing so. Complying with this or some similar proposal, he will at once consult Dr. Parr's interests as a man of letters, and will do that service to scholars which they have almost a right to demand of him. First of all, let the sermons be dismissed; they load the edition, and hang heavily upon its circulation, with no apparent benefit of any kind; none of them have ever been popular, or in the eye of the public, except the Spital Sermons; and those, being miscellaneous philosophic essays, have a special privilege of reprieve. The sermons are liable to the continual suspicion of being *in part* only of Dr. Parr's composition, from his known practice (which he even avowed) of interweaving auxiliary passages from divines who happened to meet his own views, or, in some instances, of deriving his whole groundwork from others, and simply running variations of his own, many or few, upon his adopted theme. It is possible (but the public are not aware in what degree) that the sermons selected for publication may be free from this particular objection; but, at all events, as a body, the readers of sermons are too devout a class to find their own peculiar taste gratified in a collection breathing the Parrian spirit of religion. For instance, one sermon undertakes the defence of hunting, and might very properly have come from one of the brilliant brothers of the Melton Mowbray establishment. This having been preached in the morning, I see no reason why the evening service should not have brought us an apology for steeplechases; which seem even to have the advantage in this point—that such matches *never lose sight of the church.* At least, in their origin, steeplechases obeyed that law—

Ride at the steeple, no matter what obstacles interpose. Certain it is
that the sermons, whether otherwise of merit or not, are in this respect
faulty, that they do not contemplate any determinate audience : professedly, indeed, they are parish discourses ; and yet they deal with
topics foreign to the needs and sympathies of a plain rural congregation, sometimes even inaccessible to their understandings. Doubtless all farmers would understand the hunting sermon ; but how many
would enter in any sense into the question of Christ's descent into
Hades ? However, I need not discuss the value of the sermons : good
or bad, here they are ; printed for the benefit of all readers, if any
such there are, who happen to want them ; and they are certainly
not wanted by the vast majority of scholars—of whom, on the other
hand, few but would put some value on the *philological* speculations
of Dr. Parr—and, according to their feeling and taste, all connoisseurs
in Latin composition would be glad to possess so brilliant an ἀγώνισμα
in rhetoric as the "Bellenden Preface." Thus, therefore, let the new
edition stand :—Reprint all Dr. Parr's critical tracts, essays, or fragments,—of course, not omitting (as Dr. Johnstone has done, with no
intelligible explanation, vol. i. p. 543) the long investigation of the
word *sublime* (already much abridged by Dugald Stewart), nor the
various reviews of classical works contributed to literary journals by
Dr. P., wheresoever these reviews happen to be of any value.[1] Even
the letters, when they discuss critical questions, should be detached
from the main body of miscellaneous correspondence, and united by
way of appendix to the rest of the critical matter. Points of criticism,
it is true, in the letters, are rarely insulated from occasional and personal matter, which would become irrelevant in its new situation ;
but this objection might be met by confining the extracts strictly to
those passages which *are* critical, and printing them as so many
separate notices or memoranda, under the title of *Adversaria.* These
might be accumulated in one volume, which, by means of a separate
title-page, could be sold as a distinct work, and, by means of a half-
title, could also take its place as one section of Dr. Parr's general
works. These would perhaps compose two more volumes, each offering the same recommendation, and, by means of special half-titles,
the same opportunities to separate purchasers—one being made up of
the very *élite* of his essays on political or moral subjects, the other of
his rhetorical *bravuras.*

Page 20.

Lord Wellesley [2] has been charged with a foible of the same kind—
how truly, I know not. More than one person of credit assured me,

[1] I say this because the review of Combe's "Horace," which Dr. Johnstone
has re-published, is chiefly occupied with trifling typographical minutiæ. The
obscura diligentia of such corrections will be unprofitable to *any* class of
readers (I should imagine), unless it were the class of publishers or editors
meditating new and more elaborate editions of "Horace."
[2] At the time of writing this, *Lord Wellesley* meant the Marquis Wellesley,
second Earl of Mornington, and elder brother to the Duke of Wellington.

some fifty and odd years ago, that, at his levees, when Governor-General of India, he was gratified, as by a delicate stroke of homage, upon occasionally seeing people throw their eyes to the ground—dazzled, as it were, by the effulgent lustre of his own. This is possible ; at the same time I cannot but acknowledge that my faith in the story was in some slight degree shaken by finding the same foppery attributed to Augustus Cæsar in the Memoirs of Suetonius. Meantime it is a singular coincidence that Lord Wellesley resembled Augustus Cæsar in stature, in eyes, and in delicacy of features.

Page 24.

Those who carry a spirit of distinguishing refinement into their subdivisions and classifications of colloquial talent, according to its powers and qualities, may remark one peculiar feature in Edmund Burke's style of talking, which contradistinguished it from Dr. Johnson's. It grew ; one sentence was the rebound of another ; one thought rose upon the suggestion, or more properly upon the impulse, of something which went before. Burke's motion, therefore, was all a going forward. Johnson's, on the other hand, was purely regressive and analytic. That thought which he began with contained, by involution, the whole of what he afterwards put forth. The two styles of conversation corresponded to the two theories of generation : one (Johnson's) to the theory of *Preformation* (or Evolution), where all the future products, down to the very last, lie secretly wrapped up in the original germ,—consequently nothing is positively added, everything is simply unveiled ; the other (Burke's) to the theory of *Epigenesis,* where each stage of the growth becomes a causative impulse to a new stage,—every separate element in the mysterious process of generation being, on this hypothesis, an absolute supervention of new matter, and not a mere uncovering of old, already involved at starting in the primary germ. A great gain would be obtained for intellectual philosophy, if a sufficient body of themes, Burkian and Johnsonian, were assembled, and illustrated by an ample commentary, under the distinction here indicated.

Page 29.

Dr. Parr's casuistry for regulating his practice in the case of his being called upon to read occasional forms of prayer, proclamations, &c., which he·might not approve as a politician (and, observe, he never *did* approve them), was this : read he must ; that was the text of his apology ; thus far he was bound to blind submission. *Passive* obedience was an unconditional duty, but not *active.* Now it *would* be an active obedience to read with proper emphasis and decorum. Therefore everybody sees the logical necessity of reading it into a farce, making grimaces, "inflicting one's eye," and in all ways keeping up the jest with the congregation. Was not this the boy for Ignatius Loyola ?

Page 31.

Had Mr. Fox lived a little longer, the current belief is that he would have raised Dr. Parr to the mitre ; and, had the Doctor himself survived a little longer, Lord Grey would perhaps have tried his earliest functions in that line upon him.

Page 33.

I may have an opportunity further on of showing what was Parr's conduct to the Church of which he professed himself a member, and in what sense he could be said to have betrayed it. At present I shall protect myself from misconstruction by saying that his want of fidelity to the rights and interests of the Church was not deliberate or systematic ; in this as in other things, he acted from passion—sometimes from caprice. He would allow only this or that doctrine of the Church to be defended ; he would ruinously limit the grounds of defence ; and on these great questions he gave way to the same rank personal partialities which, in the management of a school, had attracted the notice, and challenged the disrespect, of boys.

Page 39.

Even *that* was possibly barbed, in some of its consequences to Parr, by his own imprudence. The widow (his stepmother) is said to have injured Parr by her rapacity. But, if so, Parr had certainly himself laid the foundation of an early hatred between them, by refusing to lay aside his mourning for his own mother on the marriage-day of this second Mrs. Parr with his father. I do not much quarrel with his conduct on that occasion, considering his age (sixteen) and the relation of her for whom he mourned. But still the act was characteristic of the man, and led to its natural results.

Page 41.

Laying together all the incidents of that time, it is scarcely possible to doubt that Parr conducted himself with great impropriety. Benjamin Heath neither answered the letter in which Parr attempted to clear himself from the charge of exciting the boys of Harrow to insurrection against Heath's authority, nor did he so much as leave his card at Stanmore in acknowledgment of Parr's call upon himself. As to Mr. Smith, the rector, celebrated for his wit and ability, the early associate of Johnson and Garrick, he, from being "the warmest of Parr's friends" (such is Mr. Roderick's language), soon became cool, and finally ceased to speak. Mr. Roderick does not acquit his friend of the chief blame in this rupture.

Page 42.

Dr. Johnstone, however, speaking of the pamphlet as a composition, discovers in it "all the peculiarities of Parr's style—its vigour, its vehemence, its clearness," its *et cœtera, et cœtera ;* and, lastly, its "splendid imagery" ; and, obviously by way of a specimen of this last quality, he quotes the following most puerile rhetoric : "I had arrayed myself in a panoply of the trustiest armour—in the breastplate of innocence, the shield of the law, the sword of indignation, and the helmet of intrepidity.   When I first entered the lists against these hardy combatants, I determined to throw away the scabbard" : and so forth.   The *sword* of indignation !   Birch-rod he surely means. Most people will think that the bombs of contempt, and the mortars of derision, ought to open upon any person, not having the privilege of childhood, who could write such stilted fustian.

Page 45.

Parr's extreme and well-merited unpopularity with an order whom he had, through life, sneered at and misrepresented, is a little disguised to common readers by the fact that he corresponds with more than one bishop on terms of friendship and confidence.   But this arose, generally speaking, in later life, when time sufficient had been allowed for early school-fellows and pupils of his own being raised to the mitre.   The logic of the case is, therefore, naturally misinterpreted. His episcopal correspondents were such, not as bishops, but as old acquaintances.

Page 54.

As disputing with a Prince of Wales is something rarer even than waltzing with a Lord Chancellor, or smoking a cigar with the Pope— things which have been done, however—I suppose it may entertain my readers to see the rest of the discussion ; especially as it concerns two persons eminent in their day, and one of them still interesting to our literature :—

"As I knew them both so intimately " (replied the Prince), "you will not deny that I had the power of more accurately appreciating their respective merits than you can have had.   In their manner of teaching, you may judge of my estimation of Markham's superiority—his natural dignity and authority, compared with the Bishop of Worcester's smoothness and softness, and I now add (with proper submission to your authority on such a subject), his experience as a schoolmaster, and his better scholarship."—"Sir" (said Parr), "your Royal Highness began this conversation, and, if you permit it to go on, must tolerate a very different inference." — "Go on (said the Prince) ; I declare that Markham understood Greek better than Hurd ; for, when I read Homer, and hesitated about a word, Markham immediately explained it, and then we went on ; but, when I hesitated with Hurd, he always referred me to the dictionary ; I therefore concluded he wanted to be informed himself."—" Sir " (replied Parr), " I venture to differ from your Royal Highness's conclusion. I am myself a schoolmaster ; and I think that Dr. Hurd pursued the right method, and that Dr. Markham failed in his duty.[1] Hurd desired your Royal Lighness to find the word in the lexicon, not because he did not know it, but because he wished you to find by search, and learn it thoroughly. Dr. Hurd was not eminent as a scholar ; but it is not likely that he would have presumed to teach your Royal Highness without knowing the lesson himself."—" Have you not changed your opinion of Dr. Hurd ?" exclaimed the Prince ; " I have read a work in which you attack him fiercely."—" Yes, sir, I attacked him on one point which I thought important to letters ; and I summoned the whole force of my mind, and took every possible pains to do it well ; for I consider Hurd to be a great man. He is celebrated as such by foreign critics, who appreciate justly his wonderful acuteness, sagacity, and dexterity in doing what he has done with his small stock of learning. There is no comparison, in my opinion, between Markham and Hurd as men of talents. Markham was a pompous schoolmaster—Hurd was a stiff and cold, but a correct gentleman. Markham was at the head of a great school, then of a great college, and finally became an archbishop. In all these stations he had trumpeters of his fame, who called him great, though he published one *concio* only, which has already sunk into oblivion. From a farm-house and village school, Hurd emerged, the friend of Gray and a circle of distinguished men. While fellow of a small college, he sent out works praised by foreign critics, and not despised by our own scholars. He enriched his understanding by study, and sent from the obscurity of a country village a book, sir, which your royal father is said to have declared made him a bishop. He made himself unpopular in his own profession by the defence of a fantastical system. He had decriers ; he had no trumpeters ; he was great in and by himself ; and perhaps, sir, a portion of that power and adroitness you have manifested in this debate might have been owing to him." Fox, when the Prince was gone, exclaimed in his high tone of voice, " He thought he had caught you, but he caught a Tartar ! "

In the last words only Parr seems to have remembered that he was addressing a prince. In what he said of Hurd's Greek scholarship, and motive for referring the Prince to the lexicon, though probably wrong as to the matter of fact (for Hurd's impulse was laziness), he might be right as to the principle ; and at least he was there talking on a point of his own profession, which he might be presumed to understand better than the rest of the company ; or at any rate the courtesies of social life obliged the company to suppose that he did.

---

[1] *"Duty"*:—I interrupt the passage for a moment to direct the reader's attention to the preposterous word "duty." The Archbishop might be wrong, as in a matter open to large varieties of method ; but assuredly neither he, nor the Bishop of Worcester, is to be burdened for a moment with obligations of *conscience* in the exercise of an art liable to an infinite range of variations in practice.

But who can forbear smiling, and thinking of the professor who lectured Hannibal on the art of war, at that passage where Parr, addressing the Prince of Wales, undertakes to characterise Hurd's pretensions as a gentleman ?

Page 56.

Johnson had many of the elements which go to the composition of a gentleman in a very high degree, though it is true that these were neutralised, at times, by some one overmastering prejudice or caprice. His silent acquiescence in the royal praise, and the reason on which he justified this acquiescence—*that it did not become him to bandy compliments with his sovereign,*—is in the finest spirit of high breeding, and reminds me of a similar test for trying gentlemanly feeling, applied to the English ambassador (Lord Stair) by the Regent Duke of Orleans. The reader probably recollects the case. The Regent had signified, by a motion of his hand, that the Ambassador should enter the coach first ; upon which Lord Stair immediately did so, justly feeling that the slightest hesitation on *his* part would have raised a false punctilio, as though the ranks of the two men were so nearly on a level that the Regent might be forgetting himself, and might need to be set right by the Ambassador. The *act* of Lord Stair dissipated in a moment this false construction. By his instantaneous obedience to the pleasure of the Regent, he recognised at once his own precedency as a *creation* of the moment, and in that light as a silent proclamation of the supremacy as to rank and power residing in his Royal Highness.

Page 63.

"The Doctor begged me one morning to take him into S. P.'s belfry. Secure from interruption, he proceeded with his intended object, which was to raise and full (pull ?) scientifically the tenth or largest bell. He set to work in silent, solemn formality. It took some time,— I suppose, a full quarter of an hour ; for there was the raising, the full funereal toll, and the regular toll. When it was over, he stalked about the belfry in much pomposity. On recomposing himself, he looked at me with a smile, and said, 'There ; what think you of that ?' He was evidently very proud of the effort." In a Greek character of Dr. Parr by Sir William Jones, among the repositories of his Royal Highness the Duke of Sussex, neither the bell-ringing nor the ox-massacring is overlooked : "καὶ τὸ ὅλον κωδωνίζειν, δυνατὸς καὶ παρονομάζειν, καὶ δισκεύειν, καὶ ταυροκοπεῖν."—[And, to sum up the Doctor's accomplishments, he was a smart hand at bell-ringing, and as a punster, and at quoit-playing, and at slaughtering bulls.] As to bell-ringing, none but natives of England proper are judges on this art, for elsewhere it has no existence. On the Continent, wheresoever art is applied to bell-ringing, I believe that generally it takes the shape of pure clock-work, as in the *Carillons* of Ostend, &c., which admit of no aid from human hands any more than our own chimes. In

Scotland, again, there can be no bell-ringing, as there are no bells.
A peal of bells is a thing unknown. But in England, where countless
parish churches have peals of eight and ten bells, the art of bell-
ringing is very elaborate, and trying in more ways than one. It requires long-disciplined skill, and great muscular power. Dr. Parr's
arms had been kept in training by half-a-century of successful flagellation. I may add that the music from a finely-toned set of bells,
when heard upon a winding river, in summer, under the farewell lights
of setting suns, is the most pathetic in the world.

Page 69.

I am the last person to apologise for that most profligate woman.
That men of sense and honour could be found who seriously doubted
of her guilt is the strongest exemplification, to my mind, of the all-
levelling strength in party rage that history records. As little am
I likely to join the rare and weak assailants of Sir Walter Scott,
whose conduct politically was as upright and as generous as his conduct in private life. Yet, in one single instance, Sir Walter departed
from his usual chivalry of feeling, and most unseasonably joined in insulting a woman—dissolute, it is true, beyond example, but at that time
fallen, and on that very morning reaping the bitter first fruits of her
enormous guilt. Describing the morning of the Coronation, and the
memorable repulse of the poor misguided Queen, Sir Walter allowed
himself to speak of her as *the great Lady, with her body-guard of black-
guards.* These words I doubt not that Sir Walter soon, and often, and
earnestly deplored ; for the anguish of her mortification, by the testimony of all who witnessed the tumultuous succession of passions that
shook her, and convulsed her features, as she argued the point with
the officer at the entrance of Westminster Hall, was intense ; and
those pitied her then who never pitied her before. There were also
other reasons that must have drawn a generous regret from Sir Walter,
upon remembering these words afterwards. But we all know that it
was not in his nature to insult over the fallen, or to sympathise with
triumphant power. In fact, he could not foresee her near-approach-
ing death ; and he was reasonably disgusted with her violence at the
moment ; and, finally, the words escaped him under circumstances of
hurry, which allowed no time for revision. Few indeed are the
writers who have so little to blot as this distinguished man.

Page 78.

And perhaps, in candour it should be added, under happier fortunes
and more prudence in his *liaisons* with the other sex. He was in
some degree a dissolute man ; but perhaps he might have been otherwise under more noble treatment from the woman of his heart. His
unhappiness on this point latterly was great ; and there is reason to
think that he secretly wished to lay down his life, and resorted to
politics as the best means of doing so with reputation. He had a

passionate love for an unworthy woman, whom he had strong reasons for thinking unfaithful to him. And, at all events, she had the baseness to trifle with his apparent misery.

Page 81.

It is remarkable, however, that Sir William's Greek is far better than Parr's. Jones's has all the air of the genuine antique : Parr's is villainous.

Page 82.

I say Latin secretary, as indicating an office, so far as regards its duties, which really *does* exist, though the emoluments do not. There is a great deal of public work to be executed in Latin, and it is done *gratis*, and by various hands. But, were this an age for increasing the public burdens, I should suggest the propriety of creating anew the formal appointment of Latin Secretary, which ought for many reasons never to have been abolished. The Fox Ministry would have done rightly to have restored the office, and to have rewarded Dr. Parr by the first appointment.

Page 83.

But surely the brother of Sir Henry Halford (as the warden of Merton, Dr. Peter Vaughan, I believe was) needed not to have gone out of his own family connexions for such an assistance, since Sir Henry himself writes Latin with ease and effect.

Page 85.

I cannot fancy Heyne as a Latin *exegetes*. The last time I opened a book of his (perhaps it was his Virgil), some sixteen years ago, he was labouring at this well-known phrase—" *regione* viarum." As usual, a rhapsody of resemblances, more or less remote, was accumulated ; but, if I may be believed, that sole meaning of the word *regio* which throws light upon the expression, that meaning which connects it with the word *rego* in the mathematical sense (*i.e.* to drive a straight line), was unnoticed. All the rest meant nothing. I closed the book in disgust.

Page 88.

William Bellenden, a Scotch writer, flourished at the beginning of the seventeenth century, and is said to have been a professor in the University of Paris. At Paris he published, in 1608, his "Cicero Princeps," a singular work, in which he extracted from Cicero's writings detached remarks, and compressed them into one regular body, containing the rules of monarchical government, with the line of conduct to be adopted, and the virtues proper to be encouraged by the prince himself ; and this treatise, when finished, he dedicated, from a principle of patriotism and gratitude, to the son of his master,—Henry, then Prince of Wales. Four years afterwards (namely, in 1612), he proceeded to publish another work of a similar nature, which he called "Cicero Consul, Senator, Senatusque Romanus," in which he treated the nature of the consular office, and the constitution of the Roman Senate. Finding the works received, as they deserved, with the unanimous approbation of the learned, he conceived the plan of a third work, "De Statu Prisci Orbis," which was to contain a history of the progress of government and philosophy, from the times before the Flood to their various degrees of improvement under the Hebrews, Greeks, and Romans. He had proceeded so far as to print a few copies of this work in 1615, when it seems to have been suggested that, his three treatises, "De Statu Principis," "De Statu Republicæ," "De Statu Orbis," being on subjects so nearly resembling each other, there might be a propriety in uniting them into one work, by re-publishing the two former, and entitling the whole "Bellendenus de Statu Orbis." With this view, he recalled the few copies of his last work that were abroad, and, after a delay of some months, he published the three treatises together, under their new title, in the year 1615.

In the British Museum one copy of the book "De Statu Prisci Orbis," dated in 1615, still exists, which the author had probably sent into England as a present, and could not recall ; and in all the others the date appears, on a nice inspection, to have been originally MDCXV, and to have had an *I* afterwards added, on the alteration of the author's plan. The editor has shown great ingenuity in clearing up this typographical difficulty. The great work being now completed, Bellenden looked forward with a pretty well-grounded expectation for that applause which his labour and his ingenuity deserved ; but his views were disappointed by one of those events that no art of man can foresee or remedy. The vessel in which the whole impression had been embarked was overtaken by a storm before she could reach the English coasts, and foundered with all her cargo.

A very few copies only, which the learned author either kept for his own use, or had sent as presents by private hands, seem to have been preserved from the destruction which awaited the others ; and this work of Bellendenus has, therefore, from its scarcity, often escaped the notice of the most diligent collectors. It is not to be found in the library of the Duke of Argyle [Roxburghe ?], nor in that of the late Dr. Hunter ; neither Morhoffius nor Fabricius had ever seen it ; the "Observationes Literariæ" at Frankfort in 1728, which treat learnedly and copiously on scarce books, makes no mention of it. In a word, the single treatises are so rare that not above ten of them are to be found in all the libraries of England. And of the larger work it does not appear that more than six copies are known to exist : one in the public library at Cambridge ; a second in that of Emanuel College, in the same University, long admired as a well-chosen collection of excellent books ; a third in All-Souls' Library at Oxford ; and two in the possession of the editors.[1]

---

[1] There is another in the library of Shrewsbury School, left by Dr. Taylor, editor of Demosthenes, to that foundation.

Page 88.

Colman had said that the verse in the " Pursuits of Literature " was
only " a peg to hang the notes upon " : a jest too obvious, perhaps,
but also too true for the irritable author ; who had the meanness,
amongst some impotent attempts at affecting a grin of nonchalance, to
tell his readers that the jest was stolen, and stolen from Pindar !
Great was my curiosity on hearing this. A Pindaric jest ! What
could it be, and where ? Was it an Olympic or a Pythian jest ?
Why, Pindar, it seems, " said long before Mr. Colman, ἀπὸ πασσάλου
φόρμιγγα λάβε." And what then ? *He took down his harp from a*
peg ; that is to say, a literal metallic harp from a literal wooden peg.
What earthly connexion could *that* have with Mr. Colman's jest ?
Now, this, though *in re levissima*, I regard as a downright villainy.
Mathias tells a clamorous falsehood in order to convict his antagonist
of a theft. The long and the short of the case is that, being stung by
a sarcasm, and not having the magnanimity to bear it, he tries vainly
to retaliate by a consciously mendacious charge upon his assailant of
having stolen the sarcasm ; well knowing, at the time of making this
insinuation, that there was not, nor could be, in the author alleged,
any shadow of a sarcasm to steal.

For the " absolute silliness," amongst many hundred passages of
pure trifling or exquisite nonsense, let the reader look to Mathias's
long note upon Godwin, and his *" gun of generation "* ; where, under
an impression that he was lashing some peculiar conceit or caprice of
that gentleman, the satirist has unconsciously engaged himself with
Hume and his Doctrine of Causation.

I say so much upon this author because (though almost forgotten
at present) in my younger days he had a splendour of success not
much surpassed even by the most popular writers of this present more
literary generation ; and because, spite of his bad taste, his pedantry,
and his cloudy affectations, he had a demon of originality about him,
which makes him, after all, worthy of preservation, and even of study.
A strange fact it is in Dr. Parr's literary history that this same
malicious satirist, from whom he received insults so flagrant and so
public, at an after period became his all but idolised friend.   In saying this, I assume it as a thing admitted universally that Mr. Mathias
and the satirist in question were one and the same person.   Letters
from this Mr. Mathias are spoken of by Dr. Parr in another period of
his life with a fervour of devotion such as a Roman Catholic limits to
the very holiest class of relics.

Page 90.

Dr. Parr (but on what particular sense of necessity I pretend not to
conjecture) has used the words *textus* for *text*, and *margo* for *margin ;*
and he apologises for them in the following words :—
" Quod textum et marginem, et alia istiusmodi verba sine ulla

præfatione, et quasi παραμυθία usurpavi, id ne bilem moveat inter eos
qui limatulum præ cæteris et politulum habere judicium sibi
videantur : "—*i.e.* "Whereas I have used the Latin word *textus* for expressing the English word *text*, and *margo* for the *margin of a page*,
and have used other words of the same kind, without prefatory explanation, or any semblance of a conciliatory excuse ; let not this be
any cause of offence amongst those who presume themselves to have a
special refinement and delicacy of judgment in comparison with others."
And he goes on to say that spiteful critics of shallow discernment
make these cavils, which possibly they would not make if aware of
the answer made to them by Henry Stephens.   That learned and able
man has brought the question to this point : "Not so properly refined as
effeminately fastidious would those ears be which could refuse to
tolerate such words, *at any rate in a case where all other equivalent
expressions are wanting.*" Well, let the question then be rested on that
footing, and so decided.   Nobody in the world, as the reader will collect from another part of this paper, has less sympathy than myself
with idle cavillers, or less indulgence towards the scruples which grow
out of excessive *Puritanism* in style.   Yet in these instances I do not
perceive that the scruples are of that character.   For I cannot perceive that the questionable words are protected by the reservation of
Stephens—*quum alia desint.*   Surely *ora libri* expresses *margin*, and
orationis perpetuitas, or *continuitas sermonis*, might serve to express the
idea of text (for the body of the composition, as contradistinguished
from its notes).

Page 92.

Upon this subject, in its relation, not to Latin, but to classical
English, we have an essay in our own times from a writer of great
talent, Mr. Foster, the Baptist clergyman.   It is strange to say that
the tendency of that essay is in direct hostility to his own peculiar
views.   Doctrinally, he contends earnestly for the *peculiar* tenets
and mysteries of the Christian economy ; and yet, on the other hand,
as a man of taste, he would banish all the consecrated terms which
express them.   Now, this is contradictory.   With the peculiar and
characteristic language would vanish the peculiar and characteristic
doctrines.   But, apart from this consequence, it is strange that Mr.
Foster should overlook the analogical justification of a separate ter-
minology derived from so many similar cases of far less importance.
For example, who complains of the Platonic theology for its peculiar
vocabulary ?   Or what reproach has it ever been to Jamblichus, to
Proclus, to Plotinus, to Synesius, &c., that they wrote almost a sealed
dialect to the "profane,"—that is, to all the uninitiated ?

Page 95.

I may add, as equal with the very foremost of them, Immanuel
Kant, whose Latin is of the best philosophic character.   He had
studied as a fellow-pupil with the celebrated Latinist, Ruhnkenius,

and had a true sense of elegance in this particular accomplishment. By the way, on this occasion I may observe most peremptorily that Hobbes was a villainous writer of Latin ; and the common story of Lord Bacon's value for him in that character is undoubtedly false. Hobbes was amongst the hacks employed occasionally by Lord Bacon ; but not a line of the Latin " De Augmentis " could have been written by Hobbes. As Falconbridge says of his reputed father, " Could he have made this leg ? We know his workmanship."

Page 95.

Lord Bacon's style is so much moulded by his own peculiar plastic intellect that it is difficult to separate the elements of the total compound,—that part which represented individually himself, and that which represented his era and his position as a revolutionary philosopher. But from the plainer and less splendid, though perhaps more sublime, mind of Des Cartes, we receive a diction which better reflects the general standard of his era. Of this diction I venture to pronounce that, though far removed from classical Latinity, it is equally far from the other extreme of barbarism, and has an *indoles*, or genius *sui generis*, and its own peculiar laws.

Page 107.

The criticisms which Dr. Parr received upon his epitaphs he bore impatiently. He had lofty notions, with which few people had much sympathy, on the dignity of his art : *magnificabo apostolatum meum* was his motto. And in reality, having cultivated it a good deal, and meditated on it still more, he had naturally come to perceive truths and relations of truth (for everything intellectual yields, upon investigation, a world of new views) to which men in general were blind from mere defect of practice and attention. This fretted him ; and in some instances it must be acknowledged that the criticisms were both frivolous and vexatious. Could it be credited that Charles Fox, who wrote very passable Greek verses, and other scholars as good, were actually unacquainted with the true Roman sense of the word *Probabilis ?* Dr. Parr had described Johnson as *probabilis poeta*—meaning, of course, *a respectable poet*—one that wrote creditably, one upon whom a smiling or indulgent toleration might settle. This is the true and sole use of the word in classical Latinity. *Ratio probabilis* is an argument, &c., such as the understanding can submit to—a decent and respectable argument, in contradistinction to one that commands instant and universal assent. So, again, the elegant Gravina, in a passage now lying open before me, says *Probabilis orator*, for *a pretty good speaker*. But Dr. Parr's critics clearly understood the word as synonymous with *verisimilis*, or else as answering to the English word *probable*, in the sense of having an overbalance of chances in its favour. *Horresco referens !* such a use of the word *probabilis* would be the merest dog-Latin, and Dr. Parr would justly have selected his most tingling birch for the suppression of the rebellious scoundrel who could use it.

Page 111.

Dr Parr adds—'' and who had endeavoured to loosen the strongest obligations of morality.'' These words are likely to be overlooked, as though they were thrown in merely to round the rhythmus of the sentence, or (if really significant) importing not more than that relaxation of morals which naturally accompanies the shaking off religious sanctions. But more is meant than this, and there is a mystery in the matter which I cannot fathom. For elsewhere (vol. iii. p. 378) he speaks of the destructive consequences of Hume's Essays '' to the sacred interests of morality'' ; and still more pointedly in another place (on Politics, Jurisprudence, &c., vol. iii. p. 283) he speaks of Hume as having '' taught the inconsiderate and the innocent to think with diminished horror not of adultery only, but of other impurities too flagitious to be named.'' What does he mean ?

Page 111.

It is usually taken for granted that Hurd had nothing to say for himself in this case, and was on that account discreetly silent. But this is a mistake. He had enough to allege against Jortin and Leland to have turned the tables on their champion ; but his motive for silence was perhaps this : Parr threatened that, if answered, he would come back '' again and again '' upon the same ground ; and, if treated with sneers, he protested that he would give '' no quarter.'' Now, in such a war, Hurd would have had his hands tied by the restraints of his episcopal dignity.

Page 113.

Mr. Kett, whose position in Oxford enabled him to overlook the whole game, came to the same conclusion ; for, in dissuading Dr. Parr from coming forward as an active participator in the dispute, he says, '' I cannot help considering the whole affair as containing something necessarily injurious to the reputation of all who engage in it.'' He also admonished the Doctor '' that the unconditional manner in which he gave his assistance ought to induce him to be silent.'' What Mr. Kett meant by silence was abstinence from the press ; but the same reasons applied to oral communications ; and in that sense it was no longer possible for Dr. Parr to be silent. He had chattered too much.

ANECDOTAGE :

MISS HAWKINS'S ANECDOTES [1]

THIS orange we mean to squeeze for the public use. Where an author is poor, this is wrong ; but, Miss Hawkins being upon her own acknowledgment rich (p. 125), keeping " a carriage, to the *propreté* of which she is not indifferent " (p. 253), and being able to give away manors worth more than £1000 per annum (p. 140), it is most clear that her interests ought to bend to those of the public ; the public being really in very low circumstances, and quite unable to buy books of luxury and anecdotage.

Who is the author, and what is the book ? The author has descended to us from the last century, and has heard of little that has happened since the American war. She is the daughter of Sir John Hawkins, known to the world, 1st, as the historian of music, 2d, as the acquaintance and biographer of Dr. Johnson, 3d, as the object of some vulgar

---

[1] Appeared originally in the *London Magazine* for March 1823, with the signature "X. Y. Z.", and with the same title as at present, save that after the word "Anecdotage" there came "No. I," as if by way of indication that there were to be more articles of the same sort under that heading. None such followed, however. The book reviewed was "*Anecdotes, Biographical Sketches, and Memoirs,* collected by Letitia Matilda Hawkins, vol. i. London, F. C. & J. Rivington, 1823." In reprinting the paper in 1859 in vol. xiii. of the collected writings, De Quincey made some slight modifications of the original text. As the paper contains particles of literary biography, the present volume seems the fit place for it in this edition ; and, on chronological grounds, it comes naturally after that on Dr. Parr. See an apologetic reference to the paper by De Quincey himself, *ante,* vol. iii. p. 175.—M.

gossip and calumnies made current by Mr. Boswell.[1] Her era being determined, the reader can be at no loss to deduce the rest : her chronology known, all is known. She belongs to the *literati* of those early ages who saw Dr. Johnson in the body, and conversed in the flesh with Goldsmith, Garrick, Bennet Langton, Wilkes and Liberty, Sir Joshua, Hawkesworth, &c. &c. All of these good people she "*found*" (to use her own lively expression) at her father's house : that is, upon her earliest introduction to her father's drawing-room at Twickenham, most of them were already in possession. Amongst the "&c. &c.," as we have classed them, were some who really ought not to have been thus slurred over, such as Bishop Percy, Tyrwhitt, Dean Tucker, and Hurd : but others absolutely pose us. For instance, does the reader know anything of one *Israel Mauduit ?* We profess to know nothing ; no, nor at all the more for his having been the author of *Considerations on the German War* (p. 7) : in fact, there have been so many German wars since Mr. Mauduit's epoch, and the public have since then been called on to "consider" so many "considerations," that Miss Hawkins must pardon us for declaring that the illustrious Mauduit (though we remember his name in Lord Orford's Memoirs) is now defunct, and that his works have followed him.[2] Not less defunct than Mauduit is the not less illustrious Brettell. Brettell ! What Brettell ? *What* Brettell ! Why, "Wonderful old Colonel Brettell of the Middlesex Militia (p. 10), who, on my requesting him, at eighty-five years of age, to be careful in getting over a five-barred gate, replied, Take care of what ? Time was when I could have jumped over it." "Time was !" he says, *was ;* but how will *that* satisfy posterity ? What proof has the nineteenth century that he did it, or could have done it ? So much for Brettell and Mauduit. But last comes one who "hight Costard " : and here we are posed indeed. Can this be Shakspere's Costard—everybody's Costard—the Costard of *Love's Labour's Lost ?* But how is

[1] Sir John Hawkins (1719-1789) published his *History of Music* in 1776, and his *Life of Dr. Johnson* in 1787. There is a good deal about him in Boswell's *Johnson.*—M.

[2] Israel Mauduit (1708-1787) was the author, in addition to the book here mentioned, of one entitled *A Short View of the History of the Colony of Massachusetts Bay* (1774).—M.

that possible ? says a grave and learned friend at our elbow.
I will affirm it to be impossible.   How can any man celebrated by Shakspere have visited at Twickenham with Dr.
Johnson ?   *That* indeed, we answer, deserves consideration :
yet, if he can, where would Costard be more naturally found
than at Sir John Hawkins's house, who had himself anno-
tated on Shakspere, and lived in company with so many
other annotators, as Percy, Tyrwhitt, Steevens, &c. ?   Yet
again, at p. 10, and at p. 24, he is called "the learned
Costard."   Now this *is* an objection ; for Shakspere's Costard,
the old Original Costard, is far from learned.   But what of
that ?   He had plenty of time to mend his manners, and fit
himself for the company of Dr. Johnson : and at p. 80,
where Miss Hawkins again affirms that his name was "always
preceded by the epithet *learned*," she candidly admits that
"he was a feeble, ailing, emaciated man, who had all the
appearance of having sacrificed his health to his studies,"—as
well he might, if he had studied from Shakspere's time to
Dr. Johnson's.   With all his learning, however, Costard
could make nothing of a case which occurred in Sir John
Hawkins's grounds ; and we confess that we can make no
more of it than Costard.   "In a paddock," says Miss
Hawkins, "we had an oblong piece of water supplied by a
" sluice.   Keeping poultry, this was very convenient for
" ducks : on a sudden, a prodigious consternation was per-
" ceived among the ducks : they were with great difficulty
" persuaded to take to the water ; and, when there,
" shuddered, grew wet, and were drowned.   They were sup-
" posed diseased ; others were bought at other places ; but
" in vain ! none of *our* ducks could swim.   I remember the
" circumstance calling out much thought and conjecture.
" The learned George Costard, Dr. Morton, and the medical
" advisers [1] of the neighbourhood, were consulted : every one

[1] From this it should seem that Costard was a duck doctor : we
remember also a History of Astronomy by one Costard.   These facts
we mention merely as hints for inquiry to the editors of the next
Variorum Shakspere.—[As this note appeared in the original paper of
1823, it is clear that De Quincey, while making so much fun of the
name of Costard, knew something of the man to whom it belonged.   He
was the Rev. George Costard, who died 1782, author not only of a *History
of Astronomy* (1767), but also of several books of Oriental philology,

" had a different supposition ; and I well recollect my own
" dissatisfaction with all I heard.   It was told of course to
" Mr. and Mrs. Garrick.   Mrs. Garrick would not give credit
" to it : Garrick himself was not incredulous ; and, after a
" discussion, he turned to my father with his jocose impetu-
" osity, and said, ' There's my wife, who will not believe the
" story of these ducks, and yet she believes in the eleven
" thousand virgins.' "   Most probably the ducks were
descended from that " which Samuel Johnson trod on,"
which, " if it had lived and had not died, had surely been
an odd one " : its posterity therefore would be odd ones.
However, Costard could make nothing of it : and to this
hour the case is an unsolved problem, like the longitude of
the north-west passage.   Perhaps a water-snake lay basking
in the pond.

Of Lord Orford,[1] who, like Costard, was a neighbour and
an acquaintance of her father's, Miss Hawkins gives us a very
long account ; no less than thirty pages (pp. 87-117) being
dedicated to him on his first introduction.   Amongst his
eccentricities, she mentions that " he made no scruple of
avowing his thorough want of taste for Don Quixote."   This
was already known from the Walpoliana ; where it may be
seen that his objection was singularly disingenuous, because
built on an incident (the windmill adventure) which, if it
were as extravagant as it seems (though it has been palliated by
the peculiar appearance of Spanish mills), is yet of no weight,
because not *characteristic* of the work : it contradicts its
general character.   We shall extract her account of Lord
Orford's person and *abord*, his dress and his address, which is
remarkably lively and picturesque, as might have been
expected from the pen of a female observer, who was at
that time young :—

" His figure was, as every one knows, not merely tall, but
" more properly *long*, and slender to excess ; his complexion,
" and particularly his hands, of a most unhealthy paleness.

and with a reputation for Oriental learning which procured him, while
alive, the name of " Rabbi Costard."—M.]

[1] Horace Walpole (1717-1797), known as fourth Earl of Orford
during the last six years of his life, having succeeded to the title in
1791 by the death of his nephew.—M.

" I speak of him before the year 1772. His eyes were
" remarkably bright and penetrating, very dark and lively :
" his voice was not strong ; but his tones were extremely
" pleasant, and (if I may so say) highly gentlemanly. I do
" not remember his common gait : he always entered a room
" in that style of affected delicacy which fashion had then
" made almost natural ; *chapeau bras* between his hands, as if
" he wished to compress it, or under his arm ; knees bent ;
" and feet on tip-toe, as if afraid of a wet floor. His dress
" in visiting was most usually (in summer when I most saw
" him) a lavender suit ; the waistcoat embroidered with a
" little silver, or of white silk worked in the tambour ;
" partridge silk stockings ; and gold buckles ; ruffles and
" frill generally lace. I remember, when a child, thinking
" him very much under-dressed if at any time, except in
" mourning, he wore hemmed cambric. In summer, no
" powder ; but his wig combed straight, and showing his
" very smooth pale forehead, and queued behind ; in winter,
" powder."—What an amusing old coxcomb ![1]

---

[1] Further on in the volume we have five more pages (pp. 307-312)
on the same noble author ; to say nothing of three beginning at p.
278, which are imagined by Miss Hawkins to concern Horace Walpole,
but which in fact relate, by every word and syllable, to his brother Sir
Edward Walpole, and to him only. In both the first and last introduction of Lord Orford, Miss Hawkins contrives to be most amusingly
and perversely wrong in all her criticisms, both as relates to his works
and to his place in the public esteem. 1. Lord Orford's tragedy (*The
Mysterious Mother*) is not the "noxious performance" which she supposes, nor is it a work of any genius. It has no merits which can
ever bring it upon the stage ; nor, if it *were* brought upon the stage,
would it therefore be "time for the virtuous to fly their country, and
leave it a prey to wild beasts." In his *choice* of a subject, Lord Orford
showed a singular defect of judgment ; in his *treatment* of it, he is not
intentionally immoral. With depraved taste and feeble sensibilities
he is chargeable ; but not, as Miss Hawkins asserts, with an act of
"enormous indecency." 2. The *Castle of Otranto* is not "a new
creation in literature," as she seems to concede (p. 309) : on the contrary, it is a most weak and extravagant fiction, in which the coarse,
the clumsy, the palpable, and the material, are substituted for the
aërial, the spiritual, and the shadowy ; the supernatural agency being,
as Mr. Hazlitt has most happily expressed it (*Lectures on the Comic
Writers*, p. 253), "the pasteboard machinery of a pantomime." 3.
With respect to the Chatterton case, Miss Hawkins is wide of the
truth by a whole climate. She dates Lord Orford's declension "in the

Of Dr. Johnson, we have but one anecdote ; but it is very
good ; and good in the best way—because characteristic ;
being, in fact, somewhat brutal, and very witty.   Miss
Knight, the author of *Dinarbas* and of *Marcus Flaminius*,
called to pay him a farewell visit on quitting England for
the Continent : this lady (then a young lady) is remarkably
large in person ; so the old savage dismissed her with the
following memorial of his good-nature :—" *Go, go, my dear ;
for you are too big for an island.*"   As may be supposed, the
Doctor is no favourite with Miss Hawkins : but she is really
too hard upon our old friend ; for she declares " that she
never heard him say in any visit six words that could compensate for the trouble of getting to his den, and the disgust
of seeing such squalidness as she saw nowhere else."   One
thing at least Miss Hawkins might have learned from Dr.
Johnson ; and let her not suppose that we say it in ill-
nature : she might have learned to weed her pages of many
barbarisms in language which now disfigure them ; for
instance, the barbarism of " compensate *for* the trouble "—in

public favour from the time when he resisted the imposition of
Chatterton " ; and she thinks it " not the usual justice of the world to
be angry at a resistance proved so reasonable.   But, first, Lord Orford
has *not* declined in the public favour : he ranks higher now than he
did in Chatterton's lifetime, or his own : his reputation is the same in
kind as the *genuine* reputation of Voltaire : both are very spirited
memoir writers ; and, of the two, Lord Orford is the more brilliant.
The critique of his posthumous memoirs by Miss Hawkins's brother
expresses his pretensions very ably.   Secondly, if he *had* declined, it
could not have been in the way supposed.   Nobody blamed Lord
Orford for resisting the imposition of Chatterton.   He was right in
refusing to be hoaxed : he was not right in detaining Chatterton's
papers ; and, if he did this, not through negligence or inattention, but
presuming on Chatterton's rank (as Chatterton himself believed and
told him), his conduct was infamous.   Be this as it may, his treatment of Chatterton whilst living was arrogant, supercilious, and with
little or no sensibility to his claims as a man of genius ; of Chatterton
when dead, brutal, and of inhuman hypocrisy ; he himself being one
of the few men in any century who had practised at a mature age that
very sort of forgery which in a boy of seventeen he represented as
unpardonable.   Did he, or did he not, introduce his own *Castle of
Otranto* as a translation from an Italian MS. of one Onufrio Muralto ?
Do I complain of that masquerading ?   Not at all : but I say that
the same indulgence which shelters Horace, Earl of Orford, justifies
Chatterton.

the very sentence before us—instead of "compensate the trouble."

Dr. Farmer[1] disappointed Miss Hawkins by "the homeliness of his external." But surely, when a man comes to that supper at which he does not eat but is eaten, we have a deeper interest in his wit, which may chance to survive him, than in his beauty, which posterity cannot possibly enjoy any more than the *petits soupers* which it adorned. Had the Doctor been a very Adonis, he could not have done Miss Hawkins so much service as by two of his *propos* which she records :—One was, that, on a report being mentioned, at her father's table, of Sir Joshua Reynolds having shared the gains arising from the exhibition of his pictures with his man-servant, who was fortunately called Ralph, Dr. Farmer quoted against Sir Joshua these two lines from Hudibras,—

> " A squire he had whose name was Ralph,
> Who in the adventure went his half."

The other was that, speaking of Dr. Parr, he said that "he seemed to have been at a feast of learning (for *learning* read *languages*) from which he had carried off all the scraps." Miss Hawkins does not seem to be aware that this is taken from Shakspere : but, what is still more surprising, she declares herself "absolutely ignorant whether it be praise or censure." All we shall say on that question is that we most seriously advise her not to ask Dr. Parr.[2]

Of Paul Whitehead[3] we are told that his wife "was so nearly idiotic that she would call his attention in conversation to look at a cow, not as one of singular beauty, but in the words—'Mr. Whitehead, there's a cow.'" On this Miss Hawkins moralizes in a very eccentric way : "He took it," says she, "most patiently, as he did all such trials of his

[1] Richard Farmer, D.D. (1735-1797), author of *An Essay on the Learning of Shakspeare.*—M.

[2] As the wording here shows, Miss Hawkins was still alive, as well as Dr. Parr, when this paper was written. She published her *Memoirs* in more complete form in 1827.—M.

[3] Paul Whitehead, poet and miscellaneous writer, 1709-1774 ; of whom the satirist Churchill wrote—

> " May I (can worse disgrace on manhood fall ?)
> Be born a Whitehead, and baptized a Paul !"—M.

temper." Trials of his temper! why, was he jealous of the
cow? Had he any personal animosity to the cow? Not
only, however, was Paul very patient (at least under his
bovine afflictions, and his "trials" in regard to horned
cattle), but also Paul was very devout; of which he gave this
pleasant assurance: "When I go," said he, "into St. Paul's,
I admire it as a very fine, grand, beautiful building; and,
when I have contemplated its beauty, I come out: but, if I
go into Westminster Abbey, d—n me, I'm all devotion." So,
by his own account, Paul appears to have been a very pretty
fellow; d—d patient, and d—d devout.

For practical purposes, we recommend to all physicians
the following anecdote, which Sir Richard Jebb used to tell
of himself: as Miss Hawkins observes, it makes even rapacity
comical, and it suggests a very useful and practical hint.
" He was attending a nobleman, from whom he had a right
" to expect a fee of five guineas; he received only three.
" Suspecting some trick on the part of the steward, from
" whom he received it, he at the next visit contrived to drop
" the three guineas. They were picked up, and again
" deposited in his hand: but he still continued to look on
" the carpet. His lordship asked if all the guineas were
" found. 'There must be two guineas still on the carpet,'
" replied Sir Richard, 'for I have but three.' The hint was
" taken as he meant." [1]

But, of all medical stratagems, commend us to that practised by Dr. Munckley, who had lived with Sir J. Hawkins
during his bachelor days in quality of "chum": and a chum
he was, in Miss Hawkins's words, "not at all calculated to
render the chum state happy." This Dr. Munckley, by the
bye, was so huge a man-mountain that Miss Hawkins supposes the blank in the well-known epigram,

---

[1] I have heard a much neater modern version of the same story,
thus:—A rich patient, who had long paid two guineas to his doctor
for every visit, thought it time to descend to the single guinea. When
the doctor, at next visit, received the single guinea, he held it in his
hand, but stooped and fumbled on the hearthrug, as if looking for
something. "What are you looking for, doctor?" asked the patient.
"O, I have dropped the other guinea," said the doctor. "No, no,
doctor," was the answer, "it is I who have dropped that."—M.

"When —— walks the streets, the paviors cry
'God bless you, Sir !' and lay their rammers by,"

to have been originally filled up with his name,—but in this
she is mistaken. The epigram was written before he was
born ; and for about 140 years has this empty epigram, like
other epigrams *to be let*, been occupied by a succession of big
men : we believe that the original tenant was Dr. Ralph
Bathurst. Munckley, however, *might* have been the original
tenant, if it had pleased God to let him be born eighty years
sooner; for he was quite as well qualified as Bathurst to
draw down the blessings of paviors, and to play the part of a
"three-man beetle." [1] Of this Miss Hawkins gives a proof
which is droll enough. "Accidentally encountering suddenly a stout man-servant in a narrow passage, they literally
stuck." Each, like Horatius Cocles, in the words of Seneca,
solus implevit pontis angustias. One of them, it is clear, must
have backed ; unless, indeed, they are sticking there yet.
It would be curious to ascertain *which* of them backed.
For the dignity of science, one would hope it was not
Munckley. Yet we fear he was capable of any meanness, if Miss Hawkins reports accurately his stratagems
upon her father's purse. A direct attack failing, he attacked
it indirectly. But Miss Hawkins shall tell her own tale.
"He was extremely rapacious, and a very bad economist ;
" and, soon after my father's marriage, having been foiled in
" his attempt to borrow money of him, he endeavoured to
" atone to himself for this disappointment by protracting the
" duration of a low fever in which he attended him ; making
" unnecessary visits, and with his hand ever open for a fee."
Was there ever such a fellow on this terraqueous globe ?
Sir John's purse not yielding to a storm, he approaches by
mining and sapping, under cover of a low fever. Did this
Munckley really exist ; or is he but the coinage of Miss
Hawkins's brain ? If the reader wishes to know what became of this "great" man, we will gratify him. He was
" foiled," as we have seen, "in his attempt to borrow money"
of Sir J. H. : he was also soon after "foiled" in his attempt
to live. Munckley, big Munckley, being "too big for an

---

[1] "Fillip me with a three-man beetle."—Falstaff, *Henry IV.*

island" we suppose, was compelled to die : he gave up the ghost : and, what seems very absurd both to us and to Miss Hawkins, he continued talking to the last, and went off in the very act of uttering a most prosaic truism, which yet happened to be false in his case : for his final words were, that it was "hard to be taken off just then, when he was beginning to get into practice." Not at all, with such practices as his : where men enter into partnerships with low fevers, it is very fit that they should "back" out of this world as fast as possible ; as fast as, in all probability, he had backed down the narrow passage before the stout man-servant. So much for Munckley—big Munckley.

It does not strike us as any "singular feature" (p. 273), in the history of Bartleman, the great singer,[1] "that he lived to occupy the identical house in Berners Street in which his first patron resided." Knowing the house, its *pros* and *cons*, its landlord, &c., surely it was very natural that he should avail himself of his knowledge for his own convenience. But it *is* a very singular fact (p. 160) that our Government should, "merely for want of caution, have sent the *Culloden* ship of war to convoy Cardinal York from Naples." This we suppose Miss Hawkins looks upon as ominous of some disaster ; for she considers it "*fortunate*" that his Eminence "had sailed before it arrived." Of this same Cardinal York Miss Hawkins tells us further that a friend of hers, having been invited to dine with him, as all Englishmen were while he kept a table, "found him, as all " others did, a good-natured, almost superannuated gentle- " man, who had his round of civilities and jokes. He " introduced some roast beef by saying that it might not be " as good as that in England ; *for*, said he, *you know we are* " *but pretenders.*" Yes, the Cardinal was a pretender, but his beef was "legitimate" ; unless, indeed, his bulls pre-tended to be oxen.

On the subject of the Pretender, by the way, we have (at p. 63) as fine a *bon-mot* as the celebrated toast of Dr. Byrom, the Manchester Jacobite. "The Marchioness (the " Marchioness of Tweeddale) had been Lady Frances Carteret, " a daughter of the Earl of Granville, and had been brought

[1] Francis Bartleman, *alias* Barthélemon, b. 1731, d. 1808.—M.

" up by her Jacobite aunt, Lady Worsley, one of the most
" zealous of that party.   The Marchioness herself told my
" father that, on her aunt's upbraiding her when a child with
" not attending prayers, she answered that she heard her
" ladyship did not pray for the King.   'Not pray for the
" King ?' said Lady Worsley ; 'who says this ?   I will have
" you and those who sent you know that I *do* pray for the
" King ; but I do not think it necessary to tell God Almighty
" *who* is king.'"

This is *naïveté*, which becomes wit to the bystander,
though simply the natural expression of the thought to him
who utters it.   Another instance, no less lively, is the
following, mentioned at Strawberry Hill by " the sister of
one of our first statesmen, now deceased."   " She had heard
" a boy, humoured to excess, tease his mother for the remains
" of a favourite dish : mamma at length replied, ' Then do
" take it, and have done teasing me.'   He then flew into a
" passion, roaring out, 'What did you give it me for ?   I
" wanted to have snatched it.'"

The next passage we shall cite relates to a very eminent
character indeed, truly respectable, and entirely English,
viz. Plum-pudding.   The obstinate and inveterate ignorance of Frenchmen on this subject is well known.   Their
errors are grievous, pitiable, and matter of scorn and detestation to every enlightened mind.   In civilisation, in trial
by jury, and many other features of social happiness, it has
been affirmed that the French are two centuries behind us.
We believe it.   But with regard to plum-pudding they are
at least five centuries in arrear.   In the *Omniana*, we think
it is, Mr. Southey has recorded one of their insane attempts
at constructing such a pudding : the monstrous abortion
which on that occasion issued to the light the reader may
imagine, and will be at no loss to understand that volley of
" *Diables*," " *Sacres*," and " *Morbleus*," which it called forth,
when we mention that these deluded Frenchmen made cheese
the basis of their infernal preparation.   Now, under these
circumstances of national infatuation, how admirable must
have been the art of an English party who, in the very city
of Paris (that centre of darkness on this interesting subject),
and in the very teeth of Frenchmen, did absolutely extort

from French hands a **real** English plum - pudding : yes !
compelled a French apothecary, unknowing what he did, to
produce an excellent plum-pudding, and had the luxury of
a hoax into the bargain. Verily, the *ruse* was *magnifique ;*
and, though it was nearly terminating in bloodshed, yet,
doubtless, so superb a story would have been cheaply purchased by one or two lives. Here it follows in Miss Hawkins's
own words :—" Dr. Schomberg of Reading, in the early part
" of his life, spent a Christmas at Paris with some English
" friends. They were desirous to celebrate the season in the
" manner of their own country, by having, as one dish at
" their table, an English plum-pudding ; but no cook was
" found equal to the task of compounding it. A clergyman
" of the party had indeed an old receipt-book ; but this did
" not sufficiently explain the process. Dr. Schomberg, how-
" ever, supplied all that was wanting, by throwing the recipe
" into the form of a prescription, and sending it to an apothe-
" cary to be made up. To prevent all possibility of error,
" he directed that it should be boiled in a cloth, and sent in
" the same cloth, to be applied at an hour specified. At this
" hour it arrived, borne by the apothecary's assistant, and
" preceded [sweet heavens !] by the apothecary himself,
" drest, according to the professional formality of the time,
" with a sword. Seeing, when he entered the apartment,
" instead of signs of sickness, a table well filled, and sur-
" rounded by very merry faces, he perceived that he was
" made a party in a joke that turned on himself, and indig-
" nantly laid his hand on his sword ; but an invitation to
" taste his own cookery appeased him ; and all was well."

This story we pronounce altogether unique : for, as, on
the one hand, the art was divine by which the benefits of
medical punctuality and accuracy were pressed into the
service of a Christmas dinner, so, on the other hand, it is
strictly and satirically probable when told of a French
apothecary : for who but a Frenchman, whose pharmacopœia
still teems with the monstrous compounds of our ancestors,
could have believed that such a preparation was seriously
designed for a cataplasm ?

In our next extracts we come upon ground rather tender
and unsafe for obstinate sceptics. We have often heard of

learned doctors,—from Shrewsbury, suppose,—going by way
of Birmingham to Oxford, and at Birmingham, under the
unfortunate ambiguity of " the Oxford coach," getting into
that *from* Oxford, which, by nightfall, safely restored the
astonished doctor to astonished Shrewsbury.   Such a case is
sad and pitiful; but what is that to the case (p. 164) of
Wilkes the painter, who, being " anxious to get a likeness "
of " good Dr. Foster " (the same whom Pope has honoured
with the couplet,—

> " Let modest Foster, if he will, excel
> Ten metropolitans in preaching well ")

" attended his meeting one Sunday evening," and very
naturally, not being acquainted with Dr. Foster's person,
sketched a likeness of the clergyman whom he found officiating ; which clergyman happened unfortunately to be—not
the doctor—but Mr. Morris, an occasional substitute of his.
The mistake remained undiscovered : the sketch was elaborately copied in a regular picture : the picture was elaborately
engraved in mezzotinto ; and to this day the portrait of one
Mr. Morris " officiates " for that of the celebrated Dr. Foster.
Living and dead, he was Dr. Foster's substitute.   Even this,
however, is a trifle to what follows : the case " of a Baronet,
" who must be nameless, who proposed to visit Rome, and
" previously to learn the language, but by some mistake, or
" imposition, engaged a German, who taught only his own
" language, and proceeded in the study of it vigorously for
" three months before he discovered his error."   With all
deference to the authority of Horace Walpole, from whom
the anecdote originally comes, we confess that we are
staggered ; and must take leave, in the stoical phrase, to
" suspend " : in fact, we must consult our friends before we
can contract for believing it : at present, all we shall say
about it is that we greatly fear the Baronet " must," as Miss
Hawkins observes, " be nameless."

We must also consult our friends on the propriety of believing the little incident which follows, though attributed to
" a very worthy modest young man " : for it is remarkable that
of this very modest young man is recorded but one act, viz. the
most impudent in the book.   " He was walking in the Mall

" of St. James's Park, when they met two fine young women,
" drest in straw hats, and, at least to appearance, unattended.
" His friend offered him a bet that he did not go up to one
" of those rustic beauties, and salute her. He accepted the
" bet ; and in a very civil manner, and probably explaining
" the cause of his boldness, he thought himself sure of success,
" when he became aware that it was the Princess Caroline,
" daughter of George II, who, with one of her sisters, was
" taking the refreshment of a walk in complete disguise. In
" the utmost confusion he bowed, begged pardon, and re-
" treated ; whilst their Royal Highnesses, with great good
" humour, laughed at his mistake."

We shall conclude our extracts with the following story,
as likely to interest our fair readers :—

" Lady Lucy Meyrick was by birth the Lady Lucy Pitt,
" daughter to the Earl of Londonderry, and sister to the last who
" bore that title. She was, of course, nearly related to all the
" great families of that name ; and, losing her parents very
" early in life, was left under the guardianship of an uncle,
" who lived in James Street, Buckingham Gate. This house
" was a most singularly uncouth dismal dwelling, in appear-
" ance very much of the Vanburgh style of building ; and
" the very sight of it would justify almost any measure to
" get out of it. It excited every one's curiosity to ask What
" is this place ? What can it be for ? It had a front of
" very dark heavy brick-work ; very small windows, with
" sashes immensely thick. In this gay mansion, which
" looked against the blank window side of the large house in
" St. James's Park, twenty years ago Lord Milford's, but
" backwards into a market-gardener's ground, was Lady
" Lucy Meyrick to reside with her uncle and his daughter,
" a girl a little older than herself. The young ladies, who
" had formed a strict friendship, were kept under great
" restraint, which they bore as two lively girls may be sup-
" posed to have done. Their endurances soon reached the
" ear of two Westminster scholars, of one of the Welsh families
" of Meyrick, who, in the true spirit of knight-errantry, con-
" certed with them a plan for escaping, which they carried
" into effect. Having gone thus far, there was nothing for
" the courteous knights to do but to marry the fair damsels

" to whom they had rendered this essential service ; and for
" this purpose they took them to the Fleet, or to May-Fair, in
" both which places marriages were solemnised in the utmost
" privacy. Here the two couples presented themselves ; a
" baker's wife attending upon the ladies. Lady Lucy was
" then, and to the end of her life, one of the smallest women
" I ever saw : she was at the same time not more than
" fourteen years of age ; and, being in the dress of a child,
" the person officiating objected to performing the ceremony
" for her. This extraordinary scrupulosity was distressing ;
" but her ladyship met it by a lively reply—that her cousin
" might be married first, and then lend her her gown, which
" would make her look more womanly : but I suppose her
" right of precedence was regarded ; for she used to say her-
" self that she was at last married in the baker's wife's gown.
" Yet, even now, if report be true, an obstacle intervened :
" the young ladies turned fickle ; not, indeed, on the question
" 'to be or not to be' married, but on their choice of
" partners ; and I was assured that they actually changed—
" Lady Lucy taking to herself, or acquiescing in taking, the
" elder brother. What their next step was to have been
" I know not : the ladies, who had not been missed, returned
" to their place of endurance ; the young gentlemen to school,
" where they remained, keeping the secret close. When the
" school next broke up, they went home : and, probably,
" whilst waiting for courage to avow, or opportunity to dis-
" close, or accident to betray for them the matter, a newly
" arrived guest fresh from London, in reply, perhaps, to the
" usual question—What news from town ? reported an odd
" story of two Westminster scholars, names unknown, who
" had (it was said) married two girls in the neighbourhood
" of the school. The countenances of the two lads drew
" suspicions upon them ; and, confession being made, Lady
" Lucy was fetched to the house of her father-in-law. His
" lady, seeing her so very much of a child in appearance,
" said, on receiving her, in a tone of vexation—'Why, child,
" what can we do with you ? Such a baby as you are, what
" can you know ?' With equal humility and frankness
" Lady Lucy replied—'It is very true, Madam, that I am
" very young and very ignorant ; but whatever you will

" teach me I will learn.' All the good lady's prejudice was
" now overcome ; and Lady Lucy's conduct proved the
" sincerity of her submission. She lived seven years in
" Wales under the tuition of her mother-in-law, conforming
" to the manners, tempers, and prejudices of her new
" relations."

We have now "squeezed" a volume of 351 pages, according to our promise : we hope Miss Hawkins will forgive us.
She must also forgive us for gently blaming her diction.
She says (p. 277), "I read but little English." We thought
as much ; and wish she read more. The words "duple"
(p. 145), "decadence" (p. 123), and "cumbent," all point to
another language than English : as to "maux" (p. 254), we
know not what language it belongs to, unless it be Coptic.
It is certainly not "too big for an island"; but it will not
do for this island, and we beg it may be transported. Miss
Hawkins says a worse thing, however, of the English language than that she reads it but little : "instead of admiring
my native language," says she, "I feel fettered by it." That
may be : but her inability to use it without difficulty and
constraint is the very reason why she ought not to pronounce
upon its merits : we cannot allow of any person's deciding on
the value of an instrument until he has shown himself master
of its powers in their whole compass. For some purposes
(and those the highest) the English language is a divine
instrument : no language is so for all.

When Miss Hawkins says that she reads "little English,"
the form of the expression implies that she reads a good
deal of some more favoured language : may we take the
liberty of asking—what ? It is not Welsh, we hope ? nor
Syriac ? nor Sungskrita ? We say hope, for none of these
will yield her anything for her next volume : throughout
the Asiatic Researches no soul has been able to unearth a
Sanscrit bon-mot. Is it Latin ? or Greek ? Perhaps both :
for, besides some sprinklings of both throughout the volume,
she gives us at the end several copies of Latin and Greek
verses. These, she says, are her brother's : be they whose
they may, we must overhaul them. The Latin are chiefly
Sapphics, the Greek chiefly Iambics. The following is a
specimen of the Sapphics :—

" One a penny, two a penny, hot cross buns ;
   If your daughters will not eat them, give them to your sons ;
   But, if you have none of those pretty little elves,
   You cannot do better than eat them yourselves."

" *Idem Latine redditum a Viro Clariss. Henrico Hawkins.*

   " Asse placentam cupiasne solam ?
     Asse placentas cupiasne binas ?
     Ecce placentæ, teneræ, tepentes,
        Et cruce gratæ.

   " Respuant natæ ? dato, quæso, natis :
     Parvulos tales tibi si negârint
     Fata, tu tandem (superest quid ultra ?)
        Sumito : præsto est."

Our opinion of this translation is that it is worthy of the
original. We hope this criticism will prove satisfactory. At
the same time, without offence to Mr. Hawkins, may we
suggest that the baker's man has rather the advantage in
delicacy of expression and structure of verse ?   He has also
distinguished clearly the alternative of sons and daughters ;
which the unfortunate ambiguity of " na*tis* " has prevented
Mr. Hawkins from doing.   Perhaps Mr. Hawkins will consider this against a future edition.   Another, viz. a single
hexameter, is entitled, " De Amandâ, clavibus amissis."   Here
we must confess to a signal mortification, the table of " Contents " having prepared us to look for some sport ; for the
title is there printed (by mistake, as it turns out), " De
Amandâ, *clavis* amissis," *i.e. On Amanda, upon the loss of her
cudgels ;* whereas it ought to have been *clavibus amissis,* on
the loss of her keys.   Shenstone used to thank God that his
name was not adapted to the vile designs of the punster :
perhaps some future punster may take the conceit out of him
on that point by extracting a compound pun from his name
combined with some other word.   The next best thing, however, to having a name, or title, that is absolutely pun-proof,
is the having one which yields only to Greek puns, or
Carthaginian (*i.e. Punic*) puns.   Lady Moira has that felicity ;
on whom Mr. Hawkins has thus punned very seriously in a
Greek hexameter :—

   " On the death of the Countess of Moira's new-born infant."
   " Μοιρα καλη, μ᾽ ετεκες· μ᾽ ανελες μεν, Μοιρα κραταιη."

That is : " Lovely Moira, thou gavest me birth : thou also, violent Moira, tookest me away " : where the first Μοιρα means the Countess, the second is the Greek term for mortal destiny.

Of the iambics we shall give one specimen :—

" Impromptu returned with my lead pencil, which I had left on his table.

" Βοηθος ειμι· καλλιω παντ' εξ εμου·
'Εκ του μολιβδου ή νοησις ερχεται."

(Pencil is supposed to speak) : "I am a ministerial assistant : from me come all things beautiful. And thus from lead comes intellectual light."

The second clause will bear another version, which does not heal its exaggeration, in representing *all* beauty as a product of the lead pencil. And *molibdos*, we fear, which means the common household lead of cisterns, tubes, &c., will not express the *plumbago* of the artist's pencil.

The thought is pretty : some little errors there certainly are, as in the contest with the baker's man ; and in this, as in all his iambics (especially in the three from the Arabic), some little hiatuses in the metre, not adapted to the fastidious race of an Athenian audience. But these little hiatuses, these " little enormities " (to borrow a phrase from the sermon of a country clergyman), *will* occur in the best regulated verses. On the whole, our opinion of Mr. Hawkins as a Greek poet is that in seven hundred, or say seven hundred and fifty years, he may become a pretty — yes, we will say, a *very* pretty poet : as he cannot be more than one-tenth of that age at present, we look upon his performances as singularly promising. *Tantæ molis erat Romanam condere gentem.*[1]

To return to Miss Hawkins ; there are some blunders in facts up and down her book : such, for instance, as that of

[1] Seriously, however, Mr. Hawkins's translation of Lord Erskine's celebrated punning epigram on Dr. Lettsom *is* "very clever," as Miss Hawkins thinks it, and wants only a little revision. She is mistaken, however, in supposing that Lord Erskine meant to represent Dr. Lettsom " as illiterate " : the bad grammar was indispensable to the purpose of working the name—*I. Lettsom* (John Coakley Lettsom was the full name)—into the texture of the verse ; which is accomplished with great ingenuity both in the English and the Greek. [De Quincey

supposing Sir Francis Drake to have commanded in the
succession of engagements with the Spanish Armada of 1588;
which is the more remarkable, as her own ancestor [1] was so
distinguished a person in those engagements. But, upon the
whole, her work, if weeded of some trifling tales (as what
relates to the young Marquis of Tweeddale's dress, &c.), is
creditable to her talents. Her opportunities of observation
have been great; she has generally made good use of them;
and her tact for the ludicrous is striking and useful in a
book of this kind. We hope that she will soon favour us
with a second volume [2]; and, in that case, we cannot doubt
that we shall again have an orange to squeeze for the public
use.

here lops off, in 1859,—perhaps by inadvertence, but certainly with
lame effect,—the conclusion of the note as it had stood in 1823. It
was as follows :—

" Is people sick? to me apply :
I blisters, bloods, and sweats 'em ;
If after that they choose to die,
What's that to me? *I. Lets 'em.*"

" Τις νοσει ; ἐλθε· νοσων πασων οἱος τε κρατεισθαι
Ειμι· λεληθε σοφου φαρμακον ουδεν ἐμου.
Αλλ', εἰ μεν θανατον μετα ταυτα γε πικρον ἐλοιτο,
Ε'ΙΛΕΤ', ΣΩΜ' ερρει· ουδε μεμηλεν ἐμοι."—M.]

[1] The Elizabethan Sir John Hawkins, 1520-1595.—M.
[2] She did in 1827.—M.

THE MARQUESS WELLESLEY [1]

IT sounds like the tolling of funeral bells, as the annunciation is made of one death after another amongst those who supported our canopy of empire through the last most memorable generation. The eldest of the Wellesleys is gone ; he is gathered to his fathers : and here we have his life circumstantially written.

Who, and of what origin, are the Wellesleys ? There is an impression current amongst the public, or there *was* an impression, that the true name of the Wellesley family is Wesley. This is a case very much resembling some of those imagined by the old scholastic logicians, where it was impossible either to deny or to affirm : saying *yes*, or saying *no*, equally you told a falsehood. As if, being asked whether you killed your wife by strychnia, then to reply *yes* would be directly to own the crime ; but, on the other hand, to reply *no* would be indirectly to own it—since it would be argued that you admitted the killing, by denying that you did it by strychnia. The case as to the Wellesleys is briefly this :— The family was originally English ; and in England, at the earliest era, there is no doubt at all that its name was De Wellesleigh, which was pronounced in the eldest times just as it is now—viz. as a dissyllable [2]—the first syllable sound-

---

[1] In *Tait's Edinburgh Magazine* for March 1846, in the form of a notice of Mr. Robert R. Pearce's *Memoirs and Correspondence* of the Marquess, published that year. The paper was reprinted by De Quincey in 1858, in vol. viii of his Collected Writings.—M.

[2] *"As a dissyllable"* :—Just as the *Annesley* family, of which Lord Valentia is the present head, do not pronounce their name tri-

ing exactly like the cathedral city *Wells*, in Somersetshire, and the second like *lea* (a field under some modification). It is plain enough, from various records, that the true historical *genesis* of the name was precisely through that composition of words which here, for the moment, I had imagined merely to illustrate its pronunciation. Lands in the diocese of Bath and Wells, running up almost to the gates of Bristol, constituted the earliest possessions of the De Wellesleighs. They, seven centuries before Assaye and Waterloo, were " seised " of certain rich *leas* held under the Dean and Chapter of *Wells*. And, from these Saxon elements of the name, some have supposed the Wellesleys a Saxon race. They could not possibly have better blood : but still the thing does not follow from the premises. Neither does it follow from the *de* that they were Norman. The first De Wellesley known to history, the very tip-top man of the pedigree, is Avenant de Wellesleigh. About a hundred years nearer to our own times— viz. in 1239—came Michael de Wellesleigh, of whom the important fact is recorded that he was the father of Wellerand de Wellesleigh. And what did young Mr. Wellerand perform in this wicked world, that the proud muse of history should condescend to notice his rather singular name five hundred and fifty-five years [1] exactly after his decease ? Reader, he was—" killed ": that is all ; and in company with Sir Robert de Percival ; which again argues his Somersetshire descent ; for the family of Lord Egmont, the head of all Percivals, ever was, and ever will be, in Somersetshire. But *how* was he killed ? The time *when*—viz. 1303—the place *where*, are known ; but the manner *how* is not exactly stated. It was in skirmish with rascally Irish " kernes," fellows that (when presented at the font of Christ for baptism) had their right arms covered up from the baptismal waters, in order that, still remaining consecrated to the devil, those arms might inflict a devilish blow. Such a blow, with such an unbaptized arm, the Irish villain struck ; and there was an

syllabically (as strangers often suppose)—viz., Ann-es-ley—but as if *Anns* (in the possessive case)—ley. In Scotland, this ancient English name is altogether transfigured into the Scottish name of *Ainslie*.

[1] " *Five hundred and fifty-five years* " :—*i.e.* not in the year of original publication, thirteen years ago, but now, in the year of revisal and republication—viz. in 1858.

end of Wellerand de Wellesleigh. Strange that history should make an end of a man before she has made a beginning of him. These, however, are the *facts;* which, in writing a romance about Sir Wellerand and Sir Percival, I shall have great pleasure in falsifying. But how, says the too curious reader, did the De Wellesleighs find themselves amongst Irish kernes? Had these scamps the presumption to invade Somersetshire? Did they dare to intrude into Wells? Not at all: but the pugnacious De Wellesleighs had dared to intrude into Ireland. Some say in the train of Henry II. Some say —— but no matter: *there* they were; and *there* they stuck like limpets. They soon engrafted themselves into the County of Kildare, from which, by means of a fortunate marriage, they leaped into the County of Meath; and in that county, as if to refute the pretended mutability of human things, they have roosted ever since. There was once a famous copy of verses floating about Europe, which asserted that, whilst other princes were destined to fight for thrones, Austria—the handsome house of Hapsburg—should obtain thrones by marriage :

"Pugnabunt alii : tu, felix Austria, nube." [1]

So of the Wellesleighs. Sir Wellerand took quite the wrong way : not cudgelling, but courting, was the correct line of policy in Kildare. Two great estates, by two separate marriages, the De Wellesleighs obtained in Kildare ; and by a third marriage, in a third generation, they obtained, in the County of Meath, an estate known by the name of Castle Dengan (otherwise Dangan), with lordships as plentiful as blackberries. Castle Dangan came to them in the year of our Lord 1411—*i.e.* four years before Agincourt ; which memorable battle was fought exactly four hundred years before Waterloo—*ergo* in 1415. And in Castle Dangan did Field-Marshal the Man of Waterloo draw his first breath,

---

[1] "*Nube*" :—One must wink at blunders where royalties are concerned ; else, between you and me, reader, *nube* is not the right word, unless when the Austrian throne-winner happened to be a princess. *Nube* could not be applied to a man, as an old dusty pentameter will assist the reader in remembering :

"Uxorem *duco ; nubit* at illa mihi."

shed his first tears, and perpetrate his earliest trespasses. That is what one might call a pretty long spell for one family. Four hundred and thirty-five years [1] has Castle Dangan furnished a nursery for the Wellesley piccaninnies. Amongst the lordships attached to Castle Dangan was *Mornington,* which, more than three centuries afterwards, supplied an earldom for the grandfather of Waterloo. Any further memorabilia of the Castle Dangan family are not recorded, except that in 1485 (which surely was the year of Bosworth Field ?) they began to omit the *de,* and to write themselves Wellesley *tout court.* From indolence, I presume ; for a certain Lady Di. le Fleming, whom once I knew, a Howard by birth, who had condescended so far as to marry a simple baronet (Sir Michael le Fleming), told me, when a widow, as her reason for omitting the *le,* that it caused her too much additional trouble. She was a very good and kind-hearted woman ; yet still, as a daughter of the Howards (the great feudal house of Suffolk), she regarded any possible heraldic pretensions of an obscure baronet's family as visible only through powerful microscopes.

So far the evidence seems in favour of Wellesley, and against Wesley. But, on the other hand, during the last three centuries the Wellesleys themselves wrote the name Wesley. They, however, were only the *maternal* ancestors of the present Wellesleys. Garret Wellesley, the last male heir of the direct line, in the year 1745, left his whole estate to one of the Cowleys, a Staffordshire family, who had emigrated to Ireland in Queen Elizabeth's time, but who were, however, descended from the Wellesleys. This Cowley or Colley, taking, in 1745, the name of Wesley, received from George II the title of Earl Mornington ; and Colley's grandson, the Marquess Wellesley of our age, was recorded in the Irish peerage as *Wesley,* Earl of Mornington ; was uniformly so described up to the end of the eighteenth century ; and even Arthur of Waterloo, whom most of us Europeans know pretty well, on going to India a little before his brother (say early in 1799), was thus introduced by Lord Cornwallis to Sir John Shore (Lord Teignmouth, at that time

---

[1] "*Four hundred and thirty-five*"—but now (1858), on republication of this paper, hard upon four hundred and forty-seven years.

the Governor-General), " Dear sir, I beg leave to introduce to you Colonel Wesley, who is a lieutenant-colonel of my regiment. He is a sensible man, and a good officer." Posterity (for *we* are posterity in respect of Lord Cornwallis) have been very much of *his* opinion. Colonel Wesley really *was* a sensible man ; and the sensible man, soon after his arrival in Bengal, under the instigation of his brother, resumed the old name of Wellesley. In reality, the name of Wesley was merely the abbreviation of indolence, as Chumley for Cholmondeley, Pomfret for Pontefract, Cicester for Cirencester ; or, in Scotland, Marchbanks for Marjoribanks, Shatorow, as commonly pronounced, for the Duke of Hamilton's French title of Chatelherault. I remember well from my days of childhood a niece of John Wesley, the Proto-Methodist, who always spoke of the second Lord Mornington (author of the well-known glees) as a cousin, and as intimately connected with her brother, the great *foudroyant* performer on the organ. Southey, in his Life of John Wesley, the pious founder of Methodism, tells us that Charles Wesley, the brother of John, and father of the great organist, had the offer from Garret Wellesley of those same estates which eventually were left to Richard Cowley. This argues a recognition of near consanguinity. Why the offer was declined is not distinctly explained. Certainly it requires explanation, being a problem of very difficult solution to us sublunary men. But, if it had been accepted, Southey thinks that then we should have had no storming of Seringapatam, no Waterloo, and no Arminian Methodists. All that is not quite clear. Tippoo was booked for a desperate British vengeance by his own desperate enmity to our name, though no Lord Wellesley had been Governor-General in the penultimate year of the last century. Napoleon, by the same fury of hatred to us, was booked for the same fate, though the scene of it might not have been Waterloo. And, as to John Wesley, why should he not have made the same schism with the English Church because his brother Charles had become unexpectedly rich ?

The Marquess Wellesley was of the same standing, as to age, or nearly so, as Mr. Pitt ; though he outlived Pitt by almost forty years. Born in 1760, three or four months before the accession of George III, he was sent to Eton, at the age of eleven ; and from Eton, in his eighteenth year, he was sent to Christ Church, Oxford, where he matriculated as a nobleman. He then bore the courtesy title of Viscount Wellesley ; but, in 1781, when he had reached his twenty-first year, he was summoned away from Oxford by the death of his father, the second Earl of Mornington. It is interesting, at this moment, to look back on the family group of children collected at Dangan Castle. The young Earl of Mornington, future Marquess Wellesley, was within a month of his majority ; his younger brothers and sisters were these : William Wellesley Pole (since dead, under the title of Lord Maryborough), then aged eighteen ; Anne, since married to Henry, son of Lord Southampton, then aged thirteen ; *Arthur*, aged twelve ; Gerald Valerian, now in the Church, aged ten ; Mary Elizabeth (since Lady Culling Smith), aged nine ; Henry, since Lord Cowley, and British ambassador to Spain, France, &c., aged eight. The new Lord Mornington showed his conscientious nature, by assuming his father's debts, and by superintending the education of his brothers. He had distinguished himself at Oxford as a scholar ; but he returned thither no more, and took no degree. As Earl of Mornington, he sat in the Irish House of Lords ; but, not being a *British* peer, he was able to sit also in the English House of Commons ; and of this opening for a more national career he availed himself at the age of twenty-four. Except that he favoured the claims of the Irish Catholics, his policy was pretty uniformly that of Mr. Pitt. He supported that minister throughout the contests on the French Revolution, and, a little earlier, on the Regency question. This came forward in 1788, on occasion of the first insanity which attacked George III. The reader, who is likely to have been born since that era—at least I hope so—will perhaps not be acquainted with the constitutional question then at issue. It was this :—Mr. Fox held that, upon any incapacity arising in the sovereign, the regency would then settle (*ipso facto* of that incapacity, and, therefore, in defiance of Parliament) upon the Prince of Wales ; overlooking altogether the case in which there should *be* no Prince of Wales, and the case in which such a prince might be as incapable, from youth, of exercising the powers attached to the office as his father from disease. Mr. Pitt denied that a Prince of Wales simply *as* such, and apart from any moral fitness which he might have manifested, had more of *legal* title to the office of regent than any lamplighter or scavenger. It was the province of Parliament exclusively to legislate for the particular case.— The practical decision of the question was not called for, through the accident of the king's sudden recovery : but in Ireland, from the independence asserted by the two houses of the British councils, the question grew still more complex. The Lord-Lieutenant refused to transmit their address,[1] and Lord Mornington supported him powerfully in his refusal.

Ten years after this hot collision of parties, Lord Mornington was appointed Governor-General of India ; and now first he entered upon a stage worthy of his powers. I cannot myself agree with his biographer, Mr. Pearce, that "the wisdom of his policy is now universally recognised" ; because the same false view of our Indian position, which at that time caused his splendid services to be slighted in many quarters, still preponderates. All administrations alike have been intensely ignorant of Indian politics ; and for the natural reason, that the business of home politics leaves them no disposable energies for affairs so distant, and with which each man's chance of any durable connexion is so exceedingly small. What Lord Mornington did was this : he looked our prospects in the face. Two great enemies were then looming upon the horizon—viz. Mysore and the Mahrattas—both brutally ignorant of our real resources, and both deluded by our imperfect use of such resources as, even in a previous war, we had possessed. That one of these enemies who first came into play was Tippoo, the Sultan of Mysore : him, by the crushing energy of his arrangements, Lord Mornington was able utterly to destroy ; and to distribute his dominions with equity and moderation ; yet so as to prevent any new coalition arising in that quarter against the British power. There is a portrait of Tippoo,—of

---

[1] Which adopted neither view ; for, by *offering* the regency of Ireland to the Prince of Wales, they negatived Mr. Fox's view, who held it to be the prince's by inherent right, whether offered or not ; and, on the other hand, they still more openly opposed Mr. Pitt.

this very tiger, more than tiger-hearted,—in the second volume of Mr. Pearce's work, which expresses sufficiently the unparalleled ferocity of his nature ; and it is guaranteed, by its origin, as authentic. Tippoo, from the personal interest investing him, has more fixed the attention of Europe than a much more formidable enemy : that enemy was the Mahratta confederacy, chiefly concentrated in the persons of the Peishwah, of Scindia (usually pronounced Sindy), of Holkar, and the Rajah of Berar. Had these four princes been less profoundly ignorant, had they been less inveterately treacherous, they would have cost us the only [1] dreadful struggle which in India we have stood. As it was, Lord Mornington's government reduced and crippled the Mahrattas to such an extent that in 1817 Lord Hastings found it possible to crush them for ever. Three services of a profounder nature Lord Wellesley was enabled to do for India : first, to pave the way for the propagation of Christianity—mighty service, stretching to the clouds, and which, in the hour of death, must have given him consolation ; secondly, to enter upon the abolition of such Hindoo superstitions as are most shocking to humanity, particularly the practice of Suttee, and the barbarous exposure of dying persons or of first-born infants at Saugor on the Ganges ; finally, to promote an enlarged system of education, which (if his splendid scheme had been adopted) would have diffused its benefits all over India. It ought also to be mentioned that the expedition by way of the Red Sea against the French in Egypt was so entirely of his suggestion and his preparation that, to the great dishonour of Messrs. Pitt and Dundas,—whose administration, great by its general policy, was the worst as a *war* administration that ever feebly misapplied or lazily nonapplied the resources of a mighty empire,—it languished for eighteen months purely through *their* neglect.

In 1805, having staid about seven years in India, Lord Mornington was recalled ; was created Marquess Wellesley ;

[1] " *The only dreadful struggle* " :—This was written thirteen years ago, when the Sikh empire of Lahore was only beginning to be dangerous, and the *Lion* of Lahore, Runjeet Sing (the Romulus of the Sikhs), was but dimly appreciated by our own officers, when presented to him on their march to and from Affghanistan. *Sing* means *lion*.

was sent, in 1821, as Viceroy to Ireland, where there was little to do ; having previously, in 1809, been sent ambassador to the Spanish Cortes, where there was an infinity to do, but no means of doing it. The last great political act of Lord Wellesley was the smashing of the Peel ministry in 1834—viz. by the famous resolution (which he personally drew up) for appropriating to the great purpose of general education in Ireland whatever surplus might arise from the remodelled revenues of the Irish Church. Full of honours, he retired from public affairs at the age of seventy-five, and, for seven years more of life, dedicated his time to such literary pursuits as he had found most interesting in early youth.

Mr. Pearce, who is so capable of writing vigorously and sagaciously, has too much allowed himself to rely upon public journals. For example, he reprints the whole of the attorney-general's official information against eleven obscure persons, who, from the gallery of the Dublin theatre, did " wickedly, riotously, and routously " [1] hiss, groan, insult, and assault (to say nothing of their having *caused and procured to be hissed, groaned, &c.*) the Marquess Wellesley, Lord-Lieutenant General, and General Governor of Ireland. This document covers more than nine pages, and, after all, omits the only fact of the least consequence—viz. that several missiles were thrown by the rioters into the viceregal box, and amongst them a quart-bottle, which barely missed his excellency's temples. Considering the impetus acquired by the descent from the gallery, there is little doubt that such a weapon would have killed Lord Wellesley on the spot. In default, however, of this weighty fact, the attorney-general favours us with memorialising the very best piece of doggerel that I remember to have read—viz. that upon divers (to wit, three thousand) papers the rioters had wickedly and maliciously written and printed, besides, observe, *causing* to be written and printed, " No Popery," as also the following traitorous couplet :—

---

[1] " *Routously* " :—This is not altogether lawyer's surplusage : for, let the hot-blooded reader understand that to be *routous* is nothing like so criminal in law as to be *riotous*. *I* never go beyond the routous point.

" The Protestants want Talbot,
As the Papists have got *all but* " ;

meaning " all but " that which they got some years later by
means of the Clare election in favour of Dan O'Connell.
Yet if, in some instances like this, Mr. Pearce has too
largely drawn upon official papers, which he should rather
have abstracted and condensed, on the other hand, his work
has a special value in bringing forward private documents,
to which his opportunities have gained him a confidential
access. We are indebted to Mr. Pearce also for two portraits of Lord Wellesley, one in middle life, and one in old
age from a sketch by the Comte d'Orsay, felicitously
executed.

Something remains to be said of Lord Wellesley as a
literary man ; and towards such a judgment Mr. Pearce has
contributed some very pleasing materials. As a public
speaker, Lord Wellesley had that degree of brilliancy and
effectual vigour which might have been expected in a man
of great talents, possessing much native sensibility to the
charms of style, but not led by any personal accidents of
life into a separate cultivation of oratory, or into any profound investigation of its duties and its powers on the arena
of a British senate. There is less call for speaking of Lord
Wellesley in this character, where he did not seek for any
eminent distinction, than in the more general character of an
elegant *littérateur*, which furnished to him much of his recreation in all stages of his life, and much of his consolation
in the last. It is interesting to see this accomplished nobleman, in advanced age, when other resources were one by
one decaying, and the lights of life were successively fading
into darkness, still cheering his languid hours by the culture
of classical literature, and in his eighty-second year drawing
solace from those same pursuits which had given grace and
distinction to his twentieth.

One or two remarks I will make upon Lord Wellesley's
verses — Greek, as well as Latin. The Latin lines upon
Chantrey's success at Holkham in killing two woodcocks at
the first shot, which subsequently he sculptured in marble,
and presented to Lord Leicester, are perhaps the most felicitous amongst the whole. Masquerading, in Lord Welles-

ley's verses, as Praxiteles, who could not well be represented
with a Manton having a percussion lock, Chantrey is armed
with a bow and arrows :

> " En ! trajecit aves una sagitta duas."

In the Greek translation of " Parthenopœus " there are as
few faults as could reasonably be expected. But, first, one
word as to the original Latin poem : to whom does it
belong ? It is traced first to Lord Grenville, who received
it from his tutor (afterwards Bishop of London), who had
taken it as an anonymous poem from the " Censor's book " ;
and, with very little probability, it is doubtfully assigned to
" Lewis of the War Office "—meaning, no doubt, the father of
Monk Lewis. By this anxiety in tracing its pedigree, the
reader is led to exaggerate the pretensions of the little poem.
These are inconsiderable ; and there is a conspicuous fault,
which it is worth while noticing, because it is one peculiarly
besetting those who write Latin verses with the help of a
gradus—viz. that the Pentameter is often a mere reverbera-
tion of the preceding Hexameter. Thus, for instance,

> " Parthenios inter saltus non amplius erro,
> Non repeto Dryadum pascua læta choris " ;

and so of others, where the second line is but a variation of
the first. Even Ovid, with all his fertility, and partly in
consequence of his fertility, too often commits this fault.
Where, indeed, the thought is effectually varied, so that
the second line acts as a musical *minor*, succeeding to the
major in the first, there may happen to arise a peculiar
beauty. But I speak of the ordinary case, where the second
is merely the rebound of the first, presenting the same
thought in a diluted form. This is the commonest resource
of feeble thinking, and is also a standing temptation or snare
for feeble thinking. Lord Wellesley, however, is not answerable for these faults in the original, which, indeed, he notices
indulgently as "repetitions" ; and his own Greek version is
spirited and good. There are, however, some mistakes.
The second line is altogether faulty.

Χωρια Μαιναλιῳ παντ' ἐρατεινα θεῳ
Ἀχνυμενος λειπων

does not express the sense intended.   Construed correctly,
this clause of the sentence would mean—"*I sorrowfully leaving all places gracious to the Mœnalian god*"; but *that* is not
what Lord Wellesley designed : "*I leaving the woods of Cylene,
and the snowy summits of Pholoe, places that are all of them
dear to Pan*"—*that* is what was meant ; that is to say, not
leaving all places dear to Pan—far from it—but *leaving a few
places, every one of which is dear to Pan.*   In the line beginning

Καν οὐθ' ὑφ' ἡλικιας,

where the meaning is—*and if as yet, by reason of my imma-
ture age,*—there is a metrical error ; and ἡλικια will not
express immaturity of age.   I doubt whether, in the next
line,

Μηδ' ἀλκη θαλλοι γουνασιν ἠιθεος,

γουνασιν could convey the meaning without the preposition
ἐν.   And in

Σπερχομαι οὐ καλεουσι θεοι

—*I hasten whither the gods summon me*—οὐ is not the right
word : οὐ is *where*, or *in* what place ; but the call is for
whither, or *to* what place.   It is, however, difficult to write
Greek verses which shall be liable to no verbal objections ;
and the fluent movement of these verses sufficiently argues
the off-hand ease with which Lord Wellesley must have *read*
Greek, writing it so elegantly, and with so little of apparent
constraint.

Meantime the most interesting (from its circumstances)
of Lord Wellesley's metrical attempts, is one to which his
own English interpretation of it has done less than justice.
It is a Latin epitaph on the daughter (an *only* daughter) of
Lord and Lady Brougham.   She died, and (as was generally
known at the time) of an organic affection disturbing the

action of the heart, at the early age of eighteen. And the peculiar interest of the case lies in the suppression, by this pious daughter (so far as it was possible), of her own bodily anguish, in order to beguile the mental anguish of her parents. The Latin epitaph is this :

> " Blanda anima, e cunis heu ! longo exercita morbo,
>   Inter maternas heu lachrymasque patris,
> Quas risu lenire tuo jucunda solebas,
>   Et levis, et proprii vix memor ipsa mali ;
> I, pete cælestes, ubi nulla est cura, recessus :
>   Et tibi sit nullo mista dolore quies !"

The English version is this :

> " Doomed to long suffering from earliest years,
>   Amidst your parents' grief and pain alone
> Cheerful and gay, you smiled to soothe their tears ;
>   And in *their* agonies forgot your own.
> Go, gentle spirit ! and among the blest
> From grief and pain eternal be thy rest !"

In the Latin, the phrase *e cunis* hardly expresses *from your cradle upwards.* The second line is faulty in the opposition of *maternas*, an adjective, to the substantive *patris;* whilst the repetition of the *heu* in two consecutive lines is ungraceful. In the fourth line, *levis* conveys a false meaning : *levis* must mean either *physically light*—*i.e.* not heavy—which is not the sense, or else *tainted with levity*, which is still less the sense. What Lord Wellesley wished to say was *light-hearted :* this he has *not* said ; but neither is it easy to say it in good Latin.

I complain, however, of the whole, as not bringing out Lord Wellesley's own feeling—which feeling is partly expressed in his verses, and partly in his accompanying prose note on Miss Brougham's mournful destiny ("her life was a continual illness "), contrasted with her fortitude, her innocent gaiety, and the pious motives under which she supported this gaiety to the last. Not as a direct version, but as filling up the outline of Lord Wellesley, sufficiently indicated by himself, I propose the following :—

INSCRIPTION FOR THE GRAVE OF THE HON. MARIA BROUGHAM :—

" Child, that for thirteen [1] years hast fought with pain,
  Prompted by joy and depth of filial love,
Rest now at God's command.   Oh ! not in vain
  His angel ofttimes watched thee—oft, above
All pangs that would have dimmed thy parents' eyes,
Saw thy young heart victoriously rise !
Rise now for ever, self-forgetting child !
  Rise to those choirs where love like thine is blest,
From pains of flesh, from filial tears assoiled—
  Love which God's hand shall crown with God's own rest ! "

---

[1] " *For thirteen* " :—*i.e.* from the age of five to eighteen, at which age she died.

COLERIDGE AND OPIUM-EATING [1]

WHAT is the deadest of things dead ? It is, says the world, ever forward and rash, " a door-nail." But the world is wrong. There is a thing deader than a door-nail—viz. Gillman's Coleridge, Vol. I. [2] Dead, more dead, most dead, is Gillman's Coleridge—dead, deader, deadest, is volume the first, which is waiting vainly, and for thousands of years is doomed to wait, for its sister volume, viz. Vol. II. The man is not born whom prophetic destiny has appointed to the task of gilding those short-hand distinctions, *Vol. II.* The readers of *Vol. I.* languish in vain for the second course of their banquet ; the caravan that should convey it has foundered in the Arabian wilderness,

" And Mecca sickens at the long delay."

That Vol. I. is dead, through three degrees of comparison, appears certain to our mind, upon more arguments than one. The book has clearly not completed its elementary act of respiration ; the *systole* of Vol. I. is absolutely useless and lost without the *diastole* of that Vol. II which is never to exist. That is one argument ; and perhaps this second argument is stronger. Gillman's Coleridge, Vol. I., deals rashly, unjustly, and almost maliciously, with some of our own

---

[1] Published originally in *Blackwood* for January 1845, as a review of " The Life of Samuel Taylor Coleridge. By James Gillman. Vol. I. London 1838 " ; and reprinted by De Quincey in 1859, with some changes, in the twelfth volume of his collected writings.—M.

[2] As De Quincey goes on to say, there never was a second volume. M.

particular friends ; and yet, until late in this summer, *Anno Domini* 1844, we—that is, ourselves and our friends—never heard of its existence. Now, a sloth, even without the benefit of Mr. Waterton's evidence to his character, will travel faster than that ; but malice, which travels fastest of all things, must be dead and cold at starting when it can thus have lingered in the rear for six years ; and therefore, though the world was so far right that people *do* say " Dead as a door-nail," yet henceforward the weakest of these people will see the propriety of saying " Dead as Gillman's Coleridge."

The reader of experience, on sliding over the surface of this opening paragraph, begins to think there's mischief singing in the upper air. No, reader ; not at all. We never were cooler in our days. And this we protest : that, were it not for the excellence of the subject,—*Coleridge and Opium-Eating*,—Mr. Gillman would have been dismissed by us unnoticed. Indeed, we not only forgive Mr. Gillman, but we have a special kindness for him ; and on this account,—that he was good, he was generous, he was most forbearing, through twenty years, to poor Coleridge, when thrown upon his hospitality. An excellent thing *that*, Mr. Gillman, and one sufficient, in *our* estimate, to blot out a world of libels on ourselves. But still, noticing the theme suggested by this unhappy Vol. I., we are forced at times to notice its author. Nor is this to be regretted. We remember a line of Horace never yet properly translated, viz.—

" Nec scutica dignum horribili sectere flagello."

The true translation of which, as we assure the unlearned reader, is, " Nor him that is worthy of a simple rap on the knuckles, should you ' fillip ' (as Jack Falstaff observes) " with a three-man beetle." [1] Or, to give a literal version, " Nor must you pursue with the horrid knout of Christopher that man who merits only a switching." Very true. We protest against all attempts to invoke the exterminating knout or *flagellum*, for *that* sends a man to the hospital for two

---

[1] " *A three-man beetle* " :—A beetle is that heavy sort of pestle with which paviours drive home the paving-stones ; and sometimes, when it is too heavy for a single man, it is fitted up by three handles at right angles to the implement, for the use of three men.

months ; but you see that the same judicious poet who dis-
suades an appeal to the knout indirectly recommends the
switch—which, indeed, is rather pleasant than otherwise,
amiably playful in some of its lighter caprices, and, in its
very worst, suggesting only a pennyworth of diachylon.

We begin our review of this book by professing, with
hearty sincerity, our fervent admiration of that extraordinary
man who furnishes the theme for Mr. Gillman's *coup d'essai*
in biography. He was, in a literary sense, our brother ; for
he also was amongst the contributors to *Blackwood,* and will,
we presume, take his station in that Blackwood gallery of
portraits which in a century hence will possess more interest
for intellectual Europe than any merely martial series of portraits, or any gallery of statesmen assembled in congress,
except as regards one or two leaders ; for defunct major-
generals and secondary diplomatists, when their date is past,
awake no more emotion than last year's advertisements or
obsolete directories ; whereas those who in a stormy age have
swept the harps of passion, of genial wit, or of the wrestling
and gladiatorial reason, become more interesting to men when
they can no longer be seen as bodily agents than even in
the middle chorus of that intellectual music over which,
living, they presided.

Of this great camp Coleridge was a leader, and fought
among the *primipili ;* yet comparatively he is still unknown.
Heavy, indeed, are the arrears still due to philosophic curiosity on the real merits and on the separate merits of Samuel
Taylor Coleridge. Coleridge as a poet, Coleridge as a philosopher,—how extensive are those two questions, if those were
all ! And upon neither question have we yet any investigation, such as, by compass of views, by research, or even by
earnestness of sympathy with the subject, can or ought to
satisfy a philosophic demand. Blind is that man who can
persuade himself that the interest in Coleridge, taken as a
total object, is becoming an obsolete interest. We are of
opinion that even Milton, now viewed from a distance of two
centuries, is still inadequately judged or appreciated in his
character of poet, of patriot, and partisan, or, finally, in his
character of accomplished scholar. But, if so, how much
less can it be pretended that satisfaction has been rendered

to the claims of Coleridge! for upon Milton libraries have
been written. There has been time for the malice of men,
for the jealousy of men, for the enthusiasm, the scepticism,
the adoring admiration of men to expand themselves. There
has been room for a "slashing Bentley with his desperate
hook," for an Addison, for a Johnson, for a wicked Lauder,
for an avenging Douglas, for an idolising Chateaubriand, for a
wild insulting infidel Curran[1]; and yet, after all, little
enough has been done towards any comprehensive estimate
of the mighty being concerned. Piles of materials have been
gathered to the ground; but, for the monument which should
have risen from these materials, neither the first stone has
been laid nor has a qualified architect yet presented his cre-
dentials. On the other hand, upon Coleridge little comparatively has yet been written; whilst the separate characters
on which the judgment is awaited are more by one than
those which Milton sustained. Coleridge also is a poet.
Coleridge also was mixed up with the fervent politics of his
age—an age how memorably reflecting the revolutionary
agitations of Milton's age! Coleridge also was an extensive
and brilliant scholar. Whatever might be the separate proportions of the two men in each particular department of the
three here noticed,—think as the reader will upon that
point,—sure we are that either subject is ample enough to
make a strain upon the amplest faculties. How alarming,
therefore, for any *honest* critic who should undertake this
later subject of Coleridge, to recollect that, after pursuing
him through a zodiac of splendours corresponding to those of
Milton in kind, however different in degree,—after weighing
him as a poet, as a philosophic politician, as a scholar,—he
will have to wheel after him into another orbit: into the unfathomable *nimbus* of transcendental metaphysics! Weigh
him the critic must in the golden balance of philosophy the
most abstruse—a balance which even itself requires weighing
previously—or he will have done nothing that can be received for an estimate of the composite Coleridge. This
astonishing man, be it again remembered, besides being an

---

[1] The Rev. John Douglas, afterwards Bishop of Salisbury, published his exposure of Lauder's forgeries in 1751. For "Curran" see
Vol. IV. p. 105, n.—M.

exquisite poet, a profound political speculator, a philosophic
student of literature through all its chambers and recesses,
was also a circumnavigator on the most pathless waters of
scholasticism and metaphysics.   He had sounded, without
guiding-charts, the secret deeps of Proclus and Plotinus ; he
had laid down buoys on the twilight or moonlight ocean of
Jacob Boehmen [1] ; he had cruised over the broad Atlantic of
Kant and Schelling, of Fichte and Oken.   Where is the man
who shall be equal to these things ?

We, at least, make no such adventurous effort ; or, if
ever we should presume to do so, not at present.   Here we
design only to make a coasting voyage of survey round the
headlands and most conspicuous seamarks of our subject, as
they are brought forward by Mr. Gillman, or collaterally
suggested by our own reflections ; and especially we wish to
say a word or two on Coleridge as an opium-eater.

Naturally the first point to which we direct our attention
is the history and personal relations of Coleridge.   Living
with Mr. Gillman for nineteen years as a domesticated
friend, Coleridge ought to have been known intimately.
And it is reasonable to expect, from so much intercourse,
some additions to our slender knowledge of Coleridge's
adventures (if we may use so coarse a word), and of the
secret springs at work in those early struggles of Coleridge,—
at Cambridge, London, Bristol,—which have been rudely
told to the world, and repeatedly told as showy romances,
but never rationally explained.

The anecdotes, however, which Mr. Gillman has added to
the personal history of Coleridge are as little advantageous
to the effect of his own book as they are to the interest of
the memorable character which he seeks to illustrate.   Always they are told without grace, and generally are suspicious
in their details.   Mr. Gillman we believe to be too upright a
man for countenancing any untruth.   He has been deceived.

[1] " *Jacob Boehmen* " :—We ourselves had the honour of presenting
to Mr. Coleridge Law's English version of Jacob—a set of huge quartos.
Some months afterwards we saw this work lying open, and one volume,
at least, overflowing, in parts, with the commentaries and the
corollaries of Coleridge.   Whither has this work, and so many others
swathed about with Coleridge's manuscript notes, vanished from the
world ?

For example, will any man believe this ?   A certain "excellent equestrian," falling in with Coleridge on horseback,
thus accosted him : " Pray, sir, did you meet a tailor along
the road ? "   " A tailor ! " answered Coleridge.   " I did meet
a person answering such a description, who told me he had dropped
his goose ; that, if I rode a little farther, I should find it.   And
I guess he must have meant you."   In Joe Miller, this story
would read perhaps sufferably.   Joe has a privilege, and we
do not look too narrowly into the mouth of a Joe Millerism ;
" a gift horse," as the old proverb instructs us, " must not
have his mouth looked into " ; but Mr. Gillman, writing the
life of a philosopher, and no jest-book, is under a different
law of decorum.   That retort, however, which silences the
jester some people may fancy must be a good one ; and we
are desired to believe that in this case the baffled assailant
rode off in a spirit of benign candour, saying aloud to himself, like the excellent philosopher that he evidently was,
" Caught a Tartar ! "

But another story, of a sporting baronet, who was besides
a member of Parliament, is much worse, and altogether de-
grading to Coleridge.   This gentleman, by way of showing
off before a party of ladies, is represented as insulting Coleridge by putting questions to him on the qualities of his
horse,[1] so as to draw the animal's miserable defects into
public notice, and then closing his display by demanding
what he would take for the horse, "including the rider."
The supposed reply of Coleridge might seem good to those

---

[1] " His horse":—One fact, tolerably notorious, should have whispered
to Mr. Gillman that all anecdotes which presuppose for their basis any
equestrian skill or habits in Coleridge rest upon moonshine.   Samuel
Taylor Coleridge's first attempts at horsemanship were pretty nearly
his last.   What motive swayed the judgment, or what stormy impulse
drove the passionate despair of Samuel Taylor Coleridge into quitting
Jesus College, Cambridge, was never clearly or certainly made known
to the very nearest of his friends : which lends further probability to
a rumour, already in itself probable enough, that this motive which
led, or this impulse which drove, the unhappy man into headlong acts
of desperation, was—the reader will guess for himself, though ten
miles distant—a woman.   In fact, most of us play the fool at least
once in our life-career ; and the criminal cause of our doing so is
pretty well ascertained by this time in all cases to be a woman.
Coleridge was hopelessly dismissed by his proud, disdainful goddess,

who understand nothing of true dignity ; for, as an *impromptu*, it was smart, and even caustic. The baronet, it seems, was reputed to have been bought by the minister ; and the reader will at once divine that the retort took advantage of that current belief, so as to throw back the sarcasm, by proclaiming that neither horse nor rider had a price placarded in the market at which any man could become their purchaser. But this was not the temper in which Coleridge either did reply or could have replied. Coleridge showed, in the *spirit* of his manner, a profound sensibility to the nature of a gentleman ; and he felt too justly what it became a self-respecting person to say, ever to have aped the sort of flashy fencing which might seem fine to a theatrical blood.

Another story is self-refuted. " A hired partisan " had come to one of Coleridge's political lectures with the express purpose of bringing the lecturer into trouble ; and most preposterously he laid himself open to his own snare by refusing to pay for admission. Spies must be poor artists who proceed thus. Upon which Coleridge remarked " that, before the gentleman kicked up a dust, surely he would down with the dust." So far the story will not do. But what follows is possible enough. The *same* " hired " gentleman, by way of giving unity to the tale, is described as having hissed. Upon this a cry arose of " Turn him out ! " But Coleridge interfered to protect him. He insisted on the man's right to hiss if he thought fit ; it was legal to hiss ; it was natural to hiss :

although really she might have gone farther and fared worse. I am able, by female aid, to communicate a pretty close description of Samuel Taylor Coleridge as he was in the year 1796. In stature, according to the severe measurement taken down in the *studio* of a very distinguished artist, he was exactly 5 feet 10 inches in height ; with a blooming and healthy complexion ; beautiful and luxuriant hair, falling in natural curls over his shoulders ; and, as a lady (the successor of Hannah More in her most lucrative boarding-school) said to me about the year of Waterloo, " simply the most perfect realisation of a pastoral Strephon that in all her life she had looked upon." *Strephon* was the romantic name that survived from her rosy days of sweet seventeen : at present, Strephon, as well as Chloe, are at a discount ; but what she meant was an Adonis. By reason of reading too much Kant and Schelling, he grew fat and corpulent towards Waterloo ; but he was then slender and agile as an antelope.

"For what is to be expected, gentlemen, when the cool waters of reason come in contact with red-hot aristocracy, but a hiss?" *Euge!*

Amongst all the anecdotes, however, of this splendid man —often trivial, often incoherent, often unauthenticated— there is one which strikes us as both true and interesting; and we are grateful to Mr. Gillman for preserving it. We find it introduced, and partially authenticated, by the following sentence from Coleridge himself:—" From eight to fourteen I was a playless day-dreamer, a *helluo librorum*, my appetite for which was indulged by a singular incident. A stranger, who was struck by my conversation, made me free of a circulating library in King Street, Cheapside." The more circumstantial explanation of Mr. Gillman is this:—
" The incident, indeed, was singular. Going down the
" Strand in one of his day-dreams, fancying himself swimming
" across the Hellespont, thrusting his hands before him as in
" the act of swimming, his hand came in contact with a
" gentleman's pocket. The gentleman seized his hand: turn-
" ing round and looking at him with some anger,—'What!
" so young, and yet so wicked?' at the same time accusing
" him of an attempt to pick his pocket. The frightened boy
" sobbed out his denial of the intention, and explained to
" him how he thought himself Leander swimming across the
" Hellespont. The gentleman was so struck and delighted
" with the novelty of the thing, and with the simplicity and
" intelligence of the boy, that he subscribed, as before
" stated, to the library; in consequence of which Coleridge
" was further enabled to indulge his love of reading."

We fear that this slovenly narrative is the very perfection of bad story-telling. But the story itself is striking, and, by the very oddness of the incidents, not likely to have been invented. The effect, from the position of the two parties,— on the one side a simple child from Devonshire, dreaming in the Strand that he was swimming over from Sestos to Abydos; and, on the other, the experienced man, dreaming only of this world, its knaves and its thieves, but still kind and generous, and still capable of distinguishing,—is beautiful and picturesque. *O, si sic omnia!*

But the most interesting to us of the *personalities* connected with Coleridge are his feuds and his personal dislikes. Incomprehensible to us is the war of extermination which Coleridge made upon the political economists. Did Sir James Steuart in speaking of vine-dressers (not *as* vine-dressers, but generally as cultivators) tell his readers that, if such a man simply replaced his own consumption, leaving no surplus whatever or increment for the public capital, he could not be considered a useful citizen, not the beast in the Revelations is held up by Coleridge as more hateful to the spirit of truth than the Jacobite baronet. And yet we know of an author—viz. one S. T. Coleridge—who repeated the same doctrine without finding any evil in it. Look at the first part of Schiller's *Wallenstein*, where, Count Isolani having said " Poh ! we are *all* his subjects,"—*i.e.* soldiers, though unproductive labourers, not less than productive peasants,—the emperor's envoy replies, " Yet with a difference, general " ; and the difference implies Sir James's scale, —his vine-dresser being the equatorial case between the two extremes of the envoy. Malthus again, in his Population book, contends for a mathematic difference between animal and vegetable life in respect to the law of increase ; as though the first increased by geometrical ratios, the last by arithmetical ! No proposition more worthy of laughter,— since both, when permitted to expand, increase by geometrical ratios, and the latter by much higher ratios ; whereas Malthus persuaded himself of his crotchet simply by refusing the requisite condition in the vegetable case, and granting it in the other. If you take a few grains of wheat, and are required to plant all successive generations of their produce in the same flower-pot for ever, of course you neutralise its expansion by your own act of arbitrary limitation.[1] But so

---

[1] Malthus would have rejoined by saying that the flower-pot limitation was the actual limitation of Nature in our present circumstances. In America it is otherwise, he would say : but England *is* the very flower-pot you suppose ; she is a flower-pot which cannot be multiplied, and cannot even be enlarged. Very well ; so be it (which we say in order to waive irrelevant disputes) ; but then the true inference will be, not that vegetable increase proceeds under a different law from that which governs animal increase, but that, through an accident of position, the experiment cannot be tried in England. Surely the levers of Archimedes, with submission to Sir Edward B.

you would do if you tried the case of *animal* increase by still exterminating all but one replacing couple of parents. This is not to try, but merely a pretence of trying, one order of powers against another. That was folly. But Coleridge combated this idea in a manner so obscure that nobody understood it. And, leaving these speculative conundrums, in coming to the great practical interests afloat in the poor laws, Coleridge did so little real work that he left as a *res integra* to Dr. Alison the capital argument that legal and *adequate* provision for the poor, whether impotent poor or poor accidentally out of work, does not extend pauperism : no ; but is the one great resource for putting it down. Dr. Alison's overwhelming and *experimental* manifestations of that truth have prostrated Malthus and his generation for ever.[1] This comes of not attending to the Latin maxim, "*Hoc age*" (mind the object before you). Dr. Alison, a wise man, "*hoc egit*" (he minded the thing before him) ; Coleridge "*aliud egit*" (he hunted three hares at once). And we see the result. In a case which suited him, by interesting his peculiar feeling, Coleridge could command

"Attention full ten times as much as needs."

But search documents, value evidence, or thresh out bushels

Lytton, were not the less levers because he wanted the *locum standi*. It is proper, by the way, that we should inform the reader of this generation where to look for Coleridge's skirmishings with Malthus. They are to be found chiefly in the late Mr. William Hazlitt's work on that subject [Anonymous Reply in 1807 to Malthus on his Essay on Population]—a work which Coleridge so far claimed as to assert that it had been substantially made up from his own conversation.

[1] William Pulteney Alison, M.D., an elder brother of Sir Archibald Alison the historian, was Professor of the Institutes of Medicine in the University of Edinburgh from 1821 to 1842, and afterwards of the Practice of Physic in the same University from 1842 to 1855. He was a man eminent for philanthropy, and was conspicuous, as De Quincey notes, for his advocacy of a compulsory Poor Law system in opposition to the views of Malthus and others. De Quincey exaggerates, however, the influence of his advocacy of a Poor Law. Dr. Chalmers argued to the last against his contention for the compulsory Poor Law system, regarding the introduction of that system into Scotland in particular as a most woeful calamity ; and many recent reasoners on the subject, Scottish and English, have been more in accord with Chalmers than with Alison.—M.

of statistical tables, Coleridge could not, any more than he could ride with Elliot's Dragoons.[1]

Another instance of Coleridge's inaptitude for such studies as political economy is found in his fancy, by no means "rich and rare," but meagre and trite, that taxes can never injure public prosperity by mere excess of quantity. If they injure, we are to conclude that it must be by their quality and mode of operation, or by their false appropriation (as, for instance, if they are sent out of the country and spent abroad) ; because, says Coleridge, if the taxes are exhaled from the country as vapours, back they come in drenching showers. Twenty pounds ascend in a Scotch mist to the Chancellor of the Exchequer from Leeds ; but does it evaporate ? Not at all. By return of post, down comes an order for twenty pounds' worth of Leeds cloth on account of government, seeing that the poor men of the —th regiment want new gaiters. And thus thinks S. T. Coleridge. True ; but, of this return twenty pounds, not more than four will be profit—*i.e.* surplus accruing to the public capital ; whereas of the original twenty pounds every shilling was surplus. The same unsound fancy has been many times brought forward, often in England, often in France ; but it is curious that its first appearance upon any stage was precisely two centuries ago, when as yet political economy slept with the pre-Adamites—viz. in the Long Parliament. In a quarto volume of the debates during 1644, printed as an independent work, will be found the same identical doctrine, supported very sonorously by the same little love of an illustration from the see-saw of mist and rain.

Political economy was not Coleridge's forte. In politics he was happier. In mere personal politics he (like every man when reviewed from a station distant by forty years) will often appear to have erred ; nay, he will be detected and nailed in error. But this is the necessity of us all. Keen are the refutations of time ; and absolute results to posterity are the fatal touchstone of opinions in the past. It is undeniable, besides, that Coleridge had strong personal antipathies,—for instance, to Messrs. Pitt and Dundas. Yet

[1] The name of the regiment in which Coleridge had served for some months in 1793-4.—M.

why, we never could understand.   We once heard him tell a
story upon Windermere to the late Mr. Curwen, then M.P.
for Workington, which was meant apparently to account for
this feeling.   The story amounted to this : that, when a
freshman at Cambridge, Mr. Pitt had wantonly amused himself at a dinner party in smashing with filberts (discharged
in showers like grape shot) a most costly dessert set of cut
glass ; from which Samuel Taylor Coleridge inferred a principle of destructiveness in his *cerebellum*,—which, if so, was a
palliation, and no aggravation.   Now, if this dessert set
belonged to some poor suffering Trinitarian, and not to himself, we are of opinion that he was faulty, and ought, upon
his own great subsequent maxim, to have been coerced into
" indemnity for the past and security for the future."   But,
besides that this glassy *mythus* belongs to an era fifteen years
earlier than Coleridge's, so as to justify a shadow of scepticism, we really cannot find in such an *escapade* under the
boiling blood of youth any sufficient justification of that
withering malignity towards the name of Pitt which runs
through Coleridge's famous *Fire, Famine, and Slaughter*.   As
this little viperous *jeu d'esprit* (published anonymously [1]) subsequently became the subject of a celebrated after-dinner discussion in London at which Coleridge (*comme de raison*) was
the chief speaker, the reader of this generation may wish to
know the question at issue ; and, in order to judge of *that*, he
must know the outline of the devil's squib.   The writer
brings upon the scene three pleasant young ladies—viz. Miss
Fire, Miss Famine, and Miss Slaughter.   " What are you up
to ?   What's the row ? " we may suppose to be the introductory question of the poet.   And the answer of the ladies
makes us aware that they are fresh from larking in Ireland
and France.   A glorious spree they had ; lots of fun, and
laughter *à discretion*.[2]   At all times *gratus puellæ risus ab
angulo ;* so that we listen to their little gossip with interest.
They had been setting men, it seems, by the ears ; and the
drollest little atrocities they do certainly report.   Not but we

___

[1] In 1798.—M.
[2] The laughter of girls is, and ever was, among the delightful
sounds of earth.   Girls do not excel in philosophy : we have ascertained that this is not their *forte*.

have seen better in the Nenagh paper, so far as Ireland is
concerned ; but the pet little joke was in La Vendée. Miss
Famine, who is the girl for our money, raises the question
whether any of them can tell the name of the leader and
prompter to these high jinks of hell ; if so, let her
whisper it.

> " Whisper it, sister, so and so,
> In a dark hint, distinct and low."

Upon which the playful Miss Slaughter replies,—

> " Letters *four* do form his name.
>
> *   *   *   *
>
> He came by stealth and unlocked my den ;
> And I have drunk the blood since then
> Of thrice three hundred thousand men."

Good ; but the sting of the hornet lies in the conclusion. If
this quadriliteral man had done so much for *them* (though,
really, we think 6s. 8d., which is an attorney's fee, might
have settled his claim), what, says Fire, setting her arms
akimbo, would they do for *him* ? Slaughter replies, rather
crustily, that, as far as a good kicking would go, or (says
Famine) a little matter of tearing to pieces by the mob, they
would be glad to take tickets at his benefit. "How, you
bitches !" says Fire. "Is that all ?

> ' I alone am faithful ; I
> *Cling to him everlastingly.*' "

The sentiment is diabolical ; and the question argued at the
London dinner-table was, Could the writer have been other
than a devil ? The dinner was at the late excellent Mr.
Sotheby's, known advantageously in those days as the translator of Wieland's *Oberon*. Several of the great guns amongst
the literary body were present—in particular, Sir Walter
Scott ; and he, we believe, with his usual good nature, took
the apologetic side of the dispute ; in fact, he was in the
secret. Nobody else, barring the author, knew at first
whose good name was at stake. The scene must have been
high. The company kicked about the poor diabolic writer's
head as if it had been a tennis-ball. Coleridge, the yet
unknown criminal, but still as an unknown sinner, absolutely
perspired and fumed in pleading for the defendant ; the

company demurred ; the orator grew urgent; wits began to *smoke* the case, as active verbs—the advocate to *smoke,* as a neuter verb ; the "fun grew fast and furious"; until at length *delinquent arose,* burning tears in his eyes, and confessed to an audience, now bursting with stifled laughter (but whom he supposed to be bursting with fiery indignation), "Lo, I am he that wrote it!"

For our own part we side with Coleridge.   Malice is not always of the heart ; there is a malice of the understanding and the fancy.   Neither do we think the worse of a man for having invented the most horrible and old-woman-troubling curse that demons ever listened to.   We are too apt to swear horribly ourselves ; and often have we frightened the cat— to say nothing of the kettle—by our shocking (far too shocking) oaths.

There were other celebrated men whom Coleridge detested, or seemed to detest—Paley, Sir Sidney Smith, Lord Hutchinson, and Cuvier.   To Paley it might seem as if his antipathy had been purely philosophic ; but we believe that partly it was personal ; and it tallies with this belief that, in his earliest political tracts, Coleridge charged the archdeacon repeatedly with his own joke, as if it had been a serious saying—viz. "that he could not afford to keep a conscience"; such luxuries, like a carriage, for instance, being obviously beyond the finances of poor men.

With respect to the philosophic question between the parties as to the grounds of moral election, we hope it is no treason to suggest that both were perhaps in error.   Against Paley it occurs at once that he himself would not have made consequences the *practical* test in valuing the morality of an act, since these can very seldom be traced at all up to the final stages, and in the earliest stages are exceedingly different under different circumstances ; so that the same act, tried by its consequences, would bear a fluctuating appreciation.   This could not have been Paley's *revised* meaning ; consequently, had he been pressed by opposition, it would have come out that by *test* he meant only *speculative* test—a very harmless doctrine, certainly, but useless and impertinent to any purpose of his system.   The reader may catch our meaning in the following illustration.   It is a matter of general belief

that happiness, upon the whole, follows in a higher degree
from constant integrity than from the closest attention to
self-interest. Now, happiness is one of those consequences
which Paley meant by final or remotest ; but we could never
use this idea as an exponent of integrity or interchangeable
criterion ; because happiness cannot be ascertained or appreciated except upon long tracts of time, whereas the particular
act of integrity depends continually upon the election of the
moment. No man, therefore, could venture to lay down as
a rule, Do what makes you happy ; use this as your test of
actions, satisfied that in that case always you will do the
thing which is right ; for he cannot discern independently
what *will* make him happy, and he must decide on the spot.
The use of the *nexus* between morality and happiness must
therefore be inverted ; it is not practical or prospective, but
simply retrospective ; and in that form it says no more than
the good old rules hallowed in every cottage. But this
furnishes no practical guide for moral election which a man
had not before he ever thought of this *nexus*. In the sense
in which it is true, we need not go to the professor's chair
for this maxim ; in the sense in which it would serve Paley,
it is absolutely false.

On the other hand, as against Coleridge, it is certain that
many acts could be mentioned which are judged to be good
or bad only because their consequences are known to be so,
whilst the great catholic acts of life are entirely (and, if we
may so phrase it, haughtily) independent of consequences.
For instance, fidelity to a trust is a law of immutable morality
subject to no casuistry whatever. You have been left executor
to a friend ; you are to pay over his last legacy to X, though
a dissolute scoundrel ; and you are to give no shilling of it
to the poor brother of X, though a good man and a wise
man, struggling with adversity. You are absolutely excluded
from all contemplation of results. It was your deceased
friend's right to make the will ; it is yours simply to see it
executed. Now, in opposition to this primary class of actions
stands another, such as the habit of intoxication, which is
known to be wrong only by observing the consequences. If
drunkenness did not terminate, after some years, in producing
bodily weakness, irritability in the temper, and so forth, it

would *not* be a vicious act ; and accordingly, if a transcendent motive should arise in favour of drunkenness, as that it would enable you to face a degree of cold or contagion else menacing to life, a duty would arise, *pro hac vice*, of getting drunk. We had an amiable friend who suffered under the infirmity of cowardice ; an awful coward he was when sober, but when very drunk, he had courage enough for the Seven Champions of Christendom. Therefore, in an emergency, where he knew himself suddenly loaded with the responsibility of defending a family, we approved highly of his getting drunk. But to violate a trust could never become right under any change of circumstances. Coleridge, however, altogether overlooked this distinction, which, on the other hand, stirring in Paley's mind, but never brought out to distinct consciousness, nor ever investigated nor limited, has undermined his system. Perhaps it is not very important how a man *theorises* upon morality. Happily for us all, God has left no man in such questions practically to the guidance of his understanding ; but still, considering that academic bodies *are* partly instituted for the support of speculative truth as well as truth practical, we must think it a blot upon the splendour of Oxford and Cambridge that both of them, in a Christian land, make Paley the foundation of their ethics, the alternative being Aristotle. And in our mind, though far inferior as a moralist to the Stoics, Aristotle is often less of a pagan than Paley.

Coleridge's dislike to Sir Sidney Smith and the Egyptian Lord Hutchinson fell under the category of Martial's case :—

> " Non amo te, Sabidi, nec possum dicere quare ;
> Hoc solum novi—non amo te, Sabidi."

Against Lord Hutchinson we never heard him plead anything of moment except that he was finically Frenchified in his diction ; of which he gave this instance : that, having occasion to notice a brick wall (which was literally *that*, not more and not less), when reconnoitring the French defences, he called it a *revêtement*. And we ourselves remember his using the French word *gloriole* rather ostentatiously—that is, when no particular emphasis attached to the case. But every man has his foibles, and few, perhaps, are less conspicuously

annoying than this of Lord Hutchinson. Sir Sidney's crimes
were less distinctly revealed to our mind. As to Cuvier,
Coleridge's hatred of *him* was more to our taste ; for (though
quite unreasonable, we fear) it took the shape of patriotism.
He insisted on it that our British John Hunter was the
genuine article, and that Cuvier was a humbug. Now,
speaking privately to the public, we cannot go quite so far
as *that ;* but, when publicly we address that most respectable
character, *en grand costume,* we always mean to back Coleridge,
for we are a horrible John Bull ourselves. As Joseph Hume
observes, it makes no difference to us—right or wrong, black
or white—when our countrymen are concerned ; and John
Hunter, notwithstanding he had a bee in his bonnet,[1] was
really a great man, though it will not follow that Cuvier
must therefore have been a little one. We do not pretend
to be acquainted with the tenth part of Cuvier's performances ;
but we suspect that Coleridge's range in that respect was not
much greater than our own.

Other cases of monomaniac antipathy we might revive
from our recollections of Coleridge had we a sufficient motive ;
but, in compensation, and by way of redressing the balance,
he had many strange likings,—equally monomaniac,—and,
unaccountably, he chose to exhibit his whimsical partialities
by dressing up, as it were, in his own clothes, such a set of
scarecrows as eye has not beheld. Heavens ! what an ark
of unclean beasts would have been Coleridge's private
menaqerie of departed philosophers, could they all have been
trotted out in succession ! But did the reader feel them to
be the awful bores which, in fact, they were ? No ; because
Coleridge had blown upon these withered anatomies, through
the blow-pipe of his own creative genius, a stream of gas that
swelled the tissue of their antediluvian wrinkles, forced
colour upon their cheeks and splendour upon their sodden
eyes. Such a process of ventriloquism never *has* existed.
He spoke by their organs ; they were the tubes ; and he

---

[1] *Vide,* in particular, for the most exquisite specimen of pig-headedness that the world can furnish, his perverse evidence on the once
famous case at the Warwick assizes, of Captain Donellan for poisoning
his brother-in-law, Sir Theodosius Boughton. [The case occurred in
1781.—M.]

forced through their wooden machinery his own Beethoven harmonies.

First came Dr. Andrew Bell.[1] We knew him. Was he dull ? Is a wooden spoon dull ! Fishy were his eyes ; torpedinous was his manner ; and his main idea, out of two which he really had, related to the moon—from which you infer, perhaps, that he was lunatic. By no means. It was no craze, under the influence of the moon, which possessed him ; it was an idea of mere hostility to the moon. In Madras had Dr. Andrew lived. The Madras people, like many others, had an idea that she influenced the weather. Subsequently the Herschels, senior and junior, systematised this idea ; and then the wrath of Andrew, previously in a crescent state, actually dilated to a plenilunar orb. The Westmoreland people (for at the Lakes it was we knew him) expounded his condition to us by saying that he was "maffled " ; which word means "perplexed in the extreme." His wrath did not pass into lunacy ; it produced simple distraction ; an uneasy fumbling with the idea—like that of an old superannuated dog who longs to worry, but cannot for want of teeth. In this condition you will judge that he was rather tedious ; and in this condition Coleridge took him up. Andrew's other idea, because he *had* two, related to education. Perhaps six-sevenths of that also came from Madras. No matter ; Coleridge took *that* up ; Southey also ; but Southey with his usual temperate fervour. Coleridge, on the other hand, found celestial marvels both in the scheme and in the man. Then commenced the apotheosis of Andrew Bell ; and, because it happened that his opponent, Lancaster,[2] between ourselves, really *had* stolen his ideas from Bell, what between the sad wickedness of Lancaster and the celestial transfiguration of Bell, gradually Coleridge heated himself to such an extent that people, when referring to that subject, asked each other, " Have you heard Coleridge lecture on *Bel and the Dragon ?* "

The next man glorified by Coleridge was John Woolman, the Quaker.[3] Him, though we once possessed his works, it

[1] Dr. Andrew Bell, 1753-1832.—M.
[2] Joseph Lancaster, 1771-1838.—M.
[3] John Woolman, 1720-1772.—M.

cannot be truly affirmed that we ever read. Try to read
John we often did ; but read John we did not. This, however, you say, might be our fault, and not John's. Very
likely ; and we have a notion that now, with our wiser
thoughts, we *should* read John if he were here on this table.
It is certain that he was a good man, and one of the earliest
in America, if not in Christendom, who lifted up his hand to
protest against the slave trade ; but still we suspect that, had
John been all that Coleridge represented, he would not have
repelled us from reading his travels in the fearful way that
he did. But again we beg pardon, and entreat the earth of
Virginia to lie light upon the remains of John Woolman ;
for he was an Israelite indeed, in whom there was no guile.

The third person raised to divine honours by Coleridge
was Bowyer, the master of Christ's Hospital, London—a man
whose name rises into the nostrils of all who knew him with
the gracious odour of a tallow chandler's melting house upon
melting day, and whose memory is embalmed in the hearty
detestation of all his pupils. Coleridge describes this man
as a profound critic. Our idea of him is different. We are
of opinion that Bowyer was the greatest villain of the
eighteenth century. We may be wrong ; but we cannot be
far wrong. Talk of knouting indeed ! which we did at the
beginning of this paper in the mere playfulness of our hearts,
—and which the great master of the knout, Christopher, who
visited men's trespasses like the Eumenides, never resorted
to but in love for some great idea which had been outraged,
—why, this man knouted his way through life, from bloody
youth up to truculent old age. Grim idol ! whose altars
reeked with children's blood, and whose dreadful eyes never
smiled except as the stern goddess of the Thugs smiles when
the sound of human lamentations inhabits her ears. So
much had the monster fed upon this great idea of " flogging,"
and transmuted it into the very nutriment of his heart, that
he seems to have conceived the gigantic project of flogging
all mankind ; nay, worse ; for Mr. Gillman, on Coleridge's
authority, tells us (p. 24) the following anecdote :—" ' *Sirrah*,
" *I'll flog you*,' were words so familiar to him, that on one
" occasion, some *female* friend of one of the boys " [who had
come on an errand of intercession] " still lingering at the

" door, after having been abruptly told to go, Bowyer ex-
" claimed, 'Bring that woman here, and I'll flog her.'"

To this horrid incarnation of whips and scourges Coleridge, in his *Biographia Literaria*, ascribes ideas upon criticism
and taste which every man will recognise at once as the
intense peculiarities of Coleridge.   Could these notions really
have belonged to Bowyer, then how do we know but he wrote
the *Ancient Mariner?*   Yet, on consideration, no ; for even
Coleridge admitted that, spite of his fine theorising upon
composition, Mr. Bowyer did not prosper in the practice—of
which he gave us this illustration ; and, as it is supposed to
be the one only specimen of the Bowyeriana which now
survives in this sublunary world, we are glad to extend its
glory.   It is the most curious example extant of the melodi-
ous in sound :—

> " 'Twas thou that smooth'd'st the rough-rugg'd bed of pain."

"Smooth'd'st !"   Would the teeth of a crocodile not splinter
under that word ?   It seems to us as if Mr. Bowyer's verses
ought to be boiled before they can be read.   And, when he
says, *'Twas thou*, who or what is the wretch talking to ?   Can
he be apostrophising the knout ?   We very much fear it.   If
so, then you see (reader) that, even when incapacitated by
illness from operating, he still adores the image of his holy
scourge, and invokes it as alone able to smooth "his rough-
rugg'd bed."   O thou infernal Bowyer ! upon whom even
Trollope (*History of Christ's Hospital*) charges "a discipline
tinctured with more than due severity," can there be any
partners found for thee in a quadrille except Draco the
bloody lawgiver, Bishop Bonner, and Mrs. Brownrigg ?[1]

---

[1] Draco and the Bishop belong to History,—the first as bloody lawgiver in the days of the elder Athens, the Bishop as fiery disciplinarian
to weak, relapsing *perverts* (such is the modern slang) : sneaking
perverts like myself and my ever-honoured reader, who would be very
willing to give the Bishop a kick in the dark, but would find ourselves
too much of cowards to stand to it when the candles were brought.
These men are well known ; but who is Mrs. Brownrigg ?   The reader
would not have asked had he lived in the days of the Anti-Jacobin,
who describes Mrs. Brownrigg as the woman

> "who whipped two female 'prentices to death,
> And hid them in the coal-hole."

The next pet was Sir Alexander Ball.[1] Concerning
Bowyer, Coleridge did not talk much, but chiefly wrote ;
concerning Bell, he did not write much, but chiefly talked ;
concerning Ball, however, he both wrote and talked. It was
in vain to muse upon any plan for having Ball black-balled,
or for rebelling against Bell. Think of a man who had fallen
into one pit called Bell secondly falling into another pit
called Ball. This was too much. We were obliged to quote
poetry against them :

> " Letters four do form his name.
> He came by stealth and unlocked my den :
> And the nightmare I have felt since then
> Of thrice three hundred thousand men."

Not that we insinuate any disrespect to Sir Alexander Ball.
He was about the foremost, we believe, in all good qualities,
amongst Nelson's admirable captains at the Nile. He commanded a seventy-four most effectually in that battle ; he
governed Malta as well as Sancho (see *Don Quixote*) governed
Barataria ; and he was a true practical philosopher, — as,
indeed, was Sancho. But still, by all that we could ever learn,
Sir Alexander had no taste for the abstract upon any subject,
and would have read as mere delirious wanderings those
philosophic opinions which Coleridge fastened like wings
upon his respectable but astounded shoulders.

We really beg pardon for having laughed a little at these
crazes of Coleridge ; but laugh we did, of more necessity, in
those days, at Bell and Ball,[2] whenever we did not groan.
And, as the same precise alternative offers itself now,—viz.
that in recalling the case we must reverberate either the
groaning or the laughter,—we presume the reader would
vote for the last. Coleridge, we are well convinced, owed all
these wandering and exaggerated estimates of men—these
diseased impulses, that, like the *mirage*, showed lakes and
fountains where in reality there were only arid deserts—to
the derangements worked by opium. But now, for the sake

---

[1] Rear-Admiral Sir Alexander Ball, Governor of Malta from 1801
to 1809.—M.

[2] " *Bell and Ball* " :—*i.e.* not to cause any misunderstanding, I
mean, Bell and Ball, Ball and Bell, in order to impress the wearisome
iteration.

of change, let us pass to another topic. Suppose we say a word or two on Coleridge's accomplishments as a scholar. We are not going to enter on so large a field as that of his scholarship in connexion with his philosophic labours— scholarship in the result; not this, but scholarship in the means and machinery, range of *verbal* scholarship, is what we propose for a moment's review.

For instance, what sort of a German scholar was Coleridge? We dare say that, because in his version of the *Wallenstein* there are some inaccuracies, those who may have noticed them will hold him cheap in this particular pretension. But to a certain degree they will be wrong. Coleridge was not *very* accurate in anything but in the use of logic. All his philological attainments were imperfect. He did not talk German ; or so obscurely,—and, if he attempted to speak fast, so erroneously,—that in his second sentence, when conversing with a German lady of rank, he contrived to assure her that in his humble opinion she was a ———. Hard it is to fill up the hiatus decorously ; but in fact the word very coarsely expressed that she was no better than she should be. Which reminds us of a parallel misadventure to a German, whose English education had been equally neglected. Having obtained an interview with an English lady, who, having recently lost her husband, must (as he in his unwashed German condition took for granted) be open to new offers, he opened his business thus :—" Highborn madam, since your husband have kicked de bucket——" "Sir ! " interrupted the lady, astonished and displeased. " Oh, pardon !—nine, ten tousand pardon ! Now I make new beginning—quite oder beginning. Madam, since your husband have cut his stick—— " It may be supposed that this did not mend matters ; and, reading so much in the lady's countenance, the German drew out an octavo dictionary, and said, perspiring with shame at having a second time missed fire, " Madam, since your husband have gone to kingdom come—— " This he said beseechingly ; but the lady was past propitiation by this time, and rapidly moved towards the door. Things had now reached a crisis ; and, if something were not done quickly, the game was up. Now, therefore, taking a last hurried look at his dictionary, the

German flew after the lady, crying out, in a voice of despair,
" Madam, since your husband—your most respected husband
—your never-enoff-to-be-worshipped husband—have hopped
de twig——" [1] This was his sheet anchor ; and, as this
also *came home*, of course the poor man was totally wrecked.
It turned out that the dictionary he had used—(Arnold's, we
think), a work of one hundred and fifty years back, and,
from mere German ignorance, giving slang translations from
Tom Brown, L'Estrange, and other jocular writers—had put
down the verb *sterben* (*to die*) with the following worshipful
series of equivalents :—1. To kick the bucket ; 2. To cut
one's stick ; 3. To go to kingdom come ; 4. To hop the twig ;
5. To drop off the perch into Davy's locker.

But, though Coleridge did not pretend to any fluent command of conversational German, he read it with great ease.
His knowledge of German literature was, indeed, too much
limited by his rare opportunities for commanding anything
like a well-mounted library ; and particularly it surprised us
that Coleridge knew little or nothing of John Paul Richter.
But his acquaintance with the German philosophic masters
was extensive ; and his valuation of many individual German
words or phrases was delicate, and sometimes profound.

As a Grecian, Coleridge must be estimated with a reference to the state and standard of Greek literature at that
time and in this country. Porson had not yet raised our
ideal, *i.e.* had not yet *told* upon that ideal. The earliest
laurels of Coleridge were gathered, however, in that field.
Yet no man will at this day pretend that the Greek of his
prize ode is sufferable. Neither did Coleridge ever become
an accurate Grecian in later times, when better models of
scholarship and better aids to scholarship had begun to
multiply. But still we must assert this point of superiority
for Coleridge, that, whilst he never was what may be called
a well-mounted nor a well-grounded scholar in any department of verbal scholarship, he yet displayed sometimes a
brilliancy of conjectural sagacity and a felicity of philosophic
investigation, even in this path, such as better scholars do
not often attain, and of a kind which cannot be learned from

[1] *Ist eben jetzt gestorben* was his German idea, which he thus
rendered in classical English.

books.   But, as respects his accuracy, again we must recall
to the reader the state of Greek literature in England during
Coleridge's youth ; and in all equity, as a means of placing
Coleridge in the balances, specifically we must recall the state
of Greek metrical composition at that period.

To measure the condition of Greek literature, even in
Cambridge, about the initial period of Coleridge, we need
only look back to the several translations of Gray's *Elegy* by
three (if not four) of the reverend gentlemen at that time
attached to Eton College.   Mathias, no very great scholar
himself in this particular field, made himself merry, in his
Pursuits of Literature, with these Eton translations.   In that
he was right.   But he was *not* right in praising a contemporary translation by Cook, who (we believe) was the immediate
predecessor of Porson in the Greek chair.   As a specimen of
this translation,[1] we cite one stanza ; and we cannot be supposed to select unfairly, because it is the stanza which Mathias
—confessedly the *proneur* of Cook's version—praises in extravagant terms.   " Here," says he, " Gray, Cook, and
Nature do seem to contend for the mastery."   The English
quatrain must be familiar to everybody :—

> " The boast of heraldry, the pomp of power,
>   And all that beauty, all that wealth, e'er gave,
> Await alike the inevitable hour :
>   The paths of glory lead but to the grave."

And the following, we believe, though quoting from a thirty-
three years' recollection [2] of it, is the exact Greek version
of Cook :—

> ῾Α χάρις εὐγενέων, χάρις ἁ βασιληΐδος ἀρχᾶς,
> Δῶρα τύχης χρυσέης [3] ᾿Αφροδίτης καλὰ τὰ δῶρα,
> Πάνθ᾿ ἅμα ταῦτα τέθνηκε, καὶ εἶδεν μόρσιμον ἅμαρ·
> ῾Ηρώων κλέ᾿ ὄλωλε, καὶ ᾤχετο ξυνὸν ἐς ῞Αδην·

---

[1] It was printed at the end of Aristotle's *Poetics*, which Dr. Cook
edited.

[2] *A thirty-three years' recollection* in 1844 ; but now, within sixty
hours of the *Calendæ Apriles* (viz. All Fool's Festival), fourteen or
fifteen years more.

[3] χρυσέης :—It is remarkable that this epithet has been everywhere
assigned to τύχης.   Δῶρα τύχης, the gifts of Fortune, which in this

Now, really, these verses, by force of a little mosaic tessellation from genuine Greek sources, pass fluently over the tongue ; but can they be considered other than a *cento ?* Swarms of English schoolboys at this day would not feel very proud to adopt them. In fact, we remember (at a period say twelve years later than this) some iambic verses, which were really composed by a boy—viz. a son of Dr. Prettyman (afterwards Tomline), Bishop of Winchester, and, in earlier times, private tutor to Mr. Pitt. They were published by Middleton, first Bishop of Calcutta, in the preface to his work on the Greek article ; and, for racy idiomatic Greek, self-originated, and not a mere mocking-bird's iteration of alien notes, are so much superior to all the attempts of these sexagenarian doctors as distinctly to mark the growth of a new era and a new generation in this difficult accomplishment within the first decennium of this century. It is singular that only one blemish is suggested by any of the contemporary critics in Dr. Cook's verses—viz. in the word ξυνόν· ; for which this critic proposes to substitute κοινόν, to prevent, as he observes, the last syllable of ῷχετο from being lengthened by the ξ. Such considerations as these are necessary to the *trutinæ castigatio* (the trimming of the balance) before we can appraise Coleridge's place on the scale of his own day ; which day, *quoad hoc*, be it remembered, *i.e.* in reference to this particular accomplishment, was 1790.

As to French, Coleridge read it with too little freedom to find pleasure in French literature. Accordingly, we never recollect his referring for any purpose, either of argument or

place is meant to indicate *riches*, corresponding to Gray's *All that Wealth e'er gave*, might seem at first sight to justify this allocation of the epithet golden. But, on this way of understanding the appropriation, we are met by a prosaic and purely mechanic fact—the gifts of golden Fortune, as the giver of golden coins — Persian darics or English guineas. Meantime this epithet has an old traditional consecration to Venus, and in such an application springs upward like a pyramid of fire into a far more illimitable and imaginative value. A truth which Shakspere caught at once by a subtle divination of his own unfathomable sensibility. Accordingly, without needing any Grecian guidance or model, how profound is the effect of that line—

" What is't that takes from thee thy golden sleep ? "

illustration, to a French classic. Latin, from his regular
scholastic training, naturally he read with a scholar's fluency;
and indeed he read constantly in authors such as Petrarch,
Erasmus, Calvin, &c., whose *prose* works he could not then
have found in translations. But Coleridge had not cultivated an acquaintance with the delicacies of classic Latinity.
And it is remarkable that Wordsworth, educated most
negligently at Hawkshead school, subsequently, by reading
the lyric poetry of Horace, simply for his own delight as a
student of composition, made himself a master of Latinity in
its most difficult form ; whilst Coleridge, trained regularly in
a great southern school, never carried his Latin to any point
of classical polish.

There is another accomplishment of Coleridge's, less
broadly open to the judgment of this generation, and not at
all of the next—viz. his splendid art of conversation,—on
which it will be interesting to say a word. Ten years ago,
when the music of this rare performance had not yet ceased
to vibrate in men's ears, what a sensation was gathering
amongst the educated classes on this particular subject !
What a tumult of anxiety prevailed to " hear Mr. Coleridge,"
or even to talk with a man who *had* heard him. Had he
lived till this day, not Paganini would have been so much
sought after. That sensation is now decaying, because a
new generation has emerged during the ten years since his
death. But many still remain whose sympathy (whether of
curiosity in those who did *not* know him or of admiration in
those who *did*) still reflects as in a mirror the great stir upon
this subject which then was moving in the world. To these, if
they should inquire for the great distinguishing principle of
Coleridge's conversation, we might say that it was the power
of vast combination. He gathered into focal concentration
the largest body of objects, *apparently* disconnected, that any
man ever yet, by any magic, could assemble, or, *having*
assembled, could manage. His great fault was that, by not
opening sufficient spaces for reply, or suggestion, or collateral notice, he not only narrowed his own field, but he
grievously injured the final impression. For, when men's
minds are purely passive, when they are not allowed to react,
then it is that they collapse most, and that their sense of

what is said must ever be feeblest. Doubtless there must
have been great conversational masters elsewhere, and at
many periods; but in this lay Coleridge's characteristic
advantage, that he was a great natural power, and also a
great artist. He was a power in the art ; and he carried a
new art into the power.

But now, finally,—having left ourselves little room for
more,—one or two words on Coleridge as an opium-eater.

We have not often read a sentence falling from a wise
man with astonishment so profound as that particular one
in a letter of Coleridge's to Mr. Gillman which speaks of
the effort to wean one's self from opium as a trivial task.
There are, we believe, several such passages ; but we refer
to that one in particular, which assumes that a single
"week" will suffice for the whole process of so mighty a
revolution. Is, indeed, leviathan *so* tamed ? In that case,
the quarantine of the opium-eater might be finished within
Coleridge's time and with Coleridge's romantic ease. But
mark the contradictions of this extraordinary man. Not
long ago we were domesticated with a venerable rustic,
strongheaded, but incurably obstinate in his prejudices, who
treated the whole body of medical men as ignorant pretenders,
knowing absolutely nothing of the system which they professed to superintend. This, you will remark, is no very
singular case. No ; nor, as we believe, is the antagonist
case of ascribing to such men magical powers. Nor, what is
worse still, the co-existence of both cases in the same mind,
as in fact happened here ; for this same obstinate friend of
ours, who treated all medical pretensions as the mere jest of
the universe, every third day was exacting from his own
medical attendants some exquisite *tour de force*, as that they
should know or should do something, which if they *had*
known or done, all men would have suspected them reasonably of magic. He rated the whole medical body as infants ;
and yet what he exacted from them every third day, as a
matter of course, virtually presumed them to be the only
giants within the whole range of science. Parallel and equal
is the contradiction of Coleridge. He speaks of opium excess
—his own excess we mean—the excess of twenty-five years—
as a thing to be laid aside easily and for ever within seven

days ; and yet, on the other hand, he describes it pathetically, sometimes with a frantic pathos, as the scourge, the curse, the one almighty blight which had desolated his life.

This shocking contradiction we need not press. All readers will see *that*. But some will ask, Was Mr. Coleridge right in either view ? Being so atrociously wrong in the first notion (viz. that the opium of twenty-five years was a thing easily to be forsworn), where a child could know that he was wrong, was he even altogether right, secondly, in believing that his own life, root and branch, had been withered by opium ? For it will not follow, because, with a relation to happiness and tranquillity, a man may have found opium his curse, that therefore, as a creature of energies and great purposes, he must have been the wreck which he seems to suppose. Opium gives and takes away. It defeats the *steady* habit of exertion ; but it creates spasms of irregular exertion. It ruins the natural power of life ; but it develops preternatural paroxysms of intermitting power.

Let us ask of any man who holds that not Coleridge himself, but the world, as interested in Coleridge's usefulness, has suffered by his addiction to opium, whether he is aware of the way in which opium affected Coleridge ; and, secondly, whether he is aware of the actual contributions to literature —how large they were—which Coleridge made *in spite* of opium. All who were intimate with Coleridge must remember the fits of genial animation which were created continually in his manner and in his buoyancy of thought by a recent or by an *extra* dose of the omnipotent drug. A lady, who knew nothing experimentally of opium, once startled us by saying that she " could tell to a certainty when Mr. Coleridge had taken too much opium by his shining countenance." She was right, and we knew it ; but thought the secret within narrow keeping : we knew that mark of ·opium excesses well, and the cause of it ; or at least we believe the cause to lie in the quickening of the insensible perspiration which accumulates and glistens on the face. Be that as it may, a criterion it was that could not deceive us as to the condition of Coleridge. And uniformly in that condition he made his most effective

intellectual displays.   It is true that he might not be happy
under this fiery animation ; and we fully believe that he
was not.   Nobody is happy, except for a very short term of
years, under an artificial stimulation.   But in what way did
that operate upon his exertions as a writer ?   We are of
opinion that it killed Coleridge as a poet.   " The harp of
Quantock " [1] was silenced for ever by the torment of opium ;
but proportionably it roused and stung by misery his metaphysical instincts into more spasmodic life.   Poetry can
flourish only in the atmosphere of happiness.   But subtle
and perplexed investigations of difficult problems are amongst
the commonest resources for beguiling the sense of misery.
And for this we have the direct authority of Coleridge
himself, speculating on his own case.   In the beautiful
though unequal ode entitled *Dejection*, stanza sixth, occurs
the following passage :—

> " For not to think of what I needs must feel,
>   But to be still and patient all I can,
>   *And haply by abstruse research to steal*
>   *From my own nature all the natural man,* —
>   This was my sole resource, my only plan ;
>   Till that which suits a part infects the whole,
>   And now is almost grown the habit of my soul."

Considering the exquisite quality of some poems which Coleridge has composed, nobody can grieve (or *has* grieved) more
than ourselves at seeing so beautiful a fountain choked up
with weeds.   But, had Coleridge been a happier man, it is
our fixed belief that we should have had far less of his
philosophy, and perhaps *not* much more of his general literature.   In the estimate of the public, doubtless, *that* will
seem a good exchange.   Every man to his taste.   Meantime,
what we wish to show is that the loss was not absolute, but
merely relative.

It is urged, however, that, even on his philosophic specu-

----

[1] " *The Harp of Quantock* " :—Under that designation it was that
Wordsworth had apostrophised Coleridge as a poet after long years
of silence.   The *Quantock* Hills, in southern Somersetshire, are
alluded to in Wordsworth's exquisite poem of *Ruth*, and were the
early scene of joint wanderings on the part of the two poets, when
Wordsworth and his sister tenanted Alfoxton, during the minority of
Mr. St. Aubyn.

lations, opium operated unfavourably in one respect, by often causing him to leave them unfinished. This is true. Whenever Coleridge (being highly charged, or saturated, with opium) had written with distempered vigour upon any question, there occurred soon after a recoil of intense disgust, not from his own paper only, but even˜from the entire subject. All opium-eaters are tainted with the infirmity of leaving works unfinished, and suffering reactions of disgust ; but Coleridge taxed himself with that infirmity in verse before he could at all have commenced opium - eating. Besides, it is too much assumed by Coleridge and by his biographer that to leave off opium was of course to regain juvenile health. Indeed all opium-eaters, or indulgers in alcohol, make the mistake of supposing every pain or irritation which they suffer to be the product of the stimulant used, whereas a wise man will say, Suppose you *do* leave off opium, that will not deliver you from the load of years (say sixty-three) which you carry on your back. Charles Lamb, another man of true genius, and another head belonging to the Blackwood gallery, made that mistake in his *Confessions of a Drunkard*. "I looked back," says he, "to the time when always, on waking in the morning, I had a song rising to my lips." At present, it seems, being a drunkard, he has no such song. Ay, dear Lamb ; but note this, that the drunkard was fifty - six years old, while the songster was twenty - three. Take twenty-three from fifty-six, and we have heard it said that thirty-three will remain : at least Cocker, who was a very obstinate man, went to his grave in that persuasion. But that extra burthen of thirty - three years is a pretty good reason for not singing in the morning, even if brandy has been out of the question.

It is singular, as respects Coleridge, that Mr. Gillman never says one word upon the event of the great Highgate experiment for leaving off laudanum, though Coleridge came to Mr. Gillman's for no other purpose ; and in a week, this vast creation of new earth, sea, and all that in them is, was to have been accomplished. We incline to fancy that the explosion must have hung fire. But *that* is a trifle. We have another pleasing hypothesis on the subject. Mr. Wordsworth, in his exquisite lines written on a fly-leaf of his own

Castle of Indolence, having described Coleridge as a "noticeable man with large gray eyes," goes on to say, "He" (viz. Coleridge) "did that other man entice" to view his imagery. Now, we are sadly afraid that "the noticeable man with large gray eyes" did entice "that other man," viz. Gillman, to commence opium-eating. This is droll ; and it makes us laugh horribly. Gillman should have reformed *him,* viz. Samuel Taylor Coleridge ; and lo, *he* corrupts Gillman ! Coleridge visited Highgate by way of being converted from the heresy of opium ; and the issue is that in two months' time various grave men, amongst whom our friend Gillman marches first in great pomp, are found to have faces shining and glorious as that of Æsculapius—a fact of which we have already explained the secret meaning. And scandal says (but, then, what will not scandal say ?) that a hogshead of laudanum goes up every third month through Highgate tunnel. Surely one corroboration of our hypothesis may be found in the fact that Vol. I of Gillman's Coleridge is for ever to stand unpropped by Vol. II ; for we have already observed that opium-eaters, though good fellows upon the whole, never finish anything.

What then ? A man has a right never to finish anything. Certainly he has, and by Magna Charta ; but he has no right, by Magna Charta or by Parva Charta, to slander decent men like ourselves and our friend the author of the *Opium Confessions.* Here it is that our complaint arises against Mr. Gillman. If he has taken to opium-eating, can we help *that ?* If *his* face shines, must our faces be blackened ? He has very improperly published some intemperate passages from Coleridge's letters which ought to have been considered confidential unless Coleridge had left them for publication, charging upon the author of the *Opium Confessions* a reckless disregard of the temptations which in that work he was scattering abroad amongst men. Now, this author is connected with ourselves, and we cannot neglect his defence, unless in the case that he undertakes it himself.

We complain also that Coleridge raises (and is backed by Mr. Gillman in raising) a distinction, perfectly perplexing to us, between himself and the author of the *Opium Confessions,* upon the question why they severally began the practice of opium-eating.[1] In himself, it seems, this motive was to relieve pain, whereas the confessor was surreptitiously seeking for pleasure. Ay, indeed! where did he learn *that*? We have no copy of the *Confessions* here; so we cannot quote chapter and verse; but we distinctly remember that toothache is recorded in that book as the particular occasion which first introduced the author to the knowledge of opium. Whether afterwards, having been thus initiated by the demon of pain, the opium-confessor did not apply powers thus discovered to purposes of mere pleasure, is a question for himself; and the same question applies with the same cogency to Coleridge. Coleridge began in rheumatic pains. What then? This is no proof that he did not end in voluptuousness. For our part, we are slow to believe that ever any man did or could learn the somewhat awful truth, that in a certain ruby-coloured elixir there lurked a divine power to chase away the genius of pain, or secondly, of *ennui* (which it is, far more than pain, that saddens our human life), without sometimes, and to some extent, abusing this power. To taste but once from the tree of knowledge is fatal to the subsequent power of abstinence. True it is that generations have used laudanum as an anodyne (for instance, hospital patients) who have not afterwards courted its powers as a voluptuous stimulant; but that, be sure, has arisen from no abstinence in *them*. There are, in fact, two classes of temperaments as to this terrific drug—those which are, and those which are not, precon-formed to its power; those which genially expand to its temptations, and those which frostily exclude them. Not in the energies of the will, but in the qualities of the nervous organisation, lies the dread arbitration of—Fall or stand: doomed thou art to yield, or strengthened constitutionally to resist. Most of those who have but a low sense of the spells lying couchant in opium have practically none at all; for the initial fascination is for *them* effectually defeated by the sickness which nature has associated with the first stages of opium-eating. But to that other class whose nervous sensibilities vibrate to their profoundest depths under the first touch of the angelic poison, even as a lover's ear thrills on

[1] See *ante*, Vol. III. p. 225.—M.

hearing unexpectedly the voice of her whom he loves, opium is the Amreeta cup of beatitude. You know the *Paradise Lost ?* and you remember from the eleventh book, in its earlier part, that laudanum must already have existed in Eden—nay, that it was used medicinally by an archangel : for, after Michael had "purged with euphrasy and rue" the eyes of Adam, lest he should be unequal to the mere *sight* of the great visions about to unfold their draperies before him, next he fortifies his fleshly spirits against the *affliction* of these visions, of which visions the first was death.   And how ?

> " He from the well of life three drops instilled."

What was their operation ?

> " So deep the power of these ingredients pierced,
> *Even to the inmost seat of mental sight,*
> That Adam, now enforced to close his eyes,
> Sank down, and all his spirits became entranced
> But him the gentle angel by the hand
> Soon raised———"

The second of these lines it is which betrays the presence of laudanum.   It is in the faculty of mental vision, it is in the increased power of dealing with the shadowy and the dark, that the characteristic virtue of opium lies.   Now, in the original higher sensibility is found some palliation for the *practice* of opium-eating ; in the greater temptation lies a greater excuse.   And in this faculty of self-revelation is found some palliation for *reporting* the case to the world ; which palliation both Coleridge and his biographer have overlooked.[1]

---

[1] Though De Quincey cuts short the reprinted paper at this point the original in *Blackwood* for January 1845 had this dim editorial or quasi-editorial paragraph :—" On all this, however, we need say no " more ; for we have just received a note from the writer of the " *Opium Confessions,* more learned than ourselves in such mysteries, " which promises us a sequel or finale to those confessions.   And " this, which we have reason to think a record of profound experi- " ences, we shall probably publish next month."   The sequel to De Quincey's *Opium Confessions* so announced did begin to appear in *Blackwood* in March 1845.—M.

POSTSCRIPT [1]

FROM some misconception at the press, the account of Coleridge's personal appearance in the paper entitled *Coleridge and Opium - Eating* was printed off whilst yet imperfect, and, in fact, wanting its more interesting half. It had been suggested to me, as a proper offset to a very inaccurate report characterising Coleridge's person and conversation by an American traveller, who had, however, the excuse that his visit was a very hasty one, and that Coleridge had then become corpulent and heavy—wearing some indications that already (though, according to my present remembrance, not much more than forty-eight at that time) he had entered within the shadows of premature old age. The authorities for my counter-report are—1. A Bristol lady who with her sisters had become successors in a young ladies' boarding-school to the celebrated Hannah More ; 2. Wordsworth, in his supplementary stanzas to the *Castle of Indolence;* 3. Two (if not three) artists. These shall be first called into court, as deposing to Coleridge's figure, *i.e.* to the permanent *base* in the description—all the rest being fugitive accompaniments. One of these artists, who is now no longer such, took down, in the year 1810, at Allan Bank, Grasmere, the exact measurements of both Samuel Taylor Coleridge and William Wordsworth (at that time the host of Coleridge and myself). His memorandum on that occasion is missing. But, as he found the two poets agreeing in

---

[1] This, properly printed here as a Postscript, appeared as a " Prefatory Note " to the volume of De Quincey's collected writings containing the paper to which it belongs.—M.

height to a hair's-breadth,—which I myself, as an attentive
bystander, can vouch for,—it will be sufficient for me to
refer the curious reader to the Autobiography of Haydon, in
whose *studio* Wordsworth was measured with technical nicety
on a day regularly dated.   The report is—5 feet 10 inches,
within a trifling fraction ; and the same report, therefore,
stands good to a nicety for Coleridge.   Next, for the face
and bearing of Coleridge at the time referred to by the
lady (1796), an ample authority is found in Wordsworth's
fine stanzas—"Ah ! piteous sight it was " [I cannot recall
the two or three words of filling up] " when he,"

> "This man, came back to us a withered flower." [1]

That was perhaps in 1807, when he returned from Malta,
where it was that, from solitude too intense, he first took
opium in excess.   But in 1796, whilst yet apparently unacquainted with opium,

> " Noisy he was, and gamesome as a boy,
> Tossing his limbs about him in delight."

Happiest and most genial he then was of all that taste the
morning breezes of life.   From Wordsworth we learn (what
afterwards my own experience verified) that his eyes were
large, and in colour were grey :—

> "Profound his forehead was, but not severe ;
> And some did think " [viz. in the *Castle of Indolence*] "that
> *he* had little business there." [3]

The lady, as *her* little contribution to this *pic-nic* portrait,
insisted on his beautiful black hair, which lay in masses of
natural curls half - way down his back.   Among all his

---

[1] Wordsworth's lines (in his *Stanzas written in my Pocket-Copy of
Thomson's Castle of Indolence*) are :—

> " Ah ! piteous sight it was to see this Man
> When he came back to us, a withered flower."—M.

[2] Quoted more correctly, the lines are—

> "Noisy he was, and, gamesome as a boy,
> His limbs would toss about him with delight."—M.

[3] More correctly—

> " Profound his forehead was, though not severe ;
> Yet some did think that he had little business here."—M.

foibles, however, it ought to be mentioned that vanity connected with personal advantages was never one : he had been thoroughly laughed out of *that* by his long experience of life at a great public school. But that which he himself utterly ignored female eyes bore witness to ; and the lady of Bristol assured me that in the entire course of her life she had not seen a young man so engaging by his exterior. He was then a very resurrection of the old knight's son in Chaucer, of him that had jousted with infidels

"And ridden in Bélmărie."

I should add that, whereas throughout his thirty-five years of opium he was rather corpulent,—not at any period *emaciated*, as those who write romances about opium fancy to be its effect,—in 1796, when he had nearly accomplished his twenty - sixth year, he was slender in the degree most approved by ladies.

Such was Samuel Taylor Coleridge in 1796. Ask for him ten years later, and the vision had melted into air !

CHARLES LAMB[1]

It sounds paradoxical, but is not so in a bad sense, to say that in every literature of large compass some authors will be found to rest much of the interest which surrounds them on their essential *non*-popularity. They are good for the very reason that they are not in conformity to the current taste. They interest because to the world they are *not* interesting. They attract by means of their repulsion. Not as though it could separately furnish a reason for loving a book that the majority of men had found it repulsive. *Prima facie*, it must suggest some presumption *against* a book that it has failed to gain public attention. To have roused hostility, indeed, to have kindled a feud against its own principles or its temper, may happen to be a good sign. *That* argues power. Hatred may be promising. The deepest revolutions of mind sometimes begin in hatred. But simply to have left a reader unimpressed is in itself a neutral result, from which the inference is doubtful. Yet even *that*, even simple failure to impress, may happen at times to be a result from positive powers in a writer, from special originalities, such as rarely reflect themselves in the mirror of the ordinary understanding. It seems little to be perceived how much the great scriptural[2] idea of the *worldly*

[1] Appeared in the *North British Review* for November 1848,—the book reviewed being *Final Memorials of Charles Lamb*, by Thomas Noon Talfourd, 2 vols., London, 1848. Reprinted by De Quincey in 1858 in the ninth volume of his collected writings. — M.

[2] "*Scriptural*" we call it, because this element of thought, so indispensable to a profound philosophy of morals, is not simply *more* used in Scripture than elsewhere, but is so exclusively significant or

and the *unworldly* is found to emerge in literature as well as in life. In reality, the very same combinations of moral qualities, infinitely varied, which compose the harsh physiognomy of what we call worldliness in the living groups of life, must unavoidably present themselves in books. A library divides into sections of worldly and unworldly, even as a crowd of men divides into that same majority and minority. The world has an instinct for recognising its own, and recoils from certain qualities when exemplified in books, with the same disgust or defective sympathy as would have governed it in real life. From qualities, for instance, of childlike simplicity, of shy profundity, or of inspired self-communion, the world does and must turn away its face towards grosser, · bolder, more determined, or more intelligible expressions of character and intellect ; and not otherwise in literature, nor at all less in literature, than it does in the realities of life.

Charles Lamb, if any ever *was*, is amongst the class here contemplated ; he, if any ever *has*, ranks amongst writers whose works are destined to be for ever unpopular, and yet for ever interesting ; interesting, moreover, by means of those very qualities which guarantee their non-popularity. The same qualities which will be found forbidding to the world and the thoughtless, which will be found insipid to many even amongst robust and powerful minds, are exactly those which will continue to command a select audience in every generation. The prose essays, under the signature of *Elia*, form the most delightful section amongst Lamb's works. They traverse a peculiar field of observation, sequestered from general interest ; and they are composed in a spirit too delicate and unobtrusive to catch the ear of the noisy crowd, clamouring for strong sensations. But this retiring delicacy itself, the pensiveness chequered by gleams of the fanciful, and the humour that is touched with cross lights of pathos, together with the picturesque quaintness of the objects casually described, whether men, or things, or usages, and, in the rear of all this, the constant recurrence

intelligible amidst the correlative ideas of Scripture as to be absolutely insusceptible of translation into classical Greek or classical Latin.

to ancient recollections and to decaying forms of household
life, as things retiring before the tumult of new and revolutionary generations,—these traits in combination communicate to the papers a grace and strength of originality which
nothing in any literature approaches, whether for degree or
kind of excellence, except the most felicitous papers of
Addison, such as those on Sir Roger de Coverley, and some
others in the same vein of composition.   They resemble
Addison's papers also in the diction ; which is natural and
idiomatic, even to carelessness.   They are equally faithful
to the truth of nature ; and in this only they differ remarkably—that the sketches of Elia reflect the stamp and impress
of the writer's own character, whereas in all those of Addison
the personal peculiarities of the delineator (though known to
the reader from the beginning through the account of the
club) are nearly quiescent.   Now and then they are recalled
into a momentary notice, but they do not act, or at all
modify his pictures of Sir Roger or Will Wimble.   *They*
are slightly and amiably eccentric ; but the Spectator himself, in describing them, takes the station of an ordinary
observer.

Everywhere, indeed, in the writings of Lamb, and not
merely in his *Elia*, the character of the writer co-operates
in an under-current to the effect of the thing written.   To
understand, in the fullest sense, either the gaiety or the tenderness of a particular passage, you must have some insight
into the particular bias of the writer's mind, whether native
and original, or impressed gradually by the accidents of
situation ; whether simply developed out of predispositions
by the action of life, or violently scorched into the constitution by some fierce fever of calamity.   There is in
modern literature a whole class of writers, though not a
large one, standing within the same category : some marked
originality of character in the writer becomes a co-efficient
with what he says to a common result ;   you must sympathise
with this *personality* in the author before you can appreciate
the most significant parts of his views.   In most books the
writer figures as a mere abstraction, without sex or age or
local station, whom the reader banishes from his thoughts.
What is written seems to proceed from a blank intellect, not

from a man clothed with fleshly peculiarities and differences. These peculiarities and differences neither do, nor (generally speaking) *could* intermingle with the texture of the thoughts, so as to modify their force or their direction. In such books, —and they form the vast majority,—there is nothing to be found or to be looked for beyond the direct objective. (*Sit venia verbo !*) But, in a small section of books, the objective in the thought becomes confluent with the subjective in the thinker—the two forces unite for a joint product ; and, fully to enjoy the product, or fully to apprehend either element, both must be known. It is singular, and worth inquiring into, for the reason that the Greek and Roman literature had no such books. Timon of Athens, or Diogenes, one may conceive qualified for this mode of authorship, had journalism existed to rouse them in those days ; their "articles" would no doubt have been fearfully caustic. But, as *they* failed to produce anything, and Lucian in an after age is scarcely characteristic enough for the purpose, perhaps we may pronounce Rabelais and Montaigne the earliest of writers in the class described. In the century following *theirs* came Sir Thomas Browne, and immediately after *him* La Fontaine. Then came Swift, Sterne, with others less distinguished : in Germany, Hippel, the friend of Kant, Harmann the obscure, and the greatest of the whole body—John Paul Fr. Richter. In *him*, from the strength and determinateness of his nature, as well as from the great extent of his writing, the philosophy of this interaction between the author as a human agency and his theme as an intellectual re-agency might best be studied. From *him* might be derived the largest number of cases illustrating boldly this absorption of the universal into the concrete—of the pure intellect into the human nature of the author. But nowhere could illustrations be found more interesting — shy, delicate, evanescent — shy as lightning, delicate and evanescent as the coloured pencillings on a frosty night from the northern lights,—than in the better parts of Lamb.

To appreciate Lamb, therefore, it is requisite that his character and temperament should be understood in their coyest and most wayward features. A capital defect it would be if these could not be gathered silently from Lamb's works themselves. It would be a fatal mode of dependency upon an alien and separable accident if they needed an external commentary. But they do *not*. The syllables lurk up and down the writings of Lamb which decipher his eccentric nature. His character lies there dispersed in anagram ; and to any attentive reader the regathering and restoration of the total word from its scattered parts is inevitable without an effort. Still it is always a satisfaction, in knowing a result, to know also its *why* and *how ;* and in so far as every character is likely to be modified by the particular experience, sad or joyous, through which the life has travelled, it is a good contribution towards the know-ledge of that resulting character as a whole to have a sketch of that particular experience. What trials did it impose ? What energies did it task ? What temptations did it unfold ? These calls upon the moral powers, which in music so stormy many a life is doomed to hear, how were they faced ? The character in a capital degree moulds oftentimes the life, but the life *always* in a subordinate degree moulds the character. And, the character being in this case of Lamb so much of a key to the writings, it becomes important that the life should be traced, however briefly, as a key to the character.

That is *one* reason for detaining the reader with some slight record of Lamb's career. Such a record by preference and of right belongs to a case where the intellectual display, which is the sole ground of any public interest at all in the man, has been intensely modified by the *humanities* and moral *personalities* distinguishing the subject. We read a Physiology, and need no information as to the life and conversation of its author ; a meditative poem becomes far better understood by the light of such information ; but a work of genial and at the same time eccentric sentiment, wandering upon untrodden paths, is barely intelligible with-out it. There is a good reason for arresting judgment on the writer, that the court may receive evidence on the life of the man. But there is another reason, and, in any other place, a better ; which reason lies in the extraordinary value of the life considered separately for itself. Logically, it is not allowable to say that *here ;* and, considering the principal purpose of this paper, any possible *independent* value of the life must rank as a better reason for reporting it,—since, in a case where the original object is professedly to estimate the writings of a man, whatever promises to further that object must, merely by that tendency, have, in relation to that place, a momentary advantage which it would lose if valued upon a more abstract scale. Liberated from this casual office of throwing light upon a book—raised to its grander station of a solemn deposition to the moral capacities of man in conflict with calamity—viewed as a return made into the chanceries of heaven upon an issue directed from that court to try the amount of power lodged in a poor desolate pair of human creatures for facing the very anarchy of storms—this obscure life of the two Lambs, brother and sister (for the two lives were one life), rises into a grandeur that is not paralleled once in a generation.

Rich, indeed, in moral instruction was the life of Charles Lamb; and perhaps in one chief result it offers to the thoughtful observer a lesson of consolation that is awful, and of hope that ought to be immortal, viz. in the record which it furnishes that by meekness of submission, and by earnest conflict with evil in the spirit of cheerfulness, it is possible ultimately to disarm or to blunt the very heaviest of curses—even the curse of lunacy. Had it been whispered, in hours of infancy, to Lamb, by the angel who stood by his cradle—" Thou, and the sister that walks by ten years before thee, shall be through life, each to each, the solitary fountain of comfort ; and, except it be from this fountain of mutual love, except it be as brother and sister, ye shall not taste the cup of peace on earth ! "—here, if there was sorrow in reversion, there was also consolation.

But what funeral swamps would have instantly ingulfed this consolation, had some meddling fiend prolonged the revelation, and, holding up the curtain from the sad future a little longer, had said scornfully — " Peace on earth ! Peace for you two, Charles and Mary Lamb ! What peace is possible under the curse which even now is gathering against your heads ? Is there peace on earth for the lunatic —peace for the parenticide—peace for the girl that, without warning, and without time granted for a penitential cry to Heaven, sends her mother to the last audit ? " And then, without treachery, speaking bare truth, this prophet of woe might have added—" Thou also, thyself, Charles Lamb, thou in thy proper person, shalt enter the skirts of this dreadful hail-storm ; even thou shalt taste the secrets of lunacy, and enter as a captive its house of bondage [1] ; whilst over thy sister the accursed scorpion shall hang suspended through life, like Death hanging over the beds of hospitals, striking at times, but more often threatening to strike ; or withdrawing its instant menaces only to lay bare her mind more bitterly to the persecutions of a haunted memory ! " Considering the nature of the calamity, in the first place ; considering, in the second place, its life-long duration ; and, in the last place, considering the quality of the resistance by which it was met, and under what circumstances of humble resources in money or friends : we have come to the deliberate judgment that the whole range of history scarcely presents a more affecting spectacle of perpetual sorrow, humiliation, or conflict, and that was supported to the end (that is, through forty years) with more resignation, or with more absolute victory.

Charles Lamb was born in February of the year 1775. His immediate descent was humble ; for his father, though on one particular occasion civilly described as a " scrivener," was in reality a domestic servant to Mr. Salt—a bencher (and, therefore, a barrister of some standing) in the Inner Temple. John Lamb, the father, belonged by birth to Lincoln ; from which city, being transferred to London whilst yet a boy, he entered the service of Mr. Salt without delay, and apparently from this period, throughout his life, continued in this good man's household to support the honourable relation of a Roman client to his *patronus*, much more than that of a mercenary servant to a transient and capricious master. The terms on which Mr. S. seems to have lived with the family of the Lambs argue a kindness and a liberality of nature on both sides. John Lamb recommended himself as an attendant by the versatility of his accomplishments ; and Mr. Salt, being a widower without children,—which means, in effect, an old bachelor,—naturally valued

[1] Lamb was himself confined for six weeks at one period of his life in a lunatic asylum.

that encyclopædic range of dexterity which made his house independent of external aid for every mode of service. To kill one's own mutton is but an operose way of arriving at a dinner, and often a more costly way; whereas to combine one's own carpenter, locksmith, hairdresser, groom, &c., all in one man's person—to have a Robinson Crusoe, up to all emergencies of life, always in waiting—is a luxury of the highest class for one who values his ease.

A consultation is held more freely with a man familiar to one's eye, and more profitably with a man aware of one's peculiar habits. And another advantage from such an arrangement is, that one gets any little alteration or repair executed on the spot. To hear is to obey, and by an inversion of Pope's rule—

"One always *is*, and never *to be*, blest."

People of one sole accomplishment, like the *homo unius libri*, are usually within that narrow circle disagreeably perfect, and, therefore, apt to be arrogant. People who can do all things usually do every one of them ill ; and, living in a constant effort to deny this too palpable fact, they become irritably vain. But Mr. Lamb the elder seems to have been bent on perfection. He did all things ; he did them all well ; and yet was neither gloomily arrogant, nor testily vain. And, being conscious apparently that all mechanic excellencies tend to illiberal results, unless counteracted by perpetual sacrifices to the graces, he went so far as to cultivate poetry ; he even printed his poems ; and, were we possessed of a copy (which we are *not*, nor probably is the Vatican), it would give us pleasure at this point to digress for a moment, and to cut them up, purely on considerations of respect to the author's memory. It is hardly to be supposed that they did not really merit castigation ; and we should best show the sincerity of our respect for Mr. Lamb senior, in all those cases where we *could* conscientiously profess respect, by an unlimited application of the knout in the cases where we could *not*.

The whole family of the Lambs seems to have won from Mr. Salt the consideration which is granted to humble friends, and from acquaintances nearer to their own standing to have won a tenderness of esteem such as is granted to decayed gentry. Yet, naturally, the social rank of the parents, as people still living, must have operated disadvantageously for the children. It is hard, even for the practised philosopher, to distinguish aristocratic graces of manner, and capacities of delicate feeling, in people whose very hearth and dress bear witness to the servile humility of their station. Yet such distinctions, as wild gifts of nature, timidly and half unconsciously asserted themselves in the unpretending Lambs. Already in *their* favour there existed a silent privilege analogous to the famous one of Lord Kinsale.[1] He, by special grant from the crown, is allowed, when standing before the king, to forget that he is not himself a king : the bearer of that peerage, through all generations, has the privilege of wearing his hat in the royal presence. By a general though tacit concession of the same nature, the rising generation of the Lambs, John and Charles, the two sons, and Mary Lamb, the only daughter, were permitted to forget that their grandmother had been a housekeeper for sixty years, and that their father had worn a livery. Charles Lamb, individually, was so entirely humble, and so careless of social distinctions, that he has taken pleasure in recurring to these very facts in the family records amongst the most genial of his Elia recollections. He only continued to remember, without shame, and with a peculiar tenderness, these badges of plebeian rank, when everybody else, amongst the few survivors that could have known of their existence, had long dismissed them from their thoughts.

Probably through Mr. Salt's interest it was that Charles Lamb, in the autumn of 1782, when he wanted something more than four months of completing his eighth year, received a presentation to the magnificent school of Christ's Hospital. The late Dr. Arnold, when contrasting the school of his own boyish experience, Winchester, with Rugby, the school confided to his management, found nothing so much to regret in the circumstances of the latter as its forlorn condition with

---

[1] Whom, by the way, a modern Peerage tells us that, strictly speaking (or rather strictly spelling), we ought to call *Kingsale*. Very possibly. But, if so, we have been wrong throughout our whole erroneous life ; and it is too late now to correct our spelling.

respect to historical traditions. Wherever these were wanting, it occurred to Dr. Arnold that something of a compensatory effect for impressing the imagination might be obtained
by connecting every important school with the nation through
the link of annual prizes issuing from the Exchequer. An
official basis of national patronage might prove a substitute
for an antiquarian or ancestral basis. Happily for the great
educational foundations of London, none of them is in the
naked condition of Rugby. Westminster, St. Paul's, Mer-
chant Tailors', the Charter-house, &c., are all crowned with
historical recollections ; and Christ's Hospital, besides the
original honours of its foundation, so fitted to a consecrated
place in a youthful imagination—an asylum for boy-students,
provided by a boy-king (Edward VI)—a king innocent, religious, prematurely wise, and prematurely called away from
earth—has also a mode of perpetual connexion with the
state. It enjoys, therefore, *both* of Dr. Arnold's advantages.
Indeed, all the great foundation schools of London, bearing
in their very codes of organisation the impress of a double
function—viz. the conservation of sound learning and of pure
religion—wear something of a monastic or cloistral character
in their aspect and usages, which is peculiarly impressive,
and even pathetic, amidst the uproars of a capital the most
colossal and tumultuous upon earth.

Here Lamb remained until his fifteenth year ; which year
threw him on the world, and brought him alongside the
golden dawn of the French Revolution. Here he learned a
little elementary Greek, and of Latin more than a little ; for
his Latin notes to Mr. Cary (of Dante celebrity), though brief,
are sufficient to reveal a true sense of what is graceful and
idiomatic in Latinity. *We* say this, who have studied that
subject more than most men. It is not that Lamb would
have found it an easy task to compose a long paper in Latin
—nobody *can* find it easy to do what he has no motive for
habitually practising ; but a single sentence of Latin wearing
the secret countersign of the " sweet Roman hand " ascertains
sufficiently that, in reading Latin classics, a man feels and
comprehends their peculiar force or beauty. That is enough.
It is requisite to a man's expansion of mind that he should
make acquaintance with a literature so radically differing from

all modern literature as is the Latin. It is *not* requisite that he should practise Latin composition. Here, therefore, Lamb obtained in sufficient perfection one priceless accomplishment, which even singly throws a graceful air of liberality over all the rest of a man's attainments : having rarely any pecuniary value, it challenges the more attention to its intellectual value. Here also Lamb commenced the friendships of his life ; and of all which he formed he lost none. Here it was, as the consummation and crown of his advantages from the time-honoured hospital, that he came to know " Poor S. T. C."[1] τὸν θαυμάσιωτατον.

Until 1796, it is probable that he lost sight of Coleridge, who was then occupied with Cambridge, having been transferred thither as a privileged "Grecian" from Christ's Hospital. That year, 1796, was a year of change and fearful calamity for Charles Lamb. On that year revolved the wheels of his after life. During the three years succeeding to his school days, he had held a clerkship in the South Sea House. In 1795, he was transferred to the India House. As a junior clerk, he could not receive more than a slender salary ; but even this was important to the support of his parents and sister. They lived together in lodgings near Holborn ; and in the spring of 1796 Miss Lamb (having previously shown signs of lunacy at intervals), in a sudden paroxysm of her disease, seized a knife from the dinner table, and stabbed her mother, who died upon the spot. A coroner's inquest easily ascertained the nature of a case which was transparent in all its circumstances, and never for a moment indecisive as regarded the medical symptoms. The poor young lady was transferred to the establishment for lunatics at Hoxton. She soon recovered, we believe ; but her relapses were as sudden as her recoveries, and she continued through life to revisit, for periods of uncertain seclusion, that house of woe. This calamity of his fireside, followed soon after by the death of his father, who had for some time been in a state of imbecility, determined the future destiny of Lamb.

---

[1] "*Poor S. T. C.*" :—The affecting expression by which Coleridge indicates himself in the few lines written during his last illness for an inscription upon his own grave ; lines ill constructed in point of diction and compression, but otherwise speaking from the depths of his heart.

Apprehending, with the perfect grief of perfect love, that his sister's fate was sealed for life—viewing her as his own greatest benefactress, which she really *had* been through her advantage by ten years of age—yielding with impassioned readiness to the depth of his fraternal affection what at any rate he would have yielded to the sanctities of duty as interpreted by his own conscience—he resolved for ever to resign all thoughts of marriage with a young lady whom he loved, for ever to abandon all ambitious prospects that might have tempted him into uncertainties, humbly to content himself with the *certainties* of his Indian clerkship, to dedicate himself for the future to the care of his desolate and prostrate sister, and to leave the rest to God. These sacrifices he made in no hurry or tumult, but deliberately, and in religious tranquillity. These sacrifices were accepted in heaven ; and even on this earth they *had* their reward. She, for whom he gave up all, in turn gave up all for *him*. She devoted herself to his comfort. Many times she returned to the lunatic establishment, but many times she was restored to illuminate the household hearth for *him ;* and, of the happiness which for forty years and more he had, no hour seemed true that was not derived from *her*. Henceforward, therefore, until he was emancipated by the noble generosity of the East India Directors, Lamb's time, for nine-and-twenty years, was given to the India House.

" *O fortunati nimium, sua si bona nôrint,*" is applicable to more people than " *agricolæ.*" Clerks of the India House are as blind to their own advantages as the blindest of ploughmen. Lamb was summoned, it is true, through the larger and more genial section of his life, to the drudgery of a copying clerk—making confidential entries into mighty folios, on the subject of calicoes and muslins. By this means, whether he would or not, he became gradually the author of a great "serial " work, in a frightful number of volumes, on as dry a department of literature as the children of the great desert could have suggested. Nobody, he must have felt, was ever likely to study this great work of his, not even Dr. Dryasdust. He had written in vain ; which is not pleasant to know. There would be no second edition called for by a discerning public in Leadenhall Street ; not a chance of *that*.

And consequently the *opera omnia* of Lamb, drawn up in a
hideous battalion, at the cost of labour so enormous, would
be known only to certain families of spiders in one generation, and of rats in the next.   Such a labour of Sisyphus,—
the rolling up a ponderous stone to the summit of a hill only
that it might roll back again by the gravitation of its own
dulness,—seems a bad employment for a man of genius in his
meridian energies.   And yet, perhaps not.   Perhaps the collective wisdom of Europe could not have devised for Lamb a
more favourable condition of toil than this very India House
clerkship.   His works (his Leadenhall Street works) were
certainly not read ; popular they *could* not be, for they were
not read by anybody ; but then, to balance *that*, they were
not reviewed.   His folios were of that order which (in
Cowper's words) " not even critics criticise."   Is *that* nothing ?   Is it no happiness to escape the hands of merciless
reviewers ?   Many of us escape being *read ;* the worshipful
reviewer does not find time to read a line of us ; but we do
not for that reason escape being criticised, " shown up," and
martyred.   The list of *errata,* again, committed by Lamb
was probably of a magnitude to alarm any possible compositor ; and yet these *errata* will never be known to mankind.   They are dead and buried.   They have been cut off
prematurely, and, for any effect upon their generation, might
as well never have existed.   Then the returns, in a pecuniary
sense, from these folios—how important were *they !*   It is
not common, certainly, to write folios ; but neither is it
common to draw a steady income of from £300 to £400 per
annum from volumes of any size.   This will be admitted ;
but would it not have been better to draw the income without the toil ?   Doubtless it would always be more agreeable
to have the rose without the thorn.   But in the case before
us, taken with all its circumstances, we deny that the toil is
truly typified as a thorn ; so far from being a thorn in
Lamb's daily life, on the contrary, it was a second rose in-
grafted upon the original rose of the income, that he had to
earn it by a moderate but continued exertion.   Holidays, in
a national establishment so great as the India House, and in
our too fervid period, naturally could not be frequent; yet
all great English corporations are gracious masters, and in-

dulgences of this nature could be obtained on a special application. Not to count upon these accidents of favour, we find that the regular toil of those in Lamb's situation began at ten in the morning, and ended as the clock struck four in the afternoon. Six hours composed the daily contribution of labour,—that is, precisely one-fourth part of the total day. But, as Sunday was exempted, the rigorous expression of the quota was one-fourth of six-sevenths, which makes only six twenty-eighths and not six twenty-fourths of the total time. Less toil than this would hardly have availed to deepen the sense of value in that large part of the time still remaining disposable. Had there been any resumption whatever of labour in the evening, though but for half an hour, that one encroachment upon the broad continuous area of the eighteen free hours would have killed the tranquillity of the whole day, by *sowing* it (so to speak) with intermitting anxieties— anxieties that, like tides, would still be rising and falling. Whereas now, at the early hour of four, when daylight is yet lingering in the air, even at the dead of winter, in the latitude of London, and when the *enjoying* section of the day is barely commencing, everything is left which a man would care to retain. A mere *dilettante* or amateur student, having no mercenary interest concerned, would, upon a refinement of luxury—would, upon choice—give up so much time to study, were it only to sharpen the value of what remained for pleasure. And thus the only difference between the scheme of the India House distributing his time for Lamb, and the scheme of a wise voluptuary distributing his time for himself, lay, not in the *amount* of time deducted from enjoyment, but in the particular mode of appropriating that deduction. An *intellectual* appropriation of the time, though casually fatiguing, must have pleasures of its own ; pleasures denied to a task so mechanic and so monotonous as that of reiterating endless records of sales or consignments not *essentially* varying from each other. True, it is pleasanter to pursue an intellectual study than to make entries in a ledger. But even an intellectual toil is toil ; few people can support it for more than six hours in a day. And the only question, therefore, after all, is, at what period of the day a man would prefer taking this pleasure of study. Now, upon that point, as regards the case of Lamb, there is no opening for doubt. He, amongst his *Popular Fallacies*, humorously illustrates the necessity of evening and artificial lights to the prosperity of studies. After exposing, with the perfection of fun, the savage un-sociality of those elder ancestors who lived (if life it was) before lamp-light was invented,—showing that "jokes came in with candles," since "what repartees *could* have passed" when people were "grumbling at one another in the dark," and "when you must have felt about for a smile, and handled a neighbour's cheek to be sure that he understood it ?"—he goes on to say, "This accounts for the seriousness of the elder poetry," viz. because they had no candle-light. Even eating he objects to as a very imperfect thing in the dark ; you are not convinced that a dish tastes as it should do by the promise of its name, if you dine in the twilight without candles. Seeing is believing. "The senses absolutely give and take reciprocally." The sight guarantees the taste. For instance, "Can you tell pork from veal in the dark, or distinguish Sherries from pure Malaga ?" To all enjoyments whatso-ever candles are indispensable as an adjunct ; but, as to *reading*, "there is," says Lamb, "absolutely no such thing "but by a candle. We have tried the affectation of a book "at noon-day in gardens, but it was labour thrown away. "It is a mockery, all that is reported of the influential "Phœbus. No true poem ever owed its birth to the sun's "light. The mild internal light, that reveals the fine "shapings of poetry, like fires on the domestic hearth, goes "out in the sunshine. Milton's morning hymn in Paradise, "we would hold a good wager, was penned at midnight ; "and Taylor's rich description of a sunrise smells decidedly "of the taper." This view of evening and candle-light, as involved in the full delight of literature, may seem no more than a pleasant extravaganza ; and no doubt it is in the nature of such gaieties to travel a little into exaggeration ; but substantially it is certain that Lamb's sincere feelings pointed habitually in the direction here indicated. His literary studies, whether taking the colour of tasks or diver-sions, courted the aid of evening, which, by means of physical weariness, produces a more luxurious state of repose than be-longs to the labour hours of day ; they courted the aid of

lamp-light, which, as Lord Bacon remarked, gives a gorgeous-
ness to human pomps and pleasures, such as would be vainly
sought from the homeliness of day-light. The hours, therefore, which were withdrawn from his own control by the
India House happened to be exactly that part of the day which
Lamb least valued, and could least have turned to account.
The account given of Lamb's friends,—of those whom he
endeavoured to love because he admired them, or to esteem
intellectually because he loved them personally,—is too much
coloured for general acquiescence by Sergeant (since Mr. Justice) Talfourd's own early prepossessions. It is natural that
an intellectual man like the Sergeant, personally made
known in youth to people whom from childhood he had
regarded as powers in the ideal world, and in some instances
as representing the eternities of human speculation, since
their names had perhaps dawned upon his mind in concur-
rence with the very earliest suggestion of topics which they
had treated, should overrate their intrinsic grandeur. Hazlitt
accordingly is styled " the great thinker." But, had he even
been such potentially, there was an absolute bar to his
achievement of that station in act and consummation. No
man *can* be a great thinker in our days upon large and
elaborate questions without being also a great student. To
think profoundly, it is indispensable that a man should have
read down to his own starting-point, and have read as a
collating student to the particular stage at which he himself
takes up the subject. At this moment, for instance, how
could Geology be treated otherwise than childishly by one
who should rely upon the encyclopædias of 1800 ? or Comparative Physiology by the most ingenious of men unacquainted with Marshall Hall, and with the apocalyptic
glimpses of secrets unfolding under the hands of Professor
Owen ? In such a condition of undisciplined thinking, the
ablest man thinks to no purpose. He lingers upon parts of
the inquiry that have lost the importance which once they
had under imperfect charts of the subject ; he wastes his
strength upon problems that have become obsolete ; he loses
his way in paths that are not in the line of direction upon
which the improved speculation is moving ; or he gives
narrow conjectural solutions of difficulties that have long

since received sure and comprehensive ones. It is as if a
man should in these days attempt to colonize, and yet,
through inertia or through ignorance, should leave behind
him all modern resources of chemistry, of chemical agricul-
ture, or of steam-power. Hazlitt had read nothing. Unacquainted with Grecian philosophy, with Scholastic philosophy,
and with the recomposition of these philosophies in the
looms of Germany during the last seventy and odd years,
trusting merely to the untrained instincts of keen mother-
wit—whence should Hazlitt have had the materials for great
thinking? It is through the collation of many abortive
voyages to polar regions that a man gains his first chance of
entering the polar basin, or of running ahead on the true
line of approach to it. The very reason for Hazlitt's defect
in cloquence as a lecturer is sufficient also as a reason why
he could not have been a comprehensive thinker. "He
was not eloquent," says the Sergeant, "in the true sense of
the term." But why? Because it seems "his thoughts
were too weighty to be moved along by the shallow stream
of feeling which an evening's excitement can rouse,"—an
explanation which leaves us in doubt whether Hazlitt forfeited his chance of eloquence by accommodating himself to
this evening's excitement, or by gloomily resisting it. Our
own explanation is different. Hazlitt was not eloquent,
because he was discontinuous. No man can be eloquent
whose thoughts are abrupt, insulated, capricious, and (to
borrow an impressive word from Coleridge) non-sequacious.
Eloquence resides not in separate or fractional ideas, but in
the relations of manifold ideas, and in the mode of their
evolution from each other. It is not indeed enough that the
ideas should be many, and their relations coherent; the
main condition lies in the *key* of the evolution, in the *law* of
the succession. The elements are nothing without the
atmosphere that moulds, and the dynamic forces that combine. Now Hazlitt's brilliancy is seen chiefly in separate
splinterings of phrase or image which throw upon the eye a
vitreous scintillation for a moment, but spread no deep
suffusions of colour, and distribute no masses of mighty
shadow. A flash, a solitary flash, and all is gone. Rhetoric,
according to its quality, stands in many degrees of relation

to the permanencies of truth ; and all rhetoric, like all flesh, is partly unreal, and the glory of both is fleeting. Even the mighty rhetoric of Sir Thomas Browne, or Jeremy Taylor, to whom only it has been granted to open the trumpet-stop on that great organ of passion, oftentimes leaves behind it the sense of sadness which belongs to beautiful apparitions starting out of darkness upon the morbid eye, only to be reclaimed by darkness in the instant of their birth, or which belongs to pageantries in the clouds. But, if all rhetoric is a mode of pyrotechny, and all pyrotechnics are by necessity fugitive, yet even in these frail pomps there are many degrees of frailty. Some fireworks require an hour's duration for the expansion of their glory ; others, as if formed from fulminating powder, expire in the very act of birth. Precisely on that scale of duration and of power stand the glitterings of rhetoric that are not worked into the texture, but washed on from the outside. Hazlitt's thoughts were of the same fractured and discontinuous order as his illustrative images — seldom or never self-diffusive ; and *that* is a sufficient argument that he had never cultivated philosophic thinking.

Not, however, to conceal any part of the truth, we are bound to acknowledge that Lamb thought otherwise on this point, manifesting what seemed to us an extravagant admiration of Hazlitt, and perhaps even in part for that very glitter which we are denouncing—at least he did so in conversation with ourselves. But, on the other hand, as this conversation travelled a little into the tone of a disputation, and *our* frost on this point might seem to justify some undue fervour by way of balance, it is very possible that Lamb did not speak his absolute and most dispassionate judgment. And yet again, if he *did*, may we, with all reverence for Lamb's exquisite genius, have permission to say that his own constitution of intellect sinned by this very habit of discontinuity. It was a habit of mind not unlikely to be cherished by his habits of life. Amongst these habits was the excess of his social kindness. He scorned so much to deny his company and his redundant hospitality to any man who manifested a wish for either by calling upon him, that he almost seemed to think it a criminality in himself if, by

accident, he really *was* from home on your visit, rather than
by possibility a negligence in you, that had not forewarned
him of your intention. What was the consequence? All his
life, from this and other causes, he must have read in the
spirit of one liable to sudden interruption ; like a dragoon,
in fact, reading with one foot in the stirrup, when expecting
momentarily a summons to mount for action. In such situations, reading by snatches, and by intervals of precarious
leisure, people form inevitably the habit of seeking and
unduly valuing condensations of the meaning, where in
reality the truth suffers by this short-hand exhibition ; or
else they demand too vivid illustrations of the meaning.
Lord Chesterfield, so brilliant a man by nature, already
therefore making a morbid estimate of brilliancy, and so
hurried throughout his life as a public man, read under this
double coercion for craving instantaneous effects. At one
period, his only time for reading was in the morning, whilst
under the hands of his hairdresser,—who, in that age, or even
thirty years later, was an artist that, more even than a tailor,
ministered to respectability. Compelled to take the hastiest
of flying shots at his author, naturally Lord Chesterfield
demanded a very conspicuous mark to fire at. But the
author could not, in so brief a space, be always sure to crowd
any very prominent objects on the eye, unless by being
audaciously oracular and peremptory as regarded the sentiment, or flashy in excess as regarded its expression. " Come
now, my friend," was Lord Chesterfield's morning adjuration
to his author ; " come now, cut it short—don't prose—don't
hum and haw." The author had doubtless no ambition to
enter his name on the honourable and ancient roll of gentlemen - prosers ; probably he conceived himself not at all
tainted with the asthmatic infirmity of humming and haw-
ing ; but, as to "cutting it short," how could he be sure of
meeting his lordship's expectations in that point, unless by
dismissing all the limitations that might be requisite to fit
the idea for use, or the adjuncts that might be requisite to
integrate its truth, or the final consequences that might involve some deep *arrière pensée?* To be lawfully and usefully
brilliant, after this rapid fashion, a man must come forward
as a refresher of old truths, where *his* suppressions are sup-

plied by the reader's memory ; not as an expounder of new
truths, where oftentimes a dislocated fraction of the true is
not less dangerous than the false itself.

To read therefore habitually by hurried instalments has
this bad tendency—that it is likely to found a taste for
modes of composition too artificially irritating, and to disturb
the equilibrium of the judgment in relation to the colourings
of style. Lamb, however, whose constitution of mind was
even ideally sound in reference to the natural, the simple,
the genuine, might seem of all men least liable to a taint in
this direction. And undoubtedly he *was* so as regarded
those modes of beauty which nature had specially qualified
him for apprehending. Else, and in relation to other modes
of beauty, where his sense of the true, and of its distinction
from the spurious, had been an acquired sense, it is impossible
for us to hide from ourselves that, not through habits only,
not through stress of injurious accidents only, but by original
structure and temperament of mind, Lamb had a bias
towards those very defects on which rested the startling
characteristics of style which we have been noticing. He
himself, we fear, not bribed by indulgent feelings to another,
not moved by friendship, but by native tendency, shrank from
the continuous, from the sustained, from the elaborate.

The elaborate, indeed, without which much truth and
beauty must perish in germ, was by name the object of his
invectives. The instances are many, in his own beautiful
essays, where he literally collapses, literally sinks away from
openings suddenly offering themselves to flights of pathos or
solemnity in direct prosecution of his own theme. On any
such summons, where an ascending impulse and an untired
pinion were required, he *refuses* himself (to use military
language) invariably. The least observing reader of *Elia*
cannot have failed to notice that the most felicitous passages
always accomplish their circuit in a few sentences. The
gyration within which his sentiment wheels, no matter of
what kind it may be, is always the shortest possible. It
does not prolong itself—it does not repeat itself—it does not
propagate itself. But, in fact, other features in Lamb's mind
would have argued this feature by analogy, had we by accident
been left unaware of it directly. It is not by chance, or

without a deep ground in his nature, *common* to all his qualities, both affirmative and negative, that Lamb had an insensi-
bility to music more absolute than can have been often
shared by any human creature, or perhaps than was ever
before acknowledged so candidly. The sense of music—as a
pleasurable sense, or as any sense at all other than of certain
unmeaning and impertinent differences in respect to high
and low, sharp or flat—was utterly obliterated, as with a
sponge, by nature herself from Lamb's organization. It was
a corollary, from the same large *substratum* in his nature,
that Lamb had no sense of the rhythmical in prose composition. Rhythmus, or pomp of cadence, or sonorous ascent of
clauses, in the structure of sentences, were effects of art as
much thrown away upon *him* as the voice of the charmer
upon the deaf adder. We ourselves, occupying the very
station of polar opposition to that of Lamb,—being as mor-
bidly, perhaps, in the one excess as he in the other,—naturally
detected this omission in Lamb's nature at an early stage of
our acquaintance. Not the fabled Regulus, with his eyelids
torn away, and his uncurtained eyeballs exposed to the
noon-tide glare of a Carthaginian sun, could have shrieked
with more anguish of recoil from torture than we from certain sentences and periods in which Lamb perceived no fault
at all. *Pomp*, in our apprehension, was an idea of two categories : the *pompous* might be spurious, but it might also be
genuine. It is well to love the simple—*we* love it ; nor is
there any opposition at all between *that* and the very glory
of pomp. But, as we once put the case to Lamb, if, as a
musician, as the leader of a mighty orchestra, you had this
theme offered to you—" Belshazzar the King gave a great
feast to a thousand of his lords "—or this, " And, on a certain
day, Marcus Cicero stood up, and in a set speech rendered
solemn thanks to Caius Cæsar for Quintus Ligarius pardoned,
and for Marcus Marcellus restored "—surely no man would
deny that, in such a case, simplicity, though in a passive
sense not lawfully absent, must stand aside as totally insufficient for the *positive* part. Simplicity might guide even
here, but could not furnish the power ; a rudder it might be,
but not an oar or a sail. This Lamb was ready to allow ; as
an intellectual *quiddity*, he recognised pomp in the character

of a privileged thing ; he was obliged to do so ; for take
away from great ceremonial festivals, such as the solemn
rendering of thanks, the celebration of national anniversaries,
the commemoration of public benefactors, &c., the element of
pomp, and you take away their very meaning and life. But,
whilst allowing a place for it in the rubric of the logician, it
is certain that *sensuously* Lamb would not have sympathized
with it, nor have *felt* its justification in any concrete instance.
We find a difficulty in pursuing this subject without greatly
exceeding the just limits. We pause, therefore, and add
only this one suggestion as partly explanatory of the case.
Lamb had the dramatic intellect and taste, perhaps in perfection ; of the epic he had none at all. Here, as happens
sometimes to men of genius preternaturally endowed in one
direction, he might be considered as almost starved. A
favourite of nature, so eminent in some directions, by what
right could he complain that her bounties were not indiscriminate ? From this defect in his nature it arose that,
except by culture and by reflection, Lamb had no genial
appreciation of Milton. The solemn planetary wheelings of
the *Paradise Lost* were not to his taste. What he *did* com-
prehend were the motions like those of lightning, the fierce
angular coruscations of that wild agency which comes forward
so vividly in the sudden περιπέτεια, in the revolutionary
catastrophe, and in the tumultuous conflicts, through persons
or through situations, of the tragic drama.

There is another vice in Mr. Hazlitt's mode of composition,
viz. the habit of trite quotation, too common to have
challenged much notice, were it not for these reasons :—1st,
That Sergeant Talfourd speaks of it in equivocal terms, as
a fault perhaps, but as a " felicitous " fault, " trailing after
it a line of golden associations " ; 2dly, Because sometimes
it involves a dishonesty. On occasion of No. 1, we must
profess our belief that a more ample explanation from the
Sergeant would have left him in substantial harmony with
ourselves. We cannot conceive the author of *Ion*, and the
friend of Wordsworth, seriously to countenance that paralytic
" mouth-diarrhœa " (to borrow a phrase of Coleridge's)—that
fluxe de bouche (to borrow an earlier phrase of Archbishop
Huet's)—which places the reader at the mercy of a man's

tritest remembrances from his most school-boy reading. To
have the verbal memory infested with tags of verse and
"cues" of rhyme is in itself an infirmity as vulgar and as
morbid as the stable-boy's habit of whistling slang airs upon
the mere mechanical excitement of a bar or two whistled by
some other blockhead in some other stable. The very stage
has grown weary of ridiculing a folly that, having been long
since expelled from decent society, has taken refuge amongst
the most imbecile of authors. Was Mr. Hazlitt, then, of that
class ? No ; he was a man of splendid talents, and of
capacity for greater things than he ever attempted, though
without known pretensions of the philosophic kind ascribed
to him by the Sergeant. Meantime the reason for resisting
the example and practice of Hazlitt lies in this — that
essentially it is at war with sincerity, the foundation of all
good writing, to express one's own thoughts by another man's
words. This dilemma arises. The thought is, or it is not,
worthy of that emphasis which belongs to a metrical expression of it. If it is *not*, then we shall be guilty of a mere
folly in pushing into strong relief that which confessedly
cannot support it. If it *is*, then how incredible that a
thought strongly conceived, and bearing upon it the impress
of one's own individuality, should naturally, and without
dissimulation or falsehood, bend to another man's expression
of it ! Simply to back one's own view by a similar view derived from another may be useful ; a quotation that repeats
one's own sentiment, but in a varied form, has the grace
which belongs to the *idem in alio*, the same radical idea
expressed with a difference—similarity in dissimilarity ; but
to throw one's own thoughts, matter and form, through alien
organs so absolutely as to make another man one's interpreter
for evil and good, is either to confess a singular laxity of
thinking that can so flexibly adapt itself to any casual form
of words, or else to confess that sort of carelessness about the
expression which draws its real origin from a sense of indifference about the things to be expressed. Utterly at war
this distressing practice is with all simplicity and earnestness
of writing ; it argues a state of indolent ease inconsistent
with the pressure and coercion of strong fermenting thoughts
before we can be at leisure for idle or chance quotations.

But, lastly, in reference to No. 2, we must add that the practice is sometimes dishonest. It "trails after it a line of golden associations." Yes, and the burglar, who leaves an army-tailor's after a midnight visit, trails after him perhaps a long roll of gold bullion epaulettes which may look pretty by lamp-light. But *that*, in the present condition of moral philosophy amongst the police, is accounted robbery ; and to benefit too much by quotations is little less. At this moment we have in our eye a biographical work, at one time not without celebrity, which is one continued *cento* of splendid passages from other people. The natural effect from so much fine writing is that the reader rises with the impression of having been engaged upon a most eloquent work. Meantime the whole is a series of mosaics, a tessellation made up from borrowed fragments ; and, first when the reader's attention is expressly directed upon the fact, he becomes aware that the nominal author has contributed nothing more to the book than a few passages of transition or brief clauses of connexion.

In the year 1796 the main incident occurring of any importance for English Literature was the publication by Southey of an epic poem. This poem, the *Joan of Arc*, was the earliest work of much pretension amongst all that Southey wrote ; and by many degrees it was the worst. In the four great narrative poems of his later years there is a combination of two striking qualities, viz. a peculiar command over the *visually* splendid, connected with a deep-toned grandeur of moral pathos. Especially we find this union in the *Thalaba* and the *Roderick ;* but in the *Joan of Arc* we miss it. What splendour there is for the fancy and the eye belongs chiefly to the Vision, contributed by Coleridge; and this was subsequently withdrawn. The fault lay in Southey's political relations at that era ; his sympathy with the French Revolution in its earlier stages had been boundless ; in all respects it was a noble sympathy, fading only as the gorgeous colouring faded from the emblazonries of that awful event, drooping only when the promises of that golden dawn sickened under stationary eclipse. In 1796 Southey was yet under the tyranny of his own earliest fascination ; in *his* eyes the Revolution had suffered a momentary blight from refluxes of

panic ; but blight of some kind is incident to every harvest
on which human hopes are suspended. Bad auguries were
also ascending from the unchaining of martial instincts.
But that the Revolution, having ploughed its way through
unparalleled storms, was preparing to face other storms, did
but quicken the apprehensiveness of his love—did but
quicken the duty of giving utterance to this love. Hence
came the rapid composition of the poem, which cost less time
in writing than in printing. Hence, also, came the choice of
his heroine. What he needed in his central character was a
heart with a capacity for the wrath of Hebrew prophets
applied to ancient abuses, and for evangelic pity applied to
the sufferings of nations. This heart, with this double
capacity—where should he seek it ? A French heart it
must be, or how should it follow with its sympathies a
French movement ? *There* lay Southey's reason for adopting
the Maid of Orleans as the depositary of hopes and aspirations
on behalf of France as fervid as his own. In choosing this
heroine, so inadequately known at that time, Southey testified
at least his own nobility of feeling [1] ; but in executing his

[1] It is right to remind the reader of this, for a reason applying
forcibly to the present moment. Michelet has taxed Englishmen with
yielding to national animosities in the case of Joan, having no plea
whatever for that insinuation but the single one drawn from Shakspere's Henry VI. To this the answers are as follow :—First, That
Shakspere's share in that trilogy is not nicely ascertained ; not *so* nicely
as to warrant the founding upon it of any solemn accusation. Secondly,
That M. Michelet forgot (or, which is far worse, *not* forgetting it,
he dissembled) the fact that, in undertaking a series of dramas upon
the basis avowedly of national chronicles, and for the very purpose
of profiting by old traditionary recollections connected with ancestral glories, it was mere lunacy to recast the circumstances at the
bidding of antiquarian research, so as entirely to disturb these popular
traditions. Besides that, to Shakspere's age no such spirit of research had blossomed. Writing for the stage, a man would have
risked lapidation by uttering a whisper in that direction. And, even
if not, what sense could there have been in openly running counter to
the very motive that had originally prompted that particular choice of
chronicle plays ? Thirdly, If one Englishman had, in a memorable
situation, adopted the popular view of Joan's conduct (*popular* as
much in France as in England), on the other hand, fifty years before
M. Michelet was writing this flagrant injustice, another Englishman
(viz. Southey) had, in an epic poem, reversed this mis-judgment, and
invested the shepherd girl with a glory nowhere else accorded to her,

choice he and his friends overlooked two faults fatal to his purpose. One was this : sympathy with the French Revolution meant sympathy with the opening prospects of man—meant sympathy with the Pariah of every clime— with all that suffered social wrong, or saddened in hopeless bondage.

That was the movement at work in the French Revolution. But the movement of Joanna d'Arc took a different direction. In *her* day also, it is true, the human heart had yearned after the same vast enfranchisement for the children of labour as afterwards worked in the great vision of the French Revolution. In *her* days also, and shortly before them, the human hand had sought by bloody acts to realize this dream of the heart. And in her childhood Joanna had not been insensible to these premature motions upon a path too bloody and too dark to be safe. But this view of human misery had been utterly absorbed to *her* by the special misery then desolating France. The lilies of France had been trampled under foot by the conquering stranger. Within fifty years, in three pitched battles that resounded to the ends of the earth, the chivalry of France had been exterminated. Her oriflamme had been dragged through the dust. The eldest son of Baptism had been prostrated. The daughter of France had been surrendered on coercion as a bride to her English conqueror. The child of that marriage, a marriage so ignominious to the land, was King of France by the consent of Christendom ; that child's uncle domineered as regent of France ; and that child's armies were in military possession of the land. But were they undisputed masters ?

not even by Schiller. Fourthly, We are not entitled to view as an *attack* upon Joanna what, in the worst construction, is but an unex-amining adoption of the contemporary historical accounts. A poet or a dramatist is not responsible for the accuracy of chronicles. But that which *is* an attack upon Joan, being briefly the foulest and ob-scenest attempt ever made to stifle the grandeur of a great human struggle, — viz. the French burlesque poem of *La Pucelle*, — what memorable man was it that wrote *that ?* Was he a Frenchman, or was he not ? was his name Voltaire, Arouet de Voltaire, or was it not ? That M. Michelet should *pretend* to have forgotten this vilest of pasquinades is more shocking to the general sense of justice than any special untruth as to Shakspere *can* be to the particular nation-ality of an Englishman.

No ; and *there* precisely lay the sorrow of the time. Under a perfect conquest there would have been repose ; whereas the presence of the English armies did but furnish a plea, masking itself in patriotism, for gatherings everywhere of lawless marauders ; of soldiers that had deserted their banners, and of robbers by profession. This was the woe of France more even than the military dishonour. That dishonour had been palliated from the first by the genealogical pretensions of the English royal family to the French throne, and these pretensions were strengthened in the person of the present claimant. But the military desolation of France, this it was that woke the faith of Joanna in her heavenly mission of deliverance. It was the attitude of her prostrate country, crying night and day for purification from blood, and not from feudal oppression, that swallowed up the thoughts of the impassioned girl. But *that* was not the cry that uttered itself afterwards in the French Revolution. In Joanna's days, the first step towards rest for France was by expulsion of the foreigner. Independence of a foreign yoke, liberation as between people and people, was the one ransom to be paid for French honour and peace. *That* debt settled, there might come a time for thinking of civil liberties. But this time was not within the prospects of the poor shepherdess. The field, the area, of her sympathies never coincided with that of the revolutionary period. It followed, therefore, that Southey *could* not have raised Joanna (with her condition of feeling), by any management, into the interpreter of his own. *That* was the first error in his poem, and it was irremediable. The second was—and strangely enough this also escaped notice—that the heroine of Southey is made to close her career precisely at the point when its grandeur commences. She believed herself to have a mission for the deliverance of France ; and the great instrument which she was authorized to use towards this end was the king, Charles VII. Him she was to crown. With this coronation, her triumph, in the plain historical sense, ended. And *there* ends Southey's poem. But exactly at this point the grander stage of her mission commences, viz. the ransom which she, a solitary girl, paid in her own person for the national deliverance. The grander half of the story was thus sacrificed, as being irrelevant to Southey's political object; and yet, after all, the half which he retained did not at all symbolize that object. It is singular, indeed, to find a long poem, on an ancient subject, adapting itself hieroglyphically to a modern purpose; 2dly, to find it failing of this purpose; and, 3dly, if it had *not* failed, so planned that it could have succeeded only by a sacrifice of all that was grandest in the theme.

To these capital oversights Southey, Coleridge, and Lamb were all joint parties; the two first as concerned in the composition, the last as a frank though friendly reviewer of it in his private correspondence with Coleridge. It is, however, some palliation of these oversights, and a very singular fact in itself, that neither from English authorities nor from French, though the two nations were equally brought into close connexion with the career of that extraordinary girl, could any adequate view be obtained of her character and acts. The *official* records of her trial, apart from which nothing can be depended upon, were first in the course of publication from the Paris press during the currency of last [1] year. First in 1847, about four hundred and sixteen years after her ashes had been dispersed to the winds, could it be seen distinctly, through the clouds of fierce partisanships and national prejudices, what had been the frenzy of the persecution against her, and the utter desolation of her position; what had been the grandeur of her conscientious resistance.

Anxious that our readers should see Lamb from as many angles as possible, we have obtained from an old friend of his a memorial — slight, but such as the circumstances allowed—of an evening spent with Charles and Mary Lamb, in the winter of 1821-22. The record is of the most unambitious character; it pretends to nothing, as the reader will see, not so much as to a pun,—which it really required some singularity of luck to have missed from Charles Lamb, who often continued to fire puns, as minute guns, all through the evening. But, the more unpretending this record is, the more appropriate it becomes by that very fact to the memory of *him* who, amongst all authors, was the humblest and least pretending. We have often thought that the

[1] " *Last year* " :—This was written in 1848.

famous epitaph written for his own grave by Piron, the
cynical author of *La Métromanie*, might have come from
Lamb, were it not for one objection : Lamb's benign heart
would have recoiled from a sarcasm, however effective, inscribed upon a grave-stone ; or from a jest, however playful,
that tended to a vindictive sneer amongst his own farewell
words. We once translated this Piron epitaph into a kind
of rambling Drayton couplet ; and the only point needing
explanation is that, from the accident of scientific men,
Fellows of the Royal Society, being usually very solemn
men, with an extra chance, therefore, for being, or for
seeming, dull men in conversation, naturally it arose that
some wit among our great - grandfathers translated F.R.S.
into a short - hand expression for a Fellow Remarkably
Stupid ; to which version of the three letters our English
epitaph alludes. The French original of Piron is this :—

> "Ci git Piron ; qui ne fut rien ;
> Pas même académicien."

The bitter arrow of the second line was feathered to hit the
French Académie, who had declined to elect him a member.
The English version is this :—

> "Here lies Piron ; who was—nothing ; or, if *that* could be, was
> less :
> How!—nothing ? Yes, nothing ; not so much as F.R.S."

But now to our friend's memorandum [1] :—

October 6, 1848.

MY DEAR X.—You ask me for some memorial, however
trivial, of any dinner party, supper party, water party, no
matter what, that I can circumstantially recall to recollec-

---

[1] The memorandum, which begins here and extends to p. 254, and
which professes to be a letter from a friend, is, as the reader will at
once see, De Quincey's own. In an anonymous article to the *North
British Review* he could hardly announce that it was De Quincey that
was writing the article (though there have already been expressions
from which any competent reader could have inferred that fact) ; and
hence, when he wanted to insert into the article something of his own
recollections of Lamb personally, he resorted to the device of a letter supposed to be sent by a friend for the use of the writer of the article.—M.

tion, by any features whatever, puns or repartees, wisdom or wit, connecting it with Charles Lamb. I grieve to say that my meetings of *any* sort with Lamb were few, though spread through a score of years. That sounds odd for one that loved Lamb so entirely, and so much venerated his character. But the reason was that I so seldom visited London, and Lamb so seldom quitted it. Somewhere about 1810 and 1812 I must have met Lamb repeatedly at the *Courier Office* in the Strand ; that is, at Coleridge's, to whom, as an intimate friend, Mr. Daniel Stewart (a proprietor of the paper) gave up for a time the use of some rooms in the office. Thither, in the London season (May especially and June), resorted Lamb, Godwin, Sir H. Davy, and, once or twice, Wordsworth, who visited Sir George Beaumont's Leicestershire residence of Coleorton early in the spring, and then travelled up to Grosvenor Square with Sir George and Lady Beaumont, " *spectatum veniens, veniens spectetur ut ipse.*"

But in these miscellaneous gatherings Lamb said little, except when an opening arose for a pun. And how effectual that sort of small shot was from *him*, I need not say to anybody who remembers his infirmity of stammering, and his dexterous management of it for purposes of light and shade. He was often able to train the roll of stammers into settling upon the words immediately preceding the effective one ; by which means the key-note of the jest or sarcasm, benefiting by the sudden liberation of his embargoed voice, was delivered with the force of a pistol shot. That stammer was worth an annuity to him as an ally of his wit. Firing under cover of that advantage, he did triple execution : for, in the first place, the distressing sympathy of the hearers with *his* distress of utterance won for him unavoidably the silence of deep attention ; and then, whilst he had us all hoaxed into this attitude of mute suspense by an appearance of distress that he perhaps did not really feel, down came a plunging shot into the very thick of us, with ten times the effect it would else have had. If his stammering, however, often did him true " yeoman's service," sometimes it led him into scrapes. Coleridge told me of a ludicrous embarrassment which it caused him at Hastings.

Lamb had been medically advised to a course of sea-bathing; and, accordingly, at the door of his bathing-machine, whilst he stood shivering with cold, two stout fellows laid hold of him, one at each shoulder, like heraldic supporters. They waited for the word of command from their principal, who began the following oration to them : "Hear me, men! Take notice of this—I am to be dipped. But—" What more he would have said is unknown to land or sea : for, having reached the word dipped, he commenced such a rolling fire of Di—di—di—di that, when at length he descended à *plomb* upon the full word *dipped*, the two men, tired of the long suspense, became satisfied that they reached what lawyers call the "operative clause" of the sentence ; and, both exclaiming, "Oh yes, sir, we're quite aware of *that*," down they plunged him into the sea. On emerging, Lamb sobbed so much from the cold that he found no voice suitable to his indignation ; from necessity he seemed tranquil ; and, again addressing the men, who stood respectfully listening, he began thus : "Men! is it possible to obtain your attention ?" "Oh, surely, sir, by all means." "Then listen : once more I tell you, I am to be di—di—di—," and then, with a burst of indignation, "dipped, I tell you." "Oh, decidedly, sir," rejoined the men, "decidedly," and down the stammerer went for the second time. Petrified with cold and wrath, for a third time Lamb made a feeble attempt at explanation—"Grant me pa—pa—patience ; is it mum um mumum um um um um ? Again and a—ga—ga—gain, I tell you, I am to be di—di—di—dipped," now speaking furiously, with the voice of an injured man. "Oh yes, sir," the men replied, "we know that, we fully understood it," and for the third time down went Lamb into the sea. "O limbs of Satan!" he said, on coming up for the third time ; "it's now too late ; I tell you that I am—no that I *was*—by medical direction—to be di—di—di—dipped only *once*."

Since the rencontres with Lamb at Coleridge's, I had met him once or twice at literary dinner-parties. One of these occurred at the house of Messrs. Taylor and Hessey, the publishers. I myself was suffering too much from illness at the time to take any pleasure in what passed, or to notice it with any vigilance of attention. Lamb, I remember, as usual, was full of gaiety ; and, as usual, he rose too rapidly to the zenith of his gaiety ; for he shot upwards like a rocket, and, as usual, people said he was "tipsy." To me, Lamb never seemed intoxicated, but at most joyously elevated. He never talked nonsense,—which is a great point gained ; nor polemically,—which is a greater, for it is a dreadful thing to find a drunken man bent upon converting one's-self ; nor sentimentally,—which is greatest of all. You can stand a man's fraternizing with you ; or, if he swears an eternal friendship only once in an hour, you do not think of calling the police ; but once in every three minutes is too much. Lamb did none of these things ; he was always rational, quiet, and gentlemanly in his habits.. Nothing memorable, I am sure, passed upon this occasion, which was in November of 1821 ; and yet the dinner was memorable by means of one fact not discovered until some years later.

Amongst the company, all literary men, sat a murderer, —such he proved to be upon later discoveries, but even then looking prospectively towards that object,—and a murderer of a freezing class, cool, calculating, wholesale in his operations, and moving all along under the advantages of unsuspecting confidence and domestic opportunities. This was Mr. Wainewright, who was subsequently brought to trial, but not for any of his murders, and transported for life. The story has been told both by Judge Talfourd, and previously by Sir Edward B. Lytton. Both have been much blamed for the use made of this extraordinary case ; but I know not why. In itself it is a most remarkable case, for more reasons than one. It is remarkable for the appalling revelation which it makes of power spread through the hands of people not liable to suspicion, for purposes the most dreadful. It is remarkable also by the contrast which existed in this case between the murderer's dandy appearance and the terrific purposes with which he was always dallying. He was a contributor to a journal in which I also had written several papers.[1] This formed a shadowy link between us ; and, ill

[1] The journal mentioned is the *London Magazine* (see *ante*, Vol. III. pp. 5-8). De Quincey's own contributions to it at the time men-

as I was, I looked more attentively at *him* than at anybody else.   Yet there were several men of wit and genius present, —amongst whom Lamb (as I have said) and Thomas Hood, Hamilton Reynolds and Allan Cunningham.   But *them* I already knew, whereas Mr. W. I now saw for the first time and the last.   What interested me about *him* was this : the papers which had been pointed out to me as his (signed *Janus Weathercock* or else *Vinkbooms*) were written in a spirit of coxcombry that did not so much disgust as amuse.[1]   The writer could not conceal the ostentatious pleasure which he took in the luxurious fittings-up of his rooms, in the fancied splendour of his *bijouterie*, &c.   Yet it was easy for a man of any experience to read two facts in all this idle *étalage :* one being that his finery was but of a second-rate order ; the other, that he was a *parvenu*, not at home even amongst his second-rate splendour.   So far there was nothing to distinguish Mr. W.'s papers from the papers of other triflers. But in this point there *was*, viz. that in his judgments upon the great Italian masters of painting, Da Vinci, Titian, &c., there seemed a tone of sincerity and of native sensibility, as in one who spoke for himself, and was not merely a copier from books.   This it was that interested me ; as also his reviews of the chief Italian engravers, Morghen, Volpato, &c. ; not for the manner, which overflowed with levities and impertinence, but for the substance of his judgments in those cases where I happened to have had an opportunity of judging

tioned (November 1821) had consisted only of his " Confessions of an English Opium-Eater," in two articles, in the two preceding months ; but his subsequent contributions were to be numerous.—M.

[1] It is rather startling even now, in looking over the old volumes of the *London Magazine* from 1820 to 1824, to find in them, intermixed with the essays of Elia, and with papers by Hood, Hamilton Reynolds, Allan Cunningham, and De Quincey himself, the frequent, and indeed regularly recurring, contributions on art - subjects by this *Janus Weathercock* or *Vinkbooms*, alias Thomas Griffith Wainewright, the subsequently detected murderer.   Among the contents of the very numbers in which De Quincey's "Confessions" appeared, and also Lamb's Essays entitled "The Old Benchers of the Inner Temple" and "Witches and Other Night Fears," one reads "C. VAN VINKBOOMS, HIS DOGMAS FOR DILETTANTI. No. I. Recollections in a Country Churchyard," and "C. VAN VINKBOOMS, HIS DOGMAS FOR DILETTANTI. No. II. Giulio Romano."—M.

for myself. Here arose also a claim upon Lamb's attention : for Lamb and his sister, having no sensibility for music, had the deepest for painting. Accordingly, Lamb paid him a great deal of attention, and continued to speak of him for years with an interest that seemed disproportioned to his pretensions. This might be owing in part to an indirect compliment to Miss Lamb in one of W.'s papers ; else his appearance would rather have repelled Lamb ; it was commonplace, and better suited to express the dandyism which overspread the surface of his manner than the unaffected sensibility which apparently lay in his nature. Dandy or not, however, this man, on account of the schism in his papers,—so much amiable puppyism on one side, so much deep feeling on the other (feeling, applied to some of the grandest objects that earth has to show),—did really move a trifle of interest in me, on a day when I hated the face of man and woman. Yet again, if I had known this man for the murderer that even then he was, what sudden loss of interest, what sudden growth of another interest, would have changed the face of the scene ! Trivial creature, that didst carry thy dreadful eye kindling with perpetual treasons— dreadful creature, that didst carry thy trivial eye mantling with eternal levity,—over the sleeping surfaces of confiding household life,—oh, what a revolution for man wouldst thou have founded, had thy deep wickedness prospered ! What *was* that wickedness ? Here is its outline ; but his murders were more than were ever made known judicially.

At this time (October 1848 [1]) the whole British island is appalled by a new chapter in the history of poisoning. Locusta in ancient Rome, Madame Brinvilliers in Paris, were people of original genius : not in any new artifice of toxicology ; but in profiting by domestic openings for murder, unsuspected through their very atrocity. Such an opening was made some years ago by those who saw the possibility of founding purses for parents upon the murder of their children. This was done upon a larger scale than had been suspected,

---

[1] This was written ten years ago ; and doubtless I had ground sufficient for what I then said. At present [1858], however, I have entirely forgotten the particular case alluded to, unless (as I rather believe) it was a case of infant funerals with a view to the insurance-money.

and upon a plausible pretence. To bury a corpse is costly ; but, of a hundred children, only a few, in the ordinary course of mortality, will die within a given time. Five shillings apiece will produce £25 annually, and *that* will bury a considerable number. On this principle arose Infant Burial Societies. For a few shillings annually, a parent could secure a funeral for every child. If the child died, a few guineas fell due to the parent, and the funeral was accomplished without cost of *his*. But on this arose the suggestion —Why not execute an insurance of this nature twenty times over ? One single insurance pays for the funeral—the other nineteen are so much clear gain, a *lucro ponatur*, for the parents. Yes ; but on the supposition that the child dies ! Twenty are no better than one, unless they are gathered into the garner. Now, if the child died naturally, all was right ; but how if the child did *not* die ? Why, clearly this,—the child that *can* die, and won't die, may be made to die. There are many ways of doing that ; and it is shocking to know that, according to recent discoveries, poison is comparatively a very merciful mode of murder. Six years ago a dreadful communication was made to the public by a medical man, viz. that three thousand children were annually burned to death under circumstances showing too clearly that they had been left by their mothers with the means and the temptations to set themselves on fire in her absence. But more shocking, because more lingering, are the deaths by artificial appliances of wet, cold, hunger, bad diet, and disturbed sleep, to the frail constitutions of children. By that machinery it is, and not by poison, that the majority qualify themselves for claiming the funeral allowances. Here, however, there occur to any man, on reflection, two eventual restraints on the extension of this domestic curse :—1st, As there is no pretext for wanting more than one funeral on account of one child, any insurances beyond one are in themselves a ground of suspicion. Now, if any plan were devised for securing the *publication* of such insurances, the suspicions would travel as fast as the grounds for them. 2dly, It occurs that eventually the evil checks itself, since a society established on the ordinary rates of mortality would be ruined when a murderous stimulation was applied to that rate too extensively. Still it is certain that, for a season, this atrocity *has* prospered in manufacturing districts for some years, and more recently, as judicial investigations have shown, in one agricultural district of Essex. Now, Mr. W.'s scheme of murder was, in its outline, the very same, but not applied to the narrow purpose of obtaining burials from a public fund. He persuaded, for instance, two beautiful young ladies, visitors in his family, and nearly related to his wife, to insure their lives for a short period of two years. This insurance was repeated in several different offices, until a sum of £18,000 had been secured in the event of their deaths within the two years. Mr. W. took care that they *should* die, and very suddenly, within that period. I never saw either of the young women myself; but I have been assured that one of them at least was memorably distinguished by her personal attractions. In the middle of the day which Mr. Wainewright had fixed for their murder, he framed a pretence for drawing his wife out of doors upon a very long walk. His fear was that *she* might have penetration enough to notice and report the agonizing spasms caused by the poison, whereas two young servant girls, totally inexperienced, were easily persuaded to believe it a case of cholera. On returning, after a three hours' walk, Mr. and Mrs. W. found the two young ladies dead. Having previously secured from his victims an assignment to himself of their claim, he endeavoured to make this assignment available. But the offices, which had vainly endeavoured to extract from the young ladies any satisfactory account of the reasons for this limited insurance, had their suspicions at last strongly roused. One office had recently experienced a case of the same nature, in which also the young lady had been poisoned by the man in whose behalf she had effected the insurance; all the offices declined to pay; actions at law arose; in the course of the investigation which followed, Mr. W.'s character was fully exposed. Finally, in the midst of the embarrassments which ensued, he committed forgery, and was transported.[1]

[1] He was tried in 1836 on a charge of forgery; pleaded guilty; and was transported to Van Diemen's Land (now Tasmania); where he died in Hobart Town Hospital in 1852, or thereabouts.—M.

From this Mr. W., some few days afterwards, I received an invitation to a dinner party, expressed in terms that were obligingly earnest. He mentioned the names of his principal guests, and amongst them rested most upon those of Lamb and Sir David Wilkie. From an accident, I was unable to attend, and greatly regretted it. Sir David one might rarely happen to see, except at a crowded party. But, as regarded Lamb, I was sure to see him or to hear of him again in some way or other within a short time. This opportunity, in fact, offered itself within a month through the kindness of the Lambs themselves. They had heard of my being in solitary lodgings, and insisted on my coming to dine with them ; which more than once I did in the winter of 1821-22.

The mere reception by the Lambs was so full of goodness and hospitable feeling that it kindled animation in the most cheerless or torpid of invalids. I cannot imagine that any *memorabilia* occurred during the visit ; but I will use the time that would else be lost upon the settling of that point in putting down any triviality that occurs to my recollection.

There were no strangers ; Charles Lamb, his sister, and myself made up the party. Even this was done in kindness. They knew that I should have been oppressed by an effort such as must be made in the society of strangers ; and they placed me by their own fireside, where I could say as much or as little as I pleased.

We dined about five o'clock ; and it was one of the hospitalities inevitable to the Lambs that any game which they might receive from rural friends in the course of the week was reserved for the day of a friend's dining with them.

In regard to wine, Lamb and myself had the same habit —perhaps it rose to the dignity of a principle—viz. to take a great deal *during* dinner, none *after* it. Consequently, as Miss Lamb (who drank only water) retired almost with the dinner itself, nothing remained for men of our principles, the rigour of which we had illustrated by taking rather too much of old port before the cloth was drawn, except talking ; amœbean colloquy, or, in Dr. Johnson's phrase, a dialogue of " brisk reciprocation." But this was impossible ; over Lamb, at this period of his life, there passed regularly, after taking wine, a brief eclipse of sleep. It descended upon him as softly as a shadow. In a gross person, laden with superfluous flesh, and sleeping heavily, this would have been disagreeable ; but in Lamb, thin even to meagreness, spare and wiry as an Arab of the desert, or as Thomas Aquinas wasted by scholastic vigils, the affection of sleep seemed rather a network of aërial gossamer than of earthly cobweb—more like a golden haze falling upon him gently from the heavens than a cloud exhaling upwards from the flesh. Motionless in his chair as a bust, breathing so gently as scarcely to seem certainly alive, he presented the image of repose midway between life and death, like the repose of sculpture ; and, to one who knew his history, a repose affectingly contrasting with the calamities and internal storms of his life. I have heard more persons than I can now distinctly recall observe of Lamb, when sleeping, that his countenance in that state assumed an expression almost seraphic, from its intellectual beauty of outline, its child-like simplicity, and its benignity. It could not be called a transfiguration that sleep had worked in his face ; for the features wore essentially the same expression when waking ; but sleep spiritualized that expression, exalted it, and almost harmonized it. Much of the change lay in that last process. The eyes it was that disturbed the unity of effect in Lamb's waking face. They gave a restlessness to the character of his intellect, shifting, like northern lights, through every mode of combination with fantastic playfulness, and sometimes by fiery gleams obliterating for the moment that pure light of benignity which was the predominant reading on his features. Some people have supposed that Lamb had Jewish blood in his veins, which seemed to account for his gleaming eyes. It might be so ; but this notion found little countenance in Lamb's own way of treating the gloomy mediæval traditions propagated throughout Europe about the Jews, and their secret enmity to Christian races. Lamb, indeed, might not be more serious than Shakspere is supposed to have been in his Shylock ; yet he spoke at times as from a station of wilful bigotry, and seemed (whether laughingly or not) to sympathize with the barbarous Christian superstitions upon the pretended bloody practices of the Jews,

and of the early Jewish physicians. Being himself a Lincoln
man, he treated Sir Hugh of Lincoln,[1] the young child that
suffered death by secret assassination in the Jewish quarter
rather than suppress his daily anthems to the Virgin, as a
true historical personage on the rolls of martyrdom ; careless
that this fable, like that of the apprentice murdered out of
jealousy by his master the architect, had destroyed its own
authority by ubiquitous diffusion. All over Europe the same
legend of the murdered apprentice and the martyred child
reappears under different names—so that in effect the verification of the tale is none at all, because it is unanimous ;
is too narrow, because it is too impossibly broad. Lamb,
however, though it was often hard to say whether he were
not secretly laughing, swore to the truth of all these old
fables, and treated the liberalities of the present generation
on such points as mere fantastic and effeminate affectations,
—which, no doubt, they often are as regards the sincerity of
those who profess them. The bigotry which it pleased his
fancy to assume he used like a sword against the Jew, as
the official weapon of the Christian, upon the same principle
that a Capulet would have drawn upon a Montague, without
conceiving it any duty of *his* to rip up the grounds of so
ancient a quarrel ; it was a feud handed down to him by his
ancestors, and it was *their* business to see that originally it
had been an honest feud. I cannot yet believe that Lamb,
if seriously aware of any family interconnexion with Jewish
blood, would, even in jest, have held that one-sided language.
More probable it is that the fiery eye recorded not any
alliance with Jewish blood, but that disastrous alliance with
insanity which tainted his own life, and laid desolate his
sister's.

The mercurialities of Lamb were infinite, and always
uttered in a spirit of absolute recklessness for the quality
or the prosperity of the sally. It seemed to liberate his
spirits from some burthen of blackest melancholy which
oppressed it, when he had thrown off a jest : he would not
stop one instant to improve it ; nor did he care the value
of a straw whether it were good enough to be remembered,

[1] The story which furnishes a basis to the fine ballad in Percy's
Reliques, and to the Canterbury Tale of Chaucer's Lady Abbess.

or so mediocre as to extort high moral indignation from a collector who refused to receive into his collection of jests and puns any that were not felicitously good or revoltingly bad.

After tea, Lamb read to me a number of beautiful compositions, which he had himself taken the trouble to copy out into a blank paper folio, from unsuccessful authors. Neglected people in every class won the sympathy of Lamb. One of the poems, I remember, was a very beautiful sonnet from a volume recently published by Lord Thurlow—which, and Lamb's just remarks upon which, I could almost repeat *verbatim* at this moment, nearly twenty-seven years later, if your limits would allow me. But these, you tell me, allow of no such thing ; at the utmost they allow only twelve lines more. Now all the world knows that the sonnet itself would require fourteen lines ; but take fourteen from twelve and there remains very little, I fear ; besides which, I am afraid two of my twelve are already exhausted. This forces me to interrupt my account of Lamb's reading, or reporting the very accident that *did* interrupt it in fact ; since that no less characteristically expressed Lamb's peculiar spirit of kindness (always quickening itself towards the ill-used or the down-trodden) than it had previously expressed itself in his choice of obscure readings. Two ladies came in, one of whom at least had sunk in the scale of worldly consideration. They were ladies who would not have found much recreation in literary discussions,—elderly, and habitually depressed. On *their* account, Lamb proposed whist ; and in that kind effort to amuse *them*,—which naturally drew forth some momentary gaieties from himself, but not of a kind to impress themselves on the recollection,—the evening terminated.

Of Lamb's writings, some were confessedly failures, and some were so memorably beautiful as to be uniques in their class. The character of Lamb it is, and the life-struggle of Lamb, that must fix the attention of many, even amongst those wanting in sensibility to his intellectual merits. This character and this struggle, as we have already observed, impress many traces of themselves upon Lamb's writings. Even in that view, therefore, they have a ministerial value ;

but separately, for themselves, they have an independent
value of the highest order.   Upon this point we gladly adopt
the eloquent words of Sergeant Talfourd :—

" The sweetness of Lamb's character, breathed through
" his writings, was felt even by strangers ; but its heroic
" aspect was unguessed even by many of his friends.   Let
" them now consider it, and ask if the annals of self-sacrifice
" can show anything in human action and endurance more
" lovely than its self-devotion exhibits ?   It was not merely
" that he saw, through the ensanguined cloud of misfortune
" which had fallen upon his family, the unstained excellence
" of his sister, whose madness had caused it ; that he was
" ready to take her to his own home with reverential affec-
" tion, and cherish her through life, and gave up, for *her*
" sake, all meaner and more selfish love, and all the hopes
" which youth blends with the passion which disturbs and
" ennobles it ; not even that he did all this cheerfully, with-
" out pluming himself upon his brotherly nobleness as a
" virtue, or seeking to repay himself (as some uneasy martyrs
" do) by small instalments of long repining ; but that he
" carried the spirit of the hour in which he first knew and
" took his course to his last.   So far from thinking that his
" sacrifice of youth and love to his sister gave him a licence
" to follow his own caprice at the expense of her feelings,
" even in the lightest matters, he always wrote and spoke of
" her as his wiser self, his generous benefactress, of whose
" protecting care he was scarcely worthy."

It must be remembered also (which the Sergeant does not
overlook) that Lamb's efforts for the becoming support of his
sister lasted through a period of forty years.   Twelve years
before his death, the munificence of the India House, by
granting him a liberal retiring allowance, had placed his own
support under shelter from accidents of any kind.   But this
died with himself ; and he could not venture to suppose that,
in the event of his own death, the India House would grant
to his sister the same allowance as by custom is granted to a
wife.   This, however, they did ; but Lamb, not venturing to
calculate upon such nobility of patronage, had applied himself through life to the saving of a provision for his sister
under any accident to himself.   And this he did with a per-

severing prudence but little known in the literary class, amongst a continued tenor of generosities, often so princely as to be scarcely known in any class.

Was this man, so memorably good by life-long sacrifice of himself, in any profound sense a Christian? The impression is that he was *not*. We, from private communications with him, can undertake to say that, according to his knowledge and opportunities for the study of Christianity, he *was*.

What has injured Lamb on this point is that his early opinions (which, however, from the first were united with the deepest piety) are read by the inattentive as if they had been the opinions of his mature days; secondly, that he had few religious persons amongst his friends,—which made him reserved in the expression of his own views; thirdly, that, in any case where he altered opinions for the better, the credit of the improvement is assigned to Coleridge. Lamb, for example, beginning life as a Unitarian, in not many years became a Trinitarian. Coleridge passed through the same changes in the same order; and here, at least, Lamb is supposed simply to have obeyed the influence, confessedly great, of Coleridge. This, on our own knowledge of Lamb's views, we pronounce to be an error. And the following extracts from Lamb's letters will show not only that he was religiously disposed on impulses self-derived, but that, so far from obeying the bias of Coleridge, he ventured, on this one subject, firmly as regarded the matter, though humbly as regarded the manner, affectionately to reprove Coleridge.

In a letter to Coleridge, written in 1797, the year after his sister's first attack of lunacy, he says :—" Coleridge, I " have not one truly elevated character among my acquaint- " ance ; not one Christian ; not one but undervalues Christi- " anity. Singly, what am I to do? Wesley—(have you " read his life?)—was not he an elevated character? Wesley " has said religion was not a solitary thing. Alas! it is " necessarily so with me, or next to solitary. 'Tis true you " write to me ; but correspondence by letter and personal " intimacy are widely different. Do, do write to me ; and " do some good to my mind—already how much 'warped " and relaxed' by the world !"

In a letter written about three months previously, he had

not scrupled to blame Coleridge at some length for audacities
of religious speculation which seemed to him at war with the
simplicities of pure religion. He says :—" Do continue to
" write to me. I read your letters with my sister, and they
" give us both abundance of delight. Especially they please
" us two when you talk in a religious strain. Not but we
" are offended occasionally with a certain freedom of expres-
" sion, a certain air of mysticism, more consonant to the
" conceits of pagan philosophy than consistent with the
" humility of genuine piety."—Then, after some instances of
what he blames, he says :—" Be not angry with me, Cole-
" ridge. I wish not to cavil ; I know I cannot instruct
" you ; I only wish to remind you of that humility which
" best becometh the Christian character. God, in the New
" Testament, our best guide, is represented to us in the kind,
" condescending, amiable, familiar light of a parent ; and, in
" my poor mind, 'tis best for us so to consider him as our
' heavenly Father, and our best friend, without indulging
" too bold conceptions of his character."—About a month
later, he says :—" Few but laugh at me for reading my
" Testament. They talk a language I understand not; I
" conceal sentiments that would be a puzzle to *them.*"

We see by this last quotation *where* it was that Lamb
originally sought for consolation. We personally can vouch
that, at a maturer period, when he was approaching his
fiftieth year, no change had affected his opinions upon that
point ; and, on the other hand, that no changes had occurred
in his needs for consolation, we see, alas ! in the records of
his life. We do not undertake to say that in his knowledge
of Christianity he was everywhere profound or consistent ;
but he was always earnest in his aspirations after its spiritu-
alities, and had an apprehensive sense of its power.

Charles Lamb is gone. His life was a continued struggle
in the service of love the purest, and within a sphere visited
by little of contemporary applause. Even his intellectual
displays won but a narrow sympathy at any time, and in his
earlier period were saluted with positive derision and contumely on the few occasions when they were not oppressed
by entire neglect. But slowly all things right themselves.
All merit which is founded in truth, and is strong enough,

reaches by sweet exhalations in the end a higher sensory ; reaches higher organs of discernment, lodged in a selecter audience.   But the original obtuseness or vulgarity of feeling that thwarted all just estimation of Lamb in life will continue to thwart its popular diffusion.   There are even some that continue to regard him with the old hostility, and the old unmitigated scorn.   And we, therefore, standing by the side of Lamb's grave, seemed to hear, on one side (but in abated tones), strains of the ancient malice—"This man, that thought himself to be somebody, is dead, is buried, is forgotten !" and, on the other side, seemed to hear ascending as with the solemnity of a saintly requiem—"This man, that thought himself to be nobody, is dead, is buried ; his life has been searched ; and his memory is hallowed for ever !"

PROFESSOR WILSON

Sketch in 1829 [1]

My dear L.,—Among the *lions* whom you missed by one
accident or another on your late travels in Europe, I observe
that you recur to none with so much regret as Professor
Wilson. You dwell upon this one disappointment as a per-

---

[1] On the 16th of May 1829, when De Quincey had virtually settled
in Edinburgh (though still going and coming between Edinburgh and
his cottage at Grasmere), there was published the first number of a
weekly periodical called the *Edinburgh Literary Gazette*. Though
tastefully conducted and edited, it did not last much beyond a year
(the last number I have seen bearing the date "Saturday, July 10,
1830"): a fate not wonderful when the price per number of 16
quarto pages was "8d. unstamped," with 4d. extra for stamped
copies to go free by post. Not two years later, *i.e.* in February 1832,
when *Chambers's Edinburgh Journal* was started, it was at the price
of 1½d. per number; which made a difference, and may partly
account for the fact that, after nearly sixty years, that first British
pioneer of cheap literature still exists and flourishes. The short-lived
Edinburgh Literary Gazette of 1829-30 did, nevertheless, attract
local talent and win some reputation. De Quincey, though *Blackwood*
was then his mainstay, had some connexion with this humbler Edinburgh weekly. A contribution of his, entitled "Sketch of Professor
Wilson: in a Letter to an American Gentleman," spread over
three numbers — beginning in that for June 6, 1829 (the fourth
number of the periodical), and continued in the numbers for June
20 and July 11. Of three separate sketches which De Quincey has
left us of his friend Wilson, this is distinctly the best. Extracts,
I believe, have been made from it here and there; but, so far
as I know, it has never hitherto been reprinted entire anywhere
else than in the American Riverside Edition of De Quincey's Works.
In the present reprint the epistolary form of the original has been
preserved.—M.

sonal misfortune; and perhaps with reason; for, in the course of my life, I have met with no man of equally varied accomplishments, or, upon the whole, so well entitled to be ranked with that order of men, distinguished by brilliant versatility and ambidexterity, of which we find such eminent models in Alcibiades, in Cæsar, in Crichton, in that of Servan recorded by Sully, and in one or two Italians. Pity that you had not earlier communicated to me the exact route you were bound to, and the particular succession of your engagements when you visited the English Lakes; since, in that case, my interest with Professor Wilson (supposing always that you had declined to rely upon the better passport of your own merits as a naturalist) would have availed for a greater thing than at that time stood between you and the introduction which you coveted. On the day, or the night rather, when you were at Bowness and Ambleside, I happen to know that Professor Wilson's business was one which might have been executed by proxy, though it could not be delayed; and I also know that, apart from the *general* courtesy of his nature, he would, at all times, have an especial pleasure in waiving a claim of business for one of science or letters, in the person of a foreigner coming from a great distance; and that in no other instance would he make such a sacrifice so cordially as on behalf of an able naturalist. Perhaps you already know from your countryman Audubon that the Professor is himself a naturalist, and of original merit; in fact, worth a score of such meagre bookish naturalists as are formed in museums and by secondhand acts of memory; having (like Audubon) built much of his knowledge upon personal observation. Hence he has two great advantages: one, that his knowledge is accurate in a very unusual degree; and another, that this knowledge, having grown up under the inspiration of a real interest and an unaffected love for its objects,—commencing, indeed, at an age when no affectation in matters of that nature could exist,—has settled upon those facts and circumstances which have a true philosophical value. Habits, predominant affections, the direction of instincts, and the compensatory processes where these happen to be thwarted,—on all such topics he is learned and full; whilst on the science of measurements and proportions applied to dorsal-fins and tail-feathers, and on the exact arrangement of colours, &c.,—that petty upholstery of nature on which books are so tedious and elaborate,—not uncommonly he is negligent or forgetful. What may have served in later years to quicken and stimulate his knowledge in this field, and, at any rate, greatly to extend it, is the conversation of his youngest brother, Mr. James Wilson, who (as *you* know much better than I) is a naturalist *majorum gentium*.[1] He, indeed, whilst a boy of not more than sixteen or seventeen, was in correspondence (I believe) with Montague the Ornithologist, and about the same time had skill enough to pick holes in the coat of Mr. Hüber, the German reformer of our then erroneous science of bees.

You see, therefore, that no possible introduction could have stood you more in stead than your own extensive knowledge of transatlantic ornithology. Swammerdam passed his life, it is said, in a ditch. *That* was a base, earthy solitude,—and a prison. But you and Audubon have passed *your* lives in the heavenly solitudes of forests and savannahs ; and such solitude as this is no prison, but infinite liberty. The knowledge which you have gathered has been answerable to the character of your school ; and no sort of knowledge could have secured you a better welcome with Professor Wilson. Yet, had it been otherwise, I repeat that my interest (as I flatter myself) would have opened the gates of Elleray to you even at midnight ; for I am so old a friend of Mr. Wilson that I take a pride in supposing myself the oldest, and, barring relations by blood, arrogate the rights of dean in the chapter of his associates,—or at least I know of but one person whose title can probably date earlier than mine. About this very month when I am writing, I have known Professor Wilson for a cycle of twenty years and more ; which is just half of his life, and also half of mine ; for we are almost *ad apicem* of the same age : Wilson being born in May, and I in August, of the same memorable year.

My introduction to him, setting apart the introduc*ee*

[1] Author of *Illustrations of Zoology* (1826-32), *Entomologia Edinensis* (1834), and *Voyage round the Coasts of Scotland* (1842).—M.

himself, was memorable from one sole circumstance : viz.
the person of the introducer. *William Wordsworth* it was
who in the vale of Grasmere, if it can interest you to know
the place, and in the latter end of 1808, if you can be supposed to care about the time, did me the favour of making
me known to John Wilson, or, as I might say (upon the
Scottish fashion of designating men from their territorial
pretensions), to Elleray. I remember the whole scene as
circumstantially as if it belonged to but yesterday. In the
vale of Grasmere,—that peerless little vale which you and
Gray the poet and so many others have joined in admiring
as the very Eden of English beauty, peace, and pastoral
solitude,—you may possibly recall, even from that flying
glimpse you had of it, a modern house called Allan Bank,
standing under a low screen of woody rocks which descend
from the hill of Silver How, on the western side of the lake.
This house had been then recently built by a worthy mer-
chant of Liverpool, but for some reason, of no importance to
you and me, not being immediately wanted for the family
of the owner, had been let for a term of three years to Mr.
Wordsworth. At the time I speak of, both Mr. Coleridge
and myself were on a visit to Mr. Wordsworth ; and one
room on the ground-floor, designed for a breakfasting-room,
which commands a sublime view of the three mountains,—
Fairfield, Arthur's Chair, and Seat Sandal (the first of them
within about four hundred feet of the highest mountains in
Great Britain),—was then occupied by Mr. Coleridge as a
study. On this particular day, the sun having only just set,
it naturally happened that Mr. Coleridge — whose nightly
vigils were long—had not yet come down to breakfast :
meantime, and until the epoch of the Coleridgian breakfast
should arrive, his study was lawfully disposable to profaner
uses. Here, therefore, it was, that, opening the door hastily
in quest of a book, I found seated, and in earnest conversation,
two gentlemen,—one of them my host, Mr. Wordsworth, at
that time about thirty-seven or thirty-eight years old. The
other was a younger man by good sixteen or seventeen years,
in a sailor's dress, manifestly in robust health—*fervidus juventâ*,
and wearing upon his countenance a powerful expression
of ardour and animated intelligence, mixed with much good

nature. " *Mr. Wilson of Elleray* "—delivered, as the formula
of introduction, in the deep tones of Mr. Wordsworth—at
once banished the momentary surprise I felt on finding an
unknown stranger where I had expected nobody, and substituted a surprise of another kind. I now well understood
who it was that I saw ; and there was no wonder in his
being at Allan Bank, Elleray standing within nine miles ;
but (as usually happens in such cases) I felt a shock of
surprise on seeing a person so little corresponding to the one
I had half unconsciously prefigured.

And here comes the place naturally, if anywhere, for a
description of Mr. Wilson's person and general appearance in
carriage, manner, and deportment ; and a word or two I
shall certainly say on these points, simply because I know
that I *must*, else my American friends will complain that I
have left out that precise section in my whole account which
it is most impossible for them to supply for themselves by
any acquaintance with his printed works. Yet suffer me,
before I comply with this demand, to enter one word of
private protest against the childish (nay, worse than childish
—the *missy*) spirit in which such demands originate. From
my very earliest years,—that is the earliest years in which I
had any sense of what belongs to true dignity of mind,—I
declare to you that I have considered the interest which men,
grown men, take in the personal appearance of each other as
one of the meanest aspects under which human curiosity
commonly presents itself. Certainly I have the same intellectual perception of differences in such things that other
men have ; but I connect none of the feelings, whether of
admiration or contempt, liking or disliking, which are
obviously connected with these perceptions by human beings
generally. Such words as " commanding appearance," " pre-
possessing countenance," applied to the figures or faces of the
males of the human species, have no meaning in my ears :
no man commands me, no man prepossesses me, by anything
in, on, or about his carcass. What care I for any man's
legs ? I laugh at his ridiculous presumption in conceiting
that I shall trouble myself to admire or to respect anything
that he can produce in his *physics*. What ! shall I honour
Milo for the very qualities which he has in common with the

beastly ox he carries—his thews and sinews, his ponderous strength and weight, and the quantity of thumping that his hide will carry ? I disclaim and disdain any participation in such green-girl feelings. I admit that the baby feelings I am here condemning are found in connexion with the highest intellects : in particular, Mr. Coleridge, for instance, once said to me, as a justifying reason for his dislike of a certain celebrated Scotsman, with an air of infinite disgust, that—" ugh " ! (making a guttural sound as if of execration) "he (viz. the said Scotsman) was so chicken-breasted." I have been assured, by the way, that Mr. Coleridge was mistaken in the mere matter of fact : but, supposing that he were not, what a reason for a philosopher to build a disgust upon ! And Mr. Wordsworth, in or about the year 1820, in expressing the extremity of his *Nil admirari* spirit, declared that he would not go ten yards out of his road to see the finest specimen of man (intellectually speaking) that Europe had to show : and so far indeed I do not quarrel with his opinion ; but Mr. Wordsworth went on to say that this indifference did *not* extend itself to man considered physically, and that he would still exert himself to a small extent (suppose a mile or so) for the sake of seeing Belzoni. *That* was the case he instanced ; and, as I understood him, not by way of a general illustration for his meaning, but that he really felt an exclusive interest in this particular man's *physics.* Now, Belzoni was certainly a good tumbler, as I have heard ; and hopped well upon one leg, when surmounted and crested by a pyramid of men and boys ; and jumped capitally through a hoop ; and did all sorts of tricks in all sorts of styles, not at all worse than any monkey, bear, or learned pig, that ever exhibited in Great Britain. And I would myself have given a shilling to have seen him fight with that cursed Turk that assaulted him in the streets of Cairo ; and would have given him a crown for catching the circumcised dog by the throat and effectually taking the conceit out of his Mahometan carcass. But then *that* would have been for the spectacle of the passions which, in such a case, would have been let loose : as to the mere animal Belzoni,—who after all was not to be compared to Topham the Warwickshire man, that drew back by main force a cart, and its driver, and

a strong horse,—as to the mere animal Belzoni, I say, and
his bull neck, I would have much preferred to see a real bull,
or the Darlington ox.   The sum of the matter is this :—All
men, even those who are most manly in their style of
thinking and feeling, in many things retain the childishness
of their childish years : no man thoroughly weeds himself of
all.   And this particular mode of childishness is one of the
commonest, into which they fall the more readily from the
force of sympathy, and because they apprehend no reason for
directing any vigilance against it.   But I contend that
reasonably no feelings of deep interest are justifiable as applied
to any point of external form or feature in human beings,
unless under two reservations.   First, that they shall have
reference to women ; because women, being lawfully the
objects of passions and tender affections which can have no
existence as applied to men, are objects also, rationally and consistently, of all other secondary feelings (such as those derived
from their personal appearance) which have any tendency to
promote and support the first ; whereas between men the
highest mode of intercourse is merely intellectual,—which is
not of a nature to receive support or strength from any
feelings of pleasure or disgust connected with the accidents of
external appearance, but, exactly in the degree in which
these have any influence at all, they must warp and disturb
by improper biases.   And the single case of exception, where
such feelings can be honourable and laudable amongst the males
of the human species, is where they regard such deformities as
are the known products and expressions of criminal or degrad-
ing propensities.   All beyond this, I care not by whom
countenanced, is infirmity of mind, and would be baseness if
it were not excused by imbecility.

Excuse this digression, for which I have a double reason.
Chiefly I was anxious to put on record my own opinions, and
my contempt for men generally in this particular ; and here
I seemed to have a conspicuous situation for that purpose.
Secondly, apart from this purpose of offence, I was at any
rate anxious, merely on a defensive principle, to screen myself from the obvious misinterpretation incident to the case.
Saying anything minute or in detail upon a man's person, I
should necessarily be supposed to do so under the ordinary

blind feelings of interest in that subject which govern most people ; feelings which I disdain. Now, having said all this, and made my formal protest, *liberavi animam meam;* and I revert to my subject, and shall say that word or two which I was obliged to promise you on Professor Wilson's personal appearance.

Figure to yourself, then, a tall man, about six feet high, within half an inch or so, built with tolerable appearance of strength, but at the date of my description (that is, in the very spring-tide and blossom of youth) wearing, for the predominant character of his person, lightness and agility, or (in our Westmoreland phrase) *lishness.* He seemed framed with an express view to gymnastic exercises of every sort—

Ἅλμα, ποδωκείην, δίσκον, ἄκοντα, πάλην·

In the first of these exercises, indeed, and possibly (but of that I am not equally certain) in the second, I afterwards came to know that he was absolutely unrivalled ; and the best leapers at that time in the ring, Richmond the Black and others, on getting "a taste of his quality," under circumstances of considerable disadvantage (viz. after a walk from Oxford to Moulsey Hurst, which I believe is fifty miles), declined to undertake him. For this exercise he had two remarkable advantages. It is recorded of Sheffield, Duke of Buckingham, that, though otherwise a handsome man, he offended the connoisseurs in statuesque proportions by one eminent defect—perhaps the most obtrusive to which the human figure is liable—viz. a body of length disproportioned to his legs. In Mr. Wilson the proportions were fortunately reversed : a short trunk, and remarkably long legs, gave him one half of his advantages in the noble science of leaping. The other half was afterwards pointed out to me by an accurate critic in these matters as lying in the particular conformation of his foot, the instep of which is arched, and the back of the heel strengthened, in so remarkable a way that it would be worth paying a penny or so for a sight of them. It is really laughable to think of the coxcombry which eminent men of letters have displayed in connexion with their powers—real or fancied—in this art. Cardinal du Perron vapoured to the end of his life upon some remarkable

leap that he either *had* accomplished, or conceived himself to
have accomplished (not, I presume, in red stockings). Every
tenth page of the Perroniana rings with the echo of this
stupendous leap—the length of which, if I remember rightly,
is as obviously fabulous as any feat of Don Belianis of Greece.
Des Cartes also had a lurking conceit that, in some unknown
place, he had perpetrated a leap that ought to immortalise him ;
and in one of his letters he repeats and accredits a story of
some obscure person's leap, which

"At one light bound high overleaped all bound "

of reasonable credulity. Many other eminent leapers might
be cited, Pagan and Christian : but the Cardinal, by his own
account, appears to have been the flower of Popish leapers ;
and, with all deference to his Eminence, upon a better
assurance than that, Professor Wilson may be rated, at the
time I speak of, as the flower of all Protestant leapers. Not
having the Cardinal's foible of connecting any vanity with this
little accomplishment, knowing exactly what could and what
could *not* be effected in this department of gymnastics, and
speaking with the utmost simplicity and candour of his failures
and his successes alike, he might always be relied upon, and
his statements were constantly in harmony with any collateral
testimony that chance happened to turn up.

Viewed, therefore, by an eye learned in gymnastic proportions, Mr. Wilson presented a somewhat striking figure :
and by some people he was pronounced with emphasis a fine-
looking young man ; but others, who less understood, or less
valued these advantages, spoke of him as nothing extraordinary. Still greater division of voices I have heard on his
pretensions to be thought handsome. In my opinion, and
most certainly in his own, these pretensions were but
slender. His complexion was too florid ; hair of a hue quite
unsuited to that complexion ; eyes not good, having no
apparent depth, but seeming mere surfaces ; and, in fine, no
one feature that could be called fine, except the lower region
of his face, mouth, chin, and the parts adjacent, which were
then (and perhaps are now) truly elegant and Ciceronian.
Ask in one of your public libraries for that little 4to edition
of the Rhetorical Works of Cicero, edited by Schütz (the same

who edited Æschylus), and you will there see (as a frontispiece
to the 1st vol.) a reduced whole length of Cicero from the
antique ; which, in the mouth and chin, and indeed generally,
if I do not greatly forget, will give you a lively representation
of the contour and expression of Professor Wilson's face.
Taken as a whole, though not handsome (as I have already
said) when viewed in a quiescent state, the head and
countenance are massy, dignified, and expressive of tranquil
sagacity.

Thus far of Professor Wilson in his outward man, whom
(to gratify you and yours, and upon the consideration that
my letter is to cross the Atlantic) I have described with an
effort and a circumstantiation that are truly terrific to look
back upon. And now, returning to the course of my
narrative, such in personal appearance was the young man
upon whom my eyes suddenly rested, for the first time,
upwards of twenty years ago, in the study of S. T. Coleridge
— looking, as I said before, light as a Mercury to eyes
familiar with the British build ; but, with reference to the
lengthy model of you Yankees, who spindle up so tall and narrow, already rather bulky and columnar. Note, however, that
of all this array of personal features, as I have here described
them, I then saw nothing at all, my attention being altogether
occupied with Mr. Wilson's conversation and demeanour,
which were in the highest degree agreeable : the points
which chiefly struck me being the humility and gravity with
which he spoke of himself, his large expansion of heart, and
a certain air of noble frankness which overspread everything
he said. He seemed to have an intense enjoyment of life ;
indeed, being young, rich, healthy, and full of intellectual
activity, it could not be very wonderful that he should feel
happy and pleased with himself and others ; but it was
somewhat unusual to find that so rare an assemblage of
endowments had communicated no tinge of arrogance to his
manner, or at all disturbed the general temperance of his
mind.

Turn we now suddenly, and without preparation,—simply
by way of illustrating the versatile humour of the man,—from
this grave and (as in reality it was) philosophic scene, to
another first introduction, under most different circumstances,

to the same Mr. Wilson. Represent to yourself the earliest dawn of a fine summer morning, time about half-past two o'clock. A young man, anxious for an introduction to Mr. Wilson, and as yet pretty nearly a stranger to the country, has taken up his abode in Grasmere, and has strolled out at this early hour to that rocky and moorish common (called the White Moss) which overhangs the Vale of Rydal, dividing it from Grasmere. Looking southwards in the direction of Rydal, suddenly he becomes aware of a huge beast advancing at a long trot, with the heavy and thundering tread of a hippopotamus, along the public road. The creature is soon arrived within half-a-mile of his station ; and by the gray light of morning is at length made out to be a bull, apparently flying from some unseen enemy in his rear. As yet, however, all is mystery ; but suddenly three horsemen double a turn in the road, and come flying into sight with the speed of a hurricane, manifestly in pursuit of the fugitive bull. The bull labours to navigate his huge bulk to the moor; which he reaches, and then pauses, panting and blowing out clouds of smoke from his nostrils, to look back from his station amongst rocks and slippery crags upon his hunters. If he had conceited that the rockiness of the ground had secured his repose, the foolish bull is soon undeceived. The horsemen, scarcely relaxing their speed, charge up the hill, and, speedily gaining the rear of the bull, drive him at a gallop over the worst part of that impracticable ground down into the level ground below. At this point of time the stranger perceives by the increasing light of the morning that the hunters are armed with immense spears fourteen feet long. With these the bull is soon dislodged ; and, scouring down to the plain below, he and the hunters at his tail take to the common at the head of the lake, and all, in the madness of the chase, are soon half engulfed in the swamps of the morass. After plunging together for ten or fifteen minutes, all suddenly regain the *terra firma*, and the bull again makes for the rocks. Up to this moment there had been the silence of ghosts ; and the stranger had doubted whether the spectacle were not a pageant of aërial spectres, ghostly huntsmen, ghostly lances, and a ghostly bull. But just at this crisis a voice (it was the voice of Mr. Wilson) shouted aloud, " Turn the villain ;

turn that villain ; or he will take to Cumberland." The
young stranger did the service required of him ; the villain
was turned and fled southwards; the hunters, lance in
rest, rushed after him ; all bowed .their thanks as they fled
past ; the fleet cavalcade again took the high road ; they
doubled the cape which shut them out of sight ; and in a
moment all had disappeared and left the quiet valley to its
original silence, whilst the young stranger and two grave
Westmoreland statesmen (who by this time had come into
sight upon some accident or other) stood wondering in silence,
and saying to themselves perhaps,—

> " The earth hath bubbles as the water hath ;
> And these are of them ! "

But they were no bubbles. The bull was a substantial
bull, and took no harm at all from being turned out
occasionally at midnight for a chase of fifteen or eighteen
miles. The bull, no doubt, used to wonder at this nightly
visitation ; and the owner of the bull must sometimes have
pondered a little on the draggled state in which the swamps
would now and then leave his beast ; but no other harm
came of it. And so it happened, and in the very hurly-
burly of such an unheard-of chase, that my friend was
fortunate enough, by a little service, to recommend himself to
the notice of Mr. Wilson ; and so passed the scene of his
first introduction.[1]

In reading the anecdote of the bull-hunt, you must bear
in mind the period of Mr. Wilson's life to which it belongs ;
else I should here be unintentionally adding one more to the
thousand misrepresentations of his character which are
already extant in different repositories of scandal : most of
which I presume, unless in the rarer cases where they have
been the pure creations of malice, owe their origin to a little
exaggeration, and a great deal of confusion in dates. Levities
and extravagances, which find a ready excuse at twenty, ten
or fifteen years later are fatal to a man's character for good
sense. In such a case, therefore, to be careless or inaccurate
in dates, is a moral dishonesty. Understand then that the

[1] The first portion of the paper ended here.—M.

bull-hunting scenes belong to the time which immediately succeeded my first knowledge of Mr. Wilson. This particular frolic happened to fall within the earliest period of my own personal acquaintance with him. Else, and with this one exception, the era of his wildest (and, according to the common estimate, of his insane) extravagances was already past. All those stories, therefore, which you question me about with so much curiosity,—of his having joined a company of strolling players, and himself taken the leading parts both in Tragedy and Comedy,—of his having assumed the garb of a Gypsy, and settled for some time in a Gypsy encampment, out of admiration for a young Egyptian beauty,—with fifty others of the same class,—belong undoubtedly (as many of them as are not wholly fabulous) to the four years immediately preceding the time at which my personal knowledge of Mr. Wilson commenced.

From the latter end of 1803 to the spring of 1808, Mr. Wilson had studied at the University of Oxford ; and it was within that period that most of his *escapades* were crowded. He had previously studied as a mere boy, according to the Scotch fashion, at the University of Glasgow, chiefly under the tuition of the late Mr. Jardine (the Professor, I believe, of Logic) and Dr. or Mr. Young (the Professor of Greek). At both Universities he had greatly distinguished himself ; but at Oxford, where the distribution of prizes and honours of every kind is to the last degree parsimonious and select, naturally it follows that such academical distinctions are really *significant* distinctions, and proclaim an unequivocal merit in him who has carried them off from a crowd of 1600 or 2000 co-rivals to whom the contest was open ; whereas in the Scotch Universities, as I am told by Scotch-men, the multiplication of prizes and medals, and the almost indiscriminate profusion with which they are showered abroad, neutralize their whole effect and value. At least this was the case in Mr. Wilson's time ; but lately some con-spicuous changes have been introduced by a Royal Commission (not yet, I believe, dissolved) into one at least of the Scotch Universities, which have greatly improved it in this respect, by bringing it much nearer to the English model. When Mr. Wilson gained a prize of fifty guineas for fifty lines of

English verse, without further inquiry it becomes evident from the mere rarity of the distinction,—which, for a university *now* nearly of five thousand members, occurs but once a year,—and from the great over-proportion of that peculiar class (the Undergraduates) to whom the contest is open,—that such a victory was an indisputable criterion of very conspicuous merit. In fact, never in any place did Mr. Wilson play off his Proteus variety of character and talent with so much brilliant effect as at Oxford. In this great University, the most ancient, and by many degrees the most magnificent in the world, he found a stage for display perfectly congenial with the native elevation of his own character. Perhaps you are not fully aware of the characteristic differences which separate our two English Universities of Oxford and Cambridge from those of Scotland and the Continent : for I have always observed that the best informed foreigners, even after a week's personal acquaintance with the Oxford system, still adhere to the inveterate preconceptions which they had brought with them from the Continent. For instance, they continue obstinately to speak of the *Professors* as the persons to whom the students are indebted for tuition ; whereas the majority of these hold their offices as the most absolute sinecures, and the task of tuition devolves upon the tutors appointed in each particular college. These tutors are called public tutors; meaning that they do not confine their instructions to any one individual, but distribute them amongst all the Undergraduates of the college to which they belong ; and, in addition to these, *private* tutors are allowed to any student who chooses to increase his expenditure in that particular. But the main distinction, which applies to our immediate subject, is the more than regal provision for the lodging and accommodation of the students by the system of *Colleges.* Of these there are in Oxford, neglecting the technical subdivision of *Halls,* five-and-twenty ; and the main use of all, both colleges and halls, is not, as in Scotland and on the Continent, to lodge the head of the University with suitable dignity, and to provide rooms for the library and public business of the University. These purposes are met by a separate provision, distinct from the colleges ; and the colleges are applied as follows : 1st, and mainly, to the reception of the Fellows, and of the Undergraduate Students ; 2dly, to the accommodation of the head (known in different colleges by the several designations of provost, principal, dean, rector, warden, &c.) ; 3dly, to the accommodation of the private library attached to that college, and to the chapel, which is used at least twice every day for public prayers ; 4thly, to the Hall, and the whole establishment of kitchen, wine vaults, buttery, &c., &c., which may be supposed necessary for the liberal accommodation, at the public meals of dinner (and in some colleges supper) of gentlemen and visitors from the country, or from the Continent,—varying (we will suppose) from 25 to 500 heads. Everywhere else the great mass of the students are lodged in obscure nooks and corners, which may or may not be respectable, but are at all events withdrawn from the *surveillance* of the University. I shall state both the ground and the effect (or tendency rather) of this difference. Out of England, universities are not meant exclusively for professional men ; the sons of great landholders, and a large proportion of the sons of noblemen, either go through the same academic course as others, or a shorter course adapted to their particular circumstances. In England, again, the Church is supplied from the rank of gentry—not exclusively, it is true, but in a much larger proportion than anywhere else, except in Ireland. The corresponding ranks in Scotland, from their old connexions with France, have adopted (I believe) much more of the Continental plan for disposing of their sons at this period. At any rate, it will not be contended by any man that Scotland throws anything like the same proportion with England of her gentry and her peerage into her universities. Hence, a higher standard of manners and of habits presides at Oxford and Cambridge ; and, consequently, a demand for much higher accommodations would even *otherwise* have arisen, had not such a demand already been supplied by the munificence of our English princes and peers, both male and female, and, in one instance at least, of a *Scottish* Prince (Baliol). The extent of these vast Caravanseras enables the governors of the various colleges to furnish every student with a set of two rooms at the least, often with a *suite* of three—(I, who lived at Oxford on no more than my school allowance, had that

number)—or in many cases with far more.   In the superior
colleges, indeed (superior, I mean, as to their purse and
landed endowments), all these accommodations keep pace
with the refinements of the age ; and thus a connexion is
maintained between the University and the landed *Noblesse*—
upper and lower—of England, which must be reciprocally
beneficial, and which, under other circumstances, could
scarcely have taken place.

Of these advantages you may be sure that Mr. Wilson
availed himself to the utmost extent.   Instead of going to
Baliol College, he entered himself at *Magdalen*, in the class
of what are called " Gentlemen Commoners."   All of us (you
know) in Oxford and Cambridge wear an Academic dress,
which tells at once our Academic rank with all its modifications.   And the term " *Gentleman Commoner* " implies that
he has more splendid costumes, and more in number ; that
he is expected to spend a great deal more money ; that
he enjoys a few trifling immunities ; and that he has, in
particular instances, something like a king's right of
preëmption, as in the choice of rooms, &c.

Once launched in this orbit, Mr. Wilson continued to
blaze away for the four successive years, 1804, 1805, 1806,
1807, I believe without any intermission.   Possibly I myself was the one sole gownsman who had not then found my
attention fixed by his most heterogeneous reputation.   In a
similar case, Cicero tells a man that ignorance so unaccount-
able of another man's pretensions argued himself to be a
homo ignorabilis; or, in the language of the Miltonic Satan,
" Not to know *me*, argues thyself unknown."   And *that* is
true ; a *homo ignorabilis* most certainly I was.   And even with
that admission it is still difficult to account for the extent and
the duration of my ignorance.   The fact is that the case well
expresses *both* our positions : that *he* should be so conspicuous
as to challenge knowledge from the most sequestered of
anchorites expresses *his* life ; that I should have right to
absolute ignorance of him who was familiar as daylight to
all the rest of Oxford—expresses *mine*.   Never indeed before,
to judge from what I have since heard upon inquiry, did a
man, by variety of talents and variety of humours, contrive
to place himself as the connecting link between orders of

men so essentially repulsive of each other, as Mr. Wilson in
this instance.

"Omnis Aristippum decuit color, et status, et res."

From the learned president of his college, Dr. Routh, the
editor of parts of Plato, and of some Theological Selections,
with whom Wilson enjoyed an unlimited favour—from this
learned Academic Doctor, and many others of the same class,
Wilson had an infinite gamut of friends and associates,
running through every key, and the diapason closing full in
groom, cobbler, stable-boy, barber's apprentice, with every
shade and hue of blackguard and ruffian. In particular,
amongst this latter kind of worshipful society, there was no
man who had any talents real or fancied for thumping or
being thumped, but had experienced some *preeing* of his
merits from Mr. Wilson. All other pretensions in the
gymnastic arts he took a pride in humbling or in honouring ;
but chiefly his examinations fell upon pugilism ; and not a
man, who could either "give" or "take," but boasted to have
punished, or to have been punished by, *Wilson of Mallens.*[1]

A little before the time at which my acquaintance with
Mr. Wilson commenced, he had purchased a beautiful estate
on the lake of Windermere, which bore the ancient name of
Elleray—a name which, with his customary good taste, Mr.
Wilson has never disturbed. With the usual latitude of
language in such cases, I say *on* Windermere ; but in fact
this charming estate lies far above the lake ; and one of the
most interesting of its domestic features is the foreground of
the rich landscape which connects, by the most gentle scale
of declivities, this almost aërial altitude (as, for *habitable*
ground, it really is) with the sylvan margin of the deep
water which rolls a mile and a half below. When I say a
mile and a half, you will understand me to compute the

[1] The usual colloquial corruption of *Magdalen* in Ox. is *Maudlin ;*
but amongst the very *lie du peuple* it is called *Mallens.*

[The second portion of the paper ended here, but with this added
paragraph—"But this part of Wilson's life presents too wide a field,
and abounds with too many incidents, to be compressed within this
letter ; I must therefore solicit the privilege of trespassing on another
number of the *Edinburgh Literary Gazette.*"—M.]

descent according to the undulations of the ground ; because else the perpendicular elevation above the level of the lake cannot be above one half of that extent. Seated on such an eminence, but yet surrounded by foregrounds of such quiet beauty, and settling downwards towards the lake by such tranquil steps as to take away every feeling of precipitous or dangerous elevation, Elleray possesses a double character of beauty, rarely found in connexion ; and yet each, by singular good fortune, in this case absolute and unrivalled in its kind. Within a bow-shot of each other may be found stations of the deepest seclusion, fenced in by verdurous walls of insuperable forest heights, and presenting a limited scene of beauty —deep, solemn, noiseless, severely sequestered—and other stations of a magnificence so gorgeous as few estates in this island can boast, and of those few perhaps none in such close connexion with a dwelling-house. Stepping out from the very windows of the drawing-room, you find yourself on a terrace which gives you the feeling of a " specular height," such as you might expect on Ararat, or might appropriately conceive on " Athos seen from Samothrace." The whole course of a noble lake, about eleven miles long, lies subject to your view, with many of its islands, and its two opposite shores so different in character : the one stern, precipitous, and gloomy ; the other (and luckily the hither one) by the mere bounty of nature and of accident—by the happy disposition of the ground originally, and by the fortunate equilibrium between the sylvan tracts, meandering irregularly through the whole district, and the proportion left to verdant fields and meadows,—wearing the character of the richest park scenery ; except indeed that this character is here and there a little modified by a quiet hedge-row or the stealing smoke which betrays the embowered cottage of a labourer. But the sublime, peculiar, and not-to-be-forgotten feature of the scene is the great system of mountains which unite about five miles off at the head of the lake to lock in and inclose this noble landscape. The several ranges of mountains which stand at various distances within six or seven miles of the little town of Ambleside, all separately various in their forms and all eminently picturesque, when seen from Elleray appear to blend and group as parts of one connected whole ; and, when their usual drapery of clouds happens to take a fortunate arrangement, and the sunlights are properly broken and thrown from the most suitable quarter of the heavens, I cannot recollect any spectacle in England or Wales, of the many hundreds I have seen bearing a local, if not a national, reputation for magnificence of prospect, which so much dilates the heart with a sense of power and aërial sublimity as this terrace view from Elleray. It is possible that I may have stood on other mountain terraces commanding as ample a view and as happily combined; but the difference of effect must always be immense between a spectacle to which you ascend by half a day's labour, and that upon which you are launched in a second of time from the breakfast table. It is of great importance, for the enjoyment of any natural scene, to be liberated from the necessity of viewing it under circumstances of haste and anxiety, to have it in one's power to surrender one's self passively and tranquilly to the influences of the objects as they gradually reveal themselves, and to be under no summons to crowd one's whole visual energy and task of examination within a single quarter of an hour. Having seen Elleray at all times under these favourable circumstances, it is certainly not impossible that I may unconsciously have overrated in some degree its pretensions in comparison with some rival scenes. I may have committed the common error of attributing to the *objects* the whole sum of an impression which in part belonged to the *subjective* advantages of the contemplator and the benefits of his station. But, making every allowance in this direction, I am still of opinion that Elleray has, in connexion with the merits common to all scenes of its class, others peculiar to itself—and such as are indispensable conditions for the full effect of all the rest. In particular, I would instance this :—To bring any scene upon a level of competition with Elleray as to range and majesty of prospect, it is absolutely essential that it should occupy an equal elevation, or one not conspicuously inferior. Now, it is seldom indeed that eminences so commanding are not, by that very circumstance, unfitted to the picturesque aspects of things : in fact I remember no tract of ground so elevated as Elleray from which the lowest level of the adjacent country does not take a petty, dotted, and map-like appearance.

But this effect, which is so heavy a price for the sublimities of the upper regions, at Elleray is entirely intercepted by the exquisite gradations of descent by which the contiguous grounds begin their fall to the level of the lake : the moment that this fall in any quarter becomes accelerated and precipitous, it is concealed by the brows of this beautiful hanging foreground; and so happily is this remedy applied that in every instance where the lowest grounds would, if seen at all, from their immediate proximity, be seen by the spectator looking down perpendicularly as into a well, there they are uniformly hidden ; and these lowest levels first emerge to view at a remote distance—where, being necessarily viewed obliquely, they suffer no peculiar disadvantage by being viewed from an eminence. In short, to sum up the whole in one word, the splendours of Elleray, which could not have been had but at an unusual elevation, are by a rare bounty of nature obtained without one of those sacrifices for the learned eye which are usually entailed upon that one single advantage of unusual elevation.

The beautiful estate which I have thus described to you was ornamented by no suitable dwelling-house at the time when it was purchased by Mr. Wilson. There was indeed a rustic cottage, most picturesquely situated, which, with the addition of a drawing-room thrown out at one end, was made for the present (and, as it turned out, for many a year to come) capable of meeting the hospitable system of life adopted by its owner. But, with a view to more ample and luxurious accommodations, even at that early period of his possession (1808), Mr. Wilson began to build a mansion of larger and more elegant proportions. The shell, and perhaps the greater part of the internal work, was soon finished, but, for some reason which I never remember to have inquired into, was not rendered thoroughly habitable (and consequently not inhabited) till the year 1825. I think it worth while to mention this house particularly, because it has always appeared to me a silent commentary on its master's state of mind, and an exemplification of his character both as it was and as it appeared. At first sight there was an air of adventurousness, or even of extravagance, about the plan and situation of the building ; and yet, upon a considerate examination (and latterly upon a practical trial) of it, I cannot see that within the same dimensions it would have been possible to have contrived a more judicious or commodious house. Thus, for instance, the house is planted upon the boldest and most exposed point of ground that can be found on the whole estate, consequently upon that which might have been presumed (and I believe was really reputed) to be the very stormiest : yet, whether from counteracting screens of wood that have since been reared in fortunate situations, or from what other cause I know not, undoubtedly at this day no practical inconvenience is suffered ; though it is true, I believe, that in the earlier years of its history the house bore witness occasionally, by dismal wrecks of roof and windows, to the strength and fury of the wind on one particular quarter. Again, in the internal arrangements : one room was constructed of such ample proportions, with a view to dancing, that the length (as I remember) was about seventy feet ; the other dimensions I have forgotten. Now, in this instance most people saw an evidence of nothing but youthful extravagance, and a most disproportionate attention directed to one single purpose, which upon that scale could not probably be of very frequent occurrence in *any* family. This by the way was at any rate a sensible extravagance in my judgment ; for our English mode of building tends violently to the opposite and most unwholesome extravagance of giving to the very principal room of a house the beggarly proportions of closets. However, the sequel showed that, in providing for one end, Mr. Wilson had not lost sight of others : for the seventy-feet room was so divided by strong folding-doors, or temporary partitions, as in its customary state to exhibit three rooms of ordinary proportions, and unfolded its full extent only by special and extraordinary mechanism. Other instances I might give in which the plan seemed to be extravagant or inconsiderate, and yet really turned out to have been calculated with the coolest judgment and the nicest foresight of domestic needs. It is sufficient to say that I do not know a house apparently more commodiously arranged than this, which was planned and built with utmost precipitation, and in the very hey-day of a most tempestuous youth. In one thing only, upon a retrospect at this day of the whole case, there may appear to have been some imprudence,—viz. that, timber being then at a most unprecedented high price, it is probable that the building cost seven or eight hundred pounds more than it would have done a few years later. Allowing for this one oversight, the principal house on the Elleray estate, which at the time was looked upon as an evidence of Mr. Wilson's flightiness of mind, remains at this day a lasting monument of his good sense and judgment.

Whilst I justify him, however, on this head, I am obliged to admit that on another field, at that very time, Mr. Wilson was displaying the most reckless profusion. A sailing club had been established on Windermere,—by whom I never heard; very probably by Mr. Wilson himself; at all events, he was the leader and the soul of the confederation; and he applied annually nothing less than a little fortune to the maintenance of the many expenses which arose out of it. Amongst the members of the club there were more than one who had far larger fortunes than Mr. Wilson could ever have possessed; but he would permit no one to outshine him on this arena. The number of his boats was so great as to compose a little fleet; and some of them, of unusually large dimensions for this lake, had been built at an enormous expense by regular builders brought over expressly from the port of Whitehaven (distant from Elleray about forty-five miles), and kept during the whole progress of their labour at a most expensive Lakers' hotel. One of these boats in particular, a ten-oared barge, which you will find specially introduced by name in Professor Wilson's tale of "The Foresters," was generally believed at the time to have cost him at the least five hundred pounds. And, as the number of sailors which it required to man these boats was necessarily very great at particular seasons, and as the majority of these sailors lived, during the period of their services, with little or no restraint upon their expenses at the most costly inn in the neighbourhood,—it may be supposed very readily that about this time Mr. Wilson's lavish expenditure, added to the demands of architects and builders, and the recent purchase of Elleray, must have seriously injured his patrimonial property,—though generally believed to have been originally considerably more than thirty thousand (many asserted forty thousand) pounds. In fact, he had never less than three establishments going on concurrently for some years : one at the town or village of Bowness (the little port of the lake of Windermere), for his boatmen ; one at the Ambleside Hotel, about five miles distant, for himself ; and a third at Elleray, for his servants, and the occasional resort of himself and his friends. It is the opinion of some people that about this time, and during the succeeding two years, Mr. Wilson dissipated the main bulk of his patrimony in profuse expenditure. But more considerate people see no ground for that opinion : his expenses, though great, were never adequate to the dilapidation of so large an estate as he was reputed to have inherited : and the prevailing opinion is that some great loss of £20,000 at a blow, by the failure of some trustee or other, was the true cause of that diminution in his property which, within a year or two from this time, he is generally supposed to have suffered. However, as Mr. Wilson himself has always maintained an obstinate silence on the subject, and as the mere fact of the loss (however probable) is not more accurately known to me than its extent, or its particular mode, or its cause,—I shall not allow myself to make any conjectural speculations on the subject. It can be interesting to you and me only from one of its consequences,—viz. its leading him afterwards to seek a professorship : for most certain it is that, if the splendour of Mr. Wilson's youthful condition as to pecuniary matters had not been in some remarkable degree overcast, and suffered some signal eclipse, he would never have surrendered any part of that perfect liberty which was so dear to him for all the honours and rewards that could have been offered by the foremost universities of Europe.

You will have heard, no doubt, from some of those with whom you have conversed about Professor Wilson when you were in Europe, or you may have read it in Peter's Letters,[1] that in very early life (probably about the age of eighteen) he had formed a scheme for penetrating into Central Africa, visiting the city of Timbuctoo, and solving (if it were possible) the great outstanding problem of the source of the Niger. To this scheme he was attracted probably not so

[1] Lockhart's *Peter's Letters to his Kinsfolk*, published in 1819.—M.

much by any particular interest in the improvement of geographical knowledge, as by the youthful spirit of romantic adventure, and a very uncommon craving for whatever was grand, indefinite, and gigantic in conception, supposing that it required at the same time great physical powers in the execution. There cannot be a doubt for us at this day, who look back upon the melancholy list of victims in this perilous field of discovery which has been furnished by the two or three and twenty years elapsed since Mr. Wilson's plan was in agitation, that in that enterprise—had he ever irretrievably embarked himself upon it—he would infallibly have perished ; for, though reasonably strong, he was not strong upon that heroic scale which an expedition so Titanic demands ; and, what was perhaps still more important, if strong enough, he was not *hardy* enough,—as a gentleman rarely is, more especially where he has literary habits ; because the exposure to open air, which is the indispensable condition of hardiness, is at any rate interrupted—even if it were not counteracted—by the luxurious habits and the relaxing atmosphere of the library and the drawing-room. Moreover, Mr. Wilson's constitution was irritable and disposed to fever ; his temperament was too much that of a man of genius not to have furnished a mine of inflammable materials for any tropical climate ; his prudence, as regarded his health, was not remarkable ; and, if to all these internal and personal grounds of danger you add the incalculable hazards of the road itself, every friend of Mr. Wilson's must have rejoiced on hearing that in 1808, when I first met him, this Tim- (or Tom-) buctoo scheme was already laid aside.

Yet, as the stimulus of danger, in one shape or other, was at that time of life perhaps essential to his comfort, he soon substituted another scheme, which at this day might be accomplished with ease and safety enough, but in the year 1809 (under the rancorous system of Bonaparte) was full of hazard. In this scheme he was so good as to associate myself as one of his travelling companions, together with an earlier friend of his own—an Englishman, of a philosophical turn of mind, with whom he had been a fellow-student at Glasgow ; and we were certainly all three of an age and character to have enjoyed the expedition in the very highest

degree, had the events of the war allowed us to realize our
plan. The plan was as follows :—From Falmouth, by one of
the regular packets, we were to have sailed to the Tagus,
and, landing wherever accident should allow us, to purchase
mules, hire Spanish servants, and travel extensively in
Spain and Portugal for eight or nine months ; thence, by
such of the islands in the Mediterranean as particularly
interested us, we were gradually to have passed into Greece,
and thence to Constantinople. Finally, we were to have
visited the Troad, Syria, Egypt, and perhaps Nubia. I feel
it almost ludicrous to sketch the outline of so extensive a
tour, no part of which was ever executed ; such a Barmecide
feast is laughable in the very rehearsal. Yet it is bare justice
to ourselves to say that on our parts there was no slackness or
make-believe; what put an extinguisher upon our project was the
entrance of Napoleon into Spain, his immediate advance upon
Madrid, and the wretched catastrophe of the expedition so
miserably misconducted under Sir John Moore. The *prestige*
of French generalship was at that time a nightmare upon the
courage and spirit of hopeful exertion throughout Europe ;
and the earliest dawn was only then beginning to arise of
that glorious experience which was forever to dissolve it.
Sir J. Moore, and through him his gallant but unfortunate
army, was the last conspicuous victim to the mere sound and
humbug (if you will excuse a coarse expression) of the words
Napoleon Bonaparte. What he fled from was precisely those
two words. And the timid policy adopted by Sir John on
that memorable occasion would—among other greater and
national consequences—have had this little collateral interest
to us unfortunate travellers, had our movements been as
speedy as we had anticipated, that it would have cost us our
heads. A certain bulletin, issued by Bonaparte at that time,
sufficiently apprised us of that little truth. In this bulletin
Bonaparte proclaimed with a careless air, but making at the
same time somewhat of a boast of it, that, having happened
to meet a party of sixteen British travellers—persons of
whom he had ascertained nothing at all but that they did not
bear a military character—he had issued a summary order
that they should all be strung up without loss of time by
the neck. In this little facetious anecdote, as Bonaparte

seemed to think it, we read the fate that we had escaped. Had nothing occurred to retard our departure from this country, we calculated that the route we had laid down for our daily motions would have brought us to Guadarama (or what was the name of the pass ?) just in time to be hanged. Having a British general at our backs with an army of more than thirty thousand effective men, we should certainly have roamed in advance with perfect reliance upon the old British policy of fighting, for which we could never have allowed ourselves to dream of such a substitute as a flight through all the passes of Gallicia on the principle of "*the D— take the hindmost.*" Infallibly also we should have been surprised by the extraordinary rapidity at that time of the French movements ; our miserable shambling mules, with their accursed tempers, would have made but a shabby attempt at flight before a squadron of light cavalry ; and in short, as I said before, we should have come just in time to be hanged. And hanged we should all have been : though *why*, and upon what principle, it would be difficult to say ; and probably that question would have been left to after consideration in some more philosophical age. You will suppose naturally that we rejoiced at our escape ; and so undoubtedly we did. Yet, for my part, I had, among nineteen-twentieths of joy, just one-twentieth of a lingering regret that we had missed the picturesque fate that awaited us. The reason was this : it has been through life an infirmity of Mr. Wilson's (at least in my judgment an infirmity) to think too indulgently of Bonaparte, not merely in an intellectual point of view, but even with reference to his pretensions—hollower, one would think, than the wind—to moral elevation and magnanimity. Such a mistake, about a man who could never in any one instance bring himself to speak generously, or even forbearingly, of an enemy, rouses my indignation as often as I recur to it ; and in Professor Wilson I have long satisfied myself that it takes its rise from a more comprehensive weakness, the greatest in fact which besets his mind, viz. a general tendency to bend to the prevailing opinion of the world, and a constitutional predisposition to sympathise with power and whatsoever is triumphant. Hence, I could not but regret most poignantly the capital opportunity I had forfeited of throwing

in a deep and stinging sarcasm at his idol, just at the moment
when we should have been waiting to be turned off.   I know
Professor Wilson well : though a brave man, at twenty-two
he enjoyed life with a rapture that few men have ever
known, and he would have clung to it with awful tenacity.
Horribly he would have abominated the sight of the rope, and
ruefully he would have sighed if I had suggested to him on
the gallows any thoughts of that beautiful and quiet Elleray
which he had left behind in England.   Just at that moment
I acknowledge that it would have been fiendish, but yet what
a heaven of a luxury it would have been in the way of revenge
—to have stung him with some neat epigram, that I might
have composed in our walk to the gallows, or while the
ropes were getting into tune, on the generosity and
magnanimity of Bonaparte !   Perhaps, in a sober estimate,
hanging might be too heavy a price for the refutation of a
single error ; yet still, at times, when my moral sense is
roused and provoked by the obstinate blindness of Professor
Wilson to the meanness and *parvanimity* [1] of Bonaparte (a
blindness which in him, as in all other worshippers of false
idols, is connected at the moment with intense hatred for
those who refuse to partake in it), a wandering regret comes
over me that we should have missed so fine an opportunity
for gathering in our own persons some of those redundant
bounties which the Corsican's " magnanimity " at that time
scattered from his cornucopia of malice to the English name
upon all his unfortunate prisoners of that nation.

But enough of this.   An event soon occurred in Mr.
Wilson's life which made it a duty to dismiss forever all
travelling schemes that were connected with so much hazard
as this.   The fierce *acharnement* of Bonaparte so pointedly
directed to everything English, and the prostration of the
Continent, which had enabled him absolutely to seal every
port of Europe against an Englishman,—who could now no
longer venture to stray a mile beyond the range of the ship's

---

[1] I coin this word *parvanimity* as an adequate antithesis to *magnanimity ;* for the word *pusillanimity* has received from usage such a
confined determination to one single idea, viz. the defect of spirit and
courage, that it is wholly unfitted to be the antipode to the complex
idea of magnanimity.

guns which had brought him to the shore, without the
certainty of being arrested as a spy,—this unheard-of condition of things had at length compelled all English gentlemen to reconcile themselves for the present to the bounds of
their own island ; and, accordingly, in the spring of 1809, we
three unhanged friends had entirely weaned our minds from
the travelling scheme which had so completely occupied our
thoughts in 1808.   Mr. Wilson in particular gave himself up
to the pleasures and occupations furnished by the neighbourhood of Windermere, which at that time were many and
various ; living myself at a distance of nine miles from
Elleray, I did not see much of him through this year 1809 ;
in 1810 he married a young English lady, greatly admired
for her beauty and the elegance of her manners, who was
generally supposed to have brought him a fortune of about
ten thousand pounds.   In saying *that*, I violate no confidence
at any time reposed in me, for I rely only on the public
voice—which, in this instance, I have been told by well-
informed persons, was tolerably correct.   Be that as it may,
however, in other respects I have the best reasons for
believing that this marriage connexion has proved the
happiest event of Mr. Wilson's life ; and that the delightful
temper and disposition of his wife have continued to shed a
sunshine of peace and quiet happiness over his domestic
establishment, which were well worth all the fortunes in the
world.   This lady has brought him a family of two sons and
three daughters, all interesting by their personal appearance
and their manners, and at this time rapidly growing up into
young men and women.

Here I should close all further notice of Mr. Wilson's life,
and confine myself, through what remains of the space which
I have allowed myself, to a short critical notice (such as it
may be proper for a friend to write) of his literary character
and merits ; but one single event remains of a magnitude
too conspicuous in any man's life to be dismissed wholly
without mention.   I should add, therefore, that, about eight
or nine years after his marriage (for I forget the precise year),
Mr. Wilson offered himself a candidate for the chair of Moral
Philosophy in the University of Edinburgh, which had
recently become vacant by the death of Dr. Thomas Brown,

the immediate successor of Mr. Dugald Stewart. The Scotch, who know just as much about what they call " Moral [1] Philosophy " and Metaphysics as the English do, viz. exactly nothing at all, pride themselves prodigiously upon these two names of Dugald Stewart and Dr. Brown, and imagine that they filled the chair with some peculiar brilliance. Upon that subject a word or two farther on. Meantime this notion made the contest peculiarly painful and invidious, amongst ungenerous enemies, for any untried man—no matter though his real merits had been a thousand times greater than those of his predecessors. This Mr. Wilson found : he had made himself enemies,—whether by any unjustifiable violences and wanton provocations on his own part, I have no means of knowing. In whatever way created, however, these enemies now used the advantages of the occasion with rancorous malignity, and persecuted him at every step with unrelenting fury. Very different was the treatment he met with from his competitor in the contest.[2] In that one circumstance of the case, the person of his competitor, he had reason to think himself equally fortunate and unfortunate : fortunate, that he should be met by the opposition of a man whose opposition was honour—a man of birth, talents, and high breeding, a good scholar, and for extensive reading and universal knowledge of books (and especially of philosophic literature) the Magliabecchi of Scotland ; unfortunate on the other hand that this accomplished opponent, adorned by so many brilliant gifts that recommended him to the contested office, should happen to be his early and highly valued friend. The particular progress of the contest, and its circumstances, I am not able

[1] Everywhere in the world except in Scotland, by *moral* philosophy is meant the philosophy of the will, as opposed to the philosophy of the intellect : in Scotland only the word *moral* is used, by the strongest abuse, as a comprehensive designation of whatsoever is not *physical ;* so that in the cycle of knowledge undertaken by the Edinburgh Professor of Moral Philosophy are included logic, metaphysics, ethics, psychology, anthropology,—and, in one word, almost all human knowledge, with the exception of physics and mathematics.—[Not correct.—M.]

[2] Sir William Hamilton, then *Professor of History* in the University (1821-1836) ; afterwards (1836-1856) Professor of Logic and Metaphysics.—M.

to state.   In general, I have heard in Edinburgh that, from
political influences which chiefly governed the course of the
election, the conduct of the partisans (perhaps on both sides)
was intemperate, personal, and unjust; whilst that of the
principals and their immediate friends was full of forbearance and generosity.   The issue was that Mr. Wilson carried
the Professorship,[1]—by what majority of votes, I am unable
to say; and you will be pleased to hear that any little cool-
ness, which must naturally have succeeded to so warm a contest,
has long since passed away, and the two rival candidates
have been for many years restored to their early feelings of
mutual esteem and regard.

Here I pause, for everything that concerns in the remotest
way the incidents of Professor Wilson's life : one letter I
mean to add, as I have already promised, on the particular
position which he occupies in relation to modern literature ;
and then I have done.[2]   Meantime, let me hope that you have
not so far miscalculated my purpose as to have been looking
out for anecdotes (*i.e.* scandal) about Professor Wilson throughout the course of this letter ; since, if in any case I could descend
to cater for tastes of that description (which, I am persuaded,
are naturally no tastes of *your* family), you must feel, on
reflection, how peculiarly impossible it is to take that
course in sketching the character of a friend, because the
very means by which in almost every case one becomes
possessed of such private anecdotes are the opportunities
thrown in one's way by the confiding negligence of affectionate friendship, — opportunities, therefore, which must be
forever sacred to every man of honour.

Yours most faithfully,

PARMENIDES.

[1] This was in July 1820.—M.
[2] No such additional letter appeared.—M.

PROFESSOR WILSON

SKETCH IN 1850 [1]

THERE are many Newtons in England: yet, for all that, there is but one Newton for earth and the children of earth ; which Newton is Isaac, and Kepler is his prophet.[2]   There

[1] From a number of *Hogg's Instructor* in that year.   There was then running in that Edinburgh periodical a series of brief biographies of eminent persons, with the accompaniment of engraved portraits, under the title OUR PORTRAIT GALLERY ; and De Quincey had been asked, or had volunteered, to write the sketch to accompany the portrait of Christopher North.   This, accordingly, is the third sketch he has left us of that life-long friend of his,—the first in order of time having been that of 1829 in the *Edinburgh Literary Gazette* (immediately preceding this in the present volume), and the second that of 1840 in the series of his Literary and Lake Reminiscences in *Tait's Magazine* (reprinted *ante*, Vol. II).   The present sketch is slight, and contains repetitions from the others ; but it takes Wilson on to a later stage of his life.   We take it from the reprint of it in vol. xvi of the previous collective edition of De Quincey's writings.—M.

[2] I use the word *prophet* in the ordinary sense.   Yet in strictness this is not the primary sense.   Primarily it means and Scripturally it means—*interpreter of the divine purposes and thoughts.*   If those purposes and thoughts should happen to lurk in mysterious doctrines of religion, then the prophet is simply an *exegetes*, or expounder.   But, it is true, if they lurk in the dark mazes of time and futurity unrolling itself from the central present, then the prophet means a seer or reader of the future, in our ordinary modern sense.   But this modern sense is neither the Mahometan sense, nor that which prevails in the New Testament.   Mahomet is the prophet of God—not in the sense of predicter from afar, but as the organ of communication between God and man, or revealer of the divine will.   In St. Paul, again, gifts of prophecy mean uniformly any extraordinary qualifications for unfold-

are many Wilsons in Scotland, and indeed many out of
Scotland; yet, for all that, Mother Earth and her children
recognise but one, which one sits in the Edinburgh chair of
Moral Philosophy. And, when *that* is said, all is said; is
there anything to say more? Yes, there is an infinity to
say, but no need to say it !

" Cætera norunt
Et Tagus, et Ganges, forsan et Antipodes."

Such a radiance, which extinguishes all lesser lights, has
its own evils. If a man like Mr. Touchwood of the *Hottle*
in "St. Ronan's Well" should find his way to *Tim-* (or to
Tom-) *buctoo*,—no matter which, for *Tim* and *Tom* are very
like each other (especially *Tim*),—in that case, he might
have occasion to draw a bill upon England. And such a
bill would assuredly find its way to its destination. The
drawer of the bill might probably be intercepted on his
homeward route, but the bill would *not*. Now, if this bill
were drawn upon "John Wilson," *tout court*, not a post-office
in Christendom would scruple to forward it to the Professor.
The Professor, in reply, would indorse upon it "*No effects*."
But in the end he would pay it, for his heart would yearn
with brotherly admiration towards a man who had thumped
his way to the very navel of Africa.

This mention, by the way, of Timbuctoo, forced upon us
by an illustration, suddenly reminds us that the Professor
himself, in the stage of early manhood, was self-dedicated to
the adventure of Timbuctoo. What reasons arose to disturb
this African scheme, it is strange that we have forgotten, or
else that we have never heard. Possibly Major Houghton's
fate may have recalled Wilson, in the midst of his youthful
enthusiasm, to that natural but afflicting fear which, "like
the raven o'er the infected house," sweeps at intervals over
the martial hopes of most young soldiers,—viz. the fear, not

ing the meaning of Scripture doctrines, or introducing light and coherency amongst their elements, and perhaps *never* the qualifications
for inspired foresight. In the true sense of the word, therefore,
Newton was the prophet of Kepler, *i.e.* the exegetic commentator on
Kepler, not Kepler of Newton. But the best policy in this world is
to think with the wise and (generally speaking) to talk with the
vulgar.

of death, but of death incurred for no commensurate return and with no rememberable circumstances. To die, to die early, *that* belongs to the chances of the profession which the soldier has adopted. But to die as an *aide-de-camp* in the act of riding across a field of battle with some unimportant order that has not even been delivered—to feel that a sacrifice so vast for the sufferer will not stir a ripple on the surface of that mighty national interest for which the sacrifice has been made—this it is which, in such a case, makes the pang of dying. Wilson had seen Mungo Park ; from him he must have learned the sort of razor's-edge on which the traveller walks in the interior of Africa. The trackless forest, the unbridged river, the howling wilderness, the fierce Mahometan bigotry of the Moor, the lawlessness of the Pagan native, the long succession of petty despots—looking upon you with cruel contempt if you travel as a poor man, looking upon you with respect, but as a godsend ripe for wrecking, if you travel as a rich one—all these chances of ruin, with the climate superadded, leave too little of rational hopefulness to such an enterprise for sustaining those genial spirits without which nothing of that nature can prosper. A certain proportion of anxiety, or even of gloomy fear, is a stimulant ; but in this excess they become killing as the frost of Labrador. Or, if not, only where a man has a demon within him. Such a demon had Park.[1] And a far mightier demon had Wilson,—

[1] *"Park"* :—It is painful, but at the same time it is affecting, for the multitudes who respect the memory of Park [1771-1805], to know that this brave man's ruin was accomplished through a weak place in his own heart. Park, upon his second expedition [in 1805], was placed in a most trying condition. We all know the fable of the traveller that resisted Boreas and his storms—his hail, his sleet, and his blustering blasts ; *there* the traveller was strong ; but he could not resist Phœbus, could not resist his flattering gales and his luxurious wooings. He yielded to the fascinations of love what he had refused to the defiances of malice. Such temptations had Park to face when, for the second time, he reached the coast of Africa. Had the world frowned upon him, as once upon the same coast it *did*, then he would have found a nobility in his own desolation. *That* he could have faced ; and, without false bias, could have chosen what was best on the whole. But it happened that the African Association of London had shown him great confidence and great liberality. His sensitive generosity could not support the painful thought that, by delaying his expedition, he might seem to be abusing their kindness. He

but, luckily for us all, a demon that haunted the mind with objects more thoroughly intellectual.

Wilson was born, we believe, in Paisley. It is the Scottish custom, through the want of great public schools for the higher branches of education, that universities, to their own great injury, are called upon to undertake the functions of schools. It follows from this that mere schoolboys are in Scotland sent to college ; whereas, on our English system, none go to Oxford or Cambridge but young men ranging from eighteen to twenty. Agreeably to this Scottish usage, Wilson was sent at a boyish age to the university of Glasgow, and for some years was placed under the care of Professor Jardine. From Glasgow, and, we believe, in his eighteenth year, he was transferred to Oxford. The college which he selected was Magdalen, of which college Addison had been an *alumnus*. Here he entered as a *gentleman-commoner*, and, in fact, could not do otherwise ; for Magdalen receives no others, except, indeed, those who are on the foundation, and who come thither by right of election. The very existence of such a class as gentlemen-commoners has been angrily complained of, as an undue concession of licence, or privilege, or distinction to mere wealth, when all distinction should naturally rise out of learning or intellectual superiority. But the institution had probably a laudable and a wise origin. The elder sons of wealthy families, who needed no professional employments, had no particular motive for resorting to the universities ; and one motive they had against it—viz. that they must thus come under a severer code of discipline than when living at home. In order, therefore, to conciliate this class, and to attract them into association with those who would inevitably give them some tincture of literary tastes and knowledge, an easier yoke, as regarded attendance upon lectures and other college exercises, was imposed upon all who, by assuming the higher expenditure of *gentlemen-commoners*,[1] professed themselves to be rich enough for living

precipitated his motions, therefore, by one entire half-year. That original error threw him upon the wrong season, and drew after it the final error which led to the conflict in which he perished.

[1] " *Gentlemen-commoners* " :—The name is derived from our Oxford word *commons*, which in ordinary parlance means whatever is furnished at the public dinner-table, or (in those colleges which still retain public

without a profession. The purpose had been, as we have no doubt, to diffuse the liberalities of literature throughout the great body of the landed aristocracy ; and for many generations, as it would be easy to show, that object had been respectably accomplished ; for our old traditional portrait of the English country gentleman, from Fielding downwards to this ultra-democratic day, is a vulgar libel and a lie of malice. So far from being the bigoted and obtuse order described in popular harangues, the landed gentry of England has ever been the wisest order amongst us, and much ahead of the commercial body.

From Oxford, on returning to Scotland, Wilson rejoined his mother, then living in Queen Street, Edinburgh. He adopted the law as his nominal profession, with no fixed resolution, perhaps, to practise it. About 1814, we believe, he was called to the bar. In 1818, he became Professor of Moral Philosophy in the University of Edinburgh [1] ; and, we think, it was in the previous year that *Blackwood's Magazine* was established, which, from the seventh number downwards (though latterly by intermitting fits), has continued to draw more memorable support from *him* than ever journal did from the pen of an individual writer. He was not the editor of that journal at any time. The late Mr. Blackwood, a sagacious and energetic man, was his own editor ; but Wilson was its intellectual Atlas, and very probably, in one sense, its creator—viz. that he might be the first suggester (as undoubtedly he was at one time the sole executive realiser) of that great innovating principle started by this journal, under which it oscillated pretty equally between human life on the one hand and literature on the other.

suppers) at the supper-table. Reflecting at this moment upon the word, we should presume it to be the first two syllables colloquially corrupted of the Latin *commensalia*. A commoner is one who is a *fellow-tabler*, who eats his *commensalia* in company with other undergraduate students. A gentleman-commoner is one who by right may claim to be a fellow-tabler with the governing part of the college ; although in large colleges, where this order is extensive enough to justify such an arrangement, the gentle-commoners dine at a separate table. In Cambridge they bear the name of *fellow-commoners*.

[1] An error : it was in 1820.—M.

Out of these magazine articles has been drawn the occasion of a grave reproach to Professor Wilson. Had he, it is said, thrown the same weight of energy and the same fiery genius into a less desultory shape, it is hard to compute how enormous and systematic a book he might have written. *That* is true : had he worked a little at the book every day of his life, on the principle of the Greek painter—*nulla dies sine linea*—by this time the book would have towered into that altitude as to require long ladders and scaffoldings for studying it ; and, like the Vicar of Wakefield's family picture, could find its way into no human chambers without pulling down the sides of the house. In the foot-notes, where the street lamps would keep him in order, the Professor might have carried on soberly enough. But in the upper part of the page, where he would feel himself striding away *in nubibus,* oh crimini! what larkings there would have been, what sprees with the Aurora Borealis! What a rise he would have taken out of us poor wretches below! The man in the moon would have been frightened into *apogee* by the menaces of the crutch. And, after all, the book never *could* have been suffered to stay at home ; it must have been exported to central Asia on Dr. Johnson's principle, who said to Miss Knight,[1] a young Englishwoman of very large dimensions, when she communicated to the doctor her design to live on the Continent, " Do, my dear, by all means—really you are too big for an island." Certainly, awful thoughts of capsizing flit across the fancy when one sees too vast a bulk shipped on board our tight little Britannic ark. But, speaking seriously, the whole doctrine from which exhales this charge against the Professor of misapplied powers calls for revision. Wise was that old Grecian who said—Μέγα βιβλίον, μέγα κακόν—Big book, big nuisance! For books are the military " baggage " of the human understanding in its endless march. And what is baggage? Once in a hundred times it ministers to our marching necessities ; but for the other ninety-nine times it embarrasses the agility of our movement. And the Romans, therefore, who are the oldest and the best authorities on all military questions, expressed

---

[1] *" Miss Knight "* :—This young lady had offered her homage to Dr. Johnson by extending his *Rasselas* into a sequel entitled *Dinarbas.*

the upshot of these conflicting tendencies in the legionary
baggage by calling it *impedimenta*, mere hindrances. They
tolerated it, and why did they do *that*? Because, in the
case 99 + 1 the baggage might happen to be absolutely indispensable. For the mere possibility of that one case, which,
when it came, would not be evaded, they endured what was
a nuisance through all the other cases. But they took a
comic revenge by deriving the name from the ninety-nine
cases where the baggage was a nuisance, rather than from the
hundredth where it might chance to be the salvation of the
army. To the author of every big book, so far from regarding him as a benefactor, the torture ought to be administered
instantly by this interrogative dilemma : Is there anything
new (which is not false) in your book ? If he says— *no*,
then you have a man, by his own confession, ripe for the
gallows. If he says—*yes*, then you reply : What a wretch
in that case must you be, that have hidden a thing which
you suppose important to mankind in that great wilderness
of a book, where I and other honest men must spend half a
life in running about to find it ! It is, besides, the remark
of a clever French writer in our own days, that hardly any
of the cardinal works upon which revolve the capital interests of man are large works. Plato, for instance, has but
one of his many works large enough to fill a small *octavo*.
Aristotle, as to bulk, is a mere pamphleteer, if you except
perhaps four works ; and each of those might easily be
crowded into a *duodecimo*. Neither Shakspere nor Milton
has written any long work. Newton's *Principia*, indeed,
makes a small quarto ; but this arises from its large type
and its diagrams : it might be printed in a pocket shape.
And, besides all this, even when a book *is* a large one, we
usually become acquainted with it but by extracts or by abstracts and abridgments. All poets of any length are read
by snatches and fragments when once they have ascended to
great popularity ; so that the logic of the reproach against
Professor Wilson is like that logic which Mr. Bald, the
Scottish engineer, complained of in the female servants of
Edinburgh. "They insist," said he, "upon having large
blocks of coal furnished to them ; they will not put up with
any that are less : and yet every morning the cynic who

delights in laughing at female caprices may hear these same women down in areas braying to pieces the unmanageable blocks, and using severe labour, for no purpose on earth but at last to bring the coal into that very state in which, without any labour at all, they might have had it from our collieries." So of Professor Wilson's works. They lie now in short and detached papers—that is, in the very state fitted for reading ; and, if he had hearkened to his counsellors, they would have been conglutinated into one vast block, needing a quarryman's or a miner's skill to make them tractable for household use.

In so hasty a sketch of Professor Wilson, where it is inevitable to dismiss without notice much that is interesting, there is yet one aspect of his public pretensions which, having been unusually misrepresented, ought to be brought under a stronger light of examination : we mean his relation to the chair of Moral Philosophy in the University of Edinburgh. It is sometimes alleged, in disparagement of Professor Wilson, by comparison with his two immediate predecessors, Mr. Dugald Stewart and Dr. Thomas Brown,[1] that *they* did, but that he does *not*, come forward with original contributions to philosophy. He is allowed the credit of lecturing splendidly ; but the complaint is, that he does not place his own name on the roll of independent philosophers. There is some opening to demurs in this invidious statement, even as regards the facts. The quality of Wilson's lectures cannot be estimated, except by those who have attended them,—as none have been made public. On the other hand, Mr. Dugald Stewart and Dr. Thomas Brown are *not* the original philosophers which the objection supposes them. To have been multiplied through repeated editions is no argument even of notoriety or momentary acceptation ; for these editions, both at home and in America, have been absorbed by students, on whom it was compulsory to become purchasers of the books used in their academic studies. At present, when it has almost ceased to be any recommendation to these writers that once they belonged to the Whig party, and when their per-

[1] Dugald Stewart (1753-1828), Professor of Moral Philosophy in the University of Edinburgh from 1785 to 1810 ; Thomas Brown (1778-1820), Professor from 1810 to 1820.—M.

sonal connexions are fast disappearing, it is no longer doubtful that the interest in their works is undermined. Professor Ferrier of St. Andrews, one of the subtlest intellects in
modern speculation,[1] has found himself compelled to speak
with severity of both ; and since then, in his edition of Reid,
Sir William Hamilton (who chooses to lay himself under
some restraint in reference to Mr. Stewart) has not scrupled
to speak with open disrespect of Dr. Brown,[2]—once as regards
a case of plagiarism, once upon that vast umbrageousness of
superfluous wordiness which is so distressing to all readers of
his works. Even the reputation, therefore, of these men
shows signs of giving way. But that is nothing : on other
grounds, and in defiance of reputation the most flourishing,
we have always felt that the first battery of sound logic un-
masked against Dr. Brown must be fatal. That man *could*
not be a philosopher who wrote the preposterous paper
against Kant in an early number of the *Edinburgh Review.*
In reviewing a Prussian, he had not even mastered the
German language, and was indebted to a Frenchman for the
monstrous conceits which he imputed to the great founder of
the Critical Philosophy. Mr. Dugald Stewart is so much the
less vulnerable as he happens to be the more eclectic ; in the
little that is strictly his own, he is *not* less vulnerable. And
it embitters the resentment against these men, that both spoke
with unmeasured illiberality, and with entire ignorance, of
philosophers the most distinguished in the last century.

From these men, at least, Professor Wilson will have nothing to fear. He (which is a great blessing) will have nothing to *recant ;* and, assuredly, that man who has ever been
the most generous of literary men, and sometimes the most
magnanimous and self-conquering in estimating the merits of
his contemporaries, will never cause a blush upon the faces of
his descendants by putting it in the power of an enemy to
upbraid them with unbecoming language of scorn applied by
him to illustrious extenders of knowledge. "If," will be the
language of those descendants, "if our ancestor *did,* as a pro-

---

[1] James F. Ferrier, 1808-1864. He was a son-in-law of Professor
Wilson.—M.
[2] Sir William Hamilton's edition of Reid was published in 1846.
—M.

fessor, write nothing more than splendid abstracts of philosophy in its several sections, in other words a history of philosophy, even *that* is something beyond a vulgar valuation—a service to philosophy which few, indeed, have ever been in a condition to attempt. Even so, no man can doubt that he would be found a thousand times more impressive than the dull, though most respectable, Brucker, than Tennemann, than Tiedemann (not Tediousmann), than Buhle, and so forth. If he did no more than cause to transmigrate into new forms old or neglected opinions, it is not certain that in this office the philosopher whom custom treats as the secondary mind does not often transcend his principal. It is, at least, beyond a doubt that Jeremy Taylor and Paul Richter, both of whom Professor Wilson at times recalls, oftentimes, in reporting an opinion from an old cloistered casuist, or from a dyspeptic schoolman blinking upon Aristotle with a farthing rushlight, lighted it up with a triple glory of haloes, such as the dull originator could never have comprehended. If therefore," it will be said, "Professor Wilson did no more than reanimate the fading and exorcise the dead, even *so* his station as a philosopher is not necessarily a lower one."

True ; but upon *that* a word or two. We have been hitherto assuming for facts the allegations put forward—sometimes by the careless, sometimes by the interested and malignant. Now let us look out for another version of the facts.

Our own version we beg to introduce by a short preface. The British Universities *are*, but the German Universities are *not*, connected with the maintenance of the national faith. The reasons of this difference rest upon historical and political grounds. But the *consequences* of this difference are that the British professor in any faculty bearing on theology is under conscientious restraints, which a little further on we will explain, such as the German professor does not recognise, and is not by any public summons called upon to recognise.

It is ordinarily supposed,—and no person has argued the case upon that footing with more bitterness or more narrowness of view than Lord Brougham, — that Oxford, when

imposing a subscription to the Thirty-nine Articles of the
English Church, means or wishes to lay a restraint upon the
free movement of the subscriber's intellect. But the true
theory of that exaction is this—that Oxford, aiming at no
such flagrant impossibility, seeks to bind over the student, by
obligations of honour and by reverence for the sanctity of a
promise, to do—what? Is it that he will not stray in
thought beyond the limits staked out by the Thirty-nine
Articles? *That* is a promise which no man could be sure of
keeping; a promise, therefore, which an honest man would
not deliberately make, and which, for the same reason, no
honest body of men would seek to exact. Not this, not the
promise to believe as the Church of England believes, but the
promise that he will not publish or manifest his secret aber-
rations from this standard, is the promise involved in the
student's subscription. Now, mark the effects of this. Oxford has thus preoccupied the mind of the student with a
resisting force as regards the heaviest temptation to tamper
with dangerous forms of opinion, religious or irreligious,
during that period when the judgment is most rash, and the
examination most limited. The heaviest temptation lies
through the vanity connected with the conscious eccentricity
and hardihood of bold free-thinking. But this vanity cannot
be gratified in Oxford; it is doomed to be starved, unless
through a criminal breach of fidelity to engagements solemnly
contracted. That oath, which, and which only, was sacred
in the eyes of a chivalrous French king, viz. *Foi du gentil-
homme*, is thus made to reinforce and rivet the oath (more
binding, as might seem, but under the circumstances far less
so) of *Foi du chrétien*. For a case of conscientious conviction
may be imagined which would liberate the student from this
latter oath applied to his *creed ;* but no case can be imagined
which would liberate him from the other oath, enforcing
the obligation to silence. Oxford, therefore, applies a twofold check to any free-thinking pruriencies in the student's
mind : 1st, She quells them summarily, *a parte post*, by
means of the guarantee which she holds from him ; 2dly,
She silently represses the growth of such pruriencies, *a parte
ante*, by exacting bonds against all available uses of such
dallyings with heresy or infidelity. Now, on the other hand,

in the German universities generally, these restraints on excesses of free-thinking do not exist. The course of study leads,
at every point, into religious questions, or questions applicable
to religion. All modes of philosophical speculation, metaphysics, psychology, ethics, connect themselves with religion.
There is no interdict or embargo laid upon the wildest
novelties in this direction. The English subscription had
been meant to operate simply in that way ; simply to secure
an *armistitium*, a suspension of feuds, in a place where such
feuds were disrespectful to the institutions of the land, or
might be perilous, and in a stage of life when they would
too often operate as pledges given prematurely by young men
to opinions which afterwards, in riper intellect, they might
see reason, but not have the candour or the courage, to
abandon.

It follows from this state of things that a German professor is thrown upon his discretion and his own individual
conscience for the quality of his teaching. But the British
professor is thrown upon a public conscience, embodied in
usages adapted to the institutions of his country. In Edinburgh, it is true, the students are not bound by subscriptions
to any Confession of Faith. But that the whole course of
instruction, or at least of that instruction which emanates
from the chair of Moral Philosophy, is understood to be connected with the religion of the land, appears from this : that
the theological students—those who are to fill the ministerial
office in the churches of Scotland—cannot arrive at that
station without a certificate of having attended the Moral
Philosophy Lectures. There is, therefore, a secret understanding which imposes upon the professor a duty of adapting his lectures to this call upon him. He is not left at
liberty to amuse himself with scholastic subtleties ; and those
who *have* done so should be viewed as deserters of their
duty. He is called upon to give such a *representative* account
of current philosophy as may lay open those amongst its
treasures which are most in harmony with Christian
wisdom, and may arm the future clergyman against its most
contagious errors. For Fichte or for Schelling the path was
open to mere Athenian subtlety upon any subject that might
most tax their own ingenuity, or that of their hearers. But

the British professor of moral philosophy is straitened by more solemn obligations :—

> " Nobis non licet esse tam disertis,
> Qui musas colimus severiores."

Hence it would be no just blame, but the highest praise, to Professor Wilson, if his lectures really *did* wear the character imputed to him—of being rich and eloquent abstracts, rather than scholastic exercitations in untried paths. We speak in the dark as to the facts ; but at the same time we offer a new version, a new mode of interpreting, the alleged facts, supposing them to have been accurately stated.

Is *that* all ? No ; there is another, and a far ampler philosophy a philosophy of human nature, like the philosophy of Shakspere, and of Jeremy Taylor, and of Edmund Burke, which is scattered through the miscellaneous papers of Professor Wilson. Such philosophy by its very nature is of a far higher and more aspiring nature than any which lingers upon mere scholastic conundrums. It is a philosophy that cannot be presented in *abstract* forms, but hides itself as an *incarnation* in voluminous mazes of eloquence and poetic feeling. Look for this amongst the *critical* essays of Professor Wilson ; which, for continual glimpses and revelations of hidden truth, are perhaps absolutely unmatched. By such philosophy his various courses of lectures—we speak on the authority of many of his highest students—are throughout distinguished ; and more especially those numerous disquisitions on Man's Moral Being, his Passions, his Affections, and his Imagination, in which Professor Wilson displays his own genius, its originality and power.

With this brief sketch of one who walks in the van of men the most memorable and original that have adorned our memorable and original age, we conclude by saying, in a spirit of simplicity and fidelity to the truth, that from Professor Wilson's papers in *Blackwood*, but above all from his meditative examinations of great poets, Greek and English, may be formed a *florilegium* of thoughts the most profound and the most gorgeously illustrated that exist in human composition.

Of his poems or his prose tales we have not spoken : our space was limited ; and, as regards the poems in particular, there appeared some time ago in this very journal a separate critique upon them,—from whom proceeding we know not, but executed with great feeling and ability.[1]

[1] Wilson, De Quincey's most intimate Edinburgh friend to the last, died April 3, 1854, four years after this sketch of him. De Quincey outlived him nearly six years.—M.

SIR WILLIAM HAMILTON [1]

I

I BEGIN by entreating the reader, not so much in kindness (of which he may have none to spare) as in mere justice, to make allowance for this little sketch, as a sketch written under unfavourable circumstances. What circumstances? Why, written at a distance, in the first place, from the press; or, because in these days there is no such thing as distance, written under a difficulty almost incredible to myself of communicating with the press. [2] It is a fact that I can send a letter to Astrachan, or even to Bokhara (and, indeed, I meditate a letter to Bokhara, filled with reproaches to the sultan, whom I particularly detest), much more easily than I can plant a note in the hands of my publisher or his compositors. Once posted, the letter to Bokhara, like an arrow dismissed from a bow, will assuredly find out the sultan, without further " fash " on *my* part, and will cause a festering in his villainous heart [3]; and he can have no pretence for complaining of me to the Court of St. James's, since I shall pay the

---

[1] This paper, nominally on Sir William Hamilton, but actually one of the most rambling and discursive of De Quincey's essays—with only a *pinch* of Sir William Hamilton in it, flavouring a quantity of amusing matter about De Quincey himself and about anything else that occurred to him,—was begun in one of the numbers of *Hogg's Instructor* for 1852, as letterpress accompaniment to an engraved portrait of Sir William in that number, and was continued in two subsequent numbers. It was reprinted in 1871 in one of the supplementary volumes to the previous edition of De Quincey's writings.—M.

[2] Written, doubtless, in De Quincey's cottage at Lasswade.—M.

[3] And all of us detest him reasonably, who remember his treatment of poor Stoddart and Conolly, for no crime alleged but that of trusting to the hospitality and justice of his savage land.

postage to the last farthing. Fluent as the flight of a
swallow is the sultan's letter ; whereas the letter to my publisher describes a path that is zigzag, discontinuous, moving
through harsh angles, and intersected at every turn by
human negligences, or by *in*human treacheries of coachmen.
The sultan presents a point-blank mark to my bullet ; but,
to hit my publisher, I must fire round a corner ; or, indeed,
round three corners at once. That is *one* of the circumstances ; and it seems to follow that, unless my publisher
could be prevailed on kindly to " flit " to Bokhara, there is
no great prospect of opening a direct or rapid communication with him. Another of the evil circumstances is that I
have no materials—not a scrap ; my sole resource being in a
poor wearied brain, and in a memory which (although at
intervals working like a steam-engine) oftentimes yearns for
rest, and, with Themistocles, would humbly pray for some
sweet voluptuous art of forgetting. With this brain, so
time-shattered, I must work, in order to give significancy
and value to the few facts which I possess—alas ! far too
scanty as a basis for the very slightest superstructure. With
this memory, so restive on such a mission of revisiting the
past, I must go down into depths and shy recesses of time,
over which dusky draperies are hanging, and voluminous
curtains have long since fallen, such as I shrink from raising.
Wordsworth points to images and phantom recollections that
spontaneously

" will sometimes leap
From hiding-places ten years deep " ;

but in this case the earliest of my recollections must be
rekindled painfully at depths far lower. Forty years, or
near it, I must descend ; and the case becomes that of a man
forcing his way violently back into his burning house, under
a vow of recovering some special jewels : if he is repelled by
the flames, he suffers the mortification of a baffled purpose ;
if he presses forward, and accomplishes his vow, then, perhaps,
in the very midst of his success, he is scorched by the fire.
Of all curses, that which searches deepest is the violent revelation through infinite darkness—a revelation like that
" sudden blaze (Paradise Lost, b. ii.) which far round
illumined hell "—of a happiness or a glory which once and

for ever has perished. Martyrdom it is, and no less, to revivify by effect of your own, or passively to see revivified, in defiance of your own fierce resistance, the gorgeous spectacles of your visionary morning life, or of your too rapturous noontide, relieved upon a background of funeral darkness. Such poisonous transfigurations, by which the paradise of youthful hours is forced into distilling demoniac misery for ruined nerves, exist for many a profound sensibility. And, as regards myself, touch but some particular key of laughter and of echoing music, sound but for a moment one bar of preparation, and immediately the pomps and glory of all that has composed for me the delirious vision of life re-awaken for torment ; the orchestras of the earth open simultaneously to my inner ear ; and in a moment I behold, forming themselves into solemn groups and processions, and passing over sad phantom stages, all that chiefly I have loved, or in whose behalf chiefly I have abhorred and cursed the grave—all that should *not* have died, yet died the soonest—the brilliant, the noble, the wise, the innocent, the brave, the beautiful. With these dreadful masks, and under the persecution of their malicious beauty, wakens up the worm that gnaws at the heart. Under that corrosion arises a hatred, blind and vague, and incomprehensible even to one's self, as of some unknown snake-like enemy, in some unknown hostile world, brooding with secret power over the fountains of one's own vitality. Such scourges, at any rate, must be borne where the machinery of the nerves brings round the hour of torment. But it forms a hard condition towards the possibility of a sketch like this—that, by recalling such vanished scenes too vividly, one obeys a summons to an active collusion and co-operation with one's own secret suffering, and becomes a fiery *heautontimoroumenos* (or self-tormentor) in the most afflicting sense.

Another circumstance of hardship, which entitles me to the special indulgence of the reader, is, that in this paper I am writing against time. Many are the matches which I have had against time in *my* time and in *his* time (*i.e.* in Time's time). And all such matches, writing or riding, are memorably unfair. Time, the meagre shadow, carries no weight at all ; so what parity can there be in any contest with *him*? What does *he* know of anxiety, or liver-complaint, or income-tax, or of the vexations connected with the correcting of proofs for the press? Although, by the way, he *does* take upon him himself, with his villainous scrawl, to correct all the fair proofs of nature. He sows canker into the heart of rosebuds, and writes wrinkles (which are his odious attempts at pothooks) in the loveliest of female faces. No type so fair but he fancies, in his miserable conceit, that he can improve it ; no stereotype so fixed but he will alter it ; and, having spoiled one generation after another, he still persists in believing himself the universal amender and the ally of progress. Ah ! that one might, if it were but for one day in a century, be indulged with the sight of Time forced into a personal incarnation, so as to be capable of a personal insult —a cudgelling, for instance, or a ducking in a horse-pond. Or, again, that once in a century, were it but for a single summer's day, his corrected proofs might be liable to supersession by *revises*, such as I would furnish, down the margin of which should run one perpetual iteration of *stet., stet.* ; everything that the hoary scoundrel had *deleted*, rosebuds or female bloom, beauty or power, grandeur or grace, being solemnly reinstated, and having the privilege of one day's secular resurrection, like the Arabian phœnix, or any other memento of power in things earthly and in sublunary births, to mock and to defy the scythe of this crowned thief !

But this eternal blazon must not be, or the reader will think himself to have fallen into the company of a madman, and perhaps at the first convenient turning will abscond. And yet, if he knew all that I could tell him about the villainies of Time, possibly he would participate in the *acharnement* of my hatred. I know that wretch better than the reader is likely to do. For the present, what I wish to have understood is, that the time available for my little paper is not at all commensurate to the dignity of its theme. By reason of what I mentioned above in regard to my publisher's procrastination in fixing himself at Bokhara, the correspondence with him is in that condition of circuitousness and liability to *rests* (which are very good in music, but shameful and disgusting in the post-office) that three-fourths of the time otherwise disposable for my paper perishes in holes and corners amongst the embezzlements of the road ; and every contraction in the *rations* allowed as to hours and minutes regularly shows itself in a corresponding expansion of hurry and inevitable precipitancy as regards the quality of the composition. Not that always and unconditionally it is an evil to be hurried in writing for the press. I doubt not that many a score of practised writers for the press will have been self-observing enough to notice a phenomenon which *I* have many times noticed, viz. that hurry and severe compression from an instant summons that brooks no delay have a tendency to often furnish the flint and steel for eliciting sudden scintillations of originality : sometimes in what regards the picturesque felicity of the phrase, sometimes in what regards the thought itself or its illustrations. To *autoschediaze*, or improvise, is sometimes in effect to be forced into a consciousness of creative energies that would else have slumbered through life. The same stimulation to the creative faculty occurs even more notoriously in musical improvisations ; and all great executants on the organ have had reason to bemoan their inability to arrest those sudden felicities of impassioned combinations, and those flying arabesques of loveliest melody, which the magnetic inspiration of the moment has availed to excite. Meantime, this possible advantage of hurry and adventurous precipitation for the kindling of originality applies less probably to a case in which philosophy happens to be concerned. But is the present a case of that order ? A philosopher is concerned undoubtedly, and a great one ; but philosophy not so much. The public would not bear it. One man may lead a horse to a pond, but twenty will not make him drink ; and a sip is all that the public collectively ever care to take from reservoirs of abstract philosophy. Yet, even in such a case, where leisurely thought is really a possible disadvantage in regard to the immediate prosperity of the composition, it is still indispensable in regard to its revision ; so that my title still remains good to a special indulgence.

But now, reader, do not worry me any more with questions or calls for explanation. *When* I do not know, nor *how*, but not the less I feel a mesmeric impression that you have been bothering me with magnetic passes : but for which interruptions, we should have been by this time a long way on our journey. I am now going to begin. You will see a full stop or period a very few inches farther on, lurking immediately under the word *earnest* on the off side ; and, from and after that full stop, you are to consider me as having shaken off all troublesome companions, and as having once for all entered upon business in earnest.

In the year 1814 it was that I became acquainted with Sir William Hamilton, the present Professor of Logic in the University of Edinburgh. I was then in Edinburgh for the first time, on a visit to Mrs. Wilson, the mother of Professor Wilson. Him, who at that time neither *was* a professor, nor dreamed of becoming one (his intention being to pursue his profession of advocate at the Scottish bar), I had known for a little more than five years. Wordsworth it was, then living at Allan Bank in Grasmere, who had introduced me to John Wilson ; and ever afterwards I was a frequent visitor at his beautiful place of Elleray, on Windermere, not above nine miles distant from my own cottage in Grasmere. In those days, Wilson sometimes spoke to me of his friend Hamilton, as of one specially distinguished by manliness and elevation of character, and occasionally gazed at as a monster of erudition. Indeed, the extent of his reading was said to be portentous—in fact, frightful ; and, to some extent, even suspicious ; so that certain ladies thought him "no canny" ; for, if arithmetic could demonstrate that all the days of his life, ground down and pulverised into "wee wee" globules of five or eight minutes each, and strung upon threads, would not furnish a rosary anything like corresponding, in its separate beads or counters, to the books he was known to have studied and familiarly used, then it became clear that he must have had *extra* aid, and, in some way or other, must have read by proxy. Now, in that case, we all know in what direction a man turns for help, and *who* it is that he applies to when he wishes, like Dr. Faustus, to read more books than belong to his own allowance in this life. I hope sincerely there was no truth in these insinuations ; for, besides that it would be disagreeable to have a hanger-on like Mephistopheles expecting to receive a card every time that you gave a little dance, I, for my part, could have no reliance on the accuracy of his reading. The objection to Mephistopheles as a prosy reader would be absolutely fatal. Such a malicious wretch would leave out all the *nots* in critical places, as the printers fined by Laud did from the seventh commandment (reading "Thou *shalt* commit adultery"), and would discredit his principal's learning by continual falsifications of the text. I do trust and hope, therefore, that there was no ground for any such painful suspicions. Candour, however, obliges me to mention that at one time Sir William had a large dog in Great King Street, Edinburgh, very much answering to the description of the dog which Goethe, and at least *one* of our old Elizabethan dramatists, assign to poor Dr. Faustus. Surely it never could be the same identical dog, figuring first in Frankfort during the fifteenth century, and then in Edinburgh during the nineteenth !

An interest of curiosity in Sir William Hamilton had gradually, from some cause or other, combined in my mind with an interest of respect for his extraordinary attainments. Neither interest might possibly have sustained itself amongst the continual distractions of the world, had there been little prospect of forming his acquaintance. But the accident of my own visit to Edinburgh in 1814, whilst it suddenly ripened a remote chance into an instant certainty, deepened that already deep interest in Sir William's pretensions which had long given value to such a chance. Together with the certainty that I should now speedily enjoy a personal insight into the splendid accomplishments of this Titan amongst students, suddenly arose a profounder curiosity as to the exact range of these accomplishments. And I was truly happy when this anticipation was realised.

One morning I was sitting alone after breakfast, when Wilson suddenly walked in with his friend Hamilton. So exquisitely free was Sir William from all ostentation of learning that, unless the accidents of conversation made a natural opening for display, such as it would have been affectation to evade, you might have failed altogether to suspect that an extraordinary scholar was present. On this first interview with him, I saw nothing to challenge any special attention, beyond an unusual expression of kindness

and cordiality in his *abord*. There was also an air of dignity
and massy self-dependence diffused over his deportment, too
calm and unaffected to leave a doubt that it exhaled spontaneously from his nature, yet too unassuming to mortify
the pretensions of others. Men of genius I had seen before,
and men distinguished for their attainments, who shocked
everybody, and upon me in particular, nervously susceptible,
inflicted with horror as well as distress, by striving restlessly
and almost angrily for the chief share in conversation.
Some I had known who possessed themselves in effect pretty
nearly of the whole, without being distinctly aware of what
they were about ; and one autocratic gentleman there was
among them, perfectly aware of what he was about, who (in
the phrase of politicians) "went for" the whole from the
very first ; and, if things had come to that pass that he
might not have all, gave notice, with vengeance blazing in
his eyes, that he would have none. He was not to be *done*
at his time of life by frivolous offers of a compromise that
might have secured him seventy-five per cent. No, no ; all
without discount—that was his *ultimatum*. In Sir William
Hamilton, on the other hand, was an apparent carelessness
whether he took any conspicuous share or none at all in the
conversation. It is possible that, as the representative of
an ancient [1] family, he may secretly have felt his position in
life ; far less, however, in the sense of its advantages than of
its obligations and restraints. And, in general, my con-

---

[1] Hamilton of Preston was, I believe, raised to the baronetcy about
the middle of the second Charles's reign. It seems hard to reconcile
with that fact a tradition, which I have repeatedly heard in conversation, that the Hamilton of that day was a Covenanter, and even a
Drumclog rebel. If this were really so (but generally my impulse is
to regard the whole generation of anecdotes as founded in lies), it
would argue in the first baronet much obstinacy and perhaps a little
lunacy. But these are excellent qualities on which to build a house ;
for in two centuries they lose their harshness, and mellow down into
strength of will and reasonable eccentricity. In these days, when
periodic literature traverses society through sections so vastly enlarged,
and often not belonging in any sense to the classes professedly literary,
it may be necessary to inform the young reader that the order of
baronets did not arise until the reign of James I. Consequently, if
we divide the duration of the order into four successive stages, the
Preston baronetcy dates from the first.

clusion was, that at that time I had rarely seen a person
who manifested less of self-esteem, under any of the forms
by which ordinarily it reveals itself — whether of pride,
or vanity, or full - blown arrogance, or heart - chilling
reserve.

But, meantime, what was the peculiar and differential
nature of Sir William's pursuits which had won *for* him
already so much distinction, and *against* him so much
expectation ? for really a man's own merit often comes to
act against him with deadliest hostility, when, by inflaming
his reputation, it has also the power of too much inflaming
the standard by which he will be tried. Sir William's
reputation was as yet of that interesting (because somewhat
mysterious) kind which has not yet crept into newspapers,
but is moving, even locally, only through whispers. And
in these whispers, forty years ago, there was nothing like
the same principle of contagion that now exists. The cause
of this lies partly in railways, which are not only swift in
themselves, but the causes of swiftness in everything else ;
so that very soon, I am convinced, out of pure, blind sympathy with railway trains, men will begin to trot through
the streets ; and, in the next generation, unconsciously, they
will take to cantering. We may see a proof of this in the
increased vitality of slang. To my knowledge, it took
eighteen years to transplant from Germany to this country
the Greek word *mythus :* but, in more recent days, the
absurd abuse of the word *myth* for a fib has not cost three
years, when helped forward by female lips. And, as the
whispers were then far below our existing whispers in
velocity of circulation, they were no better as regarded
accuracy. The first thing I heard about Sir William
Hamilton was that he might be regarded as the modern
Magliabecchi, or even as a better Magliabecchi, if better
there could be. Now, you are aware, my youthful reader,
or (if not) you soon *shall* be aware, that the said M. (whose
long name I don't intend to spell over again) was that
librarian, a hundred and fifty years ago,[1] to some Grand
Duke of Tuscany, who, by dint of trotting and cantering
over all pages of all books, could not only repeat *verbatim et*

[1] Antonio Magliabecchi, 1633-1714.—M.

literatim any possible paragraph from any conceivable book, and, letting down his bucket into the dark ages, could fetch up for you any amount of rubbish that you might call for, but could even tell you on which side, dexter or sinister, starboard or larboard, the particular page might stand in which he had been angling. Well : I admire Indian jugglers ; I look with pleasure on rope-dancers, whether dancing the slack or the tight rope ; and I, for one, would not have grudged a subscription of five shillings towards inducing Mag. to go through his tricks. But, when all was over, I must still have asked, Now, Mag., with submission, what may be the use of all that ? It is a question through which I could never see my way, except that once a glimmering light occurred to me in the following case :—Jacob Bryant, a great scholar some fifty years ago,[1] and a dead shot at all mythological questions, had a large and lofty library, to the upper regions of which, where he kept all his cloudy and flighty authors, he was under the necessity of ascending by means of a long ladder. Now, it came to pass that, when Jacob was well stricken in years, and the sight was waxing dim in his eyes, in mounting to his mythological Olympus, whilst midway on this Jacob's ladder, Jacob fell from it ; and, by reason of falling from this ladder, Jacob broke his leg ; and, by reason of this fracture, Jacob died. Now, it occurs to one that, if Mag. had stood at the foot of the ladder, Jacob needed not to have died ; for Mag. would have told him everything that he could possibly have learned by going aloft. But still, as Jacob (being above eighty) was nearly *due* to the undertaker, and as we children of earth have contrived to crawl through the better half of the nineteenth century without Jacob, and as, after all, Mag. was *not* at the foot of the ladder when most wanted, I continue to think that, even if pleading for Mag.'s usefulness before a jury, I must submit to a non-suit.

But I do not stop there. For else, though useless, Mag.'s talent might seem admirable in the way that magic is admirable. Any intellectual gift whatever, such as Jedediah Buxton's gift of demoniac arithmetic,[2] though not only use-

---

[1] Jacob Bryant, 1715-1804.—M.
[2] Jedediah Buxton, calculator, born about 1704, died 1775.—M.

less, but perhaps even a curse to its possessor, is worth the
tribute of one moment's admiration; it is entitled to a
Bravo! though one would scruple to give it an *Ancora!*
On the other hand, as to Mag.'s mode of conjuring, I am now
satisfied that it was no talent at all, as the world has hitherto
imagined, but simply a cutaneous disease. The man ought
to have been cupped and leeched, or treated with tonics.
Experto crede. I was myself attacked by it some years ago,
for my memory is subject to frightful irregularities of spasmodic energy ; and it struck me then that corrosive sub-
limate might be required, if it were any species of *psora.*
But, inclining to try milder remedies at first, I took nitric
acid, and finished off with chalybeates. This course of
practice, accompanied by violent exercise and sudorifics,
succeeded at that time. But I have since felt the *virus* still
lurking in the system ; and am at times horribly alarmed at
the prospect of turning out a confirmed Magliab. ; which, in
point of misery to the patient, must be the next bad thing
to being a vampire.

They knew little of Sir William Hamilton who
fancied that his enormous reading tended to any result
so barren as this. But other whisperers there were, who
would have persuaded me that Sir William was simply a
great linguist. Since the time when I first came to know
him, Europe has had several monsters of that class, and,
amongst others, Cardinal Mezzofanti.[1] Perhaps the cardinal
was, on the whole, the greatest of his order. He knew, I
believe (so as to speak familiarly), thirty-four languages ;
whereas a Scandinavian clergyman (Swedish or Norse), who
has died since the cardinal, and was reputed to have mastered
fifty-six, probably only *read* them. But what ultimate value
attached to this hyperbolical acquisition ?[2] If one wrote an

---

[1] Mezzofanti, 1774-1849.—M.

[2] However, if this camel-load of languages tended to no useful
result, it ought in justice to be mentioned that at least it *originated* in
a very useful effort of benignity. One terminus lay in the useful, if
the other terminus evaporated in smoke. The army of Napoleon was
a polyglot army to a greater extent than is generally known ; and, in
attending the military hospital-beds at Milan, for the purpose of offering spiritual consolations, the pious monk Mezzofanti is reported to
have found three-and-twenty languages indispensable. These being

epitaph for his eminence, one might be tempted into saying, "Here lies a man that, in the act of dying, committed a robbery, absconding from his poor fellow-creatures with a valuable polyglot dictionary." Assuredly, any man who puts his treasures into a form which must perish in company with himself is no profound benefactor to his species. Not thus did Sir William proceed, as I soon learned after I made his acquaintance ; and the results of his reading are now sown and rooted at Paris, not less than at Berlin ; are blossoming on the Rhine ; and are bearing fruit on the Danube.

Ah, reader, at this moment I hear the fierce clamours of the press, that speaks through double trumpets of space and time, uttering inexorable edicts and interdicts as to both. Pardon me, therefore, if, by hurrying, I fall into disproportion with myself, or if, in order to hurry, I should find it necessary to be affectedly brief. My own direct acquaintance with Sir William Hamilton soon apprised me that, of all great readers, he was the one to whom it was most indispensable that he should react by his own mind upon what he read. There are different lines of approach upon which a man may force an entrance into the citadels of philosophy. Some read little or nothing: for instance, Kant, who had not (as might be proved) read even Locke— perhaps not one page of Locke—though I fully believe that he would not materially have modified what he has written if by accident he *had*. He, by blank power, integrated any imperfect hint as to a writer's doctrines that he had picked up casually in conversation or from random reading. But others make their advances by different routes. Sir William Hamilton, when I first knew him, was not properly a philosopher—nor would *then* have called himself such—but a polyhistor, of a higher class, and with far more combining powers, than Bayle,—having (or taking means to have) a pancyclopædic acquaintance with every section of knowledge wanted for the necessities of conversation, it happened naturally that they were learned radically. He that *talks* a language cannot deceive himself.—[I have heard this jest about Cardinal Mezzofanti from one who knew him : "He knew about fifty languages,—*i.e.* there were about fifty ways into his head ; and, when you got there, you found it empty."—M.]

that could furnish keys for unlocking man's inner nature. Already, in 1814, I conceive that he must have been studying physiology upon principles of investigation suggested by himself. In 1820, 1827, and the following years, up to 1832, on revisiting Edinburgh, I found him master of all the knowledge that France and Germany had then accumulated upon animal magnetism ; which he justly conceived to hide within itself shy secrets as to "the dark foundations" of our human nature, such as cannot *now* be lawfully neglected—secrets which evidently had gleamed and *cropped out* at intervals through past ages of the world in various phenomena that were tarnished or were darkened into apparent doubtfulness only by the superstitions that surrounded them. The immensity of Sir William's attainments was best laid open by consulting him (or by hearing him consulted) upon intellectual difficulties, or upon schemes literary and philosophic. Such applications, come from what point of the compass they would, found him always prepared. Nor did it seem to make any difference whether it were the erudition of words or things that was needed. Amongst the books for which I am indebted to his kindness as memorials of his regard, one which I value most is a copy of the *Scaligerana*, and for this reason, that it is intrinsically a characteristic memento of himself when first I knew him. In the Scaligers, father and son, who were both astonishing men, I fancied this resemblance to himself, that there was the same equilibrium in all three as to *thing*-knowledge and *word*-knowledge. Again, Scaliger the elder, as is well known, had been a cavalry officer up to his fortieth year ; and often, in his controversial writings, one deciphers the *quondam* trooper cutting furiously right and left in a *melée*. There, also, I fancy a resemblance : now and then, in Sir William's polemics, I seem to trace the sword-arm that charged at Drumclog ; or is that story all a dream ?

But that trumpet—both those trumpets again are sounding, and now evidently for the last time ; and it seems to me that, if ever I heard a trumpet in a passion, both of these trumpets are labouring under that infirmity. Ah, what a chaos ! In what confusion and hurry, my reader, shall we part ! I had three hundred things, at least, to say ; and, if that arithmetic is correct, it strikes me as a sad necessity that, for a matter of two hundred and ninety-nine, I must remain in your debt. In debt? Ay; but for how long? When do I mean to pay? Thirty days after date would be almost as good as cash. True, much-injured reader, it would be so; and my wish, were wishes discountable, would run exactly in that channel. But that, alas! is impossible. Hearken to the nature of the *fix* in which I find myself, and say if you ever heard of a worse. Under ordinary circumstances, if one outruns the usual allowance of space, one has but to say at the foot of the paper, *To be continued*, and all is healed. Any paper may be adjourned from month to month,—true, but not from volume to volume; and, unhappily for me, this very week's number, in which I am now writing, closes a volume. The several monthly divisions of the journal may *inosculate*, but not the several volumes. If any one volume were allowed to throw out great tap-roots into a succeeding *volume*, no section of the journal would ever be finished, or capable of being regarded as a separate and *independent* whole. To purchase any one volume of the INSTRUCTOR might pledge a man to purchasing onwards into the twentieth century, under the pain of else having on his hands a weight of unfinished articles. Rightly, therefore, it has been made a law,[1] that no subject can be carried on by adjournment from volume to volume. Yet, on the other hand, by a necessity not less cogent, the merest *silhouette*, or Indian-ink sketch in profile, of a philosopher cannot decently evade some notice of his philosophy. Is not Mallet a by-word in literature to this day for having written a life of Lord Bacon in which he remembered that the noble Lord was a chancellor, but unhappily forgot that he was a leader and a revolutionist in philosophy? And did not this hideous oversight of his make people rejoice in his having failed to keep his engagements with the Duchess of Marlborough for writing the life of her lord, since, by parity of blunder, he would carefully have remembered that the Duke had once been a gentleman of the

---

[1] From which law there is a proper dispensation in the case of papers which, although related by general title, yet in each division branch off in such way as to be always making a new beginning.

bed-chamber, and had taken a flying leap early in the morning from the bed-room window of Barbara Villiers, but would have forgotten utterly that he commanded at Blenheim, or (which is worse) would have notified it by way of "*P.S.*" among the errata and addenda that would be carefully looked after in the next edition ? Here, now, is a necessity on one side that I should *do* that which on the other side it appears to be a sheer impossibility that I should even *attempt*. Even the famous sixteen-string Jack would have recoiled a little from such a perplexity. Is there no dodge, sacred or profane, by which it can be met ? Yes, on consideration, perhaps, by this which follows :—Volume the fifteenth, it is true, cannot *succeed* to property in the fourteenth volume. It cannot receive it as an *inheritance*. But *that* will not prevent it from holding such property as an original endowment of its own. This article, for instance, cannot prolong its life into another volume ; but it may rise again—it may receive a separate birth *de novo*—in the future volume. What is to hinder me from writing a paper next March, for example, with this title, "On the Contributions of Sir William Hamilton to Philosophy" ? Publicly the law of the journal is thus maintained ; and yet, in consistency with that law, an opportunity is gained for something nearer to a reasonable estimate of an illustrious man than could have been crowded within three octavo pages.

Here is a man (it will be said by the thoughtful reviewer of his own age) able to have "made the world grow pale" with the enormity of his learned acquisitions, had he been more often confronted with that world, or, when face to face with it, more capable of ostentatious display. Make us understand in what direction his studies have moved : towards what capital objects ; with what immediate results ; followed by what testimonies of honour from the supreme tribunals in this department of literature ; and supported by what evidences or presumption of having impressed lasting changes upon some great aspects of intellectual philosophy.

II

HERE I am, viz. in vol. xv. Never ruffle your own temper, reader, or mine, by asking *how*, and with what right. I *am* here. So much is clear, and what you may call a *fait accompli*. As to saying that, though I am maybe here "de facto," nevertheless "de jure" I am *not* so,—that I have no *locus standi*; that I am an usurper, an intruder; and that any contraband process by which I can have smuggled myself from vol. xiv to this present vol. xv is not of a kind that will bear looking into,—too true, I answer : very few things *will* bear looking into! In particular, the revolution of 1688-9 will not bear looking into with eyes of philosophic purism. The object of the purist is to effect the devolution of the crown through a smooth lubricated channel known and conformable to old constitutional requisitions; and, if the word "*abdicate*" could but be established,—formally, were it, or even constructively,—all would run as sweetly as the chronometers of Greenwich. As it is, I grieve to say that there is a deadly hiatus in the harness which should connect the pre-revolutionary and post-revolutionary commonwealths of England. It is not merely a screw that is loose ; it is a link that is missing, and no use advertising for it now. But no matter : that is a grief which, being nearly two hundred years old, an extra glass of wine will do much to heal. And in reality I never heard of a man's meditating suicide because he could not harmonise the facts of our Revolution with its transcendental theory. Yet not the less the human mind does really yearn and sicken after intellectual modes of solution applied to any intellectual intricacy or nodus. Art must thaw the dilemma which art has frozen together : and never yet was there a reader of any sensibility that did not resent with clamorous indignation the removal by apoplexy from a novel or a drama of any impracticable character that ought to have been disposed of agreeably to the providential forecastings of the plot itself, and by the spontaneous evolution of the fable. My own personal embarrassment on this occasion, in effecting a transit or in evading a transit, was of a nature hardly paralleled in literature. I was to write a paper within certain assigned limits,—which paper, by its very subject and the crying necessities of its nature, utterly rebelled against limits. To transfer it (not in part but in mass) to a field of ampler limits, *i.e.* to another volume, was made impossible by certain arrangements which nailed the accompanying portrait to this punctual spot—to this instant *now*, and this momentary audience. The biographic record could not be disjoined from the portrait, and the portrait could not be removed from that particular place in that particular volume. But could I not, *secondly*, content myself with giving part, carrying forward the other parts by adjournment to another volume? No: because that would be establishing a dependency of one volume upon another, contrary to the plan and law of the whole work. But, then, *thirdly*, at least I might have hyperbolically expanded on the dimensions of that single paper which the fates allowed me to write? No: I could not do *that* even; for then I must have monopolised the entire train—first, second, and third class—and, in order to do *that*, I must have booked myself as the one sole passenger in this journal at least three months beforehand.

It is strange to see what mountains of difficulty sometimes melt away before the suggestions of a child. *Accipe principium sursus*—solved the whole case. What is to hinder me from beginning afresh upon a new foundation in a new volume, and utterly ignoring all that has gone before? I now *do* so. And what follows is to be viewed as a totally new article, standing on its own basis.

Everybody, I believe, is young at some period of his life; at least one has an old physiological prejudice in that direction. Else, to hear people talk, one must really suppose that there are celebrated persons who are born to old age as to some separate constitutional inheritance. Nobody says "Old Sophocles," but very many people say "Old Chaucer." Yet Chaucer was a younger man at his death than Sophocles. But, if not, why should men insist upon one transitory stage or phasis in a long series of changes, as if suddenly and lawfully arrested, to the exclusion of all the rest? *Old* Chaucer! why, he was also middle-aged Chaucer; he was young Chaucer; he was baby Chaucer. And the earlier distinctions of a man bear as much relation to posterity as his later distinctions. Above all, one is betrayed into such misconceptions when a man carries a false certificate of age in the very name which designates his relationship to one's self. My great-great-grandmother naturally I figured to myself as having a patriarchal beard. Could I think otherwise of one so deeply merged in grandmotherhood ? But a portrait of her taken immediately after death represented her as an attractive young woman not quite twenty-three ; which it appeared that she really was. And I remember a similar case even still more striking, which occurred in Chester about the year 1803. Some overflowing of the Dee had exposed to view the secrets of the churchyard. Amongst the coffins in the lower tiers was one which contained the corpse of a woman, particularly blooming. According to my first precipitate computation, she might be rated as one hundred and twenty years old ; for she had died in Queen Anne's reign (about 1707, I think), and by the plate on the coffin-lid had been twenty-four at the time of death. Yet her face was most blooming, her lips beautifully fresh, and her hair of the loveliest auburn. Ninety-and-three years of the eighteenth century, and two years of the nineteenth, had she spent in the grave ; and, adding these ninety-five years of rest to the twenty-four of her (doubtless unresting) life, for a moment I fell into the natural confusion of making her a very, very old woman ; and proportionably I wondered at the vernal beauty which had not ceased to adorn her in the wintry grave. This special indulgence to a special beauty had been the gift of a soil preternaturally antiseptic. But, inevitably, the sudden collision of a youthfulness so apparent with an antiquity so historical caused each idea reciprocally to illuminate the other ; so that, for a minute or two, until I had distinguished the elements of this antiquity, and had separated the ninety-five years that did not belong to the young woman herself from the twenty-four that *did*, I struggled with the impossible and contradictory conception of crazy superannuation incarnated in perfect womanly loveliness. Some metaphysical perplexity of this same nature, I observe, besets those who contemplate us, the tenants of a past generation, through the inverted tube of the present.

The Trophonian gloom which they ascribe to us, considered as present antiquities and relics, adheres to the image of the same poor *us* when traced upwards to our morning period. We that cannot attempt even to smile in this present stage of the world, is it credible that at *any* stage we can have laughed ? Child of incredulity, if not credible, it is certain. " Ginger [1] was hot in the mouth " in those long-past years ; and, " because we were virtuous " at that era, not the less there were " ale and cakes." Though transcendental philosophers (ἀεροβατοῦντες) that walked the air, we condescended to sip at times from sublunary liquors ; and at odd times it is possible that we even entered into the kingdom of " civilation."

" *Civilation !* And what may *that* be ? " Look below, reader, into the foot-note, which will explain it.[2] Whilst you are studying *that*, I'll be moving on slowly overhead ; and, when you come up from that mine to the upper air, you'll easily overtake me. *Civilation*, or (if you choose to call it so) *civilisation*, was not a state into which any of us made a regular habit of ascending : only at times we did so ; and I presume that at such times Sir William Hamilton, being

[1] I presume the reader to be familiar with the passage in Shakspere here referred to. But, if not, let him look to " Twelfth Night."

[2] And what state may that be ? As the word is a valuable word, and in some danger of being lost, I beg to rehearse its history. The late Dr. Maginn, with whom some of us may otherwise have had reason to quarrel, was, however, a man of varied accomplishments,—a wit, with singular readiness for improvising, and with very extensive scholarship. Amongst the peculiar opinions which he professed was this—that no man, however much he might *tend* towards civilisation, was to be regarded as having absolutely reached its apex. until he was drunk. Previously to which consummation, a man might be a promising subject for civilisation, but otherwise than in *posse* it must be premature ; so he must be considered as more or less of a savage. This doctrine he naturally published more loudly than ever as he was himself more and more removed from all suspicion of barbaric sobriety. He then became anxious, with tears in his eyes, to proclaim the deep sincerity of his conversion to civilisation. But, as such an odiously long word must ever be distressing to a gentleman taking his ease of an evening, unconsciously, perhaps, he abridged it always after 10 P.M. into *civilation*. Such was the genesis of the word. And I therefore, upon entering it in my neological dictionary of English, matriculated it thus : —" *Civilation*, by ellipsis, or more properly by syncope, or, rigorously speaking, by hiccup, from *civilisation*."

thoroughly social, would keep us company. From the circumstances given, I infer a probability. Else I protest
against "peaching," and revealing secrets, small or great,
though forty years old. The range of time which is concerned in my present notice stretches over a dozen years ;
within which space intermittingly, as off and on I happened
to be in Edinburgh, various persons, variously interesting,
entered for a time, or quitted for a time, our fluctuating
circle. The original nucleus had been John Wilson (*i.e. the*
Wilson) and his brothers, — amongst whom the naturalist
(James Wilson) was known to me first, — and subsequently Sir
William Hamilton. Next, and after the war had finally
reached its consummation in Waterloo—a *peripeteia* as perfect and dramatic as ever was exhibited on the stage of
Athens—others at intervals gladdened our festal company :
amongst whom, as the most memorable, I ought to mention
Colonel Mitchell, the biographer of Wallenstein, so advantageously known by his bold and original views upon strategies, upon the efficacy of the bayonet, and upon the critical
interpretation of some capital chapters in martial history ;
Captain Thomas Hamilton, the brother of Sir William, an
accomplished man, latterly known amongst us by the name
of Cyril Thornton, from the title of his novel ; Sir William
Allan, the distinguished artist, afterwards President of the
Royal Scottish Academy ; and, lastly, Mr. R. P. Gillies, the
advocate, whose name I repeat with a sigh of inexpressible
sadness, such as belongs of right to some splendid Timon of
Athens, so often as on the one hand I revivify to my mind
his gay saloons, resonant with music and festal laughter—
the abode for years of a munificent hospitality, which Wordsworth characterised as "all but princely "—and, on the
other hand, shudder at the mighty shadows of calamity, of
sorrow, of malice, of detraction, that have for thirty years
stalked after his retreating splendours, and long since have
swallowed up the very memory of his pretensions from the
children of this generation.[1]

---

[1] Robert Pearce Gillies, born 1788, was admitted to the Scottish
Bar in 1815, and for the next ten years was one of the most shining
figures in the literary society of Edinburgh. Ruined by the commercial crash of 1825, he removed to London, where he died in 1858,

But, returning to the subject of *civilation*, could it be said of Sir William Hamilton that he favoured it or promoted it? Hardly, I think. The age itself—that generation of Waterloo—sanctioned a certain degree of civilation in young and old : and Sir William, in his fervid youth, was too social and too generous to retreat austerely within the circle of absolute barbarism. But it would have been difficult to civilise *him* effectually, such was the resistance opposed to civilation by his extraordinary muscular strength. Sir William's powers, in some directions, as an athlete, were indeed unusually great, and would have attracted much more notice, had he not, upon all his personal endowments, been so systematically shy, and even so disdainful of display. Nobody, therefore, fancied that he could gratify Sir William by recalling gymnastic feats of *his*. When he relaxed at all from his habitual mood of freezing contempt for all personal acts of ostentation whatever (no matter whether intellectual or physical), it was in pure overmastering sympathy with the spirit of genial fun—the *amabilis insania*—which some special gathering of youth and youthful gaiety had concurred to kindle. It was in mere deference to the expectations or wishes of others that Sir William could be ever persuaded into a moment's display, and then not without an expression of scorn too palpable for his own compliance. A person worse qualified than myself for recording the exact extent of his athletic powers cannot be imagined ; and for the plain reason—that, having not the slightest pretensions in that way myself, I had not cultivated any interest in such powers, nor consequently any knowledge of their nature or limits. Ignorant I was of the human frame, and of its latent powers, as regarded speed, force, ambidexterity, in a degree that would have been inexcusable in an old woman. I was even proud of my own desperate ignorance to an extent that made penitence or amendment apparently hopeless. And the worst feature of my barbarism was, and *is* to this hour, that, instead of meditating occasionally on the possibility that *I* might be wrong, and the world might be right—on the contrary, with a stiff-neckedness (surely there *is* such a

after many years of misfortune. His *Memoirs of a Literary Veteran*, published in 1851, contain his Edinburgh recollections.—M.

word) that is truly criminal, I then did, and I now do,
exhaust myself in terms of bloody contempt for all the men,
and all the races of men, that ever fell down in prose or
verse to worship the idol of human physical excellence.
" The abject villains ! " was the best term (how illiberal !)
that I could afford to the ancient Greeks, when noticing
their beastly admiration of good running, good wrestling,
good cab-driving at Olympia.   Oh, heavens ! that a fist, that
a foot, that a hoof, should be viewed with a holy homage,
such as belonged of right to a revelation of truth, or after a
millennium of darkness that belonged to the first-fruits of the
rising dawn !   The Romans, it is remarkable, had no reverence for individual physical prowess.   They had no Olympic
contests.   On the contrary, they regarded all such animal
exertions as mere gladiatorial glories, *i.e.* as the distinctions
of slaves, and distinctions that were to be bought for copper
and silver amongst the savages of earth.   But the Greeks,
who, with the tremulous and half-effeminate temperament
of genius, combined a hideous defect of dignity and moral
stamina, figure as perfect lunatics in their admiration of
animal excellence :—

> " Metaque fervidis
> Evitata rotis, palmaque nobilis,
> Terrarum dominos evehit ad deos."

Horace himself, *roué* as he was, is Roman enough to squint
at his reader with a look half-aghast at this extravagance
of descent into the superstition that glorifies the fleshly.
Homer, the greatest master of traumatic surgery (*i.e.* the
philosophy of wounds) that has ever existed,—in fact (if it
were not for his profound darkness on the subject of gunshot
wounds) the only poet on record that would, *sede vacante*,
have been elected by acclamation, without needing any
interest at all or any canvass, as house-surgeon to St.
Thomas's Hospital, or the Hotel Dieu,—has absolutely left
nothing for posterity to do in what regards the description of
wounds, ulcers, &c.   That department of surgery has become
a mere sinecure since the first edition of the Iliad.   But in
Milton, raised above Homer as heaven is raised above earth,
who can tolerate the grovelling ambition of angels glorying

in " a *noble* stroke " ? [1]   To have delivered a "facer," or a
backhanded blow, or to have cut St. George with a broad-
sword over the conk of an archangel—ah, faugh! who can
blame me for being sick ? Is it I, or is it Milton, that is in
the wrong ? At all events, reader, justifying these things,
never dream yourself entitled to join the wretched and
effeminate abusers of boxing, of the ring, of the fancy, as
now languishing in England. How brutal, you pretend to
say, is that savage practice in the London ring of thumping
the human face divine into the semblance of a roasted apple
dressed with a poultice ! Doubtless. But, even as it is,
you that laud the traumatic sagacities of Homer, and even of
the heaven-born Milton, presume not to talk of brutality in
that which carried glory and illustration amongst the
heavenly host. To " fib " a man, to " punish " him, to " draw
his claret," or to get his cocoa-nut into " chancery," cannot be
so thoroughly unworthy of a bargeman, or the Tipton Slasher,
if it's quite becoming to a Grecian Milo, or a Phrygian Entellus,
or even—*horresco referens*—not beneath a Miltonic seraph.

Sir William Hamilton's prowess did not exhibit itself in
that line. Professor Wilson had *thumped* his way to consideration ; he had also *walked* and *run* into fame. But
standing leaps it was—leaps upward without any advantage
of a run—in which Sir W.'s pre-eminence was illustrated.
Even me, cased against foolish admiration in seven-fold
ignorance, they startled and astonished—me even, though
resolutely bent upon despising every pretension of that class,
and the more so at that time because Wordsworth had then
recently shocked me beyond expression by a confession that
seemed inhuman in its degradation, viz. this—that, whereas
he would not walk for a quarter of a mile to see the man
whom all the world should agree to crown as its foremost
intellectual champion, willingly he would go three days'
journey through a wilderness to see Belzoni ! [2]

[1] " So saying, a noble stroke he lifted high,
    Which hung not, but so swift with tempest fell
    On the proud crest of Satan that no sight,
    Nor motion of swift thought, less could his shield,
    Such ruin intercept. "

Paradise Lost, vi. 189-193.—M.

[2] Belzoni [1778-1823], it may be necessary to inform *this* genera-

But stop. This will not do. I must alter the scale of
this paper, or else—something will happen which would vex
me. The artist who sketched the Vicar of Wakefield's family
group, in his zeal for comprehensive fulness of details, enlarged his canvas until he forgot the narrow proportions of
the good vicar's house ; and the picture, when finished, was
too big to enter the front-door of the vicarage. One side of
the house must have been pulled down to allow of its introduction ; and, as a natural consequence, the picture was consigned to a barn—which fate will be mine, unless an instant
remedy can be applied to the desultory and expansive
tendencies which besiege all personal sketches, and especially
sketches of such men as, being largely philosophic, and controversially entangled in the questions of their own generation, stand in a possible relation to all things. A dangerous
subject is a philosopher. For, even if he has not formally
and broadly entangled himself controversially in the moving
disputes of his age, be assured that up and down his writings
will be detected hooks and eyes lurking more or less obscurely,
that are fitted to infibulate him (or perhaps meant to infibulate him) into the great draperies and arras of the philosophical speculations hanging down to coming generations.
" *Hooks and eyes !* " Is not that image strictly a plagiarism
from some respectable tailor and habit-maker ? Perhaps it
is ; but *infibulate* cannot be a plagiarism, because I never saw
the word before ; and, in fact, I have this moment invented
it, in order to express an extra interest in the subject.

The embarrassment is this : I *must* have some amusement
for my reader. Can I have it ? Is it to be looked for from
any region of philosophic speculation ? The reader has
shown himself a patient reader—he has waited : and I *must*

tion, was an Italian, who came to Liverpool originally in the character
of a posture-master, an *acrobates*, a walker on the tight-rope, a
desultor, &c. He ran towards seven feet high, was as strong as a
camel, and as agile as a horse. But he was also a very intelligent
man, and subsequently his ambition received a higher direction.
Under English patronage, he explored the tombs of Egyptian Thebes ;
gave a rude shaking to the mummies, who had slept quite long
enough ; and amongst the Arabs, Nubians, &c., but especially amongst
Turks, who have a childish reverence for physical perfections, turned
his fine person to a real diplomatic use in the service of England.

reward him. I must "take a rise" out of something or other : and nothing that connects itself with Sir W. H. is so likely to furnish it as the old-world superannuated manuals of Logic.

One-half of Sir William's laurels have been won in the fields of logic ; and a better way there cannot be for doing justice to the reforms (whether of extension or of purification) which we owe and *shall* owe to Sir William than that which lies through any fair and lively abstract of the unreformed manuals, such as have prevailed all over Europe for the last three centuries. *Lively* seems a strange epithet for the characterising of a "Logic." But, in fact, from pure misconception of their appropriate functions, the ordinary books of logic had gradually come to trespass more and more upon the regular province of Joe Miller. Here follow, for the reader's entertainment, a few of their most classical cases :—

(1) Protagoras had instructed Euathlus in the art of judicial pleading, and upon these terms,—that the stipulated fee for this instruction should not be paid by the pupil until he came to plead his first cause, and then only in the event of his winning it. Having finished his education, however, Euathlus showed no intention of fulfilling the contract by applying his knowledge practically ; and Protagoras, as the best mode of forcing him to do so, raised a suit against him for the money. The pleadings were opened by the plaintiff, who argued that it was very little matter how the court decided the case, since under *any* possible decision the result must practically be for himself—"Because," said he, "if you the judges decide in my favour, then I gain my cause by that decision ; but, on the other hand, if you decide against me, then it is true that, forensically, I lose the cause, but in that case Euathlus gains it, and it is his first cause. Now, the very agreement was that, if he gained his first cause, he should pay me *instanter*." On the other side, the defendant smilingly retorted upon him his own line of argument. "In any case," said Euathlus, "I am destined to win ; for, if the court decides in my favour, there is an end of the matter. I am absolved from paying by the highest legal authority. But, if the court makes its award in favour of the learned

gentleman, my antagonist, then I shall have lost the cause ;
and that is precisely the case in which it was agreed between
us that I was not to pay." The knavish Athenian in search
of a dinner (*Græculus esuriens*) who manufactured this
pretty conundrum of litigation flattered himself that he had
got both parties into a deadly fix, out of which they could
not stir backwards or forwards. But the summary solution
of the dilemma is this : 1st, That at any rate it is not a
dilemma within the jurisdiction of logic ; 2d, that, as a forensic dilemma, it might read prettily in the schools, but not
in the forum : since the real *nodus* of the perplexity lies in
this—that each party alternately shelters himself under the
shadow of a double law—when the one law fails him, he
runs under the shadow of the other, and *vice versa*. But in
a case of actual life the parties must previously have made
their election of the law by which they would be tried ; and,
once having done this, neither party would be at liberty to
upset the decision of the court by the specific terms of the
agreement, nor reciprocally to upset the specific agreement by
the authority of the court.

(2) Another well-known case of perplexity, falsely classed
as logical, is that denominated "The Crocodile." I recall at
this moment a little metrical tale of Southey's, in which the
dramatis personæ are pretty nearly the same, viz. a crocodile,
a woman, and her son. In that case, however, the crocodile
is introduced as a person of pattern morality, for the woman
says of him—

> " The king of the crocodiles never does wrong :
> He has no tail so stiff and strong
> Petitioners to sweep away,[1]
> But he has ears to hear what I say."

Not so the crocodile known to the Greek dialecticians. *He*
bore a very different character. If he had no tail to interfere
with Magna Charta and the imprescriptible right of petition-
ing, he had, however, teeth of the most horrid description for
crushing petition and petitioner into one indistinguishable
pulp ; and, in the particular case contemplated by the

---

[1] Forgetting this particular line, I have coined one, in order to fill
up the chasm as to sense and metre.

logicians, having made prisoner of a poor woman's son, he was
by her charged with the same purpose in regard to her beloved cub as the Cyclops in the " Odyssey " avows in regard
to Ulysses, viz. that he reserved him to his larder for an
extra bonne bouche on a gala-day.   The crocodile, who,
generally speaking, is the most uncandid of reptiles, would
not altogether deny the soft impeachment ; but, in order to
sport an air of liberality which was far from his heart, he
protested that, no matter for any private views which he
might have dallied with in respect to the young gentleman,
he would abandon them all on one condition (but, observe, a
condition which he privately held to be impossible for a
woman to fulfil), viz. that she should utter some proposition
which was incontrovertibly true.   The woman mused upon
this ; for, though she knew of propositions that no neutral
party could dispute—as this, for instance, that crocodiles are
the most odious of vermin—it was evident that her antagonist
would repel *that* as an illiberal and one-sided personality.
After some consideration, therefore, she replied thus,—" You
will eat my son."   There and then arose in the crocodile's
brain a furious self-conflict, from which it is contended that
no amount of Athenian chicanery could ever deliver him ;
since, if he *did* eat her son, then the woman had uttered the
plain truth, which the crocodile himself could not have the
face to deny ; in which case (the case of speaking truth) he
had pledged his royal word *not* to eat him : and thus he had
acted in a way to make the word of a crocodile, or his bond,
or even the tears of a crocodile, a mere jest amongst philosophers.   On the other hand, if, in contemplation of these
horrid consequences, he did *not* eat her son, then the woman
had uttered a falsehood in asserting that he would, and it became a royal duty in *him*, as a guardian of morality, to exact
the penalty of her wickedness.   Here, however, as so commonly in the case of diplomatic treaties, when the secret
object is to leave a nest-egg towards a future war as soon as
war shall become convenient, the original error lay in not
having exhausted the circle of possibilities,—that is, in having
provided for two out of three cases, but not for the third.
Truth absolute was provided for ; in that case the son was to
be spared.   Absolute falsehood was also provided for ; in

that case the son was to die. But truth conditional was *not* provided for. Supposing the woman to say something contingent on a case that might or might not be realised, then it became necessary to wait for the event. But here there was no use in waiting, since, whichever of the two possible events should occur, either equally and irretrievably landed the crocodile in a violation of his royal promise.

(3) Another and much more famous perplexity, paraded by the Greek logicians, was that known by the title of "Achilles and the Tortoise." None better illustrates the erroneous and vague conceptions which they (and universally which the popular understanding) formed of logic and its proper jurisdiction. For the sake of many who will never have heard of it, and for the sake of the metaphysical solution which it has since suggested to some original thinkers, I will here rehearse it :—Achilles, most of us know, is celebrated in the "Iliad" as the swift-footed (πόδας ὠκὺς Ἀχιλλεύς) ; and the tortoise, perhaps all of us know, is equally celebrated amongst naturalists as the slow-footed. In any race, therefore, between such parties, according to the equities of Newmarket and Doncaster, where artificial compensations as to the weight of the riders are used to redress those natural advantages that would else be unfair, Achilles must grant to the tortoise the benefit of starting first. But, if he does *that*, says the Greek sophist, then I, the sophist, back the tortoise to any amount, engaging that the goddess-born hero shall never come up with the poor reptile. Let us see. It matters little what exact amount of precedency is conceded to the tortoise ; but say that he is allowed a start of one-tenth part of the whole course. Quite as little does it matter by what ratio of speed Achilles surpasses the tortoise ; but, suppose this ratio to be that of ten to one, then, if the racecourse be ten miles long, our friend the slow-coach, being by the conditions entitled to one-tenth of the course for his starting allowance, will have finished one mile as a *solo* performer before Achilles is entitled to move. When the *duet* begins, the tortoise will be entering on the second mile precisely as Achilles enters on the first. But, because the Nob runs ten times as fast as the Snob, whilst Achilles is running his first mile the tortoise accomplishes only the

tenth-part of the second mile. Not much, you say. Certainly not very much, but quite enough to keep the reptile in advance of the hero. This hero, being very little addicted to think small beer of himself, begins to fancy that it will cost him too trivial an effort to run ahead of his opponent. But don't let him shout before he is out of the wood. For, though he soon runs over that tenth of a mile which the tortoise has already finished, even this costs him a certain time, however brief. And during that time the tortoise will have finished a corresponding sub-section of the course—viz. the tenth-part of a tenth-part. This fraction is a hundredth-part of the total distance. Trifle as that is, it constitutes a debt against Achilles, which debt *must* be paid. And, whilst he *is* paying it, behold our dull friend in the shell has run the tenth part of a hundredth part, which amounts to a thousandth-part. To the goddess-born what a flea-bite is that! True, it is so ; but still it lasts long enough to give the tortoise time for keeping his distance, and for drawing another little bill upon Achilles for a ten-thousandth part. Always, in fact, alight upon what stage you will of the race, there is a little arrear to be settled between the parties, and always *against* the hero. " Vermin, in account with the divine and long-legged Pelides, *Cr.* by one-billionth or one-decillionth of the course " : much or little, what matters it, so long as the divine man cannot pay it off before another instalment becomes due ? And pay it off he never will, though the race should last for a thousand centuries. Here, now, was a Gordian knot which never could be untied—viz. that A should be confessedly ten times fleeter than B, and yet through all ages be unable to get ahead of him. But, in fact, though baffling to the popular understanding, the problem does not turn upon any *logical* difficulty ; the difficulty is purely mathematical, and the same as is involved in a certain familiar case of decimal fractions, namely, in a repeating decimal, such as this :—Throw the vulgar fraction of 2 divided by 3 into the form of a decimal, and it will become six-tenths + six-hundredths + six-thousandths, &c. ('66666, &c., inexhaustibly to all eternity). It is, in fact, a pure mathematic or ideal case made perplexing by being incarnated in a case of physical experience. In other words, it is one amongst the many confounding consequences which may be deduced from the endless divisibility of space. But (as more than one subtle thinker has noticed) even this perplexity, as regards the *practical* antinomy (viz. the demonstrability on the one side that Achilles never can overtake the tortoise, and yet on the other side the certainty from experience that he will) is supported only by pursuing the expansion of one infinite (viz. space subdividing itself) and concealing the compensatory expansion of another infinite— viz. time subdividing itself. The infinity of space in this race of subdivision is artfully run against a *finite* time ; whereas, if the one infinite were pitted, as in reason it ought to be, against the other infinite, the endless divisibility of time against the endless divisibility of space, there would arise a reciprocal exhaustion and neutralisation that would swallow up the astounding consequences, very much as the two Kilkenny cats ate up each other. Or, as Leibnitz explains the problem to M. Foucher, in a passage called into notice by Mrs. Coleridge, "*Ne craignez point, monsieur, la tortue que les Pyrrhoniens faisaient aller aussi vite qu' Achille. Un espace divisible sans fin se passe dans un tems aussi divisible sans fin.*" [1] That is, a space that is infinitely subdivisible (and which, therefore, seems to us an abyss that never could be traversed in a finite time) is traversed without difficulty in a time that is also infinitely divisible.

III

In the case of Achilles and the Tortoise, and many others, there were concerned great metaphysical problems, and elementary perplexities, such as never cease to awaken and to interest the human mind under any condition of human development. Such questions wear always an air of permanent involution in the understanding ; and the challenge is, not to their claim upon human interest, but to their privilege of intrusion upon the field of logic. As misplaced, you reasonably protested against many of these speculations,

[1] See Appended Note at the end of this Paper for a further discussion of this famous puzzle of Achilles and the Tortoise, and of the reference made to Leibnitz in connexion with it by Mrs. Sara Coleridge.—M.

but not as in themselves trivial or wanting in philosophic importance.   Too often, on the other hand, mere tricks of verbal legerdemain, fantastic snares for puzzling the understanding by means of the equivocalities that lurk in language, entered largely into the popular books of logic, not rising in the quality of their interest at all above the level of ropedancing and thimblerigging.   Here, for instance, is an illustrative case, that has been adopted into many manuals of logic, and apparently much admired :—A great philosopher pronounces the people of Crete, one and all, liars.   But this great philosopher, whose name is Epimenides, happens himself to be a Cretan.   On his own showing, therefore, Epimenides is a liar.   But, if so, what he says is a lie.   Now, what he says is that the Cretans are liars.   This, therefore, as coming from a liar, is a lie ; and the Cretans, as is now philosophically demonstrated, are all persons of honour and veracity.   Consequently, Epimenides is such.   You may depend upon everything that he says.   But what he says most frequently is that all the Cretans are liars.   Himself, therefore, as one amongst them, he denounces as a liar. Being such, he has falsely taxed the Cretans with falsehood, and himself amongst them.   It is false, therefore, that Epimenides is a liar.   Consequently, in calling himself by implication a liar, as one amongst the Cretans, he lied.   And the proof of his veracity rests in his having lied.   And so on *da capo* for ever and ever.

A more pleasant example of the same logical see-saw occurs in the sermons[1] of Jeremy Taylor.   "That man," says the inimitable bishop, "was prettily and fantastically " troubled, who, having used to put his trust in dreams, one " night dreamed that all dreams were vain ; for he considered, " if so, then *this* was vain, and the dreams might be true for " all this. (For who pronounced them *not* true, except a " vain dream ?) But, if *they* might be true, then *this* dream " might be so upon equal reason.   And then dreams *were* " vain, because this dream, which told him so, was true ; " and so round again.   In the same circle runs the heart of " man.   All his cogitations are vain, and yet he makes especial

[1] Viz. in the sermon entitled *The Deceitfulness of the Heart*, p. 515, vol. i., in Longman's edition of the Sermons, 1826.

" use of this—that that thought which thinks so, *that* is vain.
" And, if *that* be vain, then his other thoughts, which are
" vainly declared so, may be real and relied upon." You
see, reader, the horrid American fix into which a man is
betrayed, if he obeys the command of a dream to distrust
dreams universally, for then he has no right to trust in this
particular dream which authorises his general distrust. No ;
let us have fair play. What is sauce for the goose is sauce
for the gander. And this ugly gander of a dream, that
" notes " and " protests " all dreams collectively, silently and
by inevitable consequence notes and protests itself.

So natural, indeed, to the morbid activity of man are
these revolving forms of alternate repulsion, where flight
turns suddenly into pursuit, and pursuit into flight, that I
myself, when a schoolboy, invented several : this, for instance,
which once puzzled a man in a wig ; and I believe he bore
me malice to his dying day, because he gave up the ghost, by
reason of fever, before he was able to find out satisfactorily
what screw was loose in my logical conundrum ; and thus, in
fact, " all along of me " (as he expressed it) the poor man was
forced to walk out of life *re infecta*, his business unfinished,
the one sole problem that had tortured him being unsolved.
It was this :—Somebody had told me of a dealer in gin who,
having had his attention roused to the enormous waste of
liquor caused by the unsteady hands of drunkards, invented
a counter which, through a simple set of contrivances,
gathered into a common reservoir all the spillings that previously had run to waste. St. Monday, as it was then called
in English manufacturing towns, formed the jubilee day in
each week for the drunkards ; and it was *now* ascertained
(*i.e.* subsequently to the epoch of the artificial counter) that
oftentimes the mere " spilth "[1] of St. Monday supplied the
entire demand of Tuesday. It struck me, therefore, on
reviewing this case, that the more the people drank, the
more they would *titubate ;* by which word it was that I
expressed the reeling and stumbling of intoxication. If they
drank abominably, then of course they would titubate abomi-

[1] A Shakesperian word : see *Timon of Athens.* The contrivance
of the spirit-dealer is now universally diffused, but in those days it
was only beginning.

nably ; and, titubating abominably, inevitably they would spill in the same ratio. The more they drank, the more they would titubate ; the more they titubated, the more they would spill; and the more they spilt, the more, it is clear, they did *not* drink. You can't tax a man with drinking what he spills. It is evident, from Euclid, that the more they spilt, the less they *could* have to drink. So that, if their titubation was excessive, then their spilling must have been excessive, and in that case they must have practised almost total abstinence. Spilling nearly all, how could they have left themselves anything worth speaking of to drink ? Yet, again, if they drank nothing worth speaking of, how could they titubate ? Clearly they could not ; and, not titubating, they could have had no reason for spilling; in which case they must have drunk the whole—that is, they must have drunk to the whole excess imputed ; which doing, they were dead drunk, and must have titubated to extremity ; which doing, they must have spilt nearly the whole. Spilling the whole, they could not have been drunk. *Ergo*, could not have titubated. *Ergo*, could not have spilt. *Ergo*, must have drunk the whole. *Ergo*, were dead drunk. *Ergo*, must have titubated. "And so round again," as my lord the bishop pleasantly expresses it, *in secula seculorum.*

It is not easy to state adequately the condition of Logic when overrun by a vegetation of weeds like those which I have described. The extent of the mischief would not be measured by saying that the culture of the ancient vineyard had languished. Much better it would describe the case to say that the culture had gradually been transferred to a growth of alien plants, having no relation or even resemblance to the vine, nor any tendency towards a common purpose with the vine. Logic had silently become not so much a superannuated speculation that was exhibited in decay, as a new and intrusive speculation that masquerades under an ancient name. And, undoubtedly, had it not been for the inveterate traditions of logic, which maintained their ground by means of *names*—had it not been for the hereditary necessities, which kept open a section by a sort of dull prescription for *syllogism*, for *definition*, for *division*, for *dilemma*, for *sorites*, &c.—but for this accident, the very last links that

connected the modern systems of logic with the original
Aristotelian system would probably have perished. The
heterogeneity of the materials dealt with in modish books of
logic was gradually making itself more and more conspicuous.
This taint had long been felt obscurely ; the next step would
naturally have been to brighten that feeling to the consciousness ; after which the final step would be to restore its
homogeneous character to the science, by separating the two
incoherent elements, and by expelling one or the other
of them. But *which*, whether the true or the intrusive, no
man can doubt who has watched the set of the currents in
our ordinary and popular philosophy—the philosophy which
recommends itself to the children of our own generation.
And thus, to a dead certainty, had not such a consummation
been intercepted by a splendid accident, the last stage in the
history of Logic must have been to ignore every distinguish-
able atom and fibre that continued to connect logic with
anything whatever that had originally been called or understood by that name.

The splendid accident was the critical appearance of a
great man—viz. Immanuel Kant.[1] He it was (and how
comes it that a reviewer of *Logical Revolutions* so able as Mr.
Spencer Baynes should have dropped such a fact from his
record ?)—he it was that authoritatively recalled Logic to its
proper duties as a *formal* science. In that sense, and to that
extent—viz. simply in relation to the corruptions worked or
completed by his own century—Kant was an innovator. He
was an innovator by virtue of rejecting innovation. He had
credit for a novelty, because he called back an antiquity ;
but in reality, whatever might be the openings which he

---

[1] I do not mean that, failing Kant, there have not been, since his
rising in 1755-80, other potent minds capable of the same service ;
and *eventually* that service would have been achieved by somebody.
A treason of that magnitude to a capital interest of the human intellect secretly lodges at the time a promise and a deep assurance of a
full and faithful reaction. But still, if the great impulse given to
thought, and the direction impressed upon it, by Kant, had been
wanting, how many of our great European thinkers since the French
Revolution might have been intercepted, and how long would have
been the syncope under which the life-blood of philosophy might have
stagnated !

made *elsewhere*, for going ahead and for doing or enabling to do something which should merit to be marked with the affirmative sign, the sign of *plus* (+), certainly, as regarded this special science which we are now speaking of, viz. Logic, he contented himself with cleansing the general field, and removing accumulations, whether of mere unsightly rubbish [1] or of downright obstruction.   He built nothing : simply, as an active Roman edile, he pulled down the irregular and lawless erections that preoccupied the serviceable areas where truth might pitch her tents, or that encroached upon the ancient paths along which the plain upright man might see his way into the centre of those tents.

Kant not only volunteered no extensions that I am aware of to the great Crystal Palace of Logic, with the single exception (not yet practically adopted) of the *judicia infinita* (or *limitantia*), as furnishing a basis for the arrondissement of his own categories ; but, moreover, he seems systematically to have questioned the possibility of making any *real* additions to the edifice as left by Aristotle.   Kant, therefore, in effect, bequeathed *carte blanche* on this subject to the generations that should succeed him.

But *carte blanche* is not a thing to be thankful for, unless you know of something to write upon it that may occupy the blank.   If not, it is a standing reproach to your poverty ; for who would have said "*thank ye*" for a gift of Chat Moss, unless he had happened also to possess those three million cart-loads of rubbish that were found necessary to fill its insatiable maw, and to reconcile its feelings to the torture of railway locomotives rushing and snorting, day and night, between Manchester and Liverpool ?

There are not many people who can boast of having made *discoveries* in Logic ; for the simplicity of so elementary a speculation presents at any period not very much of what can properly be made the subject of discovery.   The field is not fertile, and what little it yields is soon carried off by the

---

[1] Accordingly, he made war not only upon those *material* adulterations of logic which clouded and perplexed the truth, but also upon those *formal* refinements which did no more than disfigure the truth, as, for example, upon the spurious subtlety (*die falsche spitzfindigkeit*) of the fourth figure.

earliest reapers. But, in spite of the difficulties, Sir William
has been a discoverer. He has drawn into open daylight so
much of ancient hints that were but dimly shadowed out,
strengthening their outlines, and exposing the intellectual
necessity in which they had their roots, that even so far he
might have merited something of that gratitude which is
conceded to the earliest explorers of truth. And, apart from
these cases, there are others in which unequivocally he is the
very first revealer of what had lurked unsuspected even to
the most superstitious searchers of Aristotle's text. All the
history of letters does not present us with so remarkable a
detection of an error, that had hidden itself for a couple of
thousand years, as that made by Sir William in the Aristotelian use of the term *categorical.* There has been many a
man that would have risked his life upon the certainty that
Aristotle had employed this word as the antithesis of *hypo-
thetic :* whereas it now appears that, although corrupted into
that sense by the very earliest interpreters of the *Organon,*
it is not once so employed by Aristotle. The new doctrine
upon the Quantification of the Predicate belongs in part to
Sir William—viz. in its extension to negative propositions.
A distinguished pupil of Sir William's has recently made it
public,[1] and partially it had been published previously in the
double controversy which it had fastened upon its author.
The value of it lies, I believe, chiefly in the integration
which it gives to the theory of logic ; and everything is
valuable on that path, so long as any darkness lingers upon
it. The important distinction between the *extension and the
comprehension,* as marking two alternate wholes involved in a
syllogism, is in part a restoration, but a restoration which
owes its *improvement* (using that word in a sense confined to
the pulpit—viz. as an adaptation of a thing to the necessities
of practice) to Sir William. The material glimpses into these
innovations had dawned upon him, it now appears, so early
as 1833. But, several years before that date, I myself can

[1] Mr. Thomas Spencer Baynes ; whose *Essay on the New Analytic
of Logical Forms,* expounding Sir William Hamilton's new logical
doctrine of the Quantification of the Predicate, was published in 1850.
He was afterwards Professor of Moral Philosophy in the University
of St. Andrews, and editor of the latest edition of the *Encyclopædia
Britannica ;* and he died in May 1887.—M.

testify that Sir William was looking with a sceptical jealousy
into the old traditional notions that had become obstinate
fixtures in the received books of logic. He it was—and
certainly before 1820—that first threw light upon a very
interesting point that had perplexed me for years. Somewhere in the *Rhetoric* of Aristotle, I had, with secret astonishment, observed him speaking of the enthymeme as having
some special relation to the purposes of the orator.[1] Yet
how ? Simply that it abridged the syllogism—doubtless
fitted it better for popular use. But *that* was a matter of
course ; and Aristotle, it was clear, meant more than that.
Next came across me, in some Greek expounder of Aristotle,
the expression of ῥητορικοὶ σύλλογισμοι, *rhetorical syllogisms ;*
which certainly could not point to a mere accident of ellipsis,
but to some special differentiation as to the matter of the
particular syllogism appropriated to the orator. Sir William
Hamilton it was that threw the first ray of light into my
perplexity by a little essay of Facciolati's on this very point.
Subsequently, I learned from Sir William that a sort of controversy had existed at one time upon this particular question
of the sense attaching to this special use of the word *enthymeme.* In those years, I entertained a private intention of
publishing a translation (but largely altered for English use)
of Lambert's *Organon.*[2] It had seemed to me a sort of encyclopædia on the whole world of subjects connected with Logic.
From its great compass and variety, I had found it a most
amusing book ; and I need not say that Lambert, the friend
and correspondent of Kant, could not be otherwise than
instructive. My intention was to connect with this work a
supplement containing everything that bore upon Logic of a
revolutionary character, and suggesting either changes or
doubts,—no matter whether orthodox or heterodox, so long

---

[1] The reader must keep in mind that, whilst the Roman distinguished between the Orator and the Rhetorician, the Grecian expressed
both by the same word ; and the distinction,—which, though not
practically developed so much in Athens as in Rome, must have
existed (for such men as Isocrates were but *chamber* orators),—perished
to the Greek, as happens with many a distinction, for pure want of an
expression.

[2] Johann Heinrich Lambert (1728 - 1777). His *Organon* was
published in 1764.—M.

as it was but interesting; and, amongst the jewels of this
appendix, I relied upon this essay of Facciolati,[1] for I knew
that it was of a nature to create a lively interest amongst
scholars. However, my Lambert never made its appearance
in this world, nor will perhaps ; and in the meantime Sir
William has expanded his own knowledge of this enthymeme
dispute in a way that greatly reduces the value of Facciolati's
particular contribution, and places Sir William himself on
the central station of authority in the controversy, as the first
person who has reviewed the whole of it, and abstracted the
relations to each other of the several stages through which it
passed. There is, indeed, I am disposed to think, no great
question that has ever connected itself with Logic which Sir
William Hamilton has not glanced at, with more or less of
circumstantiality, according to its importance : except, perhaps, this one—viz. the dependency of geometrical propositions on the direct machinery of the syllogism. Once only
I have observed him to look in that direction.[2] On that
single occasion, I saw with surprise what *seemed* an insinuation that is utterly irreconcilable with any theory of the case
that I can understand.

Meantime, what the public misses chiefly, and still looks
for with hope from the hands of Sir William Hamilton, is a
comprehensive treatise on every part of Logic, adapted to
the growing necessities of the times ; for, after satire has
done its worst, and the malice is exhausted which fastens
with such genial bitterness on the errors or infirmities of our
own times, I cannot but feel a steady persuasion that this
age is labouring with a deeper fermentation of thought and
self-questioning than has ever before reached the general
heart of a nation. In such circumstances, a Logic like that
of the Jansenists does not move a step in advance towards
any real want of the times. To be free by comparison from

[1] The lexicographer Jacopo Facciolati (1682-1769) was Professor of
Logic in Padua ; and a volume of his Latin Discourses or Essays,
published at Padua in 1752, contains one "*Ad Dialecticam*" and
another "*De Dialecticæ ac Rhetoricæ Differentia.*"—M.

[2] A direction in which Reid faltered, and in effect made shipwreck : viz. in the paper on the *Organon* which he contributed to
Lord Kames's *Sketches of Men.* [*Sketches of the History of Man*,
1774.—M.]

some gross errors and impertinences that disfigure the bulk of
Logics, is not any positive service rendered to the struggling
intellect that everywhere is seeking clamorously a discipline
of art to guide its efforts towards the free movement of its
powers.   It is not a sound logic that is wanted, so much as
a potent and life-giving logic—not a logic whose merit is
simply to keep the right road, and, so far, as guaranteed
against misleading, but a logic that will break down obstruc-
tions and impediments such as make even the right road
impassable.

To sketch the outline of such a Logic, and to show that
the sketcher was not under any confusion as to the proper
functions of Logic, would require a separate paper.   The
great difficulty which besets it, and which might repel from
such a service men of the highest faculties, is that it pre-
supposes a long preparation and vigilance in noting *as they
arise* the innumerable cases of erring logic amongst parlia-
ments, governments, factions, etc.   Errors that have actually
occurred, and have recorded themselves as *operative* errors in
historical results, cannot be disputed ; whereas the errors
that are imagined for the sake of illustration always present
themselves as extravagances that express no real dangers
incident to human thinking.   It must occur, also, to anybody reflecting on this subject, that a vast proportion of bad
logic rests upon false and defective definition.   That two
ideas *can* be associated or dissociated by the mediation of a
third, depends upon the limits assigned to these ideas by
definition, and *that* again depends upon a greatly improved
valuation of words.   Or, if we look to another resource of
logic, viz. division and subdivision, how faulty is *that* in
cases innumerable ; and that inference seems good, whilst
such an idea is divided on a principle of bisection, which
would not have seemed good had the division proceeded by
trisection.   Many collateral aids are needed for a new logic
that should aim at real service.   But these are now concurrently accumulating ; and, even where they are not, Sir
William Hamilton is that man who might be relied on for
furnishing these aids from his own resources.

Whether he has any purpose of gratifying us all in that
way I do not know ; and there is an impertinence in sug-

gesting any choice of labours to a man of profound views who must be supposed long ago to have been self-determined in this or that direction ; and nothing is less truly compli-mentary, though it may clothe itself in those forms of speech, than to imagine a profound and lifelong speculator as having any freedom left him for listening to random voices of sug-gestion. Yet, if it *should* happen that Sir William were to give us a comprehensive Logic, he will in that service be making a special atonement for a special offence of Scotland against Logic. It is interesting to notice some of the fierce contradictions that have domineered over the national mind in Scotland, both in matters of religion and of literature. For instance, the nation that (1) beyond all others has put forth a rancorous intolerance of Popery and especially of Popery intruding into the civil rights of men, (2) that most angrily protests against all hallowing of times and places, and (3) against all ceremonial usages—suffers all three prin-ciples to be violated at once, and itself in one most im-portant concern of life to be laid under a yoke of slavery, such as rarely any Papal interdict has attempted to impose upon the most Popish of nations. During the month of May, in Scotland, there is neither marrying nor giving in marriage. Scotland spurns a Papal, and she allows of a Pagan, interdict. For one month out of twelve, a solemn suspension of Christianity silently takes place as regards one capital concern of life, and the nation to that extent re-enters upon its ancient allegiance to the heathen pantheon.[1] Hardly less remarkable is the self-contradiction of Scotland in its relation to Logic. We all know that everywhere throughout Christendom *since* the time of Lord Bacon, and very much *in consequence* of Lord Bacon, under the misinter-pretation given to his words,[2] the fanciful idea has arisen of an essential opposition between the Aristotelian logic and the procedure by induction—not an opposition as to the

[1] The superstition against marriages in May still exists in Scotland ; and far fewer marriages are intimated in that month in the Scottish newspapers than in any other. Still some do occur in May.—M.

[2] But not always, I fear, under a *mis*interpretation. I cannot at this moment refer to them, but my impression is that there are passages in Lord Bacon which authorise this fanciful idea.

separate conditions under which these methods could be usefully applied, but as to the comparative soundness of the methods themselves. A hundred years later than Lord Bacon, when Locke's influence began to diffuse itself, this prejudice became everywhere more obstinate. But, as to this point, Scotland outran all nations in the strength of her obstinacy. For the last hundred years, it is notorious that no expressions of hostility in relation to Aristotle so keen or so contemptuous have been avowed by the learned men of any nation as by those of Scotland. And these feelings, generally so unlimited in their verbal expression, have not usually been applied to any part of the Aristotelian physics, or psychology,—which are not much known in any country, —but almost exclusively (and, at any rate, pre eminently) to the *Organon*. Now, it is a striking fact, when ranged over against this notorious tendency amongst the Scottish thinkers, what Sir William circumstantially illustrates to us—viz. that in older times the Scotch ranked in the estimation of the most cultivated nations, especially in the universities of France, Italy, and Spain, as the most zealous and the ablest expounders of Aristotle, consequently as his most effective champions. Then, as now, they did not rank high as masters of language, — generally of what was meant by *humanity* (the "literæ *humaniores*") ; but as commentators and champions of Aristotle in his Logic they were preferred to men of all other nations. That is sharp enough in the way of contra-position ; but sharper is this which follows,— and I cannot imagine by what tortuosity of evasion a Scotch hater of Aristotle could slip his neck out of such a noose :—

The Scottish Law is notoriously an adoption from the Civil Law ; and,—for some reason, which I own myself unable to state,—in the jurisprudence which thus inoculates itself upon the Roman jurisprudence a larger use of the judicial process is conducted by written pleadings than in the English Law, which rejects the Roman. Thirty years ago I believe that this difference prevailed even more largely in Scotland ; and, as all their pleadings were printed, one natural consequence of this arrangement was that enormous masses of such papers, when once their honey had been sufficiently sucked out by my lords the judges, were served up as cold dishes to a second table, open to the public at large. They were sold as rubbish or old almanacs. Flights of them came abroad as wrappings for parcels. And in that way the public, in which mob I formed one, without needing to pick locks, or to bribe servants, wormed ourselves into the knowledge of many family secrets. We "intromitted," as Scotch Law phrases it, with many family affairs, having no more business with them than I have at this moment to "intromit" with the King of Dahomey's harem. Now, the thing which fixed my attention, and caused me to muse exceedingly, was that nowhere before in all my reading, early or late, regular or contraband, had there faced me so many cases of direct, formal, undisguised syllogism as occurred in these earnest pleadings. Misunderstand me not, reader, as meaning that some superannuated and pedantic forms of reasoning, elsewhere obsolete, had here obtained a privileged and traditional footing. Not at all. They were the mere voice and utterance of natural earnestness, extorted, perhaps, at times from men who might disapprove of them æsthetically, but to whom, nevertheless, the just consideration that the *salus clientis lex suprema* recommended them as the best form of argument. Virtually, the syllogistic elements *must* have been used and covertly dispersed through the argument upon *any* mode of pleading. This could not have been evaded. But the rigorous form of the syllogism, ostentatiously parading itself, might have been evaded. That it was *not*, argued the overpowering sense of its use. The same harsh and naked obtrusion of the scholastic syllogism I had noticed in Hackstone of Rathillet,[1] when dealing with a religious proposition, in an agony of earnestness. And thus I said to myself, Here is a succession of learned men, with a zealotry unknown to the rest of the world, violently rejecting and disowning the whole clockwork of syllogism as if it were some monstrous impediment in the way of using our natural energies with freedom ; and yet this same succession of men, when pleading for the dearest rights of property, or for the

[1] David Hackstone of Rathillet, Scottish Covenanter, taken prisoner at the fight of Airsmoss in July 1680, and hanged at Edinburgh on the 30th of that month for having carried arms against the King at Drumclog and Bothwell Bridge, and for his concern in the assassination of Archbishop Sharp in May 1679.—M.

most sacred interests of truth—that is, in situations which
throw back our human nature upon the instincts of its
native sincerity, and when the clamorous necessity is for
that resource which is most effectual to save—these very
men we find coerced and driven beyond all others in Europe
into the scholastic forms of argument, although beyond all
others in Europe they had a motive in their previous under-
valuation of such forms for strenuously rejecting them ! No
contradiction can be so broad as that between the Scotch
inordinate disparagement of the syllogism in theory and the
Scotch inordinate intrusion of it in their practice.

One may descry, indeed, a double necessity as now working towards the same end,—that is, hurrying forward Logic
to a great epoch in its evolution. There is the crying
necessity, already noticed, that besieges the human mind on
every line of advance, for a regulating discipline of exercise,
that, whilst evoking the human energies, will not suffer
them to be wasted. And, again, another necessity is arising
out of such schisms as I have just cited from Scotland. The
mere scandal of such contradictions and antinomies must
arrest the attention in a degree that will terminate in a
revolution. Even a case so broad of simple contradiction,
contradiction amongst different individuals, would finally
have that effect. But here it is evident that the contradictions were self-contradictions : for the people who, in obedience to a prevailing disparagement of scholasticism, disowned
the syllogism as any legitimate form of argument, were
precisely the same people that resorted to it in their practical extremities. And a scandal like that, I *do* say, is
unparalleled in human science. And it is a scandal which,
though not everywhere taking the amusing shape of using
as your main weapon what you denounce as no weapon at
all, nevertheless everywhere exists. *Logica Docens* is everywhere treated contemptuously, whilst *Logica Utens* is but
another name for strength of reasoning, which is everywhere
an object of intense ambition. That is, translating out of
scholastic into ordinary language, logic as a thing to be
taught and studied, logic as it is gathered into a book, is to
this hour spoken of as bearing a very dubious value : whilst
logic as a thing to be practised is so far from being dis-

paraged that it is recognised universally as the whole difference between good reasoning and bad reasoning. And
the very reason why the logic that is taught, and upon
sale, and gathered into a book, is spoken of with so much
suspicion or contempt, is, not because the natural gift of
logic is held cheap, but for the very opposite reason—viz.
because this gift is suspected to be so transcendently beyond
the reach and grasp of human systems. There is here something which reminds us of the air we breathe. Two generations back, when the popular mind had not the least tincture
of science, air was viewed as absolutely nothing ; in fact, as
the most complete cipher that exists in nature. Yet, even
then, though, as a force, or power, or chemical agent, it had
no place at all for our imagination generally, it was, however, known fearfully and allowed for in the dreadful effects
of its absence. In like manner, logic is so much of a subjective thing, confounded with our general feeling of what
constitutes ourselves, that originally we do not project it
from the dead level in which it lies sunk. It is not made
prominent if not forced into relief. The man who breathes
most healthily is least conscious of his own breathing. And,
as it is possible enough to be a most subtle logician without
any direct or vivid consciousness of this admirable endowment, it ought not to surprise us that what may by possibility
have escaped the knowledge of its possessor should exist as a
subject of scepticism to the mere observer, and still more so
that it should exist as a subject of a doubtful and variable
appreciation. The confession of Southey, always natural in
his judgments, and always faithful in reporting them, expresses accurately the general feeling upon this subject.
Having himself received no logical training whatever, and
sensible that his power of thinking had not therefore suffered,
he might have been tempted into a scornful rejection of it
as of a superfluous labour. But his candour, and his equitable disposition to acquiesce in other opinions adverse to his
own, cause him to suspend. He wishes, and we must all
wish, for a just adjudication upon this point. It would form
the best introduction to a good logic ; as, again, in its full
compass, such an adjudication could only arise as a sequel
and a sort of epilogue to such a logic.

Whether Sir W. H. will ever raise an edifice of so much labour and fatigue is (I suppose) quite uncertain to his closest friends. But so much is evident,—that, whenever, and by whomsoever, such an edifice shall be raised, the amplitude and the beauty of the superstructure will depend largely upon foundations already laid, and ground-plans already traced out, by the admirable labours of Sir William Hamilton.[1]

[1] Sir William Hamilton died May 6, 1856, *ætat.* 68, after having been Professor of Logic and Metaphysics in the University of Edinburgh for twenty years. At the date of the present sketch of him by De Quincey (1852), his philosophical fame, so far as published writings were concerned, rested chiefly on articles contributed from 1828 onwards to the *Edinburgh Review* (republished in French translation in Paris in 1840, and more completely by himself in 1852 in a volume entitled *Discussions on Philosophy and Literature, Education and University Reform*), and on an edition of Reid's Works, with Notes and Dissertations (1846). His Class-Lectures on Metaphysics and Logic were posthumously published in four volumes in 1859, under the editorship of Professor Mansel of Oxford and Professor Veitch of the University of Glasgow, and have gone through several editions. An edition of the Works of Dugald Stewart, on which he was engaged at the time of his death, was completed in 1858 by Professor Veitch ; who is also the author of the most perfect biography of him (published in 1869) and of some independent expositions of his philosophical views.—M.

THIS passage from Leibnitz is cited by Mrs. C. [Mrs. Sara Coleridge] rightly in reproof of a precipitance committed many years ago by myself, who had ascribed the detection of the fallacy to her illustrious father. In apology for my error, I must mention that somewhere or other S. T. C. has (according to my impression) given the solution as his own ; either from haste, or from forgetfulness, or because it really *was* his own—though unconsciously to himself he may have been anticipated by others. In so vast a field as literature *now* presents many and daily are the inevitable coincidences of profound thinkers when hunting in the same fields,—coincidences that will seem to argue plagiarism on one side or the other, and which yet were *not* plagiarisms. Even in this case I find a verification of that remark. For, in a memorandum of my own, dated some years *earlier* than my erroneous ascription of this idea to S. T. C., I find a reference made to Varignon, and also to some other French mathematician, flourishing about the year 1680-90 (and, therefore, contemporary with Leibnitz), as the authors of a solution virtually the same. Leibnitz, be it observed, does not formally claim the solution as his own. In a hasty letter, as in conversation, a man uses for a momentary and transient purpose many a borrowed idea, without meaning to appropriate it, and yet feeling no call upon himself to disclaim as his own what he had no thought of borrowing, not at all for its brilliancy or its felicity, but simply for its pertinence and instant application to some instant question. In his *Theodicée*, for instance, Leibnitz uses in this way many scores of alien doctrines or ideas without saying (or in honour needing to say) that these were other men's contributions to philosophy. It would not, therefore, tax him with plagiarism, if he had even *consciously* borrowed this explanation from Varignon. For it was the idea, and not the ownership of the idea, that occupied his mind at the moment of pressing it upon his correspondent's attention. The hurry of Leibnitz, I would also remark, is sufficiently evident from the gross inaccuracy of his expression, "*faisaient aller aussi vite qu'Achille*," for the Greek dialecticians were far from making the tortoise go as fast as Achilles. On the contrary, it was upon the very counterpostulate, —viz. the assumption that the speed of the tortoise was ten times less than the speed of Achilles,—that they founded the irritation of the case. Precisely upon this consideration, that Achilles was by so many degrees the fleeter, rested the whole pungency of the paradox, that nevertheless, and with all his superiority, the divine man was destined metaphysically not to come up with the tortoise. Justly, indeed, it has been noticed of Leibnitz, that, although by native constitution of mind inclined to scholastic rigour of thinking, he was yet betrayed oftentimes by the laxity of *epistolary* discussion into careless modes of expressing truths, and into a dangerous negligence as to the limitations of those truths. Much of Leibnitz's mind revealed itself in letters, and letters are a dangerous form of composition. Not the haste only, not the genial carelessness only, but also the courtesy and amenity of letter-writing, and, in L.'s particular case, his wish to combine the tone of social and Parisian urbanity with the gravity of a philosopher, tempted him into dangerous accommodations of opinion to the temper or prejudices of his particular correspondent. Accordingly, in the case now before us, a gross oversight has escaped Leibnitz, and one which he would himself have acknowledged for such, if summoned to review it · via, this,—that, in a subsequent letter to thin same M. Foucher, alleged also by Mrs. Coleridge, he says, " that P. Gregoire de St. Vincent has shown, by means of geometry, the exact place where Achilles must have caught the tortoise " : pp. 115-118 I. in Erdmann's edition of his collective works. This, *pace tanti viri,* is pure impertinence. Of course, as the ratio of motion for Achilles and the tortoise is given, together with the length of the course and the amount of grace (or "law ") conceded to the tortoise, all these things being among the data, it becomes easy, upon assuming a certain number of feet for the stride of Achilles, to mark the precise point at which that "impiger" young gentleman will fly past his antagonist like a pistol-shot, and, being also *" iracundus, inexorabilis, acer,"* will endeavour to leave his blessing with the tortoise in the shape of a kick (though, according to the picturesque remark of Sydney Smith, it is as vain to caress a tortoise, or, on the other hand, to kick him, as it is to pat and fondle, or to tickle, the dome of St. Paul's). Very little geometry would have sufficed Mr. St. Vincent for reaching such a result. But this is all beside the purpose. We know without geometry that, as the subdivisions of space narrow and narrow between the two competitors, at length they will dwindle to a point so exquisitely small that one stride of Achilles will carry him past like a gale of wind, and for ever invert the local relations of the parties. Indeed, it is evident at a glance that, upon the principle assumed of ten velocities in Achilles to one velocity in the tortoise, already by the time that the tortoise can have finished the second tenth of the course, Achilles will have finished the ten-tenths,—that is, the entire course,—and will have nothing left to do, when the tortoise still has an arrear of eight-tenths to perform. But all this only sharpens the sting of the problem. That there should exist for the reason what to a certainty would *not* exist for the actual experience, exactly this it is which constitutes the difficulty. Where and when this result will take place, at what particular point of the course, answers no question and meets no difficulty that could rationally occur to any man in his waking senses. So far from solving any difficulty, as Leibnitz supposes, St. Vincent's geometrical investigation, on the contrary, would have repeated and published the difficulty in a broader shape. It is precisely *because* Achilles will in practice go ahead of the tortoise, when, conformably to a known speculative argument, he ought *not* to go ahead—it is precisely this fact, so surely to be anticipated from all our experience, when confronted with this principle so peremptorily denying the possibility of such a fact— exactly this antinomy it is,—the *will be*, as a physical reality, ranged against the *cannot be*, as apparently a metaphysical law—this downright certainty as matched against this downright impossibility,— which, in default of the Leibnitzian solution, constitutes our perplexity, or, to use a Grecian word still more expressive, which constitutes our *aporia*, that is, our resourcelessness. Abiding by the one infinity, as the Greek sophists did, we are strictly without resource. On the other hand, arming against that infinity the counter-infinity, as suggested by Leibnitz, then we find the reason is reconciled with itself. But the resource suggested by St. Vincent is simply the re-affirmation of the *aporia*. Achilles will pass. My friend, we know he will ; we are sure of it ; and precisely in that certainty lies the perplexity of the case.

Let me illustrate this by another case of the same kind. In ancient Greece there emerged suddenly to a musing philosopher what seemed a strong *a priori* argument against motion ; that is, against the possibility of motion. Upon this another philosopher, viz. the Eleatic Zeno, without attempting to meet and to dissolve the argument, rose up from his seat, and walked,—*redarguebat ambulando ;* according to his conceit, he refuted the sophist by moving his spindle shanks, saying, "*Thus* I refute the argument. I move, as a fact ; and, if motion is a fact of the experience, then motion, as an idea, is conformable to the reason." But to me it is plain that Zeno as little comprehended the true incidence and pressure of the difficulty as G. de St. V. understood the perplexity involved in our tortoise-shell friend's Olympic contest with Achilles. The case was briefly this :—Reason, as then interpreted, said, This thing cannot be. Nature said, But, though impossible, it is a fact. Metaphysics denied it as conceivable. Experience affirmed it as actual. There was, therefore, war in the human mind, and the scandal of an irreconcilable schism. Two oracles within the human mind fought against each other. But, in such circumstances, to reaffirm or to exalt either oracle is simply to reinforce and strengthen the feud. Were some reason alleged in the very opposite direction, viz. for discrediting one of the antagonist forces, that would at least tend towards the suppression of the feud ; according to the strength of the reason, it would move at least upon the right line for accomplishing such an end. The conflict depends upon the parity of the conflicting forces ; and whatever therefore disables the authority on either side, or throws doubt upon it, must, by increasing the disparity of the forces, and unsettling their equilibrium, have a tendency *pro tanto* to terminate the feud. But the man who (like Zeno) simply parades the strength and plausibility investing one of the forces, without attempting in the smallest degree to invalidate the other, does, in fact, only publish and repeat the very ground of your perplexity. That argument, strong as the centrifugal force, which so tauntingly and so partially he causes to coruscate before your eyes, you know but too well. Knowing *that*, however, does not enable you to hide from yourself the antagonist argument, or to deny that in power it corresponds to a centripetal force. How needless to show you that motion exists as a fact ! Too sensible you are of that; for what else is it than this fact which arms with the power of perplexing and confounding the metaphysical scruples affecting the idea of motion ? But for the too great certainty of this fact, where would be the antinomy ? In a doctrine which denies, and plausibly denies, the phenomenon X, what could there be to startle or to shock, unless through some other channel you had learned continually that nevertheless X *does* exist ? The antinomy it is—the frightful co-existence of the *to be* and the *not to be*—this it is that agitates and distresses you. But how is that antinomy,—a secret word of two horns, which we may represent for the moment under the figure of two syllables,— lessened or reconciled by repeating one of these syllables, as did Zeno, leaving the secret consciousness to repeat the other ?

CHARLEMAGNE[1]

HISTORY is sometimes treated under the splendid conception of "philosophy teaching by example," and sometimes as an "old almanac"; and, agreeably to this latter estimate, we ourselves once heard a celebrated living professor of surgery,[2] who has been since distinguished by royal favour, and honoured with a title, making it his boast that he had never charged his memory with one single historical fact; that on the contrary he had, out of profound contempt for a sort of knowledge so utterly without value in his eyes, anxiously sought to extirpate from his remembrance, or, if that were impossible, to perplex and confound, any relics of historical records which might happen to survive from his youthful studies. "And I am happy to say," added he, "and it is consoling to have it in my power conscientiously to declare, that, although I have not been able to dismiss entirely from my mind some ridiculous fact about a succession of four great monarchies, since human infirmity still clings to our best efforts, and will for ever prevent our attaining perfection, still I have happily succeeded in so far confounding all distinctions of things and persons, of time and of places, that I could not assign the era of any one transaction, as I

[1] Published in *Blackwood* for November 1832, under the title "James's History of Charlemagne," as a review of "The History of Charlemagne, with a Sketch of the History of France from the Fall of the Roman Empire to the Rise of the Carlovingian Dynasty. By G. P. R. James, Esq., London, 1832." Reprinted by De Quincey in 1859 in the thirteenth volume of his Collected Writings.—M.

[2] "*A celebrated living professor*":—Living when this was written [*i.e.* in 1832].

humbly trust, within a thousand years. The whole vast
series of History is become a wilderness to me ; and my
mind, as to all such absurd knowledge, under the blessing of
Heaven, is pretty nearly a *tabula rasa.*" I was present at
this *étalage* of ignorance, as perhaps I may already have
informed the reader. And the case reminded me of one
popularly ascribed to Orator Henley, who, in disputing with
some careless fellow in a coffee-house, suddenly arrested his
noisy antagonist by telling him that in one short sentence he
had perpetrated two enormous mythologic blunders, having
interchangeably confounded *Plutus,* the blind god of wealth,
with *Pluto,* the gloomy tyrant of the infernal realms.
" Confounded them, have I ? " said the mythologic criminal.
" Well, so much the better ; confound them both for two
old rogues." " But," said Henley, " you have done them
both unspeakable wrong." " With all my heart," rejoined
the other ; " they are heartily welcome to everything unspeakable below the moon : thank God, I know very little
of such ruffians." " But how ? " said Henley ; " do I understand you to mean that you thank God for your ignorance ? "
" Well, suppose I *do,*" said the respondent, " what have *you*
to do with that ? " " Oh, nothing," cried Henley ; " only I
should say that in that case you had a great deal to be
thankful for." I was young at that time, little more than a
boy, and thirstily I sighed to repeat this little story as
applicable to the present case. In fact it was too applicable ;
and, in case Sir Anthony [1] should be of the same opinion, I
remembered seasonably that the finished and accomplished
surgeon carries a pocket case of surgical implements,—
lancets, for instance, that are loaded with *virus* in every
stage of contagion. Might he not inoculate me with *rabies,*
with *hydrophobia,* with the plague of Cairo ? On the whole,
it seemed better to make play against Sir Anthony with a
sudden coruscation of forked logic ; which accordingly I did,
insisting upon it that, as the true point of ambition was now
changed for the philosophic student (the maximum of ignor-

---

[1] Can Sir Astley Cooper (1768-1841) have been the celebrated surgeon meant ; and can De Quincey have written " Sir Anthony " here
by mistake, in momentary recollection of the two Anthony *Ashley*
Coopers who were Earls of Shaftesbury ?—M.

ance being the goal aimed at, and no longer the maximum of light), it had become outrageously vain-glorious in Sir Anthony to rehearse the steps of his own darkness ; that we, the chance-people in Mrs. Montagu's drawing-room, were young beginners, novices that had no advantages to give us a chance in such a contest with central darkness in the persons of veteran masters. Mrs. Montagu took *my* side, and said that I, for instance, myself did very well, considering how short had been my career as regarded practice ; but it was really unfair to look for perfection in a mere beginner. In this Gothic expression of self-congratulation upon the extent of his own ignorance, though doubtless founded upon what the Germans call an *einseitig* [1] or one-sided estimate, there was, however, that sort of truth which is apprehended only by strong minds,—such minds as naturally adhere to extreme courses. Certainly the blank knowledge of facts, which is all that most readers gather from their historial studies, is a mere deposition of rubbish without cohesion, and resting upon no basis of theory (that is, of general comprehensive survey) applied to the political development of nations, and accounting for the great stages of their internal movements.

Rightly and profitably to understand History, it ought to be studied in as many ways as it may be written. History, as a composition, falls into three separate arrangements, obeying three distinct laws, and addressing itself to three distinct objects. Its first and humblest office is to deliver a naked unadorned exposition of public events and their circumstances. This form of History may be styled the purely Narrative ; the second form is that which may be styled the Scenical ; and the third the Philosophic. What is meant by Philosophic History is well understood in our present advanced state of society ; and few histories are written, except in the simplest condition of human culture, which do not in part assume its functions, or which are content to rest their entire attraction upon the abstract interest of facts. The privileges of this form have, however, been greatly abused ; and the truth of facts has been so much

---

[1] Mark, reader, the progress of language, and consequently of novel ideas. This was written nearly thirty years ago, and at that time the term needed an apologetic formula.

forced to bend before preconceived theories, whereas every valid theory ought to be abstracted from the facts, that Mr. Southey and others in this day have set themselves to decry the whole genus and class, as essentially at war with the very primary purposes of the art. But, under whatever name, it is evident that philosophy, or an investigation of the true moving forces in every great train and sequence of national events, and an exhibition of the motives and the moral consequences in their largest extent which have concurred with these events, cannot be omitted in any history above the level of a childish understanding. Mr. Southey himself will be found to illustrate this necessity by his practice, whilst assailing it in principle. As to the other mode of History,—History treated scenically,—it is upon the whole the most delightful to the reader, and the most susceptible of art and ornament in the hands of a skilful composer. The most celebrated specimen in the vulgar opinion is the *Decline and Fall* of Gibbon. And to this class may in part be referred the Historical Sketches of Voltaire.[1] Histories of this class proceed upon principles of selection, presupposing in the reader a general knowledge of the great cardinal incidents, and bringing forward into especial notice those only which are susceptible of being treated with distinguished effect.

These are the three separate modes of treating history : each has its distinct purposes ; and all must contribute to

---

[1] *In part* we say, because in part also the characteristic differences of these works depend upon the particular mode of the narrative. For narration itself, as applied to History, admits of a triple arrangement, —dogmatic, sceptical, and critical : dogmatic, which adopts the current records without examination ; sceptical, as Horace Walpole's *Richard III*, Malcolm Laing's *Dissertation on Perkin Warbeck*, or on *the Gowrie Conspiracy*, which expressly undertakes to probe and try the unsound parts of the story ; and critical, which, after an examination of this nature, selects from the whole body of materials such as are coherent. There is besides another ground of difference in the quality of historical narratives : viz. between those which move by means of great public events, and those which (like the *Cæsars* of Suetonius and the French *Memoirs*), postulating all such capital events as are necessarily already known, and keeping them in the background, crowd their foreground with those personal and domestic notices which we call anecdotes.

make up a comprehensive total of historical knowledge. The first furnishes the facts; the second opens a thousand opportunities for pictures of manners and national temper in every stage of their growth; whilst the third abstracts the political or the ethical moral, and unfolds the philosophy which knits the history of one nation to that of others, and exhibits the whole under their internal connexion, as parts of one great process, carrying on the great economy of human improvement by many stages in many regions at one and the same time.

Pursued upon this comprehensive scale, the study of History is the study of human nature. But some have continued to reject it, not upon any objection to the quality of the knowledge gained, but simply on the ground of its limited extent: contending that in public and political transactions, such as compose the matter of History, human nature exhibits itself upon too narrow a scale and under too monotonous an aspect; that under different names, and in connexion with different dates and regions, events virtually the same are continually revolving; that whatever novelty may strike the ear, in passages of history taken from periods widely remote, affects the names only, and circumstances that are extra-essential; that the passions meantime, the motives, and (allowing for difference of manners) the means even, are subject to no variety; that in ancient or in modern history there is no real accession made to our knowledge of human nature; but that all proceeds by cycles of endless repetition, and in fact that, according to the old complaint, "there is nothing new under the sun."

It is not true that "there is nothing new under the sun." This is the complaint, as all men know, of a jaded voluptuary, seeking for a new pleasure and finding none, for reasons which lay in his own vitiated nature. Why did he seek for novelty? Because old pleasures had ceased to stimulate his exhausted organs; and that was reason enough why no new pleasure, had any been found, would operate as such for *him*. The weariness of spirit and the poverty of pleasure, which he bemoaned as belonging to our human condition, were not in reality *objective* (as a German philosopher would express himself), or laid in the nature of things, and thus pressing

upon all alike, but *subjective*,—that is to say, derived from
the peculiar state and affections of his own organs for
apprehending pleasure. Not the τὸ *apprehensibile*, but the
τὸ *apprehendens*, was in fault ; not the pleasures, or the
dewy freshness of pleasures, had decayed, but the sensibilities
of him who thus undertook to appraise them were *blasés* and
exhausted.

More truly and more philosophically, it may be said that
there is nothing old under the sun, no absolute repetition.
It is the well-known doctrine of Leibnitz, that amongst the
familiar objects of our daily experience there is no perfect
identity.[1] All in external nature proceeds by endless variety.
Infinite change, illimitable novelty, inexhaustible difference,
these are the foundations upon which nature builds and
ratifies her purpose of *individuality*, — so indispensable,
amongst a thousand other great uses, to the very elements
of social distinctions and social rights. But for the endless
circumstances of difference which characterize external objects,
the rights of property, for instance, would have stood upon
no certain basis, nor admitted of any general or comprehensive guarantee.

As with external objects, so with human actions : amidst
their infinite approximations and affinities, they are separated

---

[1] Leibnitz (who was *twice* in England), when walking in Kensington Gardens with the Princess of Wales,—whose admiration oscillated
between this great countryman of her own and Sir Isaac Newton, the
corresponding idol of her adopted country,—took occasion, from the
beautiful scene about them, to explain in a lively way, and at the
same time to illustrate and verify, this favourite thesis : Turning to a
gentleman in attendance upon her Royal Highness, he challenged
him to produce two leaves from any tree or shrub which should be
exact duplicates or facsimiles of each other in those lines which
variegate the surface. The challenge was accepted ; but the result
justified Leibnitz. It is in fact upon this infinite variety in the
superficial lines of the human palm that palmistry is grounded (or the
science of divination by the hieroglyphics written on each man's hand),
and has its *primâ facie* justification. Were it otherwise, this mode
of divination would not have even a *plausible* sanction ; for, without
the inexhaustible varieties which are actually found in the combination
of these lines, and which give to each separate individual his own
separate type, the same identical fortunes must be often repeated, and
there would be no foundation for assigning to each his peculiar and
characteristic destiny.

by circumstances of never-ending diversity. History may
furnish her striking correspondences, Biography her splendid
parallels; Rome may in certain cases appear but the mirror
of Athens, England of Rome; and yet, after all, no character
can be cited, no great transaction, no revolution of "high-
viced cities," no catastrophe of nations, which, in the midst
of its resemblances to distant correspondences in other ages,
does not include features of abundant distinction, and indi-
vidualizing characteristics so many and so important as to
yield its own peculiar matter for philosophical meditation
and its own separate moral.   Rare is the case in history, or
(to speak with suitable boldness) there is none, which does
not involve circumstances capable, to a learned eye, without
any external aid from chronology, of referring it to its own
age.   The doctrine of Leibnitz, on the grounds of individuality in the objects of sense, may, in fact, be profitably
extended to all the great political actions of mankind.   Many
pass, in a popular sense, for pure transcripts or duplicates of
similar cases in past times; but, accurately speaking, none
are such truly and substantially.   Neither are the differences
by which they are severally marked and featured interesting
only to the curiosity or to the spirit of minute research.   All
public acts, in the degree in which they are great and comprehensive, are steeped in living feelings and saturated
with the spirit of their own age; and the features of their
individuality, — that is, the circumstances which chiefly
distinguish them from their nearest parallels in other times,
and chiefly prevent them from lapsing into blank repetitions
of the same identical case,—are generally the very cardinal
points, the organs, and the depositories which lodge whatever
best expresses the temper and tendencies of the age to which
they belong.   So far are these special points of distinction
from being slight or trivial that in them *par excellence* is
gathered and concentrated whatever a political philosopher
would be best pleased to insulate and to converge within his
field of view.

    This indeed is evident upon consideration, and is in
some sense implied in the very verbal enunciation of the
proposition: *vi termini*, it should strike every man who
reflects, that in great national transactions of different ages,

so far resembling each other as to merit the description of
parallels, all the circumstances of agreement, all those which
compose the resemblance, for the very reason that they are
common to both periods of time, specially and characteristically belong to neither. It is the differential, and not the
common,—the points of special dissimilitude, not those of
general similitude,—which manifestly must be looked to for
the philosophic valuation of the times or the people, for the
adjudication of their peculiar claims in a comparison with
other times and other peoples, and for the appraisement of
the progress made, whether positively for its total amount,
or, relatively to itself, for its rate of advance at each separate
stage.

It is in this way of critical examination that comparison
and the collation of apparent parallels, from being a pure
amusement of ingenuity, rises to a philosophic labour, and
that the study of History becomes at once dignified, and in
a most practical sense profitable. It is the opinion of the
subtlest and the most combining (if not the most useful)
philosopher whom England has produced,[1] that a true knowledge of history confers the gift of prophecy ; or that
intelligently and sagaciously to have looked backwards is
potentially to have looked forwards. For example, he is of
opinion that any student of the great English Civil War in
the reign of Charles I. who should duly have noted the signs
precurrent and concurrent of those days, and should also
have read the contemporary political pamphlets, coming
thus prepared, could not have failed, after a corresponding
study of the French Literature from 1750 to 1788, and, in
particular, after collecting the general sense and temper of
the French people from the *Cahiers* (or codes of instruction
transmitted by the electoral bodies to the members of the
first National Assembly), to foresee in clear succession the
long career of revolutionary frenzy which soon afterwards
deluged Europe with tears and blood. This may perhaps
be conceded, and without prejudice to the doctrine just now
delivered, of endless diversity in political events. For it is
certain that the political movements of nations obey everlasting laws, and travel through the stages of known cycles,

[1] Coleridge ?—M.

which thus insure enough of resemblance to guarantee the general outline of a sagacious prophecy ; whilst, on the other hand, the times, the people, and the extraordinary minds which, in such critical eras, soon reveal themselves at the head of affairs, never fail of producing their appropriate and characteristic results of difference. Sameness enough there will always be to encourage the true political seer, with difference enough to confer upon each revolution its own separate character and its peculiar interest.

All this is strikingly illustrated in the history of those great revolutionary events which belong to the life and times of the Emperor Charlemagne. If any one period in History might be supposed to offer a barren and unprofitable picture of war, rapine, and bloodshed, unfeatured by characteristic differences, and unimproved by any peculiar moral, it is this section of the European annals. Removed from our present times by a thousand years, divided from us by the profound gulf of what we usually denominate the *dark ages*, placed, in fact, entirely upon the farther side of that great barrier,[1] this period of History can hardly be expected to receive much light from contemporary documents in an age so generally illiterate,—not from national archives, or state papers, when diplomacy was so rare, when so large a proportion of its simple transactions was conducted by personal intercourse, and after the destruction wrought amongst its slender chancery of written memorials by the revolution of one entire millennium. Still less could we have reason to hope for much light from private memoirs at a period when the means of writing were as slenderly diffused as the motives ; when the rare endowments, natural and acquired, for composing History could so seldom happen to coincide with the opportunities for obtaining accurate information ; when the writers were so few, and the audience so limited, to which any writers soever could then profitably address themselves. With or without illustration, however, the age itself, and its rapid succession of wars between barbarous and semi-barbarous tribes, might,

---

[1] According to the general estimate of Philosophical History, the *tenth* century (or perhaps the tenth and the eleventh conjointly) must be regarded as the true meridian, or the perfect midnight, of the Dark Ages.

if any one chapter in History, be presumed barren of either
interest or instruction, wearisomely monotonous ; and, by
comparison with any parallel section from the records of
other nations in the earliest stages of dawning civilisation,
offering no one feature of novelty beyond the names of the
combatants, their local and chronological relations, and the
peculiar accidents and unimportant circumstances of variety
in the conduct or issue of the several battles which they
fought.

Yet, in contradiction to all these very plausible presumptions, even this remote period teems with its own peculiar
and separate instruction.   It is the first great station, so to
speak, which we reach after entering the portals of Modern
History.[1]   It presents us with the evolution and propagation
of Christianity in its present central abodes ; with the great
march of civilisation, and the gathering within the pale of
that mighty agency for elevating human nature, and beneath
the gentle yoke of the only true and beneficent religion, of
the last rebellious recusants among the European family of
nations.   We meet also, in conjunction with the other steps
of the vast humanizing process then going on, the earliest
efforts at legislation, recording, at the same time, the barbarous condition of those for whom they were designed, and
the anti-barbarous views, alien or *exotic*, of the legislator,
in the midst of his condescensions to the infirmities of his
subjects.   Here also we meet with the elementary state,
growing and as yet imperfectly rooted, of feudalism.   Here,
too, we behold in their incunabula, forming and arranging

---

[1] It has repeatedly been made a question, at what era we ought to
date the transition from Ancient to Modern History.   This question
merits a separate dissertation.   Meantime it is sufficient to say in
this place that Justinian in the sixth century will unanimously be
referred to the ancient division, Charlemagne in the eighth to the
modern.   These, then, are two limits fixed in each direction ; and
somewhere between them must lie the frontier line.   Now the era of
Mahomet in the seventh century is evidently the exact and perfect
line of demarcation : not only as pretty nearly bisecting the debate-
able ground, but also because the rise of the Mohammedan power, as
operating so powerfully upon the Christian kingdoms of the south,
and through them upon the whole of Christendom, at that time beginning to mould themselves and to knit, marks in the most eminent
sense the birth of a new era.

themselves under the pressure of circumstances, the existing kingdoms of Christendom. So far, then, from being a mere echo, or repetition, of analogous passages in history, the period of Charlemagne is novel to the extent of ambitious originality in its instruction, and almost unique in the quality of that instruction. For here only perhaps we see the social system forming itself in the mine, and the very process, as it were, of crystallization going on beneath our eyes. Mr. James, therefore, may be regarded as not less fortunate in the choice of his subject than meritorious in its treatment; indeed, his work is not so much the best as the only History of Charlemagne which will hereafter be cited. For it reposes upon a far greater body of research and collation than has hitherto been applied even in France to this interesting theme [1]; and in effect it is the first account of the great emperor and his times which can, with a due valuation of the term, be complimented with the title of a *critical* memoir.

Charlemagne, "the greatest man of the middle ages," in the judgment of his present biographer, was born A.D. 742, seven years before his father assumed the *name* of King. This date has been disputed; but, on the whole, we may take it as settled, upon various collateral computations, that the year now assigned is the true one. The place is less certain; but we do not think Mr. James warranted in saying that it is "unknown." If everything is to be pronounced "unknown" for which there is no absolute proof of a kind to satisfy forensic rules of evidence, or which has ever been made a question for debate, in that case we may apply a sponge to the greater part of History before the era of printing. Aix-la-Chapelle, Mr. James goes on to tell us, is *implied* as the birthplace in one of the chief authorities. But our own impression is that, according to the general belief of succeeding ages, it was not Aix-la-Chapelle, but Ingelheim, a village near Mentz, to which that honour belonged. Some

---

[1] Or, in fact, than is likely to manifest itself to an unlearned reader of Mr. James's own book; for he has omitted to load his margin with references to authorities in many scores of instances where he might, and perhaps where he ought, to have accredited his narrative by those indications of research.

have supposed that Carlsburg, in Bavaria, was the true place
of his birth, and, indeed, that it drew its name from that distinguished event. Frantzius, in particular, says that in his
day the castle of that place was still shown to travellers with
the reverential interest attached to such a pretension. But,
after all, he gives his own vote for Ingelheim ; and it is
singular that he does not so much as mention Aix-la-Chapelle.
Of his education and his early years Mr. James is of
opinion that we know as little as of his birthplace. Certainly
our information upon these particulars is neither full nor circumstantial ; yet we know as much, perhaps, in these respects, of Charlemagne as of Napoleon Bonaparte. And
remarkable enough it is that, not relatively (or making
allowances for the age), but absolutely, Charlemagne was
much more accomplished than Napoleon in the ordinary
business of a *modern* education,—Charlemagne in the middle
of the eighth century than Napoleon in the latter end of the
eighteenth. Charlemagne was, in fact, the most accomplished
man of his age ; Napoleon a sciolist for any age. The tutor
of Charlemagne was Peter of Pisa, a man eminent at that
time for his attainments in literature (*in re grammaticâ*).
From him it was that Charlemagne learned Latin and
Greek : Greek in such a degree " ut sufficienter intelligeret,"
and Latin to the extent of using it familiarly and fluently in
conversation. Now, as to the man of the eighteenth century,
Greek was to him as much a sealed language as Chinese ;
and, even with regard to Latin, his own secretary doubts
upon one occasion whether he was sufficiently master of it to
translate Juvenal's expressive words *Panem et Circenses.* Yet
he had enjoyed the benefits of an education in a royal college,
in a country which regards itself self-complacently as at the
head of civilisation. Again, there is a pretty strong tradition
(which could hardly arise but upon some foundation) that
Charlemagne had cultivated the Arabic so far as to talk it,[1]
having no motive to that attainment more urgent than that

---

[1] " Arabice loquutum esse Aigolando Saracenorum regulo Turpinus
[the famous Archbishop] auctor est ; nec id fide indignum. Dum
enim in expeditione Hispanicâ præcipuam belli molem in illum vertit,
facile temporis tractu notitiam linguæ sibi comparare potuit."—
FRANTZ. *Hist. Car. Mag.* That is, he had time sufficient for this acquisition, and a motive sufficient.

political considerations made it eligible for him to undertake
an expedition against those who could negotiate in no other
language. Now, let it be considered how very much more
powerful arguments there were in Napoleon's position for
mastering the German and the English. His continental
policy moved entirely upon the pivot of central Europe,—
that is, the German system of nations, the great federation of
powers upon the Rhine and the Danube. And, as to England, his policy and his passions alike pointed in that direction as uniformly and as inevitably as the needle to the pole.
Every morning, we are told, tossing aside the Paris journals
as so many babbling echoes of his own public illusions, expressing rather what was desired than what was probable, he
required of his secretary that he should read off into French
the leading newspapers of England. And many were the
times when he started up in fury, and passionately taxed his
interpreter with mistranslation,—sometimes as softening the
expressions, sometimes as over-colouring their violence.
Evidently he lay at the mercy of one whom he knew to be
wanting in honour, and who had it in his power, either by
way of abetting any sinister views of his own, or in collusion
with others, to suppress, to add, to garble, and in every
possible way to colour and distort what he was interpreting.
Yet neither could this humiliating sense of dependency on
the one hand, nor the instant pressure of political interest on
the other, ever urge Napoleon to the effort of learning
English in the first case, German or Spanish in the second.
Charlemagne, again, cultivated most strenuously and success-
fully, as an accomplishment peculiarly belonging to the
functions of his high station, the art and practice of eloquence ; and he had this reward of his exertions—that he
was accounted the most eloquent man of his age : " totis
viribus ad orationem exercendam conversus naturalem facun-
diam ita roboravit studio ut præter [l. *propter*] promptum
ac profluens sermonis genus *facile ævi sui eloquentissimus
crederetur.*" Turn to Bonaparte. It was a saying of his
sycophants, that he sometimes spoke like a god, and sometimes worse than the feeblest of mortals. But, says one who
knew him well,—" the mortal I have often heard, unfortunately never yet the god." He, who sent down this sneer

to posterity was at Napoleon's right hand on the most
memorable occasion of his whole career—that cardinal occasion, as we may aptly term it (for upon *that* his whole
fortunes hinged), when he intruded violently upon the Legis-
lative Body, dissolved the Directory, and effected the revolution of the eighteenth Brumaire. That revolution it was
which raised him to the Consular power ; and by that
revolution, considered in its manner and style, we may judge
of Napoleon in several of his chief pretensions—courage,
presence of mind, dignity, and eloquence ; for then, if ever,
these qualities were all in instant requisition : one word
effectually urged by the antagonist parties, a breath, a gesture,
a nod, suitably followed up, would have made the total
difference between ruler of France and a traitor hurried away
à la lanterne. It is true that the miserable imbecility of all
who should have led the hostile parties, the irresolution and
the quiet-loving temper of Moreau, the base timidity of
Bernadotte,—in fact, the total defect of heroic minds amongst
the French of that day,—neutralized the defects and more
than compensated the blunders of Napoleon. But these were
advantages that could not be depended on : a glass of brandy
extraordinary might have emboldened the greatest poltroon
to do that which, by once rousing a movement of popular enthusiasm, once making a beginning in that direction, would
have precipitated the whole affair into hands which must
have carried it far beyond the power of any party to control.
Never, according to all human calculation, were eloquence
and presence of mind so requisite : never was either so de-
plorably wanting. A passionate exposition of the national
degradations inflicted by the imbecility of the Directors, an
appeal to the assembly as Frenchmen, contrasting the glories
of 1796 with the Italian disasters that had followed, might,
by connecting the new candidate for power with the public
glory, and the existing rulers with all the dishonours which
had settled on the French banners, have given an electric
shock to the patriotism of the audience, such as would have
been capable for the moment of absorbing their feelings as
partisans. In a French assembly, movements of that nature,
under a momentary impulse, are far from being uncommon.
Here, then, if never before, here, if never again, the grandeur

of the occasion demanded,—almost, we might say, implored, and clamorously invoked,—the effectual powers of eloquence and perfect self-possession.

How was the occasion met ? Let us turn to the actual scene, as painted in lively colours by a friend and an eye-witness [1] :—" The accounts brought every instant to General " Bonaparte determined him to enter the hall [of the " Ancients] and take part in the debate.   His entrance was " hasty, and in anger ; no favourable prognostics of what he " would say.   The passage by which we entered led directly " forward into the middle of the house ; our backs were to-" wards the door ; Bonaparte had the President on his right ; " he could not see him quite in front.   I found myself on the " General's right; our clothes touched : Berthier was on his left. " All the harangues composed for Bonaparte after the event differ " from each other : no miracle that.   There was, in fact, none " pronounced to the Ancients ; unless a broken conversation " with the President, carried on without nobleness, propriety, " or dignity, may be called a speech.   We heard only these " words—' Brothers in arms—frankness of a soldier.'   The " interrogatories of the President were clear.   Nothing " could be more confused or worse enounced than the am-

---

[1] Not having the French original of Bourrienne's work, we are compelled to quote from the current translation ; which, however, is everywhere incorrect, and in a degree absolutely astonishing, and, where not incorrect, offensive from vulgarisms or ludicrous expressions. Thus, it translates *un drôle*, a droll fellow, wide as the poles from the true meaning ; *ce drole-là* means *that scoundrel*.   Again, the verb *devoir*, in all tenses (that eternal stumbling-block to bad French scholars), is uniformly mistranslated.   As an instance of ignoble language, at p. 294, vol. i, he says, " Josephine was delighted with the disposition of her *goodman*," a word used only by underbred people. But, of all the absurdities which disfigure the work, what follows is perhaps the most striking :—" Kleber," he says, " took a *precognition* of the army," p. 231, vol. i.   A precognition !   What Pagan ceremony may that be ?   Know, reader, that this monster of a word is a technical term of Scotch law, and even to the Scotch, excepting those few who know a little of law, absolutely unintelligible.   In speaking thus harshly, we are far from meaning anything unkind to the individual translator ; whom, on the contrary, for his honourable sentiments in relation to the merits of Bonaparte, we greatly respect.   But that has nothing to do with French translation—the condition of which, in this country, is perfectly scandalous.

" biguous and disjointed replies of Bonaparte. He spoke
" incoherently of volcanoes—secret agitations—victories—
" constitution violated. He found fault even with the 18th
" Fructidor, of which he had himself been the prime insti-
" gator and most powerful upholder." [Not, reader, observe,
from bold time-serving neglect of his own principles, but
from absolute distraction of mind, and incoherency of purpose.] "Then came *Cæsar—Cromwell—Tyrant*"—[allusions
which, of all others, were the most unseasonable for that
crisis, and for his position]. "He repeated several times—
" *I have no more than that to tell you;* and he had told them
" nothing. Then out came the words,—*Liberty, Equality:*
" for these every one saw he had not come to St. Cloud.
" Then his action became animated, and we lost him—com-
" prehending nothing beyond 18*th Fructidor,* 30*th Prairial,*
" *hypocrites, intriguers; I am not so; I shall declare all; I*
" *will abdicate the power when the danger which threatens the*
" *Republic has passed.*" Then, after further instances of
Napoleon's falsehood, and the self-contradictory movements
of his disjointed babble, the Secretary goes on thus : "These
" interruptions, apostrophes, and interrogations, overwhelmed
" him ; he believed himself lost. The disapprobation be-
" came more violent, and his discourse still more wanting in
" method and coherence. Sometimes he addressed the repre-
" sentatives quite stultified ; sometimes the military in the
" court [*i.e.* outside], who were beyond hearing ; then, with-
" out any transition, he spoke of the thunder of war, say-
" ing, *I am accompanied by the god of war and fortune.* The
" President then calmly observed to him that he found no-
" thing, absolutely nothing, upon which they could deli-
" berate ; that all he had said was vague. *Explain yourself,*
" *unfold the plots into which you have been invited to enter.*
" Bonaparte repeated the same things ; and in what style !
" No idea in truth can be formed of the whole scene, unless
" by those present. There was not the least order in all he
" stammered out (to speak sincerely) with the most incon-
" ceivable incoherence. Bonaparte was no orator. Per-
" ceiving the bad effect produced upon the meeting by this
" rhapsody, and the progressive confusion of the speaker, I
" whispered (pulling his coat gently at the same time)—

" ' Retire, General ; you no longer know what you are say-
" ing.' I made a sign to Berthier to second me in persuad-
" ing him to leave the place ; when suddenly, after
" stammering out a few words more, he turned round, saying,
" ' Let all who love me follow.' " So ended this famous
scene—in which, more than in any other upon record,
eloquence and presence of mind were needful. And if it
should be said that vagueness was not altogether the least
eligible feature in a speech whose very purpose was to con-
fuse, and to leave no room for answer, we reply—true ; but
then it was the vagueness of art, which promised to be
serviceable, and that of preconcerted perplexity, not the
vagueness of incoherence and a rhapsody of utter contradiction.[1]

What a contrast all this to the indefeasible majesty of
Charlemagne ; to his courage and presence of mind, which
always rose with the occasion ; and, above all, to his promp-
titude of winning eloquence, that *promptum ac profluens genus
sermonis*, which caused him to be accounted *ævi sui eloquentissimus !*

Passing for a moment to minor accomplishments, we find
that Charlemagne excelled in athletic and gymnastic exercises ; he was a *pancratiast*. Bonaparte wanted those even
which were essential to his own daily security. Charlemagne swam well ; Bonaparte not at all. Charlemagne was
a first-rate horseman even amongst the Franks ; Napoleon
rode ill originally, and no practice availed to give him a firm
seat, a graceful equestrian deportment, or a skilful bridle
hand. In a barbarous age the one possessed all the
elegancies and ornamental accomplishments of a gentleman :

---

[1] Some people may fancy that this scene of that day's drama was
got up merely to save appearances by a semblance of discussion, and
that in effect it mattered not how the performance was conducted
where all was scenical, and the ultimate reliance, after all, on the
bayonet. But it is certain that this view is erroneous, and that the
final decision of the soldiery, even up to the very moment of the crisis,
was still doubtful. Some time after this exhibition, "the hesitation
reigning among the troops," says Bourrienne, "still continued."
And in reality it was a mere accident of pantomime, and a clap-trap
of sentiment, which finally gave a sudden turn in Napoleon's favour to
their wavering resolutions.

the other, in a most polished age, and in a nation of even false refinement, was the sole barbarian of his time ; presenting in his deficiencies the picture of a low mechanic, and in his positive qualities the violence and brutality of a savage.[1] Hence, by the way, the extreme folly of those who have attempted to trace a parallel between Napoleon and the first Cæsar. The heaven-born Julius, as beyond all dispute the greatest man of ancient history in moral grandeur, and therefore raised unspeakably above comparison with one who was eminent, even amongst ordinary men, for the pettiness of his passions, so also, upon an intellectual trial, will be found to challenge pretty nearly an equal precedency. Meantime, allowing for the inequality of their advantages, even Cæsar would not have disdained a comparison with Charlemagne. All the knowledge current in Rome, Athens, or Rhodes, at the period of Cæsar's youth, the entire cycle of a nobleman's education in a republic where all noblemen were from their birth dedicated to public services, this— together with much and various knowledge peculiar to himself and his own separate objects — had Cæsar mastered ; whilst, in an age of science, and in a country where the fundamental science of mathematics was generally diffused in unrivalled perfection, it is well ascertained that Bonaparte's knowledge did not go beyond an elementary acquaintance with the first six books of Euclid ; but, on the other hand, Charlemagne, even in that early age, was familiar with the intricate mathematics and the elaborate *computus* of Practical Astronomy.

But these collations, it will be said, are upon questions not primarily affecting their peculiar functions. They are

---

[1] We have occasionally such expressions as Dryden's—" When wild in woods *the noble savage* ran." These descriptions rest upon false conceptions ; in fact, no such combination anywhere exists as a man having the training of a savage, or occupying the exposed and naked situation of a savage, who is at the same time in any moral sense at liberty to be noble-minded. Men are moulded by the circumstances in which they stand habitually ; and the insecurity of savage life, by making it impossible to forgo any sort of advantages, obliterates the very idea of honour. Hence, with all savages alike, the point of honour lies in treachery, in stratagem, and the utmost excess of what is dishonourable according to the estimate of cultivated man.

questions more or less extrajudicial. The true point of
comparison is upon the talents of policy in the first place,
and strategies in the second. A trial between two celebrated
performers in these departments is at any rate difficult; and
much more so when they are separated by vast intervals of
time. Allowances must be made, so many and so various;
compensations or balances struck upon so many diversities
of situation; there is so much difference in the modes of
warfare—offensive and defensive; the financial means, the
available alliances, and other resources, are with so much
difficulty appraised, in order to raise ourselves to that
station from which the whole question can be overlooked,—
that nothing short of a general acquaintance with the history,
statistics, and diplomacy of the two periods can lay a ground
for the solid adjudication of so large a comparison. Meantime, in the absence of such an investigation, pursued upon
a scale of suitable proportions, what if we should sketch a
rapid outline (ὡς ἐν τυπῷ περιλάβειν) of its *elements* (to speak
by a metaphor borrowed from practical astronomy)—*i.e.* of
the principal and most conspicuous points which its path
would traverse? How much these two men, each central to
a mighty system in his own days, how largely and essentially
they differed, whether in kind or in degree of merit, will
appear in the course even of the hastiest sketch. The circumstances in which they agreed, and that these were sufficient to challenge an inquiry into their characteristic
differences, and to support the interest of such an inquiry,
will probably be familiar to most readers, as among the
commonplaces of general history which survive even in the
daily records of conversation. Few people can fail to know
that each of these memorable men stood at the head of a
new era in European History, and of a great movement in
the social development of nations; that each laid the foundations for a new dynasty in his own family, the one by
building forwards upon a basis already formed by his two
immediate progenitors, the other by dexterously applying to
a great political crisis his own military preponderance; and,
finally, that each forfeited within a very brief period—the
one in his own person, the other in the persons of his
immediate descendants — the giddy ascent which he had

mastered, and all the distinctions which it conferred ; in short, that "Time, which gave, did his own gifts confound,"[1] but with this mighty difference—that Time co-operated in the one case with extravagant folly in the individual, and in the other with the irresistible decrees of Providence.

Napoleon Bonaparte and Charlemagne were both, in a memorable degree, the favourites of fortune. It is true that the latter found himself by inheritance in possession of a throne which the other ascended by the fortunate use of his own military advantages. But the throne of Charlemagne had been recently won by his family, and in a way so nearly corresponding to that which was afterwards pursued by Napoleon that in effect, considering how little this usurpation had been hallowed by time, the throne might in each case, if not won precisely on the same terms, be considered to be held by the same tenure. Charlemagne, not less than Napoleon, was the privileged child of Revolution ; he was required by the times, and indispensable to the crisis which had arisen for the Franks ; and he was himself protected by the necessities to which he ministered. Clouds had risen, or were rising, at that era, on every quarter of France ; from every side she was menaced by hostile demonstrations ; and, without the counsels of a Charlemagne, and with an energy of action inferior to his, it is probable that she would have experienced misfortunes which, whilst they depressed herself, could not but have altered the destinies of Christendom for many ages to come. The resources of France, it is true, were immense ; and, as regarded the positions of her enemies, they were admirably concentrated. But, to be made available in the whole extent which the times demanded, it was essential that they should be wielded by a first-rate statesman, supported by a first-rate soldier. The statesman and the soldier were fortunately found united in the person of one man, and that man, by the rarest of combinations, the same who was clothed with the supreme power of the state. Less power, or power less harmonious, or power the most consummate administered with less absolute skill, would doubtless have been found incompetent to struggle with the tempestuous assaults which then lowered over the entire

[1] Shakspere's Sonnets.

frontier of France.   It was natural, and, upon the known
constitution of human nature, pretty nearly inevitable, that,
in the course of the very extended warfare which followed,
love for that glorious trade—so irritating and so contagious
—should be largely developed in a mind as aspiring as
Charlemagne's, and stirred by such generous sensibilities.
Yet is it in no one instance recorded that these sympathies
with the pomp and circumstance of war moved him to undertake so much as a single campaign, or an expedition which
was not otherwise demanded by his judgment, or that they
interfered even to bias or give an impulse to his judgment
where it had previously wavered.   In every case he tried
the force of negotiation before he appealed to arms ; nay,
sometimes he condescended so far in his love of peace as to
attempt purchasing with gold rights or concessions of expedi-
ency which he knew himself in a situation amply to extort
by arms.   Nor, where these courses were unavailing, and
where peace was no longer to be maintained by any sacrifices, is it ever found that Charlemagne, in adopting the
course of war, suffered himself to pursue it as an end valuable in and for itself.   And yet *that* is a result not uncommon ; for a long and conscientious resistance to a
measure originally tempting to the feelings, once being
renounced as utterly unavailing, not seldom issues in a
headlong surrender of the heart to purposes so violently
thwarted for a time.   And, even as a means, war was such
in the eyes of Charlemagne to something beyond the customary ends of victory and domestic security.   Of all conquerors whose history is known sufficiently to throw light
upon their motives, Charlemagne is the only one who looked
forward to the benefit of those he conquered as a principal
element amongst the fruits of conquest.   "Doubtless," says
his present biographer, "to defend his own infringed ter-
" ritory, and to punish the aggressors, formed a part of his
" design ; but, beyond that, he aimed at civilizing a people
" whose barbarism had been for centuries the curse of the
" neighbouring countries, and at the same time communicat-
" ing to the cruel savages, who shed the blood of their
" enemies less in the battle than in the sacrifice, the bland
" and mitigating spirit of the Christian Religion."

This applies more particularly and circumstantially to his Saxon campaigns ; but the spirit of the remark is of general application.   At that time a weak light of literature was beginning to diffuse improvement in Italy, in France, and in England.   France, by situation geographically, and politically by the prodigious advantage (which she exclusively enjoyed) of an undivided government, with the benefit consequently of an entire unity in her counsels, was peculiarly fitted for communicating the blessings of intellectual culture to the rest of the European continent, and for sustaining the great mission of civilizing conquest.   Above all, as the great central depository of Christian knowledge, she seemed specially stationed by Providence as a martial apostle for carrying by the sword that mighty blessing which, even in an earthly sense, Charlemagne could not but value as the best engine of civilisation, to the potent infidel nations on her southern and eastern frontier.   A vast revolution was at hand for Europe ; all her tribes were destined to be fused in a new crucible, to be recast in happier moulds, and to form one family of enlightened nations, to compose one great collective brotherhood, united by the tie of a common faith and a common hope, and hereafter to be known to the rest of the world, and to proclaim this unity, under the comprehensive name of *Christendom.*   Baptism, therefore, was the indispensable condition and forerunner of civilisation ; and, from the peculiar ferocity and the sanguinary superstitions which disfigured the Pagan nations in Central Europe, of which the leaders and the nearest to France were the Saxons, and from the bigotry and arrogant intolerance of the Mohammedan nations who menaced her Spanish frontier, it was evident that by the sword only it was possible that baptism should be effectually propagated.   War, therefore, for the highest purposes of peace, became the present and instant policy of France : bloodshed for the sake of a religion the most benign ; and desolation with a view to permanent security.   The Frankish Emperor was thus invited to indulge in this most captivating of luxuries—the royal tiger-hunt of war,—as being also at this time, and for a special purpose, the sternest of duties.   He had a special dispensation for wielding at times a barbarian and exterminating sword, but for the extermination of barbarism ; and he was privileged to be in a single instance an Attila, in order that Attilas might no more arise. Simply as the enemies, bitter and perfidious, of France, the Saxons were a legitimate object of war ; as the standing enemies of civilisation, who would neither receive it for themselves, nor tolerate its peaceable enjoyment in others, they and Charlemagne stood opposed to each other as it were by hostile instincts ; and this most merciful of conquerors was fully justified in departing for once, and in such a quarrel, from his general rule of conduct. And, for a paramount purpose of comprehensive service to all mankind, we entirely agree with Mr. James that Charlemagne had a sufficient plea, and that he has been censured only by calumnious libellers, or by the feeble-minded, for applying a Roman severity of punishment to treachery continually repeated. The question is one purely of policy ; and it may be, as Mr. James is disposed to think, that in point of judgment the emperor erred ; but certainly the case was one of great difficulty ; for the very infirmity even of maternal indulgence, if obstinately and continually abused, must find its ultimate limit ; and we have no right to suppose that Charlemagne made his election for the harsher course without a violent self-conflict. His former conduct towards those very people, his infinite forbearance, his long-suffering, his monitory threats, all make it a duty to presume that he suffered the acutest pangs in deciding upon a vindictive punishment ; that he adopted this course as being virtually by its consequences the least sanguinary ; and, finally, that, if he erred, it was not through his heart, but by resisting its very strongest impulses.

It is remarkable that both Charlemagne and Bonaparte succeeded as by inheritance to one great element of their enormous power : each found ready to his hands that vast development of martial enthusiasm upon which, as its first condition, their victorious career reposed. Each also found the great armoury of resources opened which such a spirit, diffused over so vast a territory, must in any age insure. Of Charlemagne, in an age when as yet the use of infantry was but imperfectly known, it may be said symbolically that he found the universal people, patrician and plebeian,

chieftain and vassal, with the left foot in the stirrup[1] ; of
Napoleon, in an age when the use of artillery was first
understood, that he found every man standing to his gun.
Both, in short, found war *in procinctu :* both found the people
whom they governed willing to support the privations and
sacrifices which war imposes : hungering and thirsting for
its glories, its pomps and triumphs ; entering even with
lively sympathy of pleasure into its hardships and its trials ;
and thus, from within and from without, prepared for
military purposes. So far both had the same good fortune[2] ;
neither had much merit. The enthusiasm of Napoleon's
days was the birth of republican sentiments, and built on a
reaction of civic and patriotic ardour. In the very plenitude
of their rage against kings, the French Republic were threatened with attack, and with the desolation of their capital by
a banded crusade of kings ; and they rose in frenzy to meet
the aggressors. The Allied Powers had themselves kindled
the popular excitement which provoked this vast development of martial power amongst the French, and first brought
their own warlike strength within their own knowledge. In
the days of Charlemagne the same martial character was the
result of ancient habits and training, encouraged and effectu-

[1] Or perhaps the *right ;* for the Prussian cavalry (who drew their
custom from some regiments in the service of Gustavus Adolphus,
and they again traditionally from others) are always trained to mount
in this way.

[2] It is painful to any man of honourable feeling that, whilst a
great rival nation is pursuing the ennobling profession of arms, his
own should be reproached contemptuously with a sordid dedication
to commerce. However, on the one hand, things are not always as
they seem : commerce has its ennobling effects, direct or indirect ;
war its barbarizing degradations. And, on the other hand, the facts
even are not exactly as *prima facie* they were supposed ; for the
truth is that, in proportion to its total population, England had more
men in arms during the last war than France. But, generally speaking, the case may be stated thus : the British nation is, by original
constitution of mind, and by long enjoyment of liberty, a far nobler
people than the French. And hence we see the reason and the
necessity that the French should, with a view to something like a
final balance in the effect, be trained to a nobler profession. Compensations are everywhere produced or encouraged by nature and by
providence ; and a nobler discipline in the one nation is doubtless
some equilibrium to a nobler nature in the other.

ally organized by the energy of the aspiring mayors of the palace, or great lieutenants of the Merovingian Kings. But, agreeing in this, that they were indebted to others for the martial spirit which they found, and that both turned to their account a power not created by themselves, Charlemagne and Napoleon differed, however, in the utmost possible extent as to the final application of their borrowed advantages. Napoleon applied them to purposes the very opposite of those which had originally given them birth. Nothing less than patriotic ardour in defence of what had at one time appeared to be the cause of civil liberty could have availed to evoke those mighty hosts which gathered in the early years of the Revolution on the German and Italian frontiers of France. Yet were these hosts applied, under the perfect despotism of Napoleon, to the final extinction of liberty ; and the armies of Jacobinism, who had gone forth on a mission of liberation for Europe, were at last employed in riveting the chains of their compatriots, and forging others for the greater part of Christendom.   Far otherwise was the conduct of Charlemagne.   The Frankish government, though we are not circumstantially acquainted with its forms, is known to have been tempered by a large infusion of popular influence. This is proved, as Mr. James observes, by the deposition of Chilperic ; by the grand national assemblies of the Champ de Mars ; and by other great historical facts.   Now, the situation of Charlemagne,—successor to a throne already firmly established, and in his own person a mighty amplifier of its glories, and a leader in whom the Franks had unlimited confidence,—threw into his hands an unexampled power of modifying the popular restraints upon himself in any degree he might desire.

"Nunquam libertas gratior exit,
Quam sub rege pio "—

is the general doctrine.   But, as to the Franks in particular, if they resembled their modern representatives in their most conspicuous moral feature, it would be more true to say that the bribe and the almost magical seduction for *them*, capable of charming away their sternest resolutions, and of relaxing the hand of the patriot when grasping his noblest birthright, has ever lain in great military success, in the power of bring-

ing victory to the national standards, and in continued offer-
ings on the altar of public vanity. In *their* estimate for
above a thousand years, it has been found true that the
harvest of a few splendid campaigns, reaped upon the fields
of neighbouring nations, far outweighs any amount of humbler
blessings in the shape of civil and political privileges.
Charlemagne, as a conqueror, and by far the greatest illus-
trator of the Frankish name, might easily have conciliated
their gratitude and admiration into a surrender of popular
rights ; or, profiting by his high situation, and the confidence
reposed in him, he might have undermined their props ; or,
by a direct exertion of his power, he might have peremptorily
resumed them. Slowly and surely, or summarily and with
violence, this great emperor had the national privileges in his
power. But the beneficence of his purposes required no such
aggression on the rights of his subjects. War brought with
it naturally some extension of power ; and a military jurisdiction is necessarily armed with some discretionary licence.
But, in the civil exercise of his authority, the Emperor was
content with the powers awarded to him by law and custom.
His great schemes of policy were all of a nature to prepare
his subjects for a condition of larger political influence ; he
could not in consistency be adverse to an end towards which
he so anxiously prepared the means. And it is certain that,
although some German writers have attempted to fasten upon
Charlemagne a charge of vexatious inquisition into the minor
police of domestic life, and into petty details of economy
below the majesty of his official character, even *their* vigilance
of research, sharpened by malice, has been unable to detect,
throughout his long reign, and in the hurry of sudden
exigencies natural to a state of uninterrupted warfare and
alarm, one single act of tyranny, personal revenge, or violation of the existing laws. Charlemagne, like Napoleon, had
bitter enemies : some who were such to his government and
his public purposes ; some again to his person upon motives
of private revenge. Tassilo, for example, the Duke of
Bavaria, and Desiderius, the King of the Lombards, acted
against him upon the bitterest instigations of feminine resentment ; each of these princes, conceiving himself concerned in
a family quarrel, pursued the cause which he had adopted in

the most ferocious spirit of revenge, and would undoubtedly
have inflicted death upon Charlemagne, had he fallen into
their power. Of this he must himself have been sensible ;
and yet, when the chance of war threw both of them into his
power, he forbore to exercise even those rights of retaliation
for their many provocations which the custom of that age
sanctioned universally : he neither mutilated nor deprived
them of sight. Confinement to religious seclusion was all
that he inflicted ; and, in the case of Tassilo, where mercy
could be more safely exercised, he pardoned him so often
that it became evident in what current his feelings ran
wherever the cruel necessities of the public service allowed
him to indulge them.

In the conspiracy formed against him upon the provocations offered to the Frankish nobility by his third wife, he
showed the same spirit of excessive clemency, a clemency
which again reminds us of the first Cæsar, and which was
not merely parental, but often recalls to us the long-suffering
and tenderness of spirit which belong to the infirmity of
maternal affection. Here are no Palms,[1] executed for no
real offence known to the laws of their country, and without
a trial such as any laws in any country would have conceded : no innocent D'Enghien,[2] murdered, without the
shadow of provocation, and purely on account of his own
reversionary rights ; not for doing or meditating wrong, but
because the claims which unfortunately he inherited might
by possibility become available in his person ; not, therefore,
even as an enemy by intention or premeditation ; not even
as an apparent competitor, but in the rare character of a
competitor presumptive,—one who might become an ideal
competitor by the extinction of a whole family, and even
then no substantial competitor until after a revolution in
France which must already have undermined the throne of
Bonaparte. To his own subjects, and his own kinsmen,
never did Charlemagne forget to be, in acts as well as words,
a parent.

[1] John Philip Palm, shot by Bonaparte's orders, August 26, 1806.
—M.
[2] The Bourbon Duke d'Enghien, shot by Bonaparte's orders, March
21, 1804.—M.

In his foreign relations, it is true, for one single purpose of effectual warning, Charlemagne put forth a solitary trait of Roman harshness. This is the case which we have already noticed and defended ; and, with a view to the comparison with Napoleon, remarkable enough it is that the numbers sacrificed on this occasion are pretty nearly the same as on the celebrated massacre at Jaffa, perpetrated by Napoleon in Council.[1] In the Saxon, as in the Syrian massacre, the numbers were between four and five thousand : not that the numbers or the scale of the transaction can affect its principle ; but it is well to know it, because then to its author, as now to us who sit as judges upon it, that circumstance cannot be supposed to have failed in drawing the very keenest attention to its previous consideration. A butchery that was in a numerical sense so vast cannot be supposed to have escaped its author in a hurry, or to be open to any of the usual palliations from precipitance or inattention. Charlemagne and Napoleon must equally be presumed to have regarded this act on all sides, to have weighed it in and for itself, and to have traversed by anticipation the whole sum of its consequences. In the one case we find a general, the leader of a *soi-disant* Christian army, the representative of the " most Christian " nation, and, as amongst infidels, specially charged with the duty of supporting the sanctity of Christian good faith, unfortunately pledged by his own most confidential and accredited agents, in a moment of weakness, to a promise which he, the commander-in-chief, regarded as ruinous. This promise, fatal to Napoleon's honour, and tarnishing for many a year to the Christian name, guaranteed " quarter " to a large body of Turkish troops, having arms in their hands, and otherwise well able to have made a desperate defence. Such a promise was peculiarly embarrassing ; provisions ran short, and, to detain them as prisoners would draw murmurs from his own troops, now suffering hardships themselves. On the other hand, to have turned them adrift

---

[1] "*In council*," we say purposely and in candour ; for the only pleas in palliation ever set up by Napoleon's apologists are these two : *necessity*, the devil's plea, in the first place ; secondly, that the guilt of the transaction, whether more or less, was divided amongst the general and the several members of his council.

would have insured their speedy reappearance as active
enemies to a diminished and debilitated army ; for, as to
sending them off by sea, that measure was impracticable, as
well from want of shipping as from the presence of the
English. Such was the dilemma, doubtless perplexing
enough, but not more so than in ten thousand other cases,
for which their own appropriate ten thousand remedies have
been found. What was the issue ? The entire body of
gallant soldiers, disarmed upon the faith of a solemn guarantee from a Christian general, standing in the very steps of
the noble (and the more noble because bigoted) Crusaders,
were all mowed down by the musketry of their thrice accursed
enemy ; and, by way of crowning treachery with treachery,
some few who had swum off to a point of rock in the sea
were lured back to destruction under a second series of
promises, violated almost at the very instant when uttered.
A larger or more damnable murder does not stain the memory
of any brigand, buccaneer, or pirate ; nor has any army,—
Huns, Vandals, or Mogul Tartars,—ever polluted itself by so
base a perfidy ; for, in this memorable tragedy the whole
army were accomplices. Now, as to Charlemagne, he had
tried the effect of forgiveness and lenity often in vain.
Clemency was misinterpreted ; it had been, and it would be,
construed into conscious weakness. Under these circumstances, with a view undoubtedly to the final extinction of
rebellions which involved infinite bloodshed on both sides,
he permitted one trial to be made of a severe and sanguinary
chastisement. It failed ; insurrections proceeded as before,
and it was not repeated. But the main difference in the
principle of the two cases is this,—that Charlemagne had
exacted no penalty but one which the laws of war in that
age conferred, and even in this age the laws of allegiance.
However bloody, therefore, this tragedy was no murder. It
was a judicial punishment, built upon known acts and admitted
laws, designed in mercy, consented to unwillingly, and
finally repented. Lastly, instead of being one in a
multitude of acts bearing the same character, it stood
alone in a long career of intercourse with wild and
ferocious nations, owning no control but that of the spear
and sword.

Many are the points of comparison, and some of them remarkable enough, in the other circumstances of the two careers, separated by a thousand years. Both effected the passage of the Great St. Bernard [1]; but the one in an age when mechanical forces, and the aids of art, were yet imperfectly developed ; the other in an age when science had armed the arts of war and of locomotion with the fabulous powers of the Titans, and with the whole resources of a mighty nation at his immediate disposal. Both, by means of this extraordinary feat, achieved the virtual conquest of Lombardy in an hour ; but Charlemagne, without once risking the original impression of this *coup-d'éclat;* Napoleon, on the other hand, so entirely squandering and forfeiting his own success that in the battle which followed he was at first utterly defeated, and, but for the blunder of his enemy, and the sudden aid of an accomplished friend, irretrievably. Both suffered politically by the repudiation of a wife ; but Charlemagne, under adequate provocation, and with no final result of evil ; Bonaparte under heavy aggravations of ingratitude and indiscretion. Each assumed the character of a patron to learning and learned men ; but Napoleon in an age when knowledge of every kind was self-patronized, when no possible exertions of power could avail to crush it, and yet, under these circumstances, with utter insincerity ; Charlemagne, on the other hand, at a time when the countenance of a powerful protector made the whole difference between revival and a long extinction, and,—what was still more to the purpose of doing honour to his memory,—not merely in a spirit of sincerity, but of fervid activity. Not content with drawing counsel and aid from the cells of Northumberland, even in the short time which he passed at Rome he had "collected a number of grammarians (that is, " *littérateurs*) and arithmeticians, the poor remains of the " orators and philosophers of the past, and engaged them to " accompany him from Italy to France."

[1] And from the fact of that corps in Charlemagne's army which effected the passage having been commanded by his uncle, Duke Bernard, this mountain, previously known as the *Mons* Jovis (and, by corruption, Mont le Joux), very justly obtained the more modern name which it still retains.

What resulted in each case from these great efforts and prodigious successes ? Each failed in laying the foundations of any permanent inheritance to his own glory in his own family. But Bonaparte lived to lay in ruins even his personal interest in this great edifice of empire, and that entirely by his own desperate presumption, precipitance, and absolute defect of self-command ; Charlemagne, on *his* part, lost nothing of what he had gained. If his posterity did not long maintain the elevation to which he had raised them, *that* did but the more proclaim the grandeur of the mind which had reared a colossal empire, that sank under any powers inferior to his own. If the empire itself lost its unity, and divided into sections, even thus it did not lose the splendour and prosperity of its separate parts ; and the praise remains entire—let succeeding princes, as conservators, have failed as much and as excusably as they might—that he erected the following splendid empire :—the whole of France and Belgium, with their natural boundaries of the Alps, the Pyrenees, the Ocean, the Mediterranean ; to the south, Spain between the Ebro and the Pyrenees ; and, to the north, the whole of Germany, up to the banks of the Elbe. Italy, as far as the lower Calabria, was either governed by his son, or tributary to his crown ; Dalmatia, Croatia, Liburnia, and Istria (with the exception of the maritime cities), were joined to the territories, which he had himself conquered, of Hungary and Bohemia. As far as the conflux of the Danube with the Teyss and the Save, the East of Europe acknowledged his power. Most of the Slavonian tribes between the Elbe and the Vistula paid tribute and professed obedience ; and Corsica and Sardinia, with the Balearic Islands, were dependent upon his possessions in Italy and Spain.

His moral were yet greater than his territorial conquests : in the eloquent language of his present historian, " he snatched " from darkness all the lands he conquered ; and may be " said to have added the whole of Germany to the world." Wherever he moved, civilisation followed his footsteps. What he conquered was emphatically the conquest of his own genius ; and his vast empire was, in a peculiar sense, his own creation. And that which, under general circumstances, would have exposed the hollowness and insufficiency of his establishment was for him in particular the seal and attestation of his extraordinary grandeur of mind. His empire dissolved after he had departed ; his dominions lost their cohesion, and slipped away from the nerveless hands which succeeded,—a sufficient evidence, were there no other, that all the vast resources of the Frankish throne, wielded by imbecile minds, were inadequate to maintain that which, in the hands of a Charlemagne, they had availed to conquer and cement.

JOAN OF ARC [1]

WHAT is to be thought of *her*? What is to be thought of the poor shepherd girl from the hills and forests of Lorraine, that—like the Hebrew shepherd boy from the hills and forests of Judea—rose suddenly out of the quiet, out of the safety, out of the religious inspiration, rooted in deep pastoral solitudes, to a station in the van of armies, and to the more perilous station at the right hand of kings? The Hebrew boy inaugurated his patriotic mission by an *act*, by a victorious *act*, such as no man could deny. But so did the girl of Lorraine, if we read her story as it was read by those

---

[1] "*Arc*":—Modern France, that should know a great deal better than myself, insists that the name is not D'Arc—*i.e.* of Arc—but *Darc*. Now it happens sometimes that, if a person whose position guarantees his access to the best information will content himself with gloomy dogmatism, striking the table with his fist, and saying in a terrific voice "It *is* so, and there's an end of it," one bows deferentially, and submits. But, if, unhappily for himself, won by this docility, he relents too amiably into reasons and arguments, probably one raises an insurrection against him that may never be crushed; for in the fields of logic one can skirmish, perhaps, as well as he. Had he confined himself to dogmatism, he would have intrenched his position in darkness, and have hidden his own vulnerable points. But, coming down to base reasons, he lets in light, and one sees where to plant the blows. Now, the worshipful reason of modern France for disturbing the old received spelling is that Jean Hordal, a descendant of *La Pucelle's* brother, spelled the name *Darc* in 1612. But what of that? It is notorious that what small matter of spelling Providence had thought fit to disburse amongst man in the seventeenth century was all monopolised by printers: now, M. Hordal was *not* a printer.

[Appeared originally in *Tait's Magazine* for March and August 1847; reprinted by De Quincey in 1854, in the third volume of his Collected Writings.—M.]

who saw her nearest. Adverse armies bore witness to the boy as no pretender ; but so they did to the gentle girl. Judged by the voices of all who saw them *from a station of good-will*, both were found true and loyal to any promises involved in their first acts. Enemies it was that made the difference between their subsequent fortunes. The boy rose to a splendour and a noonday prosperity, both personal and public, that rang through the records of his people, and became a by-word amongst his posterity for a thousand years, until the sceptre was departing from Judah. The poor, forsaken girl, on the contrary, drank not herself from that cup of rest which she had secured for France. She never sang together with the songs that rose in her native Domrémy as echoes to the departing steps of invaders. She mingled not in the festal dances at Vaucouleurs which celebrated in rapture the redemption of France. No ! for her voice was then silent ; no ! for her feet were dust. Pure, innocent, noble-hearted girl ! whom, from earliest youth, ever I believed in as full of truth and self-sacrifice, this was amongst the strongest pledges for *thy* truth, that never once—no, not for a moment of weakness—didst thou revel in the vision of coronets and honour from man. Coronets for thee ! Oh no ! Honours, if they come when all is over, are for those that share thy blood.[1] Daughter of Domrémy, when the gratitude of thy king shall awaken, thou wilt be sleeping the sleep of the dead. Call her, King of France, but she will not hear thee. Cite her by the apparitors to come and receive a robe of honour, but she will be found *en contumace*. When the thunders of universal France, as even yet may happen, shall proclaim the grandeur of the poor shepherd girl that gave up all for her country, thy ear, young shepherd girl, will have been deaf for five centuries. To suffer and to do, that was thy portion in this life ; that was thy destiny; and not for a moment was it hidden from thyself. Life, thou saidst, is short ; and the sleep which is in the grave is long ; let me use that life, so transitory, for the glory of those heavenly dreams destined to comfort the sleep which is so long ! This pure creature—pure from every suspicion of

[1] " *Those that share thy blood* " :—A collateral relative of Joanna's was subsequently ennobled by the title of *Du Lys*.

even a visionary self-interest, even as she was pure in senses
more obvious—never once did this holy child, as regarded
herself, relax from her belief in the darkness that was travelling to meet her.   She might not prefigure the very manner
of her death ; she saw not in vision, perhaps, the aerial
altitude of the fiery scaffold, the spectators without end on
every road pouring into Rouen as to a coronation, the surging
smoke, the volleying flames, the hostile faces all around, the
pitying eye that lurked but here and there, until nature and
imperishable truth broke loose from artificial restraints ;—
these might not be apparent through the mists of the hurrying future.   But the voice that called her to death, *that* she
heard for ever.

Great was the throne of France even in those days, and
great was he that sat upon it : but well Joanna knew that
not the throne, nor he that sat upon it, was for *her ;* but, on
the contrary, that she was for *them ;* not she by them, but
they by her, should rise from the dust.   Gorgeous were the
lilies of France, and for centuries had the privilege to spread
their beauty over land and sea, until, in another century, the
wrath of God and man combined to wither them ; but well
Joanna knew, early at Domrémy she had read that bitter
truth, that the lilies of France would decorate no garland
for *her.*   Flower nor bud, bell nor blossom, would ever
bloom for *her !*

·   ·   ·   ·

But stay.   What reason is there for taking up this subject
of Joanna precisely in the spring of 1847 ?   Might it not
have been left till the spring of 1947, or, perhaps, left till
called for ?   Yes, but it *is* called for, and clamorously.   You
are aware, reader, that amongst the many original thinkers
whom modern France has produced one of the reputed leaders
is M. Michelet.   All these writers are of a revolutionary cast :
not in a political sense merely, but in all senses ; mad, oftentimes, as March hares ; crazy with the laughing gas of recovered liberty ; drunk with the wine-cup of their mighty
Revolution, snorting, whinnying, throwing up their heels,
like wild horses in the boundless Pampas, and running races
of defiance with snipes, or with the winds, or with their own
shadows, if they can find nothing else to challenge.   Some

time or other I, that have leisure to read, may introduce *you*,
that have not, to two or three dozen of these writers ; of
whom I can assure you beforehand that they are often profound, and at intervals are even as impassioned as if they
were come of our best English blood. But now, confining
our attention to M. Michelet, we in England—who know him
best by his worst book, the book against priests, &c.—know
him disadvantageously. That book is a rhapsody of incoherence. But his "History of France" is quite another thing.
A man, in whatsoever craft he sails, cannot stretch away out
of sight when he is linked to the windings of the shore by
towing-ropes of History. Facts, and the consequences of
facts, draw the writer back to the falconer's lure from the
giddiest heights of speculation. Here, therefore — in his
"France"—if not always free from flightiness, if now and
then off like a rocket for an airy wheel in the clouds, M.
Michelet, with natural politeness, never forgets that he has
left a large audience waiting for him on earth, and gazing
upwards in anxiety for his return : return, therefore, he does.
But History, though clear of certain temptations in one
direction, has separate dangers of its own. It is impossible
so to write a history of France, or of England—works becoming every hour more indispensable to the inevitably-
political man of this day—without perilous openings for
error. If I, for instance, on the part of England, should
happen to turn my labours into that channel, and (on the
model of Lord Percy going to Chevy Chase)

> "A vow to God should make
> My pleasure in the Michelet woods
> Three summer days to take,"

probably, from simple delirium, I might hunt M. Michelet
into *delirium tremens*. Two strong angels stand by the side
of History, whether French History or English, as heraldic
supporters : the angel of research on the left hand, that
must read millions of dusty parchments, and of pages blotted
with lies ; the angel of meditation on the right hand, that
must cleanse these lying records with fire, even as of old the
draperies of *asbestos* were cleansed, and must quicken them
into regenerated life. Willingly I acknowledge that no man

will ever avoid innumerable errors of detail ; with so vast a
compass of ground to traverse, this is impossible ; but such
errors (though I have a bushel on hand, at M. Michelet's
service) are not the game I chase ; it is the bitter and unfair
spirit in which M. Michelet writes against England. Even
that, after all, is but my secondary object ; the real one is
Joanna, the Pucelle d'Orleans for herself.

I am not going to write the history of *La Pucelle :* to do
this, or even circumstantially to report the history of her
persecution and bitter death, of her struggle with false
witnesses and with ensnaring judges, it would be necessary
to have before us *all* the documents, and therefore the
collection only now forthcoming in Paris.[1] But *my* purpose
is narrower. There have been great thinkers, disdaining the
careless judgments of contemporaries, who have thrown themselves boldly on the judgment of a far posterity, that should
have had time to review, to ponder, to compare. There
have been great actors on the stage of tragic humanity that
might, with the same depth of confidence, have appealed
from the levity of compatriot friends—too heartless for the
sublime interest of their story, and too impatient for the
labour of sifting its perplexities—to the magnanimity and
justice of enemies. To this class belongs the Maid of Arc.
The ancient Romans were too faithful to the ideal of grandeur
in themselves not to relent, after a generation or two, before
the grandeur of Hannibal. Mithridates, a more doubtful
person, yet, merely for the magic perseverance of his indomitable malice, won from the same Romans the only real honour
that ever he received on earth. And we English have ever
shown the same homage to stubborn enmity. To work
unflinchingly for the ruin of England ; to say through life,
by word and by deed, *Delenda est Anglia Victrix !*—that one
purpose of malice, faithfully pursued, has quartered some
people upon our national funds of homage as by a perpetual
annuity. Better than an inheritance of service rendered to

---

[1] " *Only now forthcoming* " :—In 1847 *began* the publication (from
official records) of Joanna's trial. It was interrupted, I fear, by the
convulsions of 1848 ; and whether even yet finished I do not know.
[The reference seems to be to *Quicherat : Procès de condemnation et
réhabilitation de Jeanne d'Arc*, in 5 volumes, Paris 1841-9.—M.

England herself has sometimes proved the most insane hatred
to England.   Hyder Ali, even his son Tippoo, though so far
inferior, and Napoleon, have all benefited by this disposition
amongst ourselves to exaggerate the merit of diabolic enmity.
Not one of these men was ever capable, in a solitary instance,
of praising an enemy (what do you say to *that*, reader ?) ; and
yet, in *their* behalf, we consent to forget, not their crimes
only, but (which is worse) their hideous bigotry and anti-mag-
nanimous egotism,—for nationality it was not.   Suffren, and
some half-dozen of other French nautical heroes, because
rightly they did us all the mischief they could (which was
really great), are names justly reverenced in England.   On
the same principle, La Pucelle d'Orleans, the victorious enemy
of England, has been destined to receive her deepest commemoration from the magnanimous justice of Englishmen.

Joanna, as we in England should call her, but, according to
her own statement, Jeannc (or, as M. Michelet asserts, Jean [1])
D'Arc, was born at Domrémy, a village on the marches of
Lorraine and Champagne, and dependent upon the town of
Vaucouleurs.   I have called her a Lorrainer, not simply
because the word is prettier, but because Champagne too
odiously reminds us English of what are for *us* imaginary
wines,—which, undoubtedly, *La Pucelle* tasted as rarely as
we English : we English, because the Champagne of London
is chiefly grown in Devonshire ; *La Pucelle*, because the
Champagne of Champagne never, by any chance, flowed into

---

[1] "*Jean*" :—M. Michelet asserts that there was a mystical meaning at that era in calling a child *Jean ;* it implied a secret commenda-
tion of a child, if not a dedication, to St. John the evangelist, the
beloved disciple, the apostle of love and mysterious visions.   But,
really, as the name was so exceedingly common, few people will detect
a mystery in calling a *boy* by the name of Jack, though it *does* seem
mysterious to call a girl Jack.   It may be less so in France, where a
beautiful practice has always prevailed of giving a boy his mother's
name—preceded and strengthened by a male name, as *Charles Anne,*
Victor Victoire.   In cases where a mother's memory has been unusually
dear to a son, this vocal memento of her, locked into the circle of his
own name, gives to it the tenderness of a testamentary relique, or a
funeral ring.   I presume, therefore, that *La Pucelle* must have borne
the baptismal name of Jeanne Jean ; the latter with no reference,
perhaps, to so sublime a person as St. John, but simply to some
relative.

the fountain of Domrémy, from which only she drank.   M. Michelet will have her to be a *Champenoise,* and for no better reason than that she "took after her father," who happened to be a *Champenois.*

These disputes, however, turn on refinements too nice. Domrémy stood upon the frontiers, and, like other frontiers, produced a *mixed* race, representing the *cis* and the *trans.*   A river (it is true) formed the boundary-line at this point—the river Meuse ; and *that,* in old days, might have divided the populations ; but in these days it did not : there were bridges, there were ferries, and weddings crossed from the right bank to the left.   Here lay two great roads, not so much for travellers that were few, as for armies that were too many by half.   These two roads, one of which was the great high road between France and Germany, *decussated* at this very point ; which is a learned way of saying that they formed a St. Andrew's Cross, or letter Χ.   I hope the compositor will choose a good large Χ; in which case the point of intersection, the *locus* of conflux and intersection for these four diverging arms, will finish the reader's geographical education, by showing him to a hair's-breadth where it was that Domrémy stood.   These roads, so grandly situated, as great trunk arteries between two mighty realms,[1] and haunted for ever by wars or rumours of wars, decussated (for anything I know to the contrary) absolutely under Joanna's bedroom window : one rolling away to the right, past Monsieur D'Arc's old barn, and the other unaccountably preferring to sweep round that odious man's pig-sty to the left.

Oh whichever side of the border chance had thrown Joanna, the same love to France would have been nurtured. For it is a strange fact, noticed by M. Michelet and others, that the Dukes of Bar and Lorraine had for generations pursued the policy of eternal warfare with France on their own account, yet also of eternal amity and league with France in case anybody else presumed to attack her.   Let peace settle upon France, and before long you might rely upon seeing the little vixen Lorraine flying at the throat of France.   Let

---

[1] And reminding one of that inscription, so justly admired by Paul Richter, which a Russian Czarina placed on a guide-post near Moscow : *This is the road that leads to Constantinople.*

France be assailed by a formidable enemy, and instantly you saw a Duke of Lorraine insisting on having his own throat cut in support of France ; which favour accordingly was cheerfully granted to him in three great successive battles : twice by the English, viz. at Crécy and Agincourt, once by the Sultan at Nicopolis.

This sympathy with France during great eclipses, in those that during ordinary seasons were always teasing her with brawls and guerilla inroads, strengthened the natural piety to France of those that were confessedly the children of her own house. The outposts of France, as one may call the great frontier provinces, were of all localities the most devoted to the Fleurs de Lys. To witness, at any great crisis, the generous devotion to these lilies of the little fiery cousin that in gentler weather was for ever tilting at the breast of France, could not but fan the zeal of France's legitimate daughters : whilst to occupy a post of honour on the frontiers against an old hereditary enemy of France would naturally stimulate this zeal by a sentiment of martial pride, by a sense of danger always threatening, and of hatred always smouldering. That great four-headed road was a perpetual memento to patriotic ardour. To say " This way lies the road to Paris, and that other way to Aix-la-Chapelle ; this to Prague, that to Vienna," nourished the warfare of the heart by daily ministrations of sense. The eye that watched for the gleams of lance or helmet from the hostile frontier, the ear that listened for the groaning of wheels, made the high-road itself, with its relations to centres so remote, into a manual of patriotic duty.

The situation, therefore, *locally*, of Joanna was full of profound suggestions to a heart that listened for the stealthy steps of change and fear that too surely were in motion. But, if the place were grand, the time, the burden of the time, was far more so. The air overhead in its upper chambers was *hurtling* with the obscure sound ; was dark with sullen fermenting of storms that had been gathering for a hundred and thirty years. The battle of Agincourt in Joanna's childhood had reopened the wounds of France. Crécy and Poictiers, those withering overthrows for the chivalry of France, had, before Agincourt occurred, been tranquillised by more than half-a-century ; but this resurrection of their trumpet wails made the whole series of battles and endless skirmishes take their stations as parts in one drama.   The graves that had closed sixty years ago seemed to fly open in sympathy with a sorrow that echoed their own. The monarchy of France laboured in extremity, rocked and reeled like a ship fighting with the darkness of monsoons. The madness of the poor king (Charles VI) falling in at such a crisis, like the case of women labouring in childbirth during the storming of a city, trebled the awfulness of the time.   Even the wild story of the incident which had immediately occasioned the explosion of this madness—the case of a man unknown, gloomy, and perhaps maniacal himself, coming out of a forest at noonday, laying his hand upon the bridle of the king's horse, checking him for a moment to say, " Oh, king, thou art betrayed," and then vanishing, no man knew whither, as he had appeared for no man knew what—fell in with the universal prostration of mind that laid France on her knees, as before the slow unweaving of some ancient prophetic doom.   The famines, the extraordinary diseases, the insurrections of the peasantry up and down Europe—these were chords struck from the same mysterious harp ; but these were transitory chords.   There had been others of deeper and more ominous sound.   The termination of the Crusades, the destruction of the Templars, the Papal interdicts, the tragedies caused or suffered by the house of Anjou, and by the Emperor—these were full of a more permanent significance.   But, since then, the colossal figure of feudalism was seen standing, as it were on tiptoe, at Crécy, for flight from earth : that was a revolution unparalleled ; yet *that* was a trifle by comparison with the more fearful revolutions that were mining below the Church.   By her own internal schisms, by the abominable spectacle of a double pope—so that no man, except through political bias, could even guess which was Heaven's vicegerent, and which the creature of Hell—the Church was rehearsing, as in still earlier forms she had already rehearsed, those vast rents in her foundations which no man should ever heal.

These were the loftiest peaks of the cloudland in the skies that to the scientific gazer first caught the colours of the *new* morning in advance. But the whole vast range alike of sweeping glooms overhead dwelt upon all meditative minds, even upon those that could not distinguish the tendencies nor decipher the forms. It was, therefore, not her own age alone as affected by its immediate calamities that lay with such weight upon Joanna's mind, but her own age as one section in a vast mysterious drama, unweaving through a century back, and drawing nearer continually to some dreadful crisis. Cataracts and rapids were heard roaring ahead ; and signs were seen far back, by help of old men's memories, which answered secretly to signs now coming forward on the eye, even as locks answer to keys. It was not wonderful that in such a haunted solitude, with such a haunted heart, Joanna should see angelic visions, and hear angelic voices. These voices whispered to her for ever the duty, self-imposed, of delivering France. Five years she listened to these monitory voices with internal struggles. At length she could resist no longer. Doubt gave way ; and she left her home for ever in order to present herself at the dauphin's court.

The education of this poor girl was mean according to the present standard : was ineffably grand, according to a purer philosophic standard : and only not good for our age because for us it would be unattainable. She read nothing, for she could not read ; but she had heard others read parts of the Roman martyrology. She wept in sympathy with the sad *Misereres* of the Romish Church ; she rose to heaven with the glad triumphant *Te Deums* of Rome ; she drew her comfort and her vital strength from the rites of the same Church. But, next after these spiritual advantages, she owed most to the advantages of her situation. The fountain of Domrémy was on the brink of a boundless forest ; and it was haunted to that degree by fairies that the parish priest (*curé*) was obliged to read mass there once a-year, in order to keep them in any decent bounds. Fairies are important, even in a statistical view : certain weeds mark poverty in the soil ; fairies mark its solitude. As surely as the wolf retires before cities does the fairy sequester herself from the haunts of the licensed victualler. A village is too much for her nervous delicacy : at most, she can tolerate a distant view of a hamlet.

We may judge, therefore, by the uneasiness and extra trouble which they gave to the parson, in what strength the fairies mustered at Domrémy, and, by a satisfactory consequence, how thinly sown with men and women must have been that region even in its inhabited spots. But the forests of Domrémy—those were the glories of the land : for in them abode mysterious powers and ancient secrets that towered into tragic strength. " Abbeys there were, and abbey windows," —" like Moorish temples of the Hindoos,"—that exercised even princely power both in Lorraine and in the German Diets. These had their sweet bells that pierced the forests for many a league at matins or vespers, and each its own dreamy legend. Few enough, and scattered enough, were these abbeys, so as in no degree to disturb the deep solitude of the region ; yet many enough to spread a network or awning of Christian sanctity over what else might have seemed a heathen wilderness. This sort of religious talisman being secured, a man the most afraid of ghosts (like myself, suppose, or the reader) becomes armed into courage to wander for days in their sylvan recesses. The mountains of the Vosges, on the eastern frontier of France, have never attracted much notice from Europe, except in 1813-14 for a few brief months, when they fell within Napoleon's line of defence against the Allies. But they are interesting for this amongst other features, that they do not, like some loftier ranges, repel woods : the forests and the hills are on sociable terms. *Live and let live* is their motto. For this reason, in part, these tracts in Lorraine were a favourite hunting-ground with the Carlovingian princes. About six hundred years before Joanna's childhood, Charlemagne was known to have hunted there. That, of itself, was a grand incident in the traditions of a forest or a chase. In these vast forests, also, were to be found (if anywhere to be found) those mysterious fawns that tempted solitary hunters into visionary and perilous pursuits. Here was seen (if anywhere seen) that ancient stag who was already nine hundred years old, but possibly a hundred or two more, when met by Charlemagne ; and the thing was put beyond doubt by the inscription upon his golden collar. I believe Charlemagne knighted the stag ; and, if ever he is met again by a king, he ought to be made an earl, or, being upon the marches of France, a marquis. Observe, I don't absolutely vouch for all these things : my own opinion varies. On a fine breezy forenoon I am audaciously sceptical ; but as twilight sets in my credulity grows steadily, till it becomes equal to anything that could be desired. And I have heard candid sportsmen declare that, outside of these very forests, they laughed loudly at all the dim tales connected with their haunted solitudes, but, on reaching a spot notoriously eighteen miles deep within them, they agreed with Sir Roger de Coverley that a good deal might be said on both sides.

Such traditions, or any others that (like the stag) connect distant generations with each other, are, for that cause, sublime ; and the sense of the shadowy, connected with such appearances that reveal themselves or not according to circumstances, leaves a colouring of sanctity over ancient forests, even in those minds that utterly reject the legend as a fact.

But, apart from all distinct stories of that order, in any solitary frontier between two great empires,—as here, for instance, or in the desert between Syria and the Euphrates, —there is an inevitable tendency, in minds of any deep sensibility, to people the solitudes with phantom images of powers that were of old so vast. Joanna, therefore, in her quiet occupation of a shepherdess, would be led continually to brood over the political condition of her country by the traditions of the past no less than by the mementoes of the local present.

M. Michelet, indeed, says that La Pucelle was *not* a shepherdess. I beg his pardon : she *was*. What he rests upon I guess pretty well : it is the evidence of a woman called Haumette, the most confidential friend of Joanna. Now, she is a good witness, and a good girl, and I like her ; for she makes a natural and affectionate report of Joanna's ordinary life. But still, however good she may be as a witness, Joanna is better ; and she, when speaking to the dauphin, calls herself in the Latin report *Bergereta*. Even Haumette confesses that Joanna tended sheep in her girlhood. And I believe that, if Miss Haumette were taking coffee alone with me this very evening (February 12, 1847)—in which there would be no subject for scandal or for maiden blushes, because I am an intense philosopher, and Miss H. would be hard upon four hundred and fifty years old—she would admit the following comment upon her evidence to be right. A Frenchman, about forty years ago,—M. Simond, in his "Travels,"—mentions accidentally the following hideous scene as one steadily observed and watched by himself in chivalrous France not very long before the French Revolution :—A peasant was ploughing ; and the team that drew his plough was a donkey and a woman. Both were regularly harnessed : both pulled alike. This is bad enough ; but the Frenchman adds that, in distributing his lashes, the peasant was obviously desirous of being impartial : or, if either of the yoke-fellows had a right to complain, certainly it was not the donkey.[1] Now, in any country where such degradation of females could be tolerated by the state of manners, a woman of delicacy would shrink from acknowledging, either for herself or her friend, that she had ever been addicted to any mode of labour not strictly domestic ; because, if once owning herself a prædial servant, she would be sensible that this confession extended by probability in the hearer's thoughts to the having incurred indignities of this horrible kind. Haumette clearly thinks it more dignified for Joanna to have been darning the stockings of her horny-hoofed father, Monsieur D'Arc, than keeping sheep, lest she might then be suspected of having ever done something worse. But, luckily, there was no danger of *that* : Joanna never was in service ; and my opinion is that her father should have mended his own stockings, since probably he was the party to make the holes in them, as many a better man than D'Arc does,—meaning by *that* not myself, because, though probably a better man than D'Arc, I protest against doing anything of the kind. If I lived even with Friday in Juan Fernandez, either Friday must do all the darning, or else it must go undone. The better men that I meant were the sailors in the British navy, every man of whom mends his own stockings. Who else is to do it ? Do you suppose, reader, that the junior lords of the admiralty are under articles to darn for the navy ?

[1] De Quincey quotes this story more than once in the course of his writings.—M.

The reason, meantime, for my systematic hatred of D'Arc is this :—There was a story current in France before the Revolution, framed to ridicule the pauper aristocracy, who happened to have long pedigrees and short rent rolls : viz. that a head of such a house, dating from the Crusades, was overheard saying to his son, a Chevalier of St. Louis, " *Chevalier, as-tu donné au cochon à manger !*" Now, it is clearly made out by the surviving evidence that D'Arc would much have preferred continuing to say, " *Ma fille, as-tu donné au cochon à manger ?* " to saying, " *Pucelle d'Orleans, as-tu sauvé les fleurs-de-lys ?* " There is an old English copy of verses which argues thus :—

> "If the man that turnips cries
> Cry not when his father dies,
> Then 'tis plain the man had rather
> Have a turnip than his father."

I cannot say that the logic of these verses was ever *entirely* to my satisfaction. I do not see my way through it as clearly as could be wished. But I see my way most clearly through D'Arc ; and the result is—that he would greatly have preferred not merely a turnip to his father, but the saving a pound or so of bacon to saving the Oriflamme of France.

It is probable (as M. Michelet suggests) that the title of Virgin or *Pucelle* had in itself, and apart from the miraculous stories about her, a secret power over the rude soldiery and partisan chiefs of that period ; for in such a person they saw a representative manifestation of the Virgin Mary, who, in a course of centuries, had grown steadily upon the popular heart.

As to Joanna's supernatural detection of the dauphin (Charles VII) amongst three hundred lords and knights, I am surprised at the credulity which could ever lend itself to that theatrical juggle. Who admires more than myself the sublime enthusiasm, the rapturous faith in herself, of this pure creature ? But I am far from admiring stage artifices which not *La Pucelle*, but the court, must have arranged ; nor can surrender myself to the conjurer's *legerdemain*, such as may be seen every day for a shilling. Southey's " Joan of Arc " was published in 1796. Twenty years after, talking with Southey, I was surprised to find him still owning a secret bias in favour of Joan, founded on her detection of the dauphin. The story, for the benefit of the reader new to the case, was this :—*La Pucelle* was first made known to the dauphin, and presented to his court, at Chinon : and here came her first trial. By way of testing her supernatural pretensions, she was to find out the royal personage amongst the whole ark of clean and unclean creatures. Failing in this *coup d'essai*, she would not simply disappoint many a beating heart in the glittering crowd that on different motives yearned for her success, but she would ruin herself, and, as the oracle within had told her, would, by ruining herself, ruin France. Our own Sovereign Lady Victoria rehearses annually a trial not so severe in degree, but the same in kind. She "pricks" for sheriffs. Joanna pricked for a king. But observe the difference : our own Lady pricks for two men out of three ; Joanna for one man out of three hundred. Happy Lady of the Islands and the Orient ! —she *can* go astray in her choice only by one half : to the extent of one half she *must* have the satisfaction of being right. And yet, even with these tight limits to the misery of a boundless discretion, permit me, Liege Lady, with all loyalty, to submit that now and then you prick with your pin the wrong man. But the poor child from Domrémy, shrinking under the gaze of a dazzling court—not *because* dazzling (for in visions she had seen those that were more so), but because some of them wore a scoffing smile on their features—how should *she* throw her line into so deep a river to angle for a king, where many a gay creature was sporting that masqueraded as kings in dress ! Nay, even more than any true king would have done : for, in Southey's version of the story, the dauphin says, by way of trying the virgin's magnetic sympathy with royalty,

> " On the throne,
> I the while mingling with the menial throng,
> Some courtier shall be seated."

This usurper is even crowned : "the jewelled crown shines on a menial's head." But, really, that is " *un peu fort* " ; and the mob of spectators might raise a scruple whether our friend the jackdaw upon the throne, and the dauphin himself, were not grazing the shins of treason. For the dauphin could not lend more than belonged to him. According to the popular notion, he had no crown for himself; consequently none to lend, on any pretence whatever, until the consecrated Maid should take him to Rheims. This was the *popular* notion in France. But certainly it was the dauphin's interest to support the popular notion, as he meant to use the services of Joanna. For, if he were king already, what was it that she could do for him beyond Orleans? That is to say, what more than a merely *military* service could she render him? And, above all, if he were king without a coronation, and without the oil from the sacred ampulla, what advantage was yet open to him by celerity above his competitor, the English boy? Now was to be a race for a coronation: he that should win *that* race carried the superstition of France along with him : he that should first be drawn from the ovens of Rheims was under that superstition baked into a king.

La Pucelle, before she could be allowed to practise as a warrior, was put through her manual and platoon exercise, as a pupil in divinity, at the bar of six eminent men in wigs. According to Southey (v. 393, Book III, in the original edition of his "Joan of Arc"), she "appalled the doctors." It's not easy to do *that:* but they had some reason to feel bothered, as that surgeon would assuredly feel bothered who, upon proceeding to dissect a subject, should find the subject retaliating as a dissector upon himself, especially if Joanna ever made the speech to them which occupies v. 354-391, B. III. It is a double impossibility : 1st, because a piracy from Tindal's "Christianity as old as the Creation"—a piracy *a parte ante,* and by three centuries ; 2dly, it is quite contrary to the evidence on Joanna's trial. Southey's "Joan" of A.D. 1796 (Cottle, Bristol) tells the doctors, amongst other secrets, that she never in her life attended—1st, Mass ; nor 2d, the Sacramental Table ; nor 3d, Confession. In the meantime, all this deistical confession of Joanna's, besides being suicidal for the interest of her cause, is opposed to the depositions upon *both* trials. The very best witness called from first to last deposes that Joanna attended these rites of her Church even too often ; was taxed with doing so ; and, by blushing, owned the charge as a fact, though certainly not as a fault.   Joanna was a girl of natural piety, that saw God in forests, and hills, and fountains, but did not the less seek him in chapels and consecrated oratories.

This peasant girl was self-educated through her own natural meditativeness.   If the reader turns to that divine passage in " Paradise Regained " which Milton has put into the mouth of our Saviour when first entering the wilderness, and musing upon the tendency of those great impulses growing within himself—

> " Oh, what a multitude of thoughts at once
> Awakened in me swarm, while I consider
> What from within I feel myself, and hear
> What from without comes often to my ears,
> Ill sorting with my present state compared !
> When I was yet a child, no childish play
> To me was pleasing ; all my mind was set
> Serious to learn and know, and thence to do,
> What might be public good ; myself I thought
> Born to that end "—

he will have some notion of the vast reveries which brooded over the heart of Joanna in early girlhood, when the wings were budding that should carry her from Orleans to Rheims ; when the golden chariot was dimly revealing itself that should carry her from the kingdom of *France Delivered* to the Eternal Kingdom.

It is not requisite for the honour of Joanna, nor is there in this place room, to pursue her brief career of *action*. That, though wonderful, forms the earthly part of her story : the spiritual part is the saintly passion of her imprisonment, trial, and execution.   It is unfortunate, therefore, for Southey's " Joan of Arc " (which, however, should always be regarded as a *juvenile* effort), that precisely when her real glory begins the poem ends.   But this limitation of the interest grew, no doubt, from the constraint inseparably attached to the law of epic unity.   Joanna's history bisects into two opposite hemispheres, and both could not have been presented to the eye in one poem, unless by sacrificing all unity of theme, or else by involving the earlier half, as a narrative episode, in the latter ; which, however, might have been done, for it might have been communicated to a fellow-prisoner, or a confessor, by Joanna herself.   It is sufficient,

as concerns *this* section of Joanna's life, to say that she fulfilled, to the height of her promises, the restoration of the
prostrate throne.   France had become a province of England,
and for the ruin of both, if such a yoke could be maintained.
Dreadful pecuniary exhaustion caused the English energy to
droop ; and that critical opening *La Pucelle* used with a corresponding felicity of audacity and suddenness (that were in
themselves portentous) for introducing the wedge of French
native resources, for rekindling the national pride, and for
planting the dauphin once more upon his feet.   When
Joanna appeared, he had been on the point of giving up the
struggle with the English, distressed as they were, and of flying to the south of France.   She taught him to blush for
such abject counsels.   She liberated Orleans, that great city,
so decisive by its fate for the issue of the war, and then be-
leaguered by the English with an elaborate application of
engineering skill unprecedented in Europe.   Entering the
city after sunset on the 29th of April, she sang mass on
Sunday, May 8, for the entire disappearance of the besieging
force.   On the 29th of June she fought and gained over the
English the decisive battle of Patay ; on the 9th of July she
took Troyes by a coup-de-main from a mixed garrison of
English and Burgundians ; on the 15th of that month she
carried the dauphin into Rheims ; on Sunday the 17th she
crowned him ; and there she rested from her labour of
triumph.   All that was to be *done* she had now accomplished :
what remained was—to *suffer*.

All this forward movement was her own : excepting one
man, the whole Council was against her.   Her enemies were
all that drew power from earth.   Her supporters were her
own strong enthusiasm, and the headlong contagion by which
she carried this sublime frenzy into the hearts of women, of
soldiers, and of all who lived by labour.   Henceforwards she
was thwarted ; and the worst error that she committed was
to lend the sanction of her presence to counsels which she
had ceased to approve.   But she had now accomplished the
capital objects which her own visions had dictated.   These
involved all the rest.   Errors were now less important ; and
doubtless it had now become more difficult for herself to pronounce authentically what *were* errors.   The noble girl had

achieved, as by a rapture of motion, the capital end of clearing out a free space around her sovereign, giving him the power to move his arms with effect, and, secondly, the inappreciable end of winning for that sovereign what seemed to all France the heavenly ratification of his rights, by crowning him with the ancient solemnities. She had made it impossible for the English now to step before her. They were caught in an irretrievable blunder, owing partly to discord amongst the uncles of Henry VI, partly to a want of funds, but partly to the very impossibility which they believed to press with tenfold force upon any French attempt to forestall theirs. They laughed at such a thought ; and, whilst they laughed, she *did* it. Henceforth the single redress for the English of this capital oversight, but which never *could* have redressed it effectually, was to vitiate and taint the coronation of Charles VII as the work of a witch. That policy, and not malice (as M. Michelet is so happy to believe), was the moving principle in the subsequent prosecution of Joanna. Unless they unhinged the force of the first coronation in the popular mind by associating it with power given from hell, they felt that the sceptre of the invader was broken.

But she, the child that, at nineteen, had wrought wonders so great for France, was she not elated ? Did she not lose, as men so often *have* lost, all sobriety of mind when standing upon the pinnacle of success so giddy ? Let her enemies declare. During the progress of her movement, and in the centre of ferocious struggles, she had manifested the temper of her feelings by the pity which she had everywhere expressed for the suffering enemy. She forwarded to the English leaders a touching invitation to unite with the French, as brothers, in a common crusade against infidels,— thus opening the road for a soldierly retreat. She interposed to protect the captive or the wounded ; she mourned over the excesses of her countrymen ; she threw herself off her horse to kneel by the dying English soldier, and to comfort him with such ministrations, physical or spiritual, as his situation allowed. "Nolebat," says the evidence, "uti ense suo, aut quemquam interficere." She sheltered the English that invoked her aid in her own quarters. She wept as she beheld, stretched on the field of battle, so many brave enemies

that had died without confession. And, as regarded herself,
her elation expressed itself thus :—On the day when she had
finished her work, she wept ; for she knew that, when her
triumphal task was done, her end must be approaching.
Her aspirations pointed only to a place which seemed to her
more than usually full of natural piety, as one in which it
would give her pleasure to die. And she uttered, between
smiles and tears, as a wish that inexpressibly fascinated her
heart, and yet was half-fantastic, a broken prayer that God
would return her to the solitudes from which he had drawn
her, and suffer her to become a shepherdess once more. It
was a natural prayer, because nature has laid a necessity
upon every human heart to seek for rest and to shrink from
torment. Yet, again, it was a half-fantastic prayer, because,
from childhood upwards, visions that she had no power to
mistrust, and the voices which sounded in her ear for ever,
had long since persuaded her mind that for *her* no such
prayer could be granted. Too well she felt that her mission
must be worked out to the end, and that the end was now at
hand. All went wrong from this time. She herself had
created the *funds* out of which the French restoration should
grow ; but she was not suffered to witness their development,
or their prosperous application. More than one military plan
was entered upon which she did not approve. But she still
continued to expose her person as before. Severe wounds
had not taught her caution. And at length, in a sortie from
Compiègne (whether through treacherous collusion on the
part of her own friends is doubtful to this day), she was made
prisoner by the Burgundians, and finally surrendered to the
English.

Now came her trial. This trial, moving of course under
English influence, was conducted in chief by the Bishop of
Beauvais. He was a Frenchman, sold to English interests,
and hoping, by favour of the English leaders, to reach the
highest preferment. *Bishop that art, Archbishop that shalt be,*
Cardinal that mayest be, were the words that sounded continually in his ear ; and doubtless a whisper of visions still
higher, of a triple crown, and feet upon the necks of kings,
sometimes stole into his heart. M. Michelet is anxious to
keep us in mind that this bishop was but an agent of the

English. True. But it does not better the case for his countryman that, being an accomplice in the crime, making himself the leader in the persecution against the helpless girl, he was willing to be all this in the spirit, and with the conscious vileness of a cat's-paw. Never from the foundations of the earth was there such a trial as this, if it were laid open in all its beauty of defence, and all its hellishness of attack. Oh, child of France ! shepherdess, peasant girl ! trodden under foot by all around thee, how I honour thy flashing intellect, quick as God's lightning, and true as God's lightning to its mark, that ran before France and laggard Europe by many a century, confounding the malice of the ensnarer, and making dumb the oracles of falsehood ! Is it not scandalous, is it not humiliating to civilisation, that, even at this day, France exhibits the horrid spectacle of judges examining the prisoner against himself ; seducing him, by fraud, into treacherous conclusions against his own head ; using the terrors of their power for extorting confessions from the frailty of hope ; nay (which is worse), using the blandishments of condescension and snaky kindness for thawing into compliances of gratitude those whom they had failed to freeze into terror ?   Wicked judges ! barbarian jurisprudence !— that, sitting in your own conceit on the summits of social wisdom, have yet failed to learn the first principles of criminal justice,—sit ye humbly and with docility at the feet of this girl from Domrémy, that tore your webs of cruelty into shreds and dust.   "Would you examine me as a witness against myself ? " was the question by which many times she defied their arts.   Continually she showed that their interrogations were irrelevant to any business before the court, or that entered into the ridiculous charges against her. General questions were proposed to her on points of casuistical divinity ; two-edged questions, which not one of themselves could have answered, without, on the one side, landing himself in heresy (as then interpreted), or, on the other, in some presumptuous expression of self-esteem.   Next came a wretched Dominican, that pressed her with an objection, which, if applied to the Bible, would tax every one of its miracles with unsoundness.   The monk had the excuse of never having read the Bible.   M. Michelet has no such excuse ;

and it makes one blush for him, as a philosopher, to find him
describing such an argument as " weighty," whereas it is but
a varied expression of rude Mahometan metaphysics. Her
answer to this, if there were room to place the whole in a
clear light, was as shattering as it was rapid. Another
thought to entrap her by asking what language the angelic
visitors of her solitude had talked,—as though heavenly
counsels could want polyglot interpreters for every word, or
that God needed language at all in whispering thoughts to a
human heart. Then came a worse devil, who asked her
whether the Archangel Michael had appeared naked. Not
comprehending the vile insinuation, Joanna, whose poverty
suggested to her simplicity that it might be the *costliness* of
suitable robes which caused the demur, asked them if they
fancied God, who clothed the flowers of the valleys, unable
to find raiment for his servants. The answer of Joanna
moves a smile of tenderness, but the disappointment of her
judges makes one laugh exultingly. Others succeeded by
troops, who upbraided her with leaving her father ; as if that
greater Father, whom she believed herself to have been
serving, did not retain the power of dispensing with his own
rules, or had not said that for a less cause than martyrdom
man and woman should leave both father and mother.

On Easter Sunday, when the trial had been long proceeding, the poor girl fell so ill as to cause a belief that she had
been poisoned. It was not poison. Nobody had any interest
in hastening a death so certain. M. Michelet, whose sympathies with all feelings are so quick that one would gladly
see them always as justly directed, reads the case most truly.
Joanna had a twofold malady. She was visited by a
paroxysm of the complaint called *home-sickness*. The cruel
nature of her imprisonment, and its length, could not but
point her solitary thoughts, in darkness and in chains (for
chained she was), to Domrémy. And the season, which was
the most heavenly period of the spring, added stings to this
yearning. That was one of her maladies—*nostalgia*, as
medicine calls it ; the other was weariness and exhaustion
from daily combats with malice. She saw that everybody
hated her, and thirsted for her blood ; nay, many kind-
hearted creatures that would have pitied her profoundly, as

regarded all political charges, had their natural feelings warped by the belief that she had dealings with fiendish powers. She knew she was to die ; that was *not* the misery : the misery was that this consummation could not be reached without so much intermediate strife, as if she were contending for some chance (where chance was none) of happiness, or were dreaming for a moment of escaping the inevitable. Why, then, *did* she contend ? Knowing that she would reap nothing from answering her persecutors, why did she not retire by silence from the superfluous contest ? It was because her quick and eager loyalty to truth would not suffer her to see it darkened by frauds which *she* could expose, but others, even of candid listeners, perhaps, could not ; it was through that imperishable grandeur of soul which taught her to submit meekly and without a struggle to her punishment, but taught her *not* to submit—no, not for a moment—to calumny as to facts, or to misconstruction as to motives. Besides, there were secretaries all around the court taking down her words. That was meant for no good to *her*. But the end does not always correspond to the meaning. And Joanna might say to herself, " These words that will be used against me to-morrow and the next day perhaps in some nobler generation may rise again for my justification." Yes, Joanna, they *are* rising even now in Paris, and for more than justification !

Woman, sister, there are some things which you do not execute as well as your brother, man ; no, nor ever will. Pardon me if I doubt whether you will ever produce a great poet from your choirs, or a Mozart, or a Phidias, or a Michael Angelo, or a great philosopher, or a great scholar. By which last is meant—not one who depends simply on an infinite memory, but also on an infinite and electrical power of combination ; bringing together from the four winds, like the angel of the resurrection, what else were dust from dead men's bones, into the unity of breathing life. If you *can* create yourselves into any of these great creators, why have you not ?

Yet, sister woman, though I cannot consent to find a Mozart or a Michael Angelo in your sex, cheerfully, and with the love that burns in depths of admiration, I acknowledge that you can do one thing as well as the best of us men—a

greater thing than even Milton is known to have done, or
Michael Angelo : you can die grandly, and as goddesses
would die, were goddesses mortal. If any distant worlds
(which *may* be the case) are so far ahead of us Tellurians in
optical resources as to see distinctly through their telescopes
all that we do on earth, what is the grandest sight to which
we ever treat them ? St. Peter's at Rome, do you fancy, on
Easter Sunday, or Luxor, or perhaps the Himalayas ? Oh
no ! my friend : suggest something better ; these are baubles
to *them;* they see in other worlds, in their own, far better
toys of the same kind. These, take my word for it, are
nothing. Do you give it up ? The finest thing, then,
we have to show them is a scaffold on the morning of execution. I assure you there is a strong muster in those far
telescopic worlds, on any such morning, of those who happen
to find themselves occupying the right hemisphere for a peep
at *us.* How, then, if it be announced in some such telescopic
world by those who make a livelihood of catching glimpses
at our newspapers, whose language they have long since
deciphered, that the poor victim in the morning's sacrifice is
a woman ? How, if it be published in that distant world
that the sufferer wears upon her head, in the eyes of many,
the garlands of martyrdom ? How, if it should be some
Marie Antoinette, the widowed queen, coming forward on
the scaffold, and presenting to the morning air her head,
turned grey by sorrow,—daughter of Cæsars kneeling down
humbly to kiss the guillotine, as one that worships death ?
How, if it were the noble Charlotte Corday, that in the
bloom of youth, that with the loveliest of persons, that with
homage waiting upon her smiles wherever she turned her
face to scatter them—homage that followed those smiles as
surely as the carols of birds, after showers in spring, follow
the reappearing sun and the racing of sunbeams over the
hills—yet thought all these things cheaper than the dust
upon her sandals, in comparison of deliverance from hell for
her dear suffering France ! Ah ! these were spectacles
indeed for those sympathising people in distant worlds ; and
some, perhaps, would suffer a sort of martyrdom themselves,
because they could not testify their wrath, could not bear
witness to the strength of love and to the fury of hatred that

burned within them at such scenes, could not gather into golden urns some of that glorious dust which rested in the catacombs of earth.

On the Wednesday after Trinity Sunday in 1431, being then about nineteen years of age, the Maid of Arc underwent her martyrdom. She was conducted before mid-day, guarded by eight hundred spearmen, to a platform of prodigious height, constructed of wooden billets supported by occasional walls of lath and plaster, and traversed by hollow spaces in every direction for the creation of air-currents. The pile "struck terror," says M. Michelet, "by its height" ; and, as usual, the English purpose in this is viewed as one of pure malignity. But there are two ways of explaining all that. It is probable that the purpose was merciful. On the circumstances of the execution I shall not linger. Yet, to mark the almost fatal felicity of M. Michelet in finding out whatever may injure the English name, at a moment when every reader will be interested in Joanna's personal appearance, it is really edifying to notice the ingenuity by which he draws into light from a dark corner a very unjust account of it, and neglects, though lying upon the high-road, a very pleasing one. Both are from English pens. Grafton, a chronicler, but little read, being a stiffnecked John Bull, thought fit to say that no wonder Joanna should be a virgin, since her "foule face" was a satisfactory solution of that particular merit. Holinshead, on the other hand, a chronicler somewhat later, every way more important, and at one time universally read, has given a very pleasing testimony to the interesting character of Joanna's person and engaging manners. Neither of these men lived till the following century, so that personally this evidence is none at all. Grafton sullenly and carelessly believed as he wished to believe ; Holinshead took pains to inquire, and reports undoubtedly the general impression of France. But I cite the case as illustrating M. Michelet's candour.[1]

---

[1] Amongst the many ebullitions of M. Michelet's fury against us poor English are four which will be likely to amuse the reader ; and they are the more conspicuous in collision with the justice which he sometimes does us, and the very indignant admiration which, under some aspects, he grants to us.

The circumstantial incidents of the execution, unless with more space than I can now command, I should be unwilling to relate. I should fear to injure, by imperfect report, a martyrdom which to myself appears so unspeakably grand. Yet, for a purpose, pointing not at Joanna, but at

1. Our English Literature he admires with some gnashing of teeth. He pronounces it "fine and sombre," but, I lament to add, "sceptical, Judaic, Satanic—in a word, antichristian." That Lord Byron should figure as a member of this diabolical corporation will not surprise men. It *will* surprise them to hear that Milton is one of its Satanic leaders. Many are the generous and eloquent Frenchmen, besides Chateaubriand, who have, in the course of the last thirty years, nobly suspended their own burning nationality, in order to render a more rapturous homage at the feet of Milton ; and some of them have raised Milton almost to a level with angelic natures. Not one of them has thought of looking for him *below* the earth. As to Shakspere, M. Michelet detects in him a most extraordinary mare's nest. It is this : he does "not recollect to have seen the name of God " in any part of his works. On reading such words, it is natural to rub one's eyes, and suspect that all one has ever seen in this world may have been a pure ocular delusion. In particular, I begin myself to suspect that the word "*la gloire*" never occurs in any Parisian journal. "The great English nation," says M. Michelet, ''has one immense profound vice "—to wit, "pride." Why, really that may be true ; but we have a neighbour not absolutely clear of an "immense profound vice," as like ours in colour and shape as cherry to cherry. In short, M. Michelet thinks us, by fits and starts, admirable,—only that we are detestable ; and he would adore some of our authors, were it not that so intensely he could have wished to kick them.

2. M. Michelet thinks to lodge an arrow in our sides by a very odd remark upon Thomas à Kempis : which is, that a man of any conceivable European blood—a Finlander, suppose, or a Zantiote—might have written Tom ; only not an Englishman. Whether an Englishman could have forged Tom must remain a matter of doubt, unless the thing had been tried long ago. That problem was intercepted for ever by Tom's perverseness in choosing to manufacture himself. Yet, since nobody is better aware than M. Michelet that this very point of Kempis *having* manufactured Kempis is furiously and hopelessly litigated, three or four nations claiming to have forged his work for him, the shocking old doubt will raise its snaky head once more—whether this forger, who rests in so much darkness, might not, after all, be of English blood. Tom, it may be feared, is known to modern English literature chiefly by an irreverent mention of his name in a line of Peter Pindar's (Dr. Wolcot) fifty years back, where he is described as

" Kempis Tom,
Who clearly shows the way to Kingdom Come."

Few in these days can have read him, unless in the Methodist version

M. Michelet—viz. to convince him that an Englishman is
capable of thinking more highly of *La Pucelle* than even her
admiring countrymen—I shall, in parting, allude to one or

of John Wesley. Amongst those few, however, happens to be myself;
which arose from the accident of having, when a boy of eleven,
received a copy of the "De Imitatione Christi" as a bequest from a
relation who died very young; from which cause, and from the external prettiness of the book,—being a Glasgow reprint by the celebrated
Foulis, and gaily bound,—I was induced to look into it, and finally
read it many times over, partly out of some sympathy which, even in
those days, I had with its simplicity and devotional fervour, but
much more from the savage delight I found in laughing at Tom's
Latinity. *That*, I freely grant to M. Michelet, is inimitable. Yet,
after all, it is not certain whether the original *was* Latin. But, however *that* may have been, if it is possible that M. Michelet[1] can be
accurate in saying that there are no less than *sixty* French versions
(not editions, observe, but separate versions) existing of the "De Imitatione," how prodigious must have been the adaptation of the book
to the religious heart of the fifteenth century! Excepting the Bible,
but excepting *that* only in Protestant lands, no book known to man
has had the same distinction. It is the most marvellous bibliographi-
cal fact on record.

3. Our English girls, it seems, are as faulty in one way as we
English males in another. None of us men could have written the
Opera Omnia of Mr. à Kempis; neither could any of our girls have
assumed male attire like *La Pucelle*. But why? Because, says
Michelet, English girls and German think so much of an indecorum.
Well, that is a good fault, generally speaking. But M. Michelet
ought to have remembered a fact in the martyrologies which justifies
both parties—the French heroine for doing, and the general choir of
English girls for *not* doing. A female saint, specially renowned in
France, had, for a reason as weighty as Joanna's—viz. expressly to
shield her modesty amongst men—worn a male military harness.
That reason and that example authorised *La Pucelle;* but our English
girls, as a body, have seldom any such reason, and certainly no such
saintly example, to plead. This excuses *them*. Yet, still, if it is
indispensable to the national character that our young women should
now and then trespass over the frontier of decorum, it then becomes a

---

[1] *"If M. Michelet can be accurate"* :—However, on consideration, this statement does not depend on Michelet. The bibliographer Barbier has absolutely
specified sixty in a separate dissertation, *soixante traductions*, amongst those
even that have not escaped the search. The Italian translations are said to be
thirty. As to mere *editions*, not counting the early MSS. for half-a-century
before printing was introduced, those in Latin amount to two thousand, and
those in French to one thousand. Meantime, it is very clear to me that this
astonishing popularity, so entirely unparalleled in literature, could not have
existed except in Roman Catholic times, nor subsequently have lingered in
any Protestant land. It was the denial of Scripture fountains to thirsty lands
which made this slender rill of Scripture truth so passionately welcome.

two traits in Joanna's demeanour on the scaffold, and to one
or two in that of the bystanders, which authorise me in
questioning an opinion of his upon this martyr's firmness.

patriotic duty in me to assure M. Michelet that we *have* such ardent
females amongst us, and in a long series : some detected in naval
hospitals when too sick to remember their disguise ; some on fields of
battle ; multitudes never detected at all ; some only suspected ; and
others discharged without noise by war offices and other absurd
people.   In our navy, both royal and commercial, and generally from
deep remembrances of slighted love, women have sometimes served in
disguise for many years, taking contentedly their daily allowance of
burgoo, biscuit, or cannon-balls—anything, in short, digestible or
indigestible, that it might please Providence to send.   One thing, at
least, is to their credit : never any of these poor masks, with their
deep silent remembrances, have been detected through murmuring,
or what is nautically understood by "skulking."   So, for once, M.
Michelet has an *erratum* to enter upon the fly-leaf of his book in
presentation copies.

4. But the last of these ebullitions is the most lively.   We English,
at Orleans, and after Orleans (which is not quite so extraordinary, if
all were told), fled before the Maid of Arc.   Yes, says M. Michelet,
you *did :* deny it, if you can.   Deny it, *mon cher ?*   I don't mean to
deny it.   Running away, in many cases, is a thing so excellent that no
philosopher would, at times, condescend to adopt any other step.   All
of us nations in Europe, without one exception, have shown our
philosophy in that way at times.   Even people "*qui ne se rendent
pas*" have deigned both to run and to shout "*Sauve qui peut !*" at
odd times of sunset ; though, for my part, I have no pleasure in recalling
unpleasant remembrances to brave men ; and yet, really, being so
philosophic, they ought *not* to be unpleasant.   But the amusing
feature in M. Michelet's reproach is the way in which he *improves* and
varies against us the charge of running, as if he were singing a catch.
Listen to him.   They "*showed their backs*," did these English.   (Hip,
hip, hurrah ! three times three !)   "*Behind good walls they let themselves be taken.*"   (Hip, hip ! nine times nine !)   They "*ran as fast
as their legs could carry them.*"   (Hurrah ! twenty-seven times twenty-
seven !)   They "*ran before a girl*"; they did.   (Hurrah ! eighty-one
times eighty-one !)   This reminds one of criminal indictments on the
old model in English courts, where (for fear the prisoner should
escape) the crown lawyer varied the charge perhaps through forty
counts.   The law laid its guns so as to rake the accused at every
possible angle.   Whilst the indictment was reading, he seemed a
monster of crime in his own eyes ; and yet, after all, the poor fellow
had but committed one offence, and not always *that.*   N.B.—Not
having the French original at hand, I make my quotations from a
friend's copy of Mr. Walter Kelly's translation ; which seems to me
faithful, spirited, and idiomatically English—liable, in fact, only to
the single reproach of occasional provincialisms.

The reader ought to be reminded that Joanna D'Arc was subjected to an unusually unfair trial of opinion. Any of the elder Christian martyrs had not much to fear of *personal* rancour. The martyr was chiefly regarded as the enemy of Cæsar ; at times, also, where any knowledge of the Christian faith and morals existed, with the enmity that arises spontaneously in the worldly against the spiritual. But the martyr, though disloyal, was not supposed to be therefore anti-national ; and still less was *individually* hateful. What was hated (if anything) belonged to his class, not to himself separately. Now, Joanna, if hated at all, was hated personally, and in Rouen on national grounds. Hence there would be a certainty of calumny arising against *her*, such as would not affect martyrs in general. That being the case, it would follow of necessity that some people would impute to her a willingness to recant. No innocence could escape *that*. Now, had she really testified this willingness on the scaffold, it would have argued nothing at all but the weakness of a genial nature shrinking from the instant approach of torment. And those will often pity that weakness most who, in their own persons, would yield to it least. Meantime, there never was a calumny uttered that drew less support from the recorded circumstances. It rests upon no *positive* testimony, and it has a weight of contradicting testimony to stem. And yet, strange to say, M. Michelet, who at times seems to admire the Maid of Arc as much as I do, is the one sole writer amongst her *friends* who lends some countenance to this odious slander. His words are that, if she did not utter this word *recant* with her lips, she uttered it in her heart. " Whether she *said* the word is uncertain : but I affirm that she *thought* it."

Now, I affirm that she did not ; not in any sense of the word " *thought* " applicable to the case. Here is France calumniating *La Pucelle :* here is England defending her. M. Michelet can only mean that, on *a priori* principles, every woman must be presumed liable to such a weakness ; that Joanna was a woman ; *ergo*, that she was liable to such a weakness. That is, he only supposes her to have uttered the word by an argument which presumes it impossible for anybody to have done otherwise. I, on the contrary, throw the *onus* of the argument not on presumable tendencies of nature, but on the known facts of that morning's execution, as recorded by multitudes. What else, I demand, than mere weight of metal, absolute nobility of deportment, broke the vast line of battle then arrayed against her ? What else but her meek, saintly demeanour won, from the enemies that till now had believed her a witch, tears of rapturous admiration ? "Ten thousand men," says M. Michelet himself — "ten thousand men wept"; and of these ten thousand the majority were political enemies knitted together by cords of superstition. What else was it but her constancy, united with her angelic gentleness, that drove the fanatic English soldier—who had sworn to throw a faggot on her scaffold, as *his* tribute of abhorrence, that *did* so, that fulfilled his vow — suddenly to turn away a penitent for life, saying everywhere that he had seen a dove rising upon wings to heaven from the ashes where she had stood ? What else drove the executioner to kneel at every shrine for pardon to *his* share in the tragedy ? And, if all this were insufficient, then I cite the closing act of her life as valid on her behalf, were all other testimonies against her. The executioner had been directed to apply his torch from below. He did so. The fiery smoke rose upwards in billowing volumes. A Dominican monk was then standing almost at her side. Wrapped up in his sublime office, he saw not the danger, but still persisted in his prayers. Even then, when the last enemy was racing up the fiery stairs to seize her, even at that moment did this noblest of girls think only for *him*, the one friend that would not forsake her, and not for herself ; bidding him with her last breath to care for his own preservation, but to leave *her* to God. That girl, whose latest breath ascended in this sublime expression of self-oblivion, did not utter the word *recant* either with her lips or in her heart. No ; she did not, though one should rise from the dead to swear it.

Bishop of Beauvais ! thy victim died in fire upon a scaffold — thou upon a down bed. But, for the departing minutes of life, both are oftentimes alike. At the farewell crisis, when the gates of death are opening, and flesh is resting from its struggles, oftentimes the tortured and the torturer have the same truce from carnal torment; both sink together into sleep; together both sometimes kindle into dreams. When the mortal mists were gathering fast upon you two, bishop and shepherd girl—when the pavilions of life were closing up their shadowy curtains about you— let us try, through the gigantic glooms, to decipher the flying features of your separate visions.

The shepherd girl that had delivered France—she, from her dungeon, she, from her baiting at the stake, she, from her duel with fire, as she entered her last dream — saw Domrémy, saw the fountain of Domrémy, saw the pomp of forests in which her childhood had wandered. That Easter festival which man had denied to her languishing heart—that resurrection of spring-time, which the darkness of dungeons had intercepted from *her*, hungering after the glorious liberty of forests—were by God given back into her hands, as jewels that had been stolen from her by robbers. With those, perhaps (for the minutes of dreams can stretch into ages), was given back to her by God the bliss of child-hood. By special privilege for *her* might be created, in this farewell dream, a second childhood, innocent as the first; but not, like *that*, sad with the gloom of a fearful mission in the rear. This mission had now been fulfilled. The storm was weathered; the skirts even of that mighty storm were drawing off. The blood that she was to reckon for had been exacted; the tears that she was to shed in secret had been paid to the last. The hatred to herself in all eyes had been faced steadily, had been suffered, had been survived. And in her last fight upon the scaffold she had triumphed gloriously; victoriously she had tasted the stings of death. For all, except this comfort from her farewell dream, she had died—died, amidst the tears of ten thousand enemies— died, amidst the drums and trumpets of armies—died, amidst peals redoubling upon peals, volleys upon volleys, from the saluting clarions of martyrs.

Bishop of Beauvais! because the guilt-burdened man is in dreams haunted and waylaid by the most frightful of his crimes, and because upon that fluctuating mirror—rising (like the mocking mirrors of *mirage* in Arabian deserts) from the fens of death—most of all are reflected the sweet countenances which the man has laid in ruins ; therefore I know, bishop, that you also, entering your final dream, saw Domrémy. That fountain, of which the witnesses spoke so much, showed itself to your eyes in pure morning dews : but neither dews, nor the holy dawn, could cleanse away the bright spots of innocent blood upon its surface. By the fountain, bishop, you saw a woman seated, that hid her face. But, as *you* draw near, the woman raises her wasted features. Would Domrémy know them again for the features of her child ? Ah, but *you* know them, bishop, well ! Oh, mercy ! what a groan was *that* which the servants, waiting outside the bishop's dream at his bedside, heard from his labouring heart, as at this moment he turned away from the fountain and the woman, seeking rest in the forests afar off. Yet not *so* to escape the woman, whom once again he must behold before he dies. In the forests to which he prays for pity, will he find a respite ? What a tumult, what a gathering of feet is there ! In glades where only wild deer should run armies and nations are assembling ; towering in the fluctuating crowd are phantoms that belong to departed hours. There is the great English Prince, Regent of France. There is my Lord of Winchester, the princely cardinal, that died and made no sign. There is the Bishop of Beauvais, clinging to the shelter of thickets. What building is that which hands so rapid are raising ? Is it a martyr's scaffold ? Will they burn the child of Domrémy a second time ? No : it is a tribunal that rises to the clouds ; and two nations stand around it, waiting for a trial. Shall my Lord of Beauvais sit again upon the judgment-seat, and again number the hours for the innocent ? Ah no ! he is the prisoner at the bar. Already all is waiting: the mighty audience is gathered, the Court is hurrying to their seats, the witnesses are arrayed, the trumpets are sounding, the judge is taking his place. Oh ! but this is sudden. My lord, have you no counsel ? " Counsel I have none : in heaven above, or on earth beneath, counsellor there is none now that would take a brief from *me :* all are silent." Is it, indeed, come to this ? Alas ! the time is short, the tumult is wondrous, the crowd stretches away into infinity ; but yet I will search in it for somebody to take your brief : I know of somebody that will be your counsel. Who is this that cometh from Domrémy ? Who is she in bloody coronation robes from Rheims ? Who is she that cometh with blackened flesh from walking the furnaces of Rouen ? This is she, the shepherd girl, counsellor that had none for herself, whom I choose, bishop, for yours. She it is, I engage, that shall take my lord's brief. She it is, bishop, that would plead for you : yes, bishop, SHE,—when heaven and earth are silent.

END OF VOL. V